TOTALITARIANISM

TOTALITARIANISM

EDITED WITH AN INTRODUCTION

By CARL J. FRIEDRICH

The Universal Library

GROSSET & DUNLAP

NEW YORK

PARTICIPANTS IN THE CONFERENCE

HANNAH ARENDT

RAYMOND BAUER

ERWIN CANHAM

WILLIAM HENRY CHAMBERLIN

GEORGE DENICKE

KARL W. DEUTSCH

IVO DUCHACEK

ERIK H. ERIKSON

MERLE FAINSOD

PHILIPP FRANK

ELSE FRENKEL-BRUNSWIK

CARL J. FRIEDRICH

ALEXANDER GERSCHENKRON

JERZY G. GLIKSMAN

WALDEMAR GURIAN

ALEX INKELES

MARIE JAHODA

MICHAEL KARPOVICH

PAUL KECSKEMETI

GEORGE F. KENNAN

EDWIN C. LAND

HAROLD D. LASSWELL

ALBERT LAUTERBACH

PAUL LEHMAN

W. W. LEONTIEF

FRANKLIN H. LITTELL

LEO LOWENTHAL

BORIS MIRKINE-GUÉTZÉVITCH

H. J. MULLER

LOUIS NEMZER

J. P. NETTL

SIGMUND NEUMANN

DAVID RIESMAN

GEROID T. ROBINSON

FRANK W. ROUNDS, JR.

GEORGE DE SANTILLANA

N. S. TIMASHEFF

ADAM ULAM

EDWARD WEEKS

BERTRAM D. WOLFE

Preface

This volume is the outgrowth of a conference on totalitarianism held by the American Academy of Arts and Sciences in Boston, March 6 to 8, 1953. In the view of the Council of the Academy, totalitarianism is such an extraordinary and all-pervading phenomenon of our time that the best scholarly and scientific efforts should be marshaled, and the necessary funds provided, for a comparative and interdisciplinary exploration of the basic issues involved.

The conference was prepared by a committee consisting of Erwin D. Canham, Karl W. Deutsch, Merle Fainsod, Carl J. Friedrich (Chairman), Alexander Gerschenkron, and Harold D. Lasswell. The list of participants precedes this preface. A number of others had been invited but were unable to attend. The conference was open to regular members of the Academy, and quite a few attended one session or another.

The material here presented consists of the papers submitted to the conference and an abstract of the discussions. The papers are largely in their original form, but some have been slightly expanded and others reduced, in order to have them of more equal length. Also, some portions were revised by the authors in the light of the discussions, in order to improve formulations and sharpen positions.

Two papers presented to the conference have appeared as parts of other books. Mr. Frank W. Rounds has published his paper in his book *A Window on Red Square*, pages 250–293; similarly William Henry Chamberlin incorporated his paper in his *Beyond Containment*. These papers are therefore not contained in this volume. Finally, Mr. Kennan's paper, which was presented in the evening session of the first day of the conference, seemed admirably suited to open this volume and is hence put first.

These papers were submitted to all participants some weeks prior to the conference, and only brief summaries were presented at the meetings, so that a large part of the available time could be devoted to discussion. The discussions were taken down by a team of younger scholars, including T. S. Baer, Zbigniew Brzezinski, Martin Malia, Herbert Spiro, and Judith Shklar, under the general supervision of T. S. Baer. The responsibility for editing these notes, and it was a crucial one, fell to Dr. Baer, who deserves nothing but praise for the able manner in which he performed this task. His abstract of the discussions was submitted to all those who participated in those discussions and was amended by them. Miss Hannah Arendt, at the request of the editor, somewhat extended her remarks, so that these taken together constitute what amounts to the substance of a paper. Similarly, Mr. Andrew Gyorgy offered additional comments, which are given at the end of the volume, although they were not presented to the conference.

Any volume of this nature is bound to leave some important *lacunae*, but the subject of totalitarianism is of such central importance at the present time that the material here presented ought to prove valuable. The interdisciplinary approach to totalitarianism has, to our knowledge, not previously been attempted, and deserves to be pursued further. The American Philosophical Society held a symposium in 1940 on the *Totalitarian State*, which was published in their proceedings as Volume LXXXII that year. As the title suggests, it was focused on the governmental aspect.

In conclusion, I should like to thank President Edwin Land and Secretary Ralph Burhoe of the Academy, as well as Taylor Starck, Chairman of the Publications Committee, for their generous and unflinching support during the long months of preparation and the heavy work during and since the conference. I should also like to express my very warm appreciation for the devoted work of editorial and secretarial assistance rendered by Mrs. Clacia Healy, Miss Roberta G. Hill and Mrs. June Lombardi.

C. J. F.

Cambridge, Massachusetts
May 25, 1953

Contents

The Problem of Totalitarianism — An Introduction

CARL J. FRIEDRICH

In the general studies concerned with man and society, totalitarianism is the most perplexing problem of our time. It has burst upon mankind more or less unexpected and unannounced. There are antecedents, to be sure, both in thought and in action, but they do not add up to the reality with which the mid-twentieth century finds itself confronted and by which it finds itself persistently challenged. Virtually no one before 1914 anticipated the course of development which has overtaken Western civilization since then. Prophets of gloom there were who direly predicted the downfall of culture and all that, and there are glimpses of the new age of tyrants in Nietzsche's late works. But how spiritual and high-minded, and how far removed from the dictators who built the totalitarian dictatorships, was Nietzsche's superman! Indeed, this superman was Plato's philosopher-king under a new name.[1] And if Nietzsche correctly foresaw the structure of world politics — he suggested that the supermen would be Britons, Americans, Russians — if he anticipated something of the anti-Christian, amoral tendencies of the twentieth century, he had no conception of the Leviathan that totalitarian dictatorship has turned out to be. It is striking, indeed, that none of the outstanding scholars in history, law, and the social sciences discerned what was ahead. Neither Veblen nor Durkheim, Jellinek nor Duguit, Max Weber nor Pareto sensed the trend which culminated in totalitarianism.

To this failure to foresee corresponds a difficulty in comprehend-

[1] *Der Wille zur Macht*, para. 972–980.

ing. For while everybody talks about totalitarianism, the greatest divergencies persist in the view taken of these societies. Does the Soviet Union represent a new civilization, as the Webbs once argued in a lengthy two-volume work? [2] In the perspective of a score of years later, it would seem that they had overlooked some of the most significant features of the "system," such as the terror. But there are many who even now are of the opinion that you can discuss various aspects of totalitarian society without dealing with the terror. And what of the question of the comparability of different totalitarian regimes, more especially the possibility of equating the dictatorship of Stalin in the Soviet Union and that of Hitler in Germany? Soviet spokesmen argue, of course, that radical differences divide them, not only in terms of objectives, but also in terms of work accomplished (so they say). But there is room for sharp disagreement among more detached observers. Yet upon this degree of equivalence, much depends for an analysis of totalitarianism.[3]

It is evident that a conference of scholars, representing different disciplines, which undertook to adumbrate some of the issues surrounding the discussion of totalitarianism would not try to "cover" the ground. It would have to pick and choose, to highlight for special attention some of the areas in which significant research has been done, and to set up the line of argument in such a way that no one-sided approach in terms of one of the social sciences could readily preëmpt the discussion. For this issue is part of the fundamental range of controversy. Is totalitarianism primarily an economic or an anthropological or a political phenomenon? That is to say, does the total planning of the economy constitute its crucial feature, or the fact that Russians (or Germans) developed it, or yet that one man or a small group rule over it autocratically? It will be seen that the participants in the conference differed sharply on some of these aspects of basic interpretation.

The conference first explored the challenge of totalitarianism, and more especially the issue of freedom and totalitarianism. Upon the general basis laid by these discussions, it took up successively the

---

[2] Sidney and Beatrice Webb, *Soviet Communism — A New Civilization* (1936).

[3] Scholarly analysis has been impeded by the recurrent sharp reversals in American public opinion on this subject. About 1936, for instance, the difference was strongly emphasized; in 1939–40 it was gainsaid; in 1943–45 it was considered very marked indeed; since 1947 it has been all but obliterated.

ideological and the psychological aspects, and then considered totalitarianism in its relation to intellectual life and to social and economic organization. Finally, it considered totalitarianism and the future. But at no time did it undertake to "cover" these subjects, that is, to deal systematically with all that might be said concerning them. There is a good deal of elementary material, both informative and analytical, which the conference took for granted, and was bound to take for granted, if it was to make any progress on its basic concern, the clarification of totalitarianism as the central problem of our time.

Nor did the conference seek in any sense to achieve geographical coverage. Indeed the references to Japan, China, and the Soviet satellites are rather inadequate and we are therefore glad to include Professor Gyorgy's paper which suggests some of the key problems in the last-named area.

Nor did the conference consider it its task to evolve "practical" solutions. In the English and American tradition any problem is likely to be seen as a problem of action, as something about which something can and ought to be done. But such is not the case in fact with totalitarianism. For if "practical" means to assist the totalitarians in making a success of their enterprise, this could hardly be considered an urgent task for Americans at the present time, even if it were feasible to tackle it. In fact, it may confidently be left to the Russians and their friends to do what can be done. If on the other hand a "practical" solution means how to deal with the threat of totalitarianism to our free society, both the threat from without and the threat from within, such a practical guide presupposes that the "problem" of what totalitarianism in fact is has been solved. We are, however, quite far from solving it. In the meantime, men of action have to shift for themselves as best they can, learning as it were from experience (though not much so far, it would seem).

Finally, the conference did not seek to establish firm agreement among the participants. I doubt that it would have been possible. As the discussion will show, there are "emergent" areas of agreement, but they are limited in scope. It would be tempting to formulate some of these agreements and disagreements and thus to mark out an area of agreement among the conferees, but considering the fact that we never sought an expression of opinion by all members of the conference, it seemed too perilous to undertake such a statement. The reader will probably be able to form a judgment of his own on the basis of comment in the discussions concerning this aspect of the conference. Even the effort of one of the participants to indicate a broad range of agreement on certain basic aspects of totalitarian dictatorship served to precipitate disagreement as much as it did agreement. In short, the papers which follow will disappoint him who comes to them in the hope of finding ready-made answers. It is the clarification of the issues, rather than the settlement of them which the conference aimed at and which it is hoped actually was achieved in the course of it.

It is evident that totalitarianism is not only, nor even primarily, a form of government. The prevailing oratory in the market place, employing as it does such terms as "tyranny," "despotism," and the even more general one of "authoritarianism," has created in many minds such a presumption, and the employment of the expression "dictatorship" has further contributed to this notion. But totalitarianism, as the papers here presented will show, is indeed "total": it engulfs the whole man who participates in it, and hence has its economic, sociological, and other aspects beyond the political and governmental. At the same time, totalitarianism has once again revealed the crucial role of politics. Long ago, Aristotle called the science of what pertains to the *polis* or the state, the "master science." What he meant, of course, was not that it was more scientific than other sciences, far from it. He had in mind what has recently been brought to the attention of many scientists, and that is the impossibility of making any science contribute to the good life without understanding how the community is governed and thus kept functioning well.

And yet the symposium did not specifically include a treatment of the government of these totalitarian societies. The reason is that this issue runs like a red threat through all the papers and discussions. Government in the totalitarian societies affects every human activity, and a number of papers are specifically concerned with some dominant aspects of this all-pervading governmental activity, such as the terror. But here, as elsewhere, it was a matter of picking and choosing.

As previously indicated, the writers of these papers and the participants in these discussions approached the subject of totalitarianism with the problems and methods of their particular disciplines in mind. Especially the discussions show clearly that it is often difficult to adjust to the approaches of related disciplines. This is, of course, no peculiarity of the subject of totalitarianism, but a recurrent experience of those who today insist that interdisciplinary teamwork is essential for a comprehensive empirical study of many of the broader problems and situations to which formerly historical, legal, economic, governmental-political, and sociological as well as psychological and anthropological studies have been addressed in isolation and often in duplication. Such interdisciplinary approach often reveals, as it does in these papers, that the range of problems is greater and their structure more complex than had been anticipated, because common-sense notions which had been retained in one field as if they were a "matter of course" turn out upon closer inspection to be themselves highly problematical and in need of careful investigation. Numerous illustrations will be found for this in the discussions on totalitarianism here presented. At the same time it was one of the striking features of the conference that there developed a cumulative cross-reference between the several disciplines and approaches as the discussions proceeded. It is hoped that something of this pulling together is reflected in the report on the discussions.

George F. Kennan's paper on "Totalitarianism and Freedom" seeks to establish the contrast between the two kinds of societies, free and totalitarian ones, on a broad basis of humanist concern for the values involved. But its primary effort is directed toward sketching the basic issues which totalitarianism presents, and as Mr. Kennan sees them in the perspective of his practical observation and experience. In his discussion of freedom he limits himself to indicating dangers that lie in some of the more radically democratic and equalitarian elements of the American tradition, insisting that restraints are vital to the survival of freedom.

The two papers on the nature of totalitarianism address themselves to some basic issues of the phenomenon. Their points of view are sharply contrasting, as is shown in the discussion. The focal point of their disagreement is over the question whether totalitarian regimes are to be equated with older forms of despotism and tyranny, or are to be treated as "historically unique," that is to say sufficiently novel so as to defy precedent. This fundamental issue was in a sense illustrated by an analysis of terror in the Soviet Union, which the author, Jerzy Gliksman, interpreted as a kind of social prophylaxis, arguing that its prime function is to eliminate offenders, actual and potential, against the regime by terrorizing them into submission. This view was sharply challenged in the discussion by Hannah Arendt, who insisted that the terror had no such rational basis. She also felt there should be great emphasis on the fact that terror was directed against the entire people, a view which Paul Kecskemeti shared. The juxtaposition of this paper on the terror with the two more general papers on totalitarianism may seem arbitrary, until it is recalled that the totalitarian terror is one of the key aspects of these regimes, and its nature is therefore of vital importance to an understanding of the phenomenon in its entirety.

The next part of the conference was concerned with the role of ideology in totalitarianism. This has been a hotly disputed issue among students of totalitarianism. Does ideology influence the ruling groups, as well as the followers, in such a system? Are ideas, to put it more philosophically, an independent force and an autonomous factor in the molding of totalitarian systems? Or are these merely "superstructure," rationalizations of underlying economic and social forces? All three papers tended to lean toward the first of these alternatives, although Alex Inkeles' interpretation of ideology as mystique may be taken as something of a qualification. His use of the term "mystique" aroused sharp controversy, however. His pointed contrast of this mystique with ideology is based upon the conclusion that important aspects of totalitarian *society* (as contrasted with its politics) cannot be explained adequately either by formal ideology, such as Marxism, or by mere power-seeking. The mystique is based upon the totalitarian's express belief in his knowledge of a "law of social development" which both obliges and enables him to act in its furtherance. The mystique thus is primarily a quality of the leaders, at least initially, but in time comes to characterize totalitarian society as such. Mr. Inkeles sees this mystique as correlative, and not as either superior to or supplanting the two other factors of power-seeking and ideology. As the discussion showed, the problem is partly a semantic one; others would present what is essentially an analogous analysis by stressing the changing pattern and content of totalitarian ideology as it is transformed into what Mr. Inkeles calls mystique. Mr. Inkeles, however, was disinclined to accept such interpretations of the dichotomy which he proposed between the rational ideology and the nonrational mystique. It is obvious that only an acceptance of this dichotomy (much emphasized in the sociology of Max Weber, for example) would secure general agreement.

The papers by Franklin Littell and Waldemar Gurian address themselves to some of the problems of religion under totalitarianism. Mr. Littell argues that only a church grounded firmly in orthodox dogma can marshal the discipline needed to withstand the ordeal of a totalitarian onslaught, and offers evidence from the sharply divergent behavior of Protestants in Germany. Mr. Gurian considers the other side of the medal and shows totalitarian ideologies to be "secular religions" — which in any case replace the older religions. Such phenomena as the deification of the leaders and the sanctification of the history of the movement illustrate this trend. Sacred formulas and rituals appear to be instituted, albeit in strictly secular form. "Transcendent beliefs are changed into immanent ones." Hence the hostility to established Christian religion is seen as related to the totalitarians' own religious orientation. If objection is raised to employing the term "religion" for describing this phenomenon of totalitarian societies, Mr. Gurian would suggest the term "ideocracy" — for which Miss Arendt in turn would substitute "logocracy," since she would lay stress on the abstract logical derivations employed by the totalitarians, rather than on their ideas. Clearly, Mr. Gurian's concept of the totalitarian ideology brings it close to the mystique of Mr. Inkeles. Ultimately, the totalitarian ideology is in Mr. Gurian's view the deification of a power system which is needed in order to execute the laws of history.

The papers of the session on Totalitarianism and Psychology struck a rather different note. They were concerned with what light modern psychology might be able to shed upon totalitarianism in order to explain it at least in part. Characteristically, and in keeping with the methodological premises of modern empirical modes of approach, the papers dealt with situations which were at least in part experimental and based upon an assumed pattern of totalitarianism which the experiment sought to re-create.

The first paper, by Raymond Bauer, in a sense belongs as much in the preceding and the subsequent part, as in that on psychology. He resumes the discussion of ideology and explores what it does to the totalitarian approach to science, which is, of course, an important part of the problem of totalitarianism and intellectual life. But Mr. Bauer is a psychologist, and his handling of the problem is influenced by this fact. Since his central concern was to show that Marxist ideas were a factor, though by no means the only factor, shaping Soviet attitudes toward science, his paper resuscitated several of the themes previously explored. His inclination is to claim that since 1931 Soviet theoreticians have selected those statements of Lenin's that can be used to support a pragmatic position and that they are themselves thoroughgoing pragmatists, even though they go to great pains to disguise the fact.

Erik Erikson, approaching his paper on wholeness and totality as a psycho-pathologist in the light of the assumption that "totalitarianism is based on universal human potentialities and is thus related to all aspects of human nature," concentrated on the psychological prerequisites of a totalitarian ideology. He thus related the psychological problems of this part of the conference to the ideological ones of the preceding one. Contrasting balanced, organic wholeness with one-sided, mechanic totality, Mr. Erikson suggests that when a human being loses his confidence in "whole" solutions, "he restructures himself and the world by taking recourse to what we may call totalism." He traces through three stages of childhood the recurrent propensity to adopt total realignment as a solution. He pleads for continued exploration of the possibilities of genuine wholeness and integration in our own society as against fearful attempts of totalizing it in turn.

Else Frenkel-Brunswik in her paper on environmental controls and the impoverishment of thought more particularly considered the issue of authoritarianism in personality structure. She "attempted to throw light on the psychological mechanisms by which the totalitarian outlook is transmitted and the role it plays in the adjustment balance of the individual." Her findings tend to support the notion that there is a parallelism between totalitarianism in society and government on one side, and the totalitarian tendencies in the individuals susceptible to this kind of ideology. There is, she believes, a "pronounced preponderance of mechanization, standardization, and dehumanization of social contacts, a marked rigidity and intolerance of ambiguity growing out of a need for absolutes and a corresponding lack of spontaneity . . ." Her views precipitated a sharp challenge in terms of the beneficent role of authority in human society and a consequent differentiation on her own part of two kinds of authority. Miss Frenkel-Brunswik concentrated on the theme of the eradication of independent and critical judgment which she believes "lies at the very core of totalitarianism." But she would not assert that there is "necessarily a direct or exclusive causal relationship between family structure and the rise of totalitarianism." (It was later argued in the discussion that authoritarian family structure was characteristic of societies, such as New England Puritanism, which in fact evolved patterns of free and democratic societies.) In an assessment of totalitarian propensities prevalent in contemporary America, Miss Frenkel-Brunswik, although clearly recognizing the danger signs, expressed a long-range optimism.

The final psychological paper, by Marie Jahoda and Stuart W. Cook, dealt with ideological compliance as a social-psychological process; as a model for this process it used experiments by Solomon Asch which tended to show that individuals when confronted with (prearranged) isolation in a group, tended to surrender their own judgment and conform. Some criticism was voiced, because the model involved sense-data, rather than more strictly rational thoughts. Miss Jahoda stated in a rejoinder that she recognized the distinction between perceptual and ideological compliance; while the model should not be literally applied to political matters, further experiments might show that for the great mass of a population there is no significant difference between the processes of perceptual and ideological compliance. In any case, the material seemed to suggest very interesting lines of analysis and corresponding insights into the kind of mass support the totalitarian systems have been able to marshal.

The next session of the conference was concerned with totalitarianism and intellectual life. Focal areas of analysis were those of science under soviet totalitarianism and totalitarianism and history, with a special paper on phases of the conflict between totalitarianism and science which high-lighted the issue which arose between Galileo and the Catholic Church. All the papers tended to corroborate the deleterious effect of totalitarianism and indeed authoritarianism upon scientific inquiry and progress. H. J. Muller specifically shows how the directive procedures of governmentally controlled scientific research lead "more and more in the direction of submissive mediocrity" and he warned against similar tendencies in the United States. George de Santillana, after recalling the precedent of Plato's *Laws*, insisted that "the Catholic Church could not but proceed along the lines suggested by Plato." Yet, he shows the trial of Galileo to have been the last such attempt, and in a discriminating analysis shows that Galileo got into trouble not because he was a progressive, but because he was a conservative. "The Church of the Counter Reformation is the 'pilot project' of the modern totalitarian state and stands for the streamlined and the new in executive efficiency." After a brief parallel on Comte, Mr. Santillana in conclusion applies his analysis to the problems of science in the Soviet Union, with some critical hints about parallel trends in the West. He is not as sure as Mr. Muller that Soviet science will fail to produce under conditions of totalitarian direction and suggests that the West also has its difficulties, including "programmatic research." And in conclusion, he states that "the analogy with the Galileo trial which seemed so clear in the beginning, appears misleading. We are not facing a static idealist orthodoxy, but a moving operationalist one."

Bertram Wolfe, in his paper on totalitarianism and history, gave specific evidence for the way in which historical data are doctored. These attitudes thus correspond to shifts of the ruling group. "What the totalitiarian is sure of is what the rest of us are most unsure of. Historians find it hard enough to determine what really happened in the past, more difficult to apprehend what is happening in the present, and impossible to foretell the future. It is the totalitarian's certainty as to the future which makes him so ruthless in manipulating the present." His facts are in line with George Orwell's fantasy *1984*, which Mr. Kennan had suggested as one of the sources for the type or image in the mind of people when they speak of totalitarianism (rather than the reality as he saw it). Mr. Wolfe's material and analysis, for one, implies that these fantasies are pretty close to that reality. Yet, Mr. Wolfe's facts were challenged by Michael Karpovich, who insisted that this systematic distortion of the historical record is less pronounced for ancient history and by no means complete. Similarly, Mr. Santillana's facts were implemented by suggestions of other aspects, including the tensions arising from rapid shifts of knowledge and hence problems of learning. His equating of the authoritarianism of the church and of totalitarianism was seriously questioned. There are, of course, points of similarity; Mr. Santillana himself suggested some discriminating points in the concluding statement already referred to.

Totalitarian social and economic organization is, in the minds of many, the core of the whole enterprise. Especially central economic planning is often considered the prime aspect of totalitarianism. Albert Lauterbach, in his paper on totalitarian appeal and economic reform, is more discriminating. "For the bulk of their followers, the economic reforms proposed represent a rationalization of deeper emotional needs," he writes. Linking his analysis to some of the preceding psychological and ideological positions, Lauterbach shows how the "solutions" of totalitarian economics frequently consist in mere suppression of criticism and of possible alternative approaches. And while stressing the basic similarity of Communist and fascist totalitarians, he nonetheless would differentiate between them in terms of social roots, claiming that Communism initially addresses itself to aspirations of the lower classes, fascism at first to the upper and middle classes. In the discussion he agreed to modify this statement to take account of the frequent peasant support of fascism. All in all, Lauterbach tended to minimize the long-run achievements of totalitarian regimes in developing patterns of genuine economic reforms, especially in the West. W. W. Leontieff on the other hand drew attention to the vast economic gains in the Soviet Union and their prospective continuance.

In a paper on the economy of the Soviet zone of Germany, J. P. Nettl, contrasting the Communist economic policy and action with its Nazi predecessor, arrived at the conclusion that "the difference between Communism and other types of totalitarianism is fundamental as far as economics is concerned." This view was explicitly challenged by several of the discussants. (In the politico-governmental field the difference is, according to Nettl, merely a matter of degree in method.)

In the concluding paper of this session, Karl Deutsch addressed himself to the disintegrative forces operating in totalitarian systems. He premised his remarks upon a three-pronged characterization of totalitarianism: mobilization of effort, unity of command, and effective power of enforcement. This characterization aroused some adverse comment. Whether one accepts or not this particular set of traits (and Mr. Deutsch himself professed a willingness to adopt Friedrich's traits, while Mr. Timasheff once again insisted that the proper method was to identify one central aspect, such as "state control"), significant insights were recognized in Mr. Deutsch's analyses of specific weaknesses of the totalitarian systems. Among them he noted the limited capacity for decision-making; the instability of hierarchical power; some technological limitations, such as those of weapons and of supervision instruments. Finally he discussed some of the totalitarian policies to resist the disintegration which threatened their systems. He thought that these faced a decreasing prospect of success, but only within the time-span of twenty-five to fifty years from the present. He therefore felt that the free countries cannot rely upon this disintegration in the near future. This explicit *caveat* rather invalidated a point made in the discussion by Mr. Leontieff, who stressed the success of the Soviet Union in industrializing Russia and even insisted that the Soviets were gaining on the rest of the world (a view which was contested). A sharp disagreement developed between Mr. Deutsch and Miss Arendt over the success of the *Fuehrerprinzip*, which Mr. Deutsch considered an unsuccessful organizational device, while Ivo Duchacek, seconded by others, stressed the tremendous compulsive force resulting from the complete control of jobs in a totalitarian system.

The conclusion of Deutsch's paper actually opened up the issues of the last session, devoted to Totalitarianism and the Future. Paul Kecskemeti, after noting the unrevolutionary nature of the war and postwar period at the beginning of his paper, briefly dealt with possible aspects of a future war between totalitarians and democrats, and then turned to the issues presented for both camps by peaceful coexistence. He did not expect spontaneous upheavals in either camp but saw some threat to the stability of totalitarian systems in connection with the problem of succession. "It is possible that the 'wave' of totalitarianism has reached its high-water mark."

In a concluding paper on the world-revolutionary situation, Harold Lasswell sketched a projection in terms of two "developmental constructs" or "speculative models" for which he claimed no scientific validity, though they are based upon our presently existing knowledge. The first construct would culminate in a free man's commonwealth on a global scale, the second in the establishment of two or more garrison-police states and the reëstablishment of caste systems in new forms. After an extended analysis, he concluded that the garrison-police alternative is more probable, though he added that the recognition of this probability might reverse the trend. In the discussion, several divergent views were voiced. I stressed the intrinsic difficulty of predicting, after pointing out that neither of his constructs were likely, and that all things considered it was more likely that the world would be in 1980 much like the world of 1950. Mr. Kecskemeti also questioned this simple "monolithic" alternative. There was considerable argument about what means might be adopted to fight totalitarianism, whether a religious revival, economic activity, or, as David Riesman put it, a "nylon war" of flooding the Russian population with consumer goods (which reminds one of the recent efforts of the United States to feed the Eastern German population) might be effective. Erwin Canham brought the discussion to a close by stressing voluntary groupings in democratic societies and by calling them "our greatest source of strength in the contest with totalitarianism."

The perusal of these papers and discussions suggests a considerable number of topics on which further research is not only urgently needed but distinctly promising. Very large amounts of documentary materials are now available with reference to Germany, Italy, and Japan to mention only the three main examples which deserve much fuller exploration than they have hitherto received. Only in Germany does there seem to have come into existence a center for research in this general field, the Institut für Zeitgeschichte at the University of Munich. It publishes monographs as well as a journal in which current findings are reported: *Zeitschrift für Zeitgeschichte*. It would seem highly desirable that similar centers be established both in Italy and Japan, but such research by scholars in these countries should without a doubt be reinforced and implemented by American workers, whose participation could stress the comparative and more general lines of approach and could mitigate the parochial impact of national prejudices and presumptions.

By way of a conclusion, I should like to invite the reader to draw his own. As I stated at the outset, it cannot be the purpose of a conference such as this to arrive at conclusions embodied in resolutions adopted and agreed upon. Numerous issues were explored, and most of the participants came away with a clearer view of what were some of the outstanding problems with which totalitarianism confronts us. They also revised some of their views and were confirmed in others. The reader of these papers and discussions ought likewise to be in a better position to avoid some of the more obvious pitfalls into which those plunge who deal with totalitarianism today. Knowledge insufficient for prediction may yet be valuable for guidance, John Stuart Mill says somewhere in his *Logic*. It is so with what knowledge can be garnered about totalitarianism here. There is a long road ahead, before we shall fully understand the cataclysmic developments of our time, embodied in totalitarianism, which destroyed the facile optimism and the ready belief in progress. This conference marked a way-station in the view of its participants. It is my hope that others through reading this record will come to share our view.

PART ONE

Totalitarianism and Freedom

■

1. Totalitarianism in the Modern World

GEORGE F. KENNAN

We have come together to discuss a phenomenon of our time that has brought the deepest possible misery to untold millions of our contemporaries, even to the point of rendering life itself a hated burden to them. As a source of sorrow and suffering to the human race, I suppose this phenomenon has overshadowed every other source of human woe in our times; for it has demeaned humanity in its own sight, attacked man's confidence in himself, made him realize that he can be his own most terrible and dangerous enemy, more bestial than the beasts, more cruel than nature. And although we Americans have not been directly affected by it, to many of our countrymen it has come to appear as the greatest of all our American problems — to some of them, I fear, as the only one.

The phenomenon of which I am speaking is, of course, modern totalitarianism; and if we have come together at this conference to study and discuss it, it is because we wonder how such a thing could have come into our world, what are the prospects for its passing in the areas where it is now dominant, and what we can do to keep it from spreading and completing the ruin of our environment and our society.

I would like to say at the outset that I find this subject a difficult one to discuss in any general way. It is one in which I have no theoretical erudition. My experience with it has been largely pragmatical. It began against an educational background which I recognize today to have been wholly inadequate, and it has proceeded in ways that failed to correct that deficiency.

I first came into close contact with totalitarianism when I served in the Baltic countries — Estonia and Latvia — in the late twenties and early thirties. Those countries were of course not themselves totalitarian at that time; but both had only recently been through periods of Bolshevik rule. The traces were still fresh; and the shadow of the neighboring Communist power still lay heavily across the lives of their peoples. I was repelled from the start by certain features of Russian Communism apparent even in the shadow: notably, its reckless injustice, its shocking physical cruelty, and its congenital untruthfulness. This repulsion was so great that I never could take very seriously the theory that lay behind it — the theoretical pretensions of Communism seemed, when you saw them at that time from the vantage points of Reval and Riga, so obviously hypocritical. In this way I missed the period of preoccupation with the theoretical aspects of Communism that so many other people passed through who were interested in the Soviet Union. That had both advantages and disadvantages; but among the latter was the fact that it left unfilled an existing educational gap.

Later it fell to me to reside and serve for long periods of time in both the Soviet Union and Nazi Germany. Again, duties were practical, and experience related largely to minor problems of our relations. Never, as it seems to me in retrospect, did we foreign service officers have occasion to systematize what we knew about the regimes of those countries, to attempt the general assessment of that sort of power from the standpoint of its place in history and its relation to our civilization as a whole. We were always too busy dealing with individual manifestations of it that posed immediate and specific problems for our government.

When, therefore, I look into my own mind today to see what might be in there in the way of general appreciations about the nature of totalitarianism, I find a great disorder of undigested impressions and a number of actual blanks where I know that knowledge and deduction ought to be present and aren't. And that being so, I don't think that I can hope to add anything valuable in the way of historical or theoretical appreciation to the fund of analysis that we already have before us — much of it from the minds and pens of people far more learned than myself — many of them actually with us in this hall tonight. The only thing I can do, as it seems to me, is to expose to you, in all humility, the state of such progress as I have been able to make and not to make in my own thinking on this subject to date and the nature of the questionings with which that progress has left me — for I am bound to say that I have far more questions on this point than I have conclusions. What I am afraid you must expect, therefore, is merely something in the way of a personal confession; and I can only hope that the rather unusual experience from which it flows will give it a significance that it would not otherwise have.

When I begin to think of totalitarianism as a general phenomenon, the first thing that assails me is, as usual, the problem of definition. That there is such a thing, I have no doubt; but how does one delimit the term in such a way as to make it a useful one for purposes of group discussion? We have all noted totalitarian elements and tendencies in every human society, including sometimes our own; but to me the only places where these tendencies have really flowered and revealed their true nature seem to have been Germany and the Soviet Union. Some people would argue about this, I know. They would suggest that other countries as well should be included under this heading. Let us leave this argument aside for the moment, and agree that there are at least no *better* examples than Germany and Russia, and that these might then be permitted to serve as a basis for discussion.

But even here I run at once into difficulties; for I see that the Russian and German phenomenon were highly disparate things, in nature as in origin; and I am moved to wonder whether there is any generic phenomenon that we can identify and describe from actual experience as totalitarianism. Is there really some identity of essence as between Russian Communism and German National Socialism? Or is it simply that two countries have both had certain national experiences in our time and that those experiences have simply had points in common, perhaps accidentally?

When I try to picture totalitarianism to myself as a general phenomenon, what comes into my mind most prominently is neither the Soviet picture nor the Nazi picture as I have known them in the flesh, but rather the fictional and symbolic images created by such people as Orwell or Kafka or Koestler or the early Soviet satirists.

The purest expression of the phenomenon, in other words, seems to me to have been rendered not in its physical reality but in its power as a dream, or a nightmare. Not that it lacks the physical reality, or that this reality is lacking in power; but it is precisely in the way it appears to people, in the impact it has on the subconscious, in the state of mind it creates in its victims, that totalitarianism reveals most deeply its meaning and its nature. Here, then, we seem to have a phenomenon of which it can be said that it is both a reality and a bad dream, but that its deepest reality lies strangely enough in its manifestation as a dream, and it is by this manifestation that it can best be known and judged and discussed. This conclusion, involving as it does a most profound contradiction, is already an unsettling and baffling one to the simple bureaucratic mind; and I can only back off from it and pass it on to the philosophers with my best wishes and regards.

Leaving aside, then, the question of definitions, and turning to the nature of whatever it is we conceive to be totalitarianism: there are a number of things that occur to me about it and seem to me to be significant. Whether they constitute an adequate list of its important attributes, I strongly doubt. I cannot say that they build up to any reliable conclusions. They remind me of the observation (I forget the origin) that "we have chaos, but not enough to make a world." Anyway, let me list some of them for you and tell you what I think they may mean.

First of all, I have been greatly impressed with the primary importance, in the totalitarian picture, of modern police weapons and their use. I am thinking here not merely of arms and munitions; I am also thinking of such things as modern means of transportation and communication. Whenever, today, a group of men obtains a monopolistic control over these things and exercises that control with sufficient ruthlessness and with suitable techniques, for the purpose of perpetuating its own power, and so long as that group retains its internal unity and does not suffer violent interference from outside, popular revolt is simply impossible. In this fact there seems to me to lie the fundamental reality of modern totalitarianism; and I would point out that this is a reality derived from the progress of modern technology.

Whether totalitarianism was conceivable apart from modern technology, I do not know. I have heard it said by well informed people that all the essential features of Soviet Communism could be observed in certain ancient oriental despotisms. I cannot be a good judge of this, for I know nothing about oriental history. I would be inclined to doubt that this could be wholly true, precisely because of the importance of the technological component in the totalitarian system as we know it today. In any case, so far as the West is concerned, totalitarianism does seem to have been something made possible only by the technological developments of the past century and a half, which have operated to enhance enormously the potential scope and intensity of absolute power.

Noting that, my mind turns next to the question of popular support — that is, the relation of totalitarian power to the feelings of people. Here I notice that there have been great differences between the Nazi and Soviet phenomena. In Germany, Nazi rule certainly enjoyed at most times a fairly high degree of mass support — although whether this would have continued much longer, had Nazi power not been destroyed when it was, seems to me to be doubtful. In the Soviet Union, Communism was introduced by a small minority and has been maintained the same way. The Soviet regime enjoyed the passive tolerance of the masses at the time of the seizure of power, largely because of the lack of promising alternatives, and in consequence of certain demagogic concessions it made to popular feeling at the moment; but it has never been the product or the object of mass enthusiasm. No majority was ever necessary to Bolshevism. People in this country have a seemingly incurable tendency to overrate the propaganda successes of Bolshevism. I am not aware that anywhere in the world, unless you insist on including China in this picture, has Soviet Communism ever won over a majority or commanded mass support; in no case, certainly, has propaganda been the main source of the establishment or maintenance of its power; in no place has it ever come into power except by force of arms — by pressure, that is, exerted either by the direct application or by the threat of armed force.

This being the case, a great deal that has been written about totalitarianism on the basis of experience with National Socialism has turned out to be not fully applicable to Soviet Communism. This is true, it seems to me, of a good part of the teaching concerning the importance of the cultivation of mass delusions, and the creation of scapegoat elements on which to focus mass emotion. These things always have been present in totalitarianism in one degree or another; they have been really important, on occasions, to the seizure of power; but they are important to the maintenance of power only if a serious attempt be made to maintain real mass enthusiasm. The Soviet rulers make no such attempt. They do, of course, in a rather half-hearted and routine way, employ both devices: the myth and the scapegoat. Now, for example, two decades after the final and official liquidation of the "remnants of capitalism" in Soviet society, lacking any other plausible scapegoat element, the Soviet rulers are not averse to gleaning such meager profit as can be gleaned from the exploitation of the endemic, and not really very powerful, anti-Semitism in certain sections of the Soviet population. But they do this only when it coincides with considerations of foreign policy. And as a domestic measure, they do not exaggerate its importance. Their rule actually rests not on the cultivation of illusions but on a bitter reality: which is the existence of a monopoly of physical force and a readiness to employ that monopoly quite ruthlessly in the interests of the perpetuation of the power of the ruling group. The mystique and semi-religious appeal are important for the promotion of Soviet purposes in areas where Soviet power is not yet dominant; where it already reigns supreme, they become subsidiary elements.

It is true that the effective application of Soviet police power involves the use of certain devices peculiar, as far as I know, to modern totalitarianism, namely, the maintenance of a system of artificial tensions within society (as a substitute for the natural ones, which might be dangerous to the system) and the employment of coercion on a vast scale for what might be called prophylactic purposes (that is, the concentration-camp system) in place of, or in addition to, its use on a small scale for the punishment of actual offenses, as in bourgeois democracy. It involves, in other words, as you all know, the punishment of people primarily for the crimes they have not committed, rather than for those they have — the punishment of those who *might* rebel, rather than those who *do*. It even involves, precisely for this reason, a species of intimacy and collaboration with the real criminal element in society, since the latter are necessary to provide certain of the essential features of the earthly purgatory:

the trusties and the yegg-men, the tormentors of the political prisoners and exiles. These — not, as many people suppose, the degree of terror — are the features of modern totalitarianism, incidentally, that seem to distinguish it from most of the traditional forms of despotism.

But none of these things have anything to do with mass support, really. They are only addenda to the system of police intimidation. This being so, popular emotional support must be viewed as something which may or may not be a feature of totalitarianism, but is certainly not essential to it. What is essential is only the seizure, organization, and ruthless exercise of power. For the seizure of power, a certain degree of mass bewilderment and passivity are required — in other words, certain negative rather than positive states of the mass mind. Once power has been seized, even these states of mind are not vitally important.

Now modern police weapons are of course only one of the essential components of the totalitarian situation. Another is the presence of a body of men — namely, the natural bureaucrats and enthusiasts of a police regime — ready to use those weapons for the purpose indicated. I would like to say that I think such people are always present in any human society, to some degree or another. They are not a product of the political movement itself. They are something that is always there and needs only to be activated. They represent a mutation of the human species. I do not need to describe these people to you, nor is it pleasant to do so. They merge with the born criminal element, to which I have already referred. They are the brutal, aggressive, unsuccessful natures, deficient in moral courage, in self-confidence, in self-respect, in the ability to compete on any even terms. They are the ghouls of human society. In the sunlight of normalcy you do not see them. But let society be overtaken by the darkness of some special weakness, which leaves it helpless and vulnerable, and they are suddenly there, slinking out of the shadows, ready to take over, ready to flog, to intimidate, to torture, to do all those things in the company of armed men, and preferably against unarmed ones, that help to give them the illusion of success and security, that dispel for the moment the nightmare of inadequacy by which they are haunted.

Such people, I reiterate, are always there in every human society.

They are all around us. They are the people of whom Dostoyevsky's totalitarian, Verkhovensky, said in *The Possessed*: they "are ours, though they do not know it." They are the Judases of whom any political society would be justified in saying: "Behold, the hand of him that betrayeth me is with me on the table." But in most instances, they become real dangers only when the weakness of society is already present.

It is these reflections that bring me to think of modern totalitarianism as a sort of a strait jacket which can conceivably be clamped on to any great modern society if and when circumstances so dispose. To use another word picture: it is a condition made possible by modern police weapons, a state into which any great national entity *can* relapse, if it doesn't watch its step. Whether it might be considered a natural state for peoples of other climes and eras, I do not know. But for Western man, taught as he has been to look for hope and solace in the dignity of the human spirit, it is surely a pathological, abnormal state — a sick state, devoid of hope, characterized by the deepest sort of agony and misery and depression.

It is a state, furthermore, from which there is no recovery, I fear, by the patient's own effort. Only three things can, as far as I can see, operate to bring it to an end. One is successful military intervention by external power. A second is forgetfulness and lack of due vigilance and zeal on the part of the totalitarian rulers themselves. The last is the disruption of the unity of the ruling group. But to the last development, totalitarianism surely has a certain congenital vulnerability in its dependence on the individual dictator and in its lack of any reliable institutional framework for the transfer of power from one individual to another. The lack of such a framework is precisely one of the things that distinguishes it from dynastic absolutism, as indeed also from bourgeois democracy. Just in these days it is useful for us to bear in mind, I think, that the ultimate test of totalitarianism lies not in its ability to surmount peaceably any single crisis of succession but rather in its ability to survive what is bound to be a long series of such crises, each attended by great nervousness and fear and secret intrigue, and sure to open up many possibilities for misunderstanding, division, and paralysis of the central will. This long series of crises must always present an even greater danger in the case of a regime that has projected its

power on to other national societies and is attempting to hold together a far-flung empire than in the case of the indigenous totalitarian regime alone. This type of power is most safely exerted within
the intimacy of the national society, so far as the intrinsic relationships of power are concerned. But on the other hand, totalitarian
rulers are always moved to try to eliminate the awkward standard
of comparison involved in the existence of freedom elsewhere, particularly in the country just next door. This is their dilemma — the
reconciling of the requirements of domestic totalitarianism with the
urge to imperialism. It is on the horns of this dilemma, in my view,
that they are most likely to be at some stage impaled and destroyed.

This view of the likely impermanence of totalitarian systems (a
view which, I must say, is not shared by all of my good friends)
naturally has its implications for our attitude toward Soviet power,
lending force to the counsels of patience and caution. But I am well
aware that it gives us no grounds for complacency as to the extent
of the damage done by totalitarianism where it comes and while it
lasts. It is like a flood; the fact that the water is bound some day to
recede does not mitigate the damage it does while it lasts. Thus it
is small comfort that totalitarianism may be by nature impermanent.
It can still encompass in the course of a few short years a destruction
of human and cultural values that cannot be overcome in generations, if at all. And for this reason we cannot leave the consideration
of it without glancing at the all-important subject of its causes.

This is, above all, a subject on which I have no firm and rounded
and demonstrable conclusions that in any way satisfy me. What I
have are more in the way of suspicions and hunches, and I offer
them here with particular diffidence and doubt as to their value.
They are based simply on thoughts about the places where totalitarianism *has* appeared and has *not* appeared, and particularly on
those few elements of background which the German and Russian
manifestations of it appear to have had in common.

We see, first of all, that both Germany and Russia are great countries. Hannah Arendt has pointed out that totalitarianism seems to
be a phenomenon of the numerical great entities; and I think that
this is a profound and useful observation. Perhaps we are witnessing
today in Tito's Yugoslavia the inevitable rejection by the small
country of many of the typical features of modern totalitarianism.

Am I right in suspecting that the totalitarian process is something that takes place in the grand manner, or not at all? If so, we may have here one of the clues to its origin. Perhaps it is important to the establishment and maintenance of an indigenous totalitarian system that the scale of society be so vast and complicated that the individual can no longer sense or survey his relation to the whole and is obliged to feel himself, in the absence of the totalitarian illusions, as a helpless and superfluous entity in the hands of demoniac forces beyond his power to understand or influence. This is not so apt to occur in smaller societies characterized by a greater degree of intimacy as between ruler and ruled.

Second, I note that in both of these countries totalitarianism came in the wake of a terribly costly and exhausting military effort, namely World War I, which in each case overstrained the existing structure of society and culminated in the overthrow of the monarchical system and the decisive disruption of the power of the aristocracy. We in this country have a tendency to judge war too much in relation to its ostensible and stated purposes; we judge it, in other words, by whether it does or does not achieve on the field of battle that specific and momentary result that we call "victory." By the same token, we are relatively unreceptive to the understanding of war as a social phenomenon in its own right, quite independent of its military result. This quality, however, has been tremendously important in recent European history, and particularly in the case of World War I. That war strained more than any other the faith and credulity of the men who participated in it. It tended to appear to these men either as a wholly senseless and tragic undertaking or as the product of the criminal manipulations of mysterious and malicious conspiratorial forces. This was particularly true, quite naturally, in the case of the defeated countries; and it is useful to remember that both Germany and Russia, though they were on opposite sides of the war, fell into this catergory.

Third, there were certain *other* highly significant similarities in the recent social and political histories of these two countries. Let us work backward from the revolution. In each case, the advent of totalitarianism had been immediately preceded by the overthrow of a monarchy and by a brief and unsuccessful liberal era. In Germany, this embraced the period of the Weimar Republic and in part the final years of the Empire. In Russia, this embraced the brief months of the provisional government, but also, it is important to note, in some measure the years from the revolution of 1905 to the great war.

Back of these abortive liberal experiences there lay, in each case, the relatively late survival of feudal institutions, reaching even into the memory of living man, and, accordingly, a relatively shallow, brief, and imperfect development of bourgeois-democratic institutions.

Next, I would note that in both countries the growth of secular national feeling occurred largely in the nineteenth century and was subject to the influences of the romantic concepts of the nation-state evolved by German thinkers in the early part of that century: concepts that glorified the bonds of race and tongue, surrounded these bonds with vague and mystical overtones of emotional association, and tended to disintegrate rather suddenly and contemptuously the old hierarchical break-downs of national and international life. It is significant, I suspect, that liberal thought in both countries tended to associate itself with this new concept of the nation-state, and to be incredulous of the need for the preservation of any continuity with the dying feudal order.

Finally, I note that both of these countries were great military landpowers, characterized long before their respective revolutions by a relatively high degree of centralization and bureaucratization. In the overseas trading nations, the growth of centralized, bureaucratic power had been impeded by various realities, notably by the vital importance of the great urban trading communities, such as London or Liverpool or Amsterdam, by the influence of business circles generally, and by the complicated compromises always involved in the overseas relationship. Similarly, the outlooks of people in these countries had been kept varied and flexible and cosmopolitan by the constant experience of travel and contact with other environments. In the military land powers there was relatively little to stop the march of centralization, both in administration and in outlook. Both Russia and Germany were relatively receptive, by virtue of their national experience, to the sort of administrative and ideological centralization which totalitarianism involves.

Now these are only fragmentary and impressionistic points. It would be hard, in the space of time allotted to us, to bring them forward in any other way. To me, they prove little; but they do point in a direction. And if I were to be asked to describe that direction, I would do so substantially as follows.

All societies have varying degrees of vulnerability to totalitarian tendencies and of resistance to them.

The powers of resistance are partly connected with, and dependent on, the requisite degree of gradualness in evolution — a decent and sedate pace of social change — a pace that permits change to occur without disrupting the continuity of the generations or destroying the individual's confidence in his environment. Where peoples have had a decent time to prepare themselves for the strains of modern life they are better able to resist the totalitarian virus than where these things have come too suddenly upon them.

Furthermore, variety and decentralization of every sort have increased the powers of resistance. The dispersion of interests and tastes and outlooks through maritime and overseas activities, the experience of far-flung commercial and political empires, the necessity for compromise between competing linguistic groups; these things have kept open the vistas of men, preserved the heterogeneity of their outlook, sustained the need and capacity for compromise and adjustment.

We see, also, how important it is, if men are not to fall into the illness of totalitarianism, that they should not be subjected without adequate ideological preparation to the strains of the great apocalyptic disasters of society; that without such preparation they should not know on their own territories the infinite horrors of modern warfare, that they should not be asked to sit for dreary long years in filthy, vermin-infested trenches and to witness what can only seem to them to be the senseless agony and slaughter of their fellow creatures, just as they must not be thrown out onto the streets by unemployment through processes they cannot understand, and thus be forced to lose their sense of usefulness and belonging in society. If democracy does not wish its members to turn to the morbid and despairing delusions of totalitarianism, it must take care to spare them these harrowing and excruciating experiences. This does not mean that it must always avoid war, or that it must baby its people in the extreme paternalism of the welfare state. But it must never ask men to undergo such experiences unless it also enables them to understand their rationale. If democracy cannot make men understand why life is sometimes hard and dangerous, it will not be able to continue successfully to subject men to hardship and danger. It will have only itself to blame if by so doing it drives them to seek refuge in the purgatory of totalitarianism. For even a purgatory in which there seems initially to be some semblance of meaning, however crude and irrational, is preferable, from the standpoint of the human soul, to a liberal chaos from which the sense of community is absent and in which freedom means only the sense of being lost and lonely and helpless.

I suspect, furthermore, that a neurotic sense of tidiness in political arrangements can be a great danger to any society. Too great an urge for symmetry and order, too strong an insistence on uniformity and conformity, too little tolerance for the atypical and minority phenomenon: these are all things that can grease the path by which nations slide into totalitarianism. Lucky, in this respect, are countries like Great Britain, with its bizarre pattern of nationalities and dialects, its far-flung bonds of blood and interest, and its picturesque ceremonies and traditions; lucky is Switzerland, with mountain barriers, its unique historical path, and its multilingual balance. Lucky, even, we Americans have been up to this time, with our sectional diversities, our checks and balances, and our deference to the vital interests of competing minorities. Woe to any of us, if these things begin to yield to the leveling influences of the perfectionist, to utopian dreams of progress and equality, to the glorification of conformity in tongue or outlook that have been embraced in the concept of romantic nationalism and have gone before the disasters of totalitarian triumph. Diversity, in all the glorious disorder of nature, is the best defense of healthy societies.

In short, I suspect totalitarianism to be the retribution that befalls all peoples who give free rein to extremists and extremisms, who forget the golden rule of political life, which is that ideas are never good except in moderation, and that anything carried to its logical conclusion becomes a menacing caricature of itself. For this reason one must not be too morbid about incipient totalitarian tendencies, which are only a part of life — so long as they remain incipient and counterbalanced. All totalitarianism is only a matter of degree; but it is precisely in this fact that its mortal danger lies. Who says differences of degree are not vital differences? Remember Shakespeare's words:

> Take but degree away, untune that string,
> And, hark! what discord follows . . .
> Then every thing includes itself in power,
> Power into will, will into appetite;
> And appetite, a universal wolf . . .
> Must make perforce a universal prey,
> And last eat up himself . . .

Now I have said many things this evening about totalitarianism, and very few about freedom — which was supposed to be the other side of my topic. I am sure the interconnection of all these things has been apparent to you throughout. But I would like to suggest to you, in conclusion, that these words of Shakespeare are no less important in their relation to liberty than in relation to authority. There is, of course, no such thing as freedom in the abstract. There is only a freedom *from* something, and a freedom *to* something. It is therefore not just "freedom," but the kind of freedom that is important as an antidote and an alternative to totalitarianism. And here I would only like to say that it is by no means the maximum absence of restraint that is demanded. On the contrary, I sometimes think that totalitarianism finds it hardest to enter where the framework of individual obligation is firmest, and where certain forms of restraint are most highly developed. Those forms of restraint are of course the voluntarily accepted ones — the ones that deal most gently and considerately with the real needs of men — and not just those needs that lend themselves to idealization, but the absurd needs, the pathetic ones, the anarchic ones. These are the forms of restraint that give recognition to charity and to humor and to sadness — the ones that take man as he is, not as other people would like to make him. They are ones that make it possible for him to arrive at acceptable compromises with himself and his fellows, and to live life without destroying its meaning, or disgracing the Image in which he was created.

Such a system of restraints — in reality, the highest form of freedom — must be sought in the wisdom of the ages, and in the ethical codes that the great religions of civilization have developed. Never, but really never, will it be found in utopian visions and undertakings that set out to change the nature of man and the order of human affairs within our time. If we Americans wish, then, to hold aloft at this time a standard of freedom that will truly serve to rally and inspire the forces of resistance to modern totalitarianism, we will have to reject many of our favored predilections, outstandingly our belief in human perfectibility and the miracle of progress. We will have to see to it that our visions of the human future, unlike those of totalitarianism, are tuned to the deepest needs of man, that they show a certain tenderness to his weakness, and a forbearance for all the childishness and helplessness of his nature.

DISCUSSION

Mr. Merle Fainsod: I should like to ask Mr. Kennan to expand his remarks on the "erosion" of totalitarian power. So far, at any rate, no totalitarian system has been transformed from within. Overthrow has come only from without.

We know further that all such systems create internal strains and conflicts behind the monolithic façade. There is this pluralism, but there is also a drive toward unity and totality. The two contradictory pressures are always active.

Do you think, Mr. Kennan, that the pluralistic forces will triumph in the Soviet Union?

Mr. Kennan: I have never felt that erosion is inevitable, but I see no proof that it is impossible. In an article in *Foreign Affairs*, Isaiah Berlin has suggested that the Soviet leadership, by creating artificial tensions, can control the process of change, and that "evolution" in the nature of political power will therefore not occur.

I am not convinced. I concede that the Soviet Union presents an impression of great sameness — the theoretical basis of Soviet social- ism is essentially the same today as it was in the twenties or thirties, and one can't tell the date of an issue of *Pravda* merely by reading the articles in it.

But I see some signs of evolution. I can recall the great enthusiasm of young people in the late twenties and early thirties: voluntary labor, passionate devotion to the ideals of communism, constant preaching of the faith. Today there is none of that. Youth has be- come conditioned to the regime. They never challenge its power. They are very discreet in its presence, but in its absence they don't

care about it. There is a loss of interest, throughout the whole population, in the workings of the regime.

And the regime has lost interest in the people too. So long as
they do not challenge it, it leaves them alone. People are permitted
to pursue their private interests to a degree never tolerated before.
The regime sets the "line," laying down what is expected and
wherein it must be obeyed. But on the margins of the line there is
a kind of freedom. People make love, people drink, people commit
crimes. The leaders don't seem to care how the people feel; for,
within the limits of the line, the regime seems to have confidence in
its methods of exacting obedience.

Another significant change is the stagnation of the bureaucracy.
There is little turnover of personnel at the higher levels. These
people are getting accustomed to a favored status in society. There
is snobbery, and there is a *jeunesse dorée*. I can recall watching
Vassily Stalin in the central box at the Opera, acting as if he were a
crown prince.

And now — beginning today — the post-revolutionary generation
is in power. Malenkov and his friends have a far narrower outlook
and experience than did Lenin and Stalin. Are they adequate to the
problem of keeping the power together? It may be that there will be
further evolution in the direction of a kind of constitutionalism —
if World War III doesn't prevent it.

Mr. Edward Weeks: What is the position of the church in the
Soviet Union?

Mr. Kennan: The Orthodox faith has survived much more widely
than is generally realized, but the Orthodox Church has not survived to the same degree. In Moscow, about one-third of the people
want to have their children baptized, but only about one-tenth of
the churches are open. These facts lead to crowding, which may
help to account for one's impression of an intense piety. In many
churches, funerals, weddings, and baptisms take place simultaneously. Nevertheless, it is clear that those who want to get ahead in
Soviet society do not find it wise to go to church.

The present position of the Church in the Soviet Union is a result of Hitler's propaganda coup during the war, when the Nazis
opened the Russian churches behind their lines. In Pskov, for example, ten thousand people stood in subzero weather waiting for

the reopening on Christmas night. The Soviet government, alarmed at the German success, followed suit, but characteristically placed Church affairs under the control of the secret police. At the present time, there are in Russia three seminaries and a religious journal.

I spoke to one Orthodox priest, who told me that he and his fellows do not expect any government to be good, and that they are reconciled to shepherding a flock of martyrs.

It is a very mixed picture, and conclusions are hard to draw.

Questioner: Is the relation of scientists to the regime like that of the clergymen?

Mr. Kennan: Roughly speaking, yes: the scientists also know that collaboration with the system is the price of doing one's work. But the scientists lack the centuries of experience at collaboration which the Church has accumulated. The social sciences are beneath contempt, the humanities are in a very bad way. The exact sciences, however, are able to avoid social judgments, by and large, and in them there is very fine work which bears close watching.

Mr. Waldemar Gurian: I have two questions. The first relates to the role of ideology in the Soviet regime. Has the original Marxist promise of worldwide Utopia been replaced by an appeal to traditional Russian nationalism, and would this not perhaps account for the declining enthusiasm of which you spoke in replying to Mr. Fainsod?

My second question is one about ourselves. In your book, Mr. Kennan, you reminded us that we defeated the Nazi totalitarians only by allying with the Soviet ones. Is there not a danger today that we can fight the Soviet totalitarians only at the cost of creating other totalitarianisms elsewhere in the world? May we not become totalitarian ourselves, accepting and practicing a totalitarianism under the name of anti-totalitarianism?

Mr. Kennan: Well, the Soviet regime certainly is having its ideological difficulties. The basic problem is the relevance of Marxism in a society which has had no capitalism for thirty-five years. Marx, as you well know, made no detailed predictions as to the state of society that long after the revolution.

This problem explains, I think, the appearance last year of Stalin's articles on the relevance of the Marxist laws of history in the Soviet system today. Stalin evidently recognized that if one denies their applicability, one is reduced to reliance on a single man, who cannot but be more fallible than the inflexible laws of history. It is clear, I think, that objective laws of historical development are still held to be valid, and the Soviet leaders constantly insist on this.

But this insistence creates other problems of its own. It is difficult to motivate masses of people with an inexorable future, and the Soviet leaders, therefore, must make use of emotional appeals, such as nationalism and the recent appearance of anti-Semitism. The wartime resort to national sentiment was a success, and criticism from abroad gives it even greater force. Perhaps we should be wiser to praise them.

Now, as to your second question. I should certainly agree that the danger exists. One of Stalin's great talents was his ability to provoke his opponents to behave much more badly than they really were. We seem to be bent on the same tack. We tend more and more to confine ourselves to military methods and to adopt our opponents' tactics. If we go too far in behaving as they do, we are lost.

Mr. Paul Lehman: You have spoken of the gulf between the regime and the people as an evidence of evolution in Soviet society. Do you think the separation itself will inhibit future evolution? Given the existence of such a gap, how can we, from the outside, try to influence the evolution into the channels we should like to see it follow?

Mr. Kennan: Until we are certain that it doesn't evolve and that it won't evolve further, we have no moral right to resort to war, which may destroy both the Soviet system and our own.

After all, the basic weakness of totalitarianism is its reliance upon the manipulation of millions by a small group of men who forget that they are themselves human too. Over the periods of time through which the Nazi system endured and the Soviet system has so far survived, this may be feasible, but I very much doubt that it can continue indefinitely. The job is just too big. Ultimately, I feel, the Soviet leaders will realize that they, too, are human, with human limitations, and I think that then the totalitarianism will be relaxed.

I think that our task is to give them time.

Mr. Sigmund Neumann: Those of us who analyze totalitarianism, Mr. Kennan, must make use of comparisons between the Nazi and the Soviet varieties. One obviously central element in Nazism was its expansionist emphasis. Now in the case of the Soviet, the ideology does not contain that component, but there is the complicating factor that in Russia, and in China too, the Marxist revolution coincides with the nationalistic revolution and the revolution of a democratic awakening. I remember Jakob Burckhardt's aphorism: "When two revolutions meet, the stronger destroys the weaker." Here we have three, all going on at once, and historically the latter two have bred expansionism. Which revolution do you think will win out in Russia and China?

Mr. Kennan: There is, I think, a constant tendency to expand, but I would immediately add that it arises from deep-seated *defensive* considerations. Totalitarianism of the Soviet sort is like the filament of an incandescent bulb — it works only if it is surrounded by an inert gas in a protective envelope. The Soviet leaders feel that they must keep out foreign influences, and in particular they cannot abide free societies on their frontiers. The contrast is too sharp and too attractive to the Russian people. This is why Western Berlin is such a horror to them, and why its maintenance as an oasis of freedom in a desert of totalitarianism is so important to us.

Real security for them lies only in the elimination of all surrounding freedom, for the knowledge of another way of life would unsettle the Russian people more than any other single factor. Hence, I think, the expansive tendency is built into the system.

But this is combined with a desire to minimize their responsibilities. I happen to believe that the men in the Kremlin *don't* want to take over France or Germany — they *don't* want the Red Flag to fly over the Ruhr. They would like to control these areas indirectly from afar, and they would like to get us out of them, but they don't, I think, want to expand their direct responsibility that much. These men are military realists. These thoughts, by the way, are why I yet believe that containment is still the best policy for us to follow, because I am convinced that they will not pay the price of a general war merely to expand somewhat the European protective zone they already have.

In the East, the situation is different. I am not sure that Soviet power is revolutionary any longer in those parts of the world. Western ideas have been brought to the Far East too fast, and there is a reaction against them. The same process may have gone on in Russia itself. This reaction may therefore be a bond between the Russians and the Chinese, but on the other hand, we must realize that Marxism is itself a Western system, and that insofar as the Chinese react against the West they may also react against its most recent manifestation there. I'm just not sure.

Mr. Edwin Land: Perhaps I might exercise the prerogatives of the President of the American Academy by asking a question which shall be the last one. Mr. Kennan, you have painted for us a bleak and complex picture. What is it that gives you your faith in our success?

Mr. Kennan: I believe, sir, that Soviet power is active evil. But the closer one comes to its horrors — and I have been very close — the less one fears it. It is the unknown and the unfamiliar that one fears the most.

PART TWO

The Nature of Totalitarianism

■

2. Totalitarianism, Despotism, Dictatorship

N. S. TIMASHEFF

The term "totalitarian society" is applied in two closely related but nevertheless distinct meanings. In the first meaning it
connotes a *type* of society characterized by a number of traits such
as concentration of power in the hands of a few; the absence of
rights ascribed to the individuals *vs.* the collectivity; and an unlimited extension of the functions of the state making the state
almost tantamount with society. Other combinations of traits are
possible; for example, the addition of the ideocratic nature of the
state, of imperialism, of the organization of atomized men.[1] In another meaning the term connotes one definite *trait*, namely the unlimited extension of state functions; then, the term designates not a
concrete type of society, but a trait isolated by means of abstraction
and apt to appear in societies of various types.

Definitions, as is well known, cannot be proved to be right or
wrong. They are verbal equations equalizing the term with a combination of attributes; the formula is: N is that which possesses
traits or properties A, B, C. These verbal equations can be tested
from the point of view of their adequacy. The test of adequacy
must establish (1) whether the traits chosen coincide with clusters
of traits observable in reality; (2) whether the meaning ascribed to
the term approximately coincides with common speech and etymol-
ogy; (3) whether the definition is a satisfactory tool for scientific
inquiry.[2]

[1] The last two traits form the central core of Hannah Arendt's conception of
totalitarianism (*The Origins of Totalitarianism*, 1951).

[2] See my paper, "Definitions in the Social Sciences," *American Journal of Sociology*,
LIII, 201–209.

Since this is an exploratory paper, no assertion is made that one of the two defintions is more adequate than the other. But the position is hypothetically taken that the second definition, identifying totalitarianism with one definite trait appearing in society rather than identifying it with a type of society, is at least plausible and fruitful.

Let us begin by establishing a few differences which obtain depending on the definition chosen. If the first definition is chosen, totalitarian society may be considered as a unique phenomenon having appeared in our day, though this is subject to doubt. G. Ferrero applies the term "totalitarian" to the Consulate and Empire [3] while Pitirim Sorokin points to totalitarian periods in the history of Ancient Egypt, the late Roman Empire (since Diocletian), China, and the state of the Incas.[4]

If the second definition is chosen, the term "totalitarian" may be applied to a society which differs significantly from the concrete totalitarian societies of our day, Communist, Fascist, and National Socialist. One could then combine the term "totalitarian" with the term "democratic," which is obviously impossible if Definition 1 is chosen. There recently appeared a book, by Professor J. L. Talmon, entitled *The Rise of Totalitarian Democracy*.[5] This combination of terms is used to designate the type of society which was being created in France under the Jacobins. Finally, if Definition 2 is chosen, correlations of isolated traits may be studied, while under the first definition, comparative study of total social configurations is the adequate approach.

Definition 2, to be explored in this paper, is logically connected with the requirements of a multidimensional analysis of the political phase of social life. This multidimensional analysis must be logically embedded in the essential properties of the structure and functions of the state.

The organization of the state presents enormous variations. For our purposes, these variations may be reduced to a formula expressing the basis of the political status of those in power, in other words, answering the question: why are these men and not other ones in

---

[3] *The Reconstruction of Europe* (1941), p. 51.
[4] *Social and Cultural Dynamics* (1937), III, 188–192; see also II, 575.
[5] Published in 1952.

power, while the other ones obey orders issued by the former?[6] The foundation of the political status of those in power may be, first, explicit and periodically checked consent of the governed; then, the government is democratic. Second, the foundation of the political status of those in power may be implicit but unchecked consent of the ruled, derived from the fact that obedience to those in power and their predecessors is consecrated by tradition; then, the government is traditional. Or, third, the political status of those in power may be based upon the seizure of power by the rulers and their ability to maintain it against attempts to dislodge them. Then, the government is dictatorial.

It is obvious that the three types are ideal or pure types. In concrete situations, there may be mixtures of two or even all the three. The government of this country is primarily democratic, but secondarily traditional since the rules of the democratic game have been received into America's culture tradition. The government of the Soviet Union is dictatorial, but it makes attempts to invoke, in its favor, both the results of elections and the millennial tradition of Russia. The government of Napoleon also was dictatorial; but it made attempts to restore in its favor the tradition of the *ancien régime* and to strengthen itself by democratic consent in the form of plebiscites.

Other lines of analysis must be related to the three main divisions of the functions of the state. Two of them cover the state's essential functions, i.e., functions without which the state cannot exist.

The first of them is self-assertion in the framework of the greater society consisting of bodies politic in interaction. The second is maintenance of law and order which is manifested mainly in criminal and civil justice and is a substitute for conflict solution by means of violence; later on, it will be called protective. The two functions, by inner necessity, must be carried on by one organization or, eventually, a system of organizations forming a hierarchy. This is so because each function can be adequately performed only by an organization possessing overwhelming power — that is, power sufficient to break the resistance of reluctant individuals. It is obvious that, in a

---

[6] The classification offered in the text follows the lines of those offered by Ferrero, pp. 53–54, and R. MacIver, *The Web of Government* (1947), pp. 147ff. Both obviously develop ideas expressed by Max Weber in *Wirtschaft und Gesellschaft* (1925).

given area, there cannot be two overwhelmingly strong organizations, for each of them would be deprived of this attribute by the
very existence of the other.

The third division of the state's functions is residual. It covers all
functions which are not ramifications of the self-assertive and protective functions. These functions which can be called auxiliary arise
on the background of the principle of the heterogeny of ends. An
organization exists and is endowed with overwhelming power. It
is there primarily for self-assertion and maintenance of law and
order. Then, under most diversified conditions, part of its energy
is diverted to achieve other ends. This happens if their achievement
receives positive social evaluation, and the possibility and/or de-
sirability of their achievement in nonpolitical ways is questioned.

Depending on the scope and modalities of the exertion of the
three types of functions, the politically organized societies may be
distributed along continua, each, in principle, independent of the
others.[7]

With respect to the self-assertive function, the states may be distributed along a continuum beginning with peace-loving societies
and finishing by warlike, highly aggressive, morbidly nationalistic
or imperialistic societies. This position of the individual units (states)
can be measured. Such a measurement has been carried out, with
interesting results, by L. T. Hobhouse and associates relating to
primitive societies,[8] and by Pitirim Sorokin[9] and Q. Wright[10] relating to advanced societies. The latter measurement could be re-
fined if the individual wars counted in the two works were divided
into defensive and aggressive ones.

Concerning the protective function of the state, units can be distributed along a continuum beginning with that which, in German,
is called *Rechtsstaat* and, in English, is covered by the phrase, "due
process of law," and ending by the despotic state. A society is
despotic if, in the relationship between the state and the citizens,

[7] This is well understood by Sorokin (III, 182ff), who identifies the dimension
liberalism–totalitarianism with the *number* of relationships (activities) controlled by
the state and the dimension legalism-despotism (though he does not use the terms)
with the *intensity* of the measures of control.

[8] *The Material Culture and the Social Institutions of Simpler Peoples* (1915).

[9] Sorokin, III, 289ff.

[10] *A Study of War* (1942), I, 218ff.

the state ascribes to itself all the rights and imposes on its citizens a heavy burden of duties. A society is legalistic (let us use tentatively this term), if the opposite is the case. The position of the individual states can be indirectly measured by comparing the average intensity of the criminal sanctions they use.[11]

Concerning the auxiliary functions of the state, the units can be distributed along a continuum beginning with liberal society and finishing with totalitarian society. A society is totalitarian if the number of the auxiliary functions of the state is so high that almost all human activities are regulated by it. A society is liberal if the number of the auxiliary functions is so small that the state's activities are almost confined to its logical minimum. The contradistinction between the two extreme positions on the continuum can be best illustrated by two quotations, one from Jefferson, another from Mussolini. Jefferson advocates a government "which shall restrain men from injuring one another, which shall leave them otherwise free to regulate their own pursuits of industry and improvement." Mussolini declares that everything must be done within the nation (in the meaning of the state), nothing against the nation or outside the nation; the individuals are related to each other through the medium of the whole, or of one of its spheres (political, economic, and so on).

It is noteworthy that the exertion of the auxiliary functions of the state can appear in at least three forms: (1) state regulation of activities of individuals or corporations carrying out a function; (2) licensing of individuals or corporations desirous to perform a function; or (3) absorption of the function, manifested in the annexation of the corresponding organizations by the bureaucratic machinery of the state.

This is a continuum relating to which indirect measurement is possible. The auxiliary functions of the state must be enforced, and the main instrument of enforcement is, of course, criminal law. Consequently, the larger the scope of the auxiliary functions, the larger is the number of types of conduct punished by criminal law.[12]

[11] The present writer had the opportunity to carry out such a computation relating to five advanced societies and seven epochs beginning with the early Middle Ages and finishing with our day. The results were incorporated, with Sorokin's interpretations, into his *Social and Cultural Dynamics*, II, chap. xv.

[12] Such a computation has been carried out simultaneously with the one mentioned

The scientific problem which arises when confronting and corre-lating the distribution of the units (i.e., states) among the classes or positions in the four-dimensional space just traced is this: are, or are not, the positions of the units in the four dimensions related in such a way that, from the position along one of the dimensions, positions along the other dimensions can be predicted? This is of course an enormous problem, the solution of which would require years of team work. At this place only a tentative answer can be given: There are incompatible locations; there are, on the other hand, frequent and naturally recurring combinations; there is, how-ever, also a significant area of freedom characterized by the appear-ance of diverse combinations.

We observe, or have recently observed, a number of political units whose position on the four coördinates must be termed as dicta-torial, highly aggressive, despotic, and totalitarian (in the meaning of Definition 2), and we are inclined to construct, to cover them, an historical, or concrete, type (totalitarian in the meaning of Defi-nition 1). Such are, or have been, Communist Russia, now also Communist China, National Socialist Germany, Fascist Italy, per-haps also Franco's Spain.[13] But relating to the Western satellites, the classification would not be exactly the same. These societies are dictatorial and despotic, but they cannot be aggressive (since they are themselves victims of aggression), and they have not yet reached the climax of totalitarianism. Salazar's Portugal is a dictatorship; it is far advanced toward totalitarianism (but without reaching the limit); it is not aggressive and is not so much despotic as authori-tarian, a position midway between legalism and despotism. In the twenties, thirties, and early forties, there were in Europe many semi-fascist societies, such as Spain under Primo de Rivera, Poland under Pilsudski and his successors, Lithuania under Waldemaras and his successors, Latvia under Ulmanis, Rumania under Carol II and Antonescu, Bulgaria under K. Gueorguiev and his successors, Greece under Metaxas, Vichy France. They all were dictatorships, close to despotism, inclined to aggression (*vide* Lithuania *vs.* the Memelland,

---

in the preceding footnote. Other computations pertinent to the subject of this paper appear in chapters iv, vi, and vii of vol. III of Sorokin's work.

[13] H. Arendt, in the *Origins of Totalitarianism*, narrows down the concept of totali-tarian society to cover only Hitler's Germany and Stalin's (not Lenin's) Russia.

Poland *vs.* Lithuania and Teschen, Hungary *vs.* the provinces lost in 1918, Rumania *vs.* Bessarabia and a vast area East of it, Bulgaria *vs.* the lands granted her by the treaty of San Stefano, but lost through the treaty of Berlin). They were also inclined to totalitarianism without going, however, more than halfway.[14]

As a contrast to these combinations, let us mention the combination of democracy, legalism, and liberalism in the United States, Belgium, and Switzerland, and the combination of democracy, legalism, and significant expansion of the functions of the state toward totalitarianism in Great Britain, Australia, New Zealand, France, Italy, and many other, formerly liberal countries.

If we leave the contemporary European scene, we find other combinations. France, under the Jacobins, was a combination of democracy (the convention having been elected by universal suffrage!), aggressiveness, despotism, and far-advanced totalitarianism (tendency to regulate everything, including religion). The mercantilistic states of continental Europe in the seventeenth and eighteenth centuries were also well advanced toward the totalitarian regulation of life (especially, economic life); they were however traditional in their organization, but despotic as to the relations between the state and the individuals, with a few striking exceptions: Frederick the Great's Prussia approximated the ideal of legalism. At the same time England was a traditional body politic with incipient concessions toward democracy, as inclined to totalitarianism as the continental nations, but, like Prussia, approximating legalism. Some of the English colonies in America presented peculiar combinations of democracy, legalism, and quasi-totalitarianism, especially relative to religion and the connected regulations of everyday life.

Russia under Nicholas I was traditional, despotic, aggressive, and inclined to totalitarianism, as were the Western states fifty years earlier. Under Nicholas II, Russia was traditional, but with significant concessions to democracy; closer to legalism than to despotism; aggressive, but closer to the liberal than to the totalitarian position on the fourth continuum.

The Latin American dictatorships are commonly despotic (sometimes only authoritarian), but little inclined to totalitarianism: life

[14] On the scope of the functions of the state in these societies see N. S. Timasheff, *Three Worlds* (Milwaukee, 1949), pp. 76–101.

is politically regulated only so far as it is relevant for the maintenance in power of those who hold it. But Paraguay under the Jesuits
was close to totalitarianism; Peron's Argentina is midway between
the liberal and totalitarian positions.

The Ancient World presents instances of combinations closely
resembling totalitarian society (Definition 1) of our day, but also
combinations of democracy with despotism and inclination toward
totalitarianism.[15]

It is worth while to conclude this survey by comparing the lists
of actions considered criminal in the Middle Ages, the climax of
liberalism (from the French Revolution up to the last quarter of
the nineteenth century), and the postliberal period characterized by
the rise of modern totalitarianism (Definition 1). This comparison
shows that (1) there is a hard core of such actions perpetuated from
period to period and approximately corresponding to the "maintenance of law and order" function of the state; (2) in the Middle
Ages, and well into the eighteenth century, such actions appeared
punishable as apostasy, heresy, schism, conversion to another religion, sorcery, nonperformance of the rites of the official religion,
contact with Jews, fornication, sodomy, wearing of prohibited ap-
parel (thus violating the symbolic separation of the social classes),
infringement of government regulations concerning the production
of specified commodities; (3) in the postliberal period, many subtle
types of sexual abuse and many complex modalities of the violation
of the order of production and exchange made their appearance,
even in nontotalitarian societies. But even the totalitarian societies
do not penalize many of the actions enumerated above, thus testify-
ing to the fact that they are not interested in the corresponding activities; of course, they punish deviations from their secular ideologies and the principles of action derived therefrom.[16] The number
of types of action punishable in modern totalitarian societies and in
typical medieval societies is perhaps not very much different.[17]

Of course, this survey is very superficial. It proves, however, that
the extreme positions along the four dimensions discussed above

[15] See J. Bryce, *Modern Democracies* (1921), I, 166ff.

[16] The statements above condense material appearing in Sorokin, II, chap. xv.

[17] The idea that the totalitarianism is a unique, purely modern phenomenon is
probably generated by the fact that it emerged after a long period of liberalism.

do not necessarily go together. In the survey, some of the theoretically possible combinations are conspicuous by their absence. No traditional society has been simultaneously despotic *and* liberal; no democratic society either; no dictatorial society has been legalistic. But this is not sufficient evidence in favor of the proposition that such combinations are impossible.

For further study of totalitarian society as of an historical type these conclusions may be drawn: (1) it is worth while analyzing it into elements; (2) it is desirable to establish, throughout history, the fluctuations of concrete societies along the types of organization and the continua corresponding to the three divisions of the functions of the state, applying, whenever possible, quantitative methods; (3) it is desirable to find out the conditions directing societies toward the choice of dictatorship and of extreme positions on each of the continua; (4) it is desirable to reach, by case study, the understanding of conditions favorable to the *simultaneous* movement of a society in the directions just stated. This is, perhaps, the most promising way to understand the compound which is totalitarian society (Definition 1), and eventually to control movements conducive to its emergence and expansion.

3. The Unique Character of Totalitarian Society

CARL J. FRIEDRICH

It is the contention of this paper that (*a*) fascist and Communist totalitarian society are basically alike, that is to say are more nearly alike to each other than to any other systems of government and society, and (*b*) totalitarian society is historically unique and *sui generis*. These two theses are closely linked and must be examined together. At the outset, it should be stated that these contentions do not presuppose that our understanding of totalitarian society is complete or even adequate; these theses are based upon what we at present know reasonably surely about them. Nor do the two theses presuppose that totalitarian societies are fixed and static entities — on the contrary, it is being assumed that they have undergone and continue to undergo a steady evolution; presumably involv-

ing both growth and deterioration.[1] The debate about these causes
or origins of totalitarianism, and more especially of fascism, has
run all the way from a primitive bad-man theory to the "moral
crisis of our time" kind of argument. A detailed inspection of the
available evidence would seem to suggest that virtually everyone of
the factors which has been stressed as offering by itself an explanation of the origin of totalitarianism has played its role. For example,
in the German case, Hitler's moral and personal defects, weaknesses in the German constitutional tradition, certain traits involved
in the German "national character," the Versailles Treaty and its
aftermath, the economic crisis and the "contradictions" of an aging

---

[1] Mr. George Kennan, in his discussion (see above, pp. 31–32), stresses this point.
As for the problem of uniqueness, existing literature varies widely, as it does on the
question whether fascist and Communist totalitarianism are basically alike or not.
Sigmund Neumann, in *Permanent Revolution* (1942), treats them as basically alike;
indeed his is the first comprehensive treatment of the general problems of totalitarian
dictatorship. Franz Neumann, in *Behemoth* (1942 and later), on the other hand, deals
with the Hitler dictatorship as something quite distinctive, essentially the creation if
not the creature of big business, the bureaucracy, and the army. Among earlier works,
Alfred Cobban's *Dictatorship, Its History and Theory* (1939) on the one hand definitely links modern dictatorship with enlightened despotism, Bonapartism, and other
tyrannical systems of the past, while on the other definitely treating fascist and
Communist dictatorship as alike. His book also undertakes to suggest the derivation
of totalitarian dictatorship from Hobbes, Rousseau, and the French Revolution's doctrine of popular sovereignty; this theme has lately been developed brilliantly, though
unconvincingly, by J. L. Talmon in *Totalitarian Democracy* (1952). Two other vol-
umes also stressed the connection between fascist and Communist dictatorship:
Dictatorship in the Modern World (edited by Guy Stanton Ford, 1935 and 1939),
and Hans Kohn's *Revolutions and Dictatorships* (1939). Among the books emphasizing either explicitly or by implication the distinctness of fascism, mention might be
made of E. B. Ashton (pseudonym), *The Fascist — His State and His Mind* (1937);
Herbert W. Schneider, *Making the Fascist State* (1928); G. A. Borgese, *Goliath, the
March of Fascism* (1937); Max Ascoli and Arthur Feiler, *Fascism for Whom?* (1938);
and several books on Nazi Germany, including Frederick L. Schumann, *The Nazi
Dictatorship* (1935 and later); Fritz Morstein Marx, *Government in the Third Reich*
(1936 and later); Karl Loewenstein, *Hitler's Germany* (1939 and later). Konrad
Heiden's *Der Führer — Hitler's Rise to Power* (1944), like the recent work by Alan
Bullock, *Hitler — A Study in Tyranny* (1952), brings out the personal side of totalitarian dictatorship; this approach, while important, tends to obscure the uniqueness
of totalitarianism. Bertram Wolfe's *Three Who Made a Revolution* (1938), and other
works on Stalin, serve the same good purpose. The most searching study on the
level where the impact of ideas upon political practice occurrs is Hannah Arendt's
The Origins of Totalitarianism (1951); it bears a certain resemblance to Herrmann
Rauschning's *The Revolution of Nihilism* (1939), and to Borgese's book cited above,
but it develops the important thesis that totalitarianism is an outgrowth of the establishment of dictatorship under modern conditions.

capitalism, the "threat" of communism, the decline of Christianity
and other spiritual moorings, and so forth have all played a role in
the total configuration of factors contributing to the over-all result.
As in the case of other broad developments in history, only a
multiple-factor analysis will do. In keeping with his general philosophical methodological position, the author is presupposing that
ta politika are decisive for the patterning of any society.[2]

The argument of historical uniqueness of any configuration does
not mean that it is "wholly" unique; for nothing is. All historical
phenomena belong to broad classes of analytical objects. When we
say that the Greek *polis* was historically unique, we do not mean
that there were never any cities, or city-states, but we do mean that
the Greek and more particularly the Athenian *polis* had so many
and such striking traits peculiar to it that it deserves to be considered "historically unique." History is primarily concerned with
individualities, whether these be persons, things, or events, and a
sufficiently variegated pattern of distinctive elements therefore constitutes historical uniqueness.[3] In passing, one should perhaps safe-
guard oneself against the objection that everything historically considered is "historically unique." This objection, while often made,
is not actually correct. A great many events (as well as persons and
things) are so nearly alike that they lack that distinctive quality
which constitutes historical uniqueness; but it is true that when
taken in sufficiently large "classes" and broad enough perspective,
their uniqueness often appears. Thus the monarchy in this or that
German territory in the eighteenth century is not in any sense historically unique, but the monarchical paternalism of all these and a
number of related societies in the seventeenth and eighteenth centuries does indeed constitute what we may call a "historically unique"
configuration.

[2] See *Constitutional Government and Democracy* (1941 ed.), chap. xxv. The understanding of these political relationships is the most important aspect of societies
with which the student must be concerned; in the words of Aristotle, political science
is the highest or most important science. See also footnote 28.

[3] This distinction was elaborated by Heinrich Rickert, *Kulturwissenschaft und
Naturwissenschaft* (1898, 1910, and later), building upon studies of Wilhelm Dilthey,
especially his *Einleitung in die Geisteswissenschaften* (1883). The point was central
to the famous argument between Eduard Meyer and Max Weber, of which Max
Weber's part is found in *Gesammelte Aufsaetze zur Wissenschaftslehre* (1922), "Kriti-
sche Studien auf dem Gebiet der kulturwissenschaftlichen Logik," pp. 215-290.

Why do we say that fascist and Communist totalitarian society and government are *basically alike*? In the first instance, the qualifying adverb "basically" is intended to indicate that they are *not wholly alike*. Popular and journalistic interpretation has oscillated between these two extremes of proclaiming the two societies as wholly alike or as not at all basically alike. The latter was the prevailing mood during the popular front days in Europe, and in "liberal" circles in the United States; it was even more popular during the Second World War, and more especially among Allied propagandists. It is, of course, the insistently promoted official Soviet and Hitler party line. The proposition that they are wholly alike is presently favored in the United States and Western Europe, and hence it may seem unnecessary to labor the point. But there is, in the first place, a lingering doubt remaining from former days, and there is secondly and perhaps more importantly the problem of the range of alikeness, or to put it another way, the question of what makes them "basically" alike. For it is obvious that they are not alike in intention. The sharply divergent content of their ideologies proves it.[4] So do the historical facts which show the fascist movements to arise in reaction to the Communist challenge and to offer themselves to a frightened bourgeoisie as saviors from the Communist threat. These facts are so familiar that they do not require documentation. The well-known frauds involved in the argument are part of the pattern of psychic antagonism and combative projection.

It is equally obvious that more of the preceding liberal and constitutional society survives in the fascist than in the Communist society; but this is in part due to the fact that no liberal, constitutional society preceded Soviet Communism. It is conceivable that at least for a considerable initial period, the situation in this respect would be sharply different in, say, Great Britain or the United States. This tendency of isolated fragments of the preceding state of society to survive has been a most potent source of misinterpretation of the fascist totalitarian society. In the twenties, Italian totalitarianism was very commonly misinterpreted as being "merely" this and that, with the "trains on time" and "the beggars off the street"

---

[4] Mr. Inkeles' paper rightly comments, on the other hand, that totalitarian dictatorships are alike in having such ideology. See below, pp. 87–108.

thrown in for symbolic measure.[5] In the thirties, various authors, some Marxist, others of Marxist antecedents, still others just befuddled, undertook to interpret German totalitarianism as either "the end phase of capitalism"[6] or of "militarist imperialism" (in the manner of Veblen).[7] It is not generally appreciated, even by scholars, how profound a shock to Marxist orthodoxy the rise of German fascism turned out to be. Men of the dogmatic acumen of Hilferding were so struck by it that they felt a complete reassessment of Marxist doctrine was called for.[8] For there was no trace in Marx and Engels of this eventuality emerging. To be sure, Marx was not unaware (how could he be?) that a frightened bourgeoisie might rally behind a rider on horseback, such as Napoleon III, but this kind of amiable *opera bouffe* of mid-nineteenth-century politics is a far cry indeed from the totalitarian society of our time. All one has to do is to look at the intellectual life of France in that period to sense the difference. It was a natural escape for such Marxist and Veblenian interpreters to try and depict the totalitarian society Hitler and Himmler were building as nothing but a capitalist one, totally at variance with the socialist society which was being formed in the Soviet Union. Blinded by the dichotomy of capitalism and socialism of the Marxian heritage, and afflicted by its preoccupation with the economic as contrasted with the governmental and political aspects of society, they did not see that the "planned," that is to say the thoroughly coördinated and governmentally controlled, economy of the Nazi state was different from that of the Soviet state only by the degree of thoroughness with which the coördination and subordination of the "managerial" as well as "labor" elements had been carried forward; this process was advancing apace and given another ten to twenty years would probably have become as nearly

[5] Borgese, *Goliath*, sarcastically comments upon this very symptomatic escapism of the Western liberal. A striking instance of it, as far as the Soviet Union is concerned, is found in Maurice Hindus' *Mother Russia* (1942), but there are many others.

[6] See Neumann, *Permanent Revolution*; Maxine B. Sweezey, *The Structure of the Nazi Economy* (1941); and R. A. Brady, *The Spiritual Structure of German Fascism* (1937).

[7] Karl Loewenstein, *Hitler's Germany* (1940), and W. Ebenstein, *The Nazi State* (1943).

[8] R. Hilferding, "State Capitalism or Totalitarian Economy," in *Modern Review* I, 266–271.

complete as in the Soviet Union.[9] Characteristically, however (to
mention only one common feature), strikes are completely barred,
as criminal sabotage of the "workers' state" in both totalitarian
societies. Having said this much, one has at the same time indicated
once more some significant divergences between the two totalitarian
societies as well: they do not advance toward the totality of their
economic controls either by the same stages, or at the same tempo.
(It might, as an amusing variant of this line of reasoning, be recalled that Sidney and Beatrice Webb in *The Truth about Soviet
Russia* (1942) argued that Stalin was no dictator at all, but had
brought not only political but economic democracy to Russia,
whereas the real dictator appeared to them to be the American
president, Franklin D. Roosevelt.)

Other attempts at differentiating sharply between the Soviet Communist and the fascist regimes turn upon such items as the content
of their divergent ideologies, the national characters of the peoples
within which they arise, the stage of respective economic development, and the like. It would be tedious to refute these various lines
of reasoning, especially as their positions will by implication be denied through a more positive analysis of the basic features which,
according to general agreement, they have in common. These same
features do at the same time constitute the ground for asserting that
these totalitarian societies are historically unique.

The factors or aspects which basically are shared by all totalitarian
societies of our time are five, or can be grouped around five closely
linked clusters of characteristic features. These societies all possess:

1. An official ideology, consisting of an official body of doctrine
covering all vital aspects of man's existence, to which everyone living
in that society is supposed to adhere at least passively; this ideology
is characteristically focused in terms of chiliastic claims as to the
"perfect" final society of mankind.[10]

2. A single mass party consisting of a relatively small percentage
of the total population (up to 10 per cent) of men and women passionately and unquestioningly dedicated to the ideology and pre-

[9] James Burnham, *The Managerial Revolution* (1941).
[10] The role of ideology is penetratingly discussed by Arendt, *Origins*, and in the
article cited below, footnote 30.

pared to assist in every way in promoting its general acceptance, such party being organized in strictly hierarchical, oligarchical manner, usually under a single leader and typically either superior to or completely commingled with the bureaucratic governmental organization.

3. A technologically conditioned near-complete monopoly of control (in the hands of the party and its subservient cadres, such as the bureaucracy and the armed forces) of all means of effective armed combat.

4. A similarly technologically conditioned near-complete monopoly of control (in the same hands) of all means of effective mass communication, such as the press, radio, motion pictures, and so on.

5. A system of terroristic police control, depending for its effectiveness upon points 3 and 4 and characteristically directed not only against demonstrable "enemies" of the regime, but against arbitrarily selected classes of the population; such arbitrary selection turning upon exigencies of the regime's survival, as well as ideological "implications," and systematically exploiting scientific psychology.

The suggestion that to these five clusters of basic traits there should be added that of the secret police gaining ascendancy over the army,[11] seems unacceptable, because both of these factors are controversial, whereas the five which have been delineated are quite generally admitted to be factually established features of these regimes. In the nature of the case, it is very difficult to determine whether, when, and to what extent the secret police gained ascendancy over the army; another difficulty arises from the fact that in so far as the police is a branch of the civilian government, it is in the ascendancy in constitutional states as well.

The argument that total subversion is another distinctive feature of totalitarian systems[12] has merit, but it is arguable whether this aspect of totalitarianism constitutes a sufficiently separate item. It would seem to me that it is comprehended under the first of the five characteristics, where we state that the official ideology is one "to which everyone living in that society is supposed to adhere." The

[11] See the remarks by Hannah Arendt below, pp. 75–79, as well as Lasswell, pp. 360–372.
[12] See the remarks by Paul Kecskemeti below, pp. 345–360.

five main clusters of traits, for the sake of clarity, ought not to be
unnecessarily expanded.

Within this broad similarity, there are many significant variations,
both in time and in place, as already mentioned. For instance, the
party appears to play less of a role in the Soviet Union today than
earlier; [13] the ideology of the Soviet Union is more rigid, because
of its Marxist bible, than that of Italian or German fascism, where
ideology was formulated by the leader of the party; [14] and — to give
a third illustration at random — Hitler's extermination of the Jews

[13] This was written at the time Stalin was still living; there are some indications,
such as the appointment of Kushchev instead of Malenkov to be general secretary of
the party, that this may be less true in the future. But the searching inquiries of
Merle Fainsod definitely point in this direction. See his "Controls and Tensions in
the Soviet System," *American Political Science Review*, xliv, 266–282, and "The
Komsomols — A Study of Youth under Dictatorship," *ibid*, xlv, 18–40, as well as
his forthcoming *How Russia Is Ruled*, which I have been privileged to catch glimpses
of in seminar discussions and conversations.

[14] There have been considerable controversies on the question of the degree of
rigidity of Soviet ideology. During the war it was customary among all those who
wished to soft-pedal the potential conflict between the Soviet Union and the West
to claim that ideology had become unimportant, in spite of the fact that Stalin and
others repeatedly stressed it. For an indication of the "line," see as representative
Robert E. Sherwood, *Roosevelt and Hopkins* (1948), especially pp. 301–308. However,
not only those who wished to play it soft, but also the self-styled "realist" school,
denying the real significance of ideas and talking in terms of geographical and other
kinds of "real" interest, have tended to take the line that Stalin was pursuing the
policy of the Tsars of Russia and that ideology was little more than camouflage. Very
interesting in this connection is Walter Lippmann's *U.S. Foreign Policy: Shield of the
Republic* (1943), in which the two tendencies are combined. Lippmann, after demonstrating that the United States has never been willing to permit a power in continental Europe to become predominant, and then clearly recognizing that Russia will
be the dominant power after the war (p. 149), fails to draw the inevitable conclusion, except by way of insisting that the alliance must be maintained. He has some
shrewd things to say about what will happen, if it is not (note the remark on p. 148
on the conflict over territorial settlements), but characteristically Lippmann discusses
the matter in terms of Russia rather than the Soviet Union, just as he speaks of Germany and the "German war" rather than Hitler and the Nazi state, thereby displaying his desire to minimize the ideological factor in terms of which this first world
revolutionary war was actually fought. Barrington Moore, Jr., in *Soviet Politics —
The Dilemma of Power* (1950), gives a discriminating discussion of the role of the
ideology, to which he assigns a central role in the analysis of Soviet politics, while
Julian Towster, in *Political Power in the U.S.S.R.* (1948), rightly started his discussion
of Soviet government with a sketch of the underlying ideology. He speaks of it as
"avowed theory" and comments at the outset that "an understanding of its [the
USSR's] operative constitutional order would lack coherence without due attention
to avowed theory." That the USSR's government is no "constitutional order" in
terms of our analysis is obvious.

was ideologically motivated and contrary to the apparent immediate needs of the regime, whereas Stalin's recent Jewish purges appear to be taking place in response to exigencies of the international situation, rather than to ideology, hence the vigorous denial of anti-Semitism.[15]

It is submitted that every one of these factors to a large extent, and all of them in combination, are certainly lacking from all historically known despotic, let alone authoritarian, societies of the past. It might be mentioned in passing that many authoritarian societies of the past should in point of fact be sharply differentiated from autocratic societies. The medieval and early modern distinction of monarchy and tyranny was in many ways sounder than our common differentiation of "democratic" and "autocratic." [16] Neither the oriental despotisms of the more remote past nor the absolute monarchies of modern Europe, neither the tyrannies of the ancient Greek *polis* nor the imperial establishment of Rome, nor yet the tyrannies of the city-states of the Italian Renaissance exhibit any one of these factors to any marked extent. Attempts, such as Thornton Wilder's *The Ides of March* (in which he tries to show Caesar to have been a totalitarian dictator in the making) or more learned efforts along similar lines,[17] collapse when subjected to a more detailed scrutiny in terms of these five factors. To be sure, there have often been made efforts to organize some kind of secret police, but they are not even horse-and-buggy affairs compared to the enterprises of a Himmler or a Beria. Similarly, there have been in the past both military and propagandistic concentrations of power and control, but as in the previous case, the limits of technology pre-

---

[15] Recent developments suggest that the Soviet Union is abandoning this line again. As for Hitler's anti-Semitism, the damage done to his foreign policy, as well as the weakening of his domestic support are obvious. The problem has been explored in its ramifications by Hannah Arendt, *Origins of Totalitarianism*, chaps. vi–ix. However, her tendency is to overrate this aspect of fascist ideology. Even early in the regime, mass support for Hitler was primarily based upon other factors, and anti-Semitism tended to weaken rather than strengthen Hitler's appeal with many, as was shown very convincingly on the basis of numerous psychological interviews by Theodore Abel, *Why Hitler Came into Power* (1938).

[16] Reference may be had to my remarks below regarding authority, pp. 274–275. See also Harold D. Lasswell, *Power and Society*, § 6.5.

[17] See Alfred Cobban, *Dictatorship — Its History and Theory* (1939); Carl Schmitt, *Die Diktatur von den Anfaengen des modernen Souveraenitaetsgedankens bis zum proletarischen Klassenkampf* (2nd ed., 1928).

vented any thorough-going development along totalitarian lines. Rather than elaborate this point, which is obvious enough, once one has faced up to it, it seems more urgent to stress the common reason for the uniqueness of factors 3, 4, and 5, and thus to turn back to the other side of the general thesis.

This common cause appears to be our advanced technology. Without the inventions of the last few generations, none of these features could have been created, no matter how glad Peter or Frederick the Great might have been to do so. This technological aspect of totalitarianism is, of course, particularly striking in the matter of arms and communications. The constitution of the United States guarantees to every citizen the "right to bear arms." In the days of the Minutemen this was a very important right, and the freedom of the citizen was indeed symbolized by the gun over the hearth, as it is in Switzerland to this day. But who can "bear" such arms as a tank, a bomber, or a flame-thrower, let alone an atom bomb? The citizen as an individual, and indeed in larger groups, is simply defenseless against the overwhelming technological superiority of those who can centralize in their hands the means wherewith to wield these modern arms and thereby physically to coerce. Similar observations readily apply concerning the press, the radio, and so forth. "Freedom" does not have the same intrinsic value, resting upon individual effort and exertion, which it had a hundred and fifty years ago. The trend of technological advance carries with it, with relatively few exceptions, the trend toward greater and greater size of organization. Thus, totalitarian societies appear in this respect to be merely exaggerations, but nonetheless logical exaggerations, of inherent implications of the technological state in which we find ourselves.[18]

The situation is rather different with respect to the first two distinctive features of totalitarian societies. Neither ideology nor party have any significant relation to the state of technology.[19] But they

[18] See the comment of Karl Deutsch, below pp. 308–333. The role of technology in the development of modern politics has received inadequate attention. Charles A. Beard, following Thorstein Veblen, occasionally lays stress upon it. James Burnham's *The Managerial Revolution* (1941) is built upon it, but the conclusions go beyond the evidence.

[19] This is not strictly true, since the mass conversion continually attempted by totalitarian propaganda through the effective use of its monopoly of communications (factor 4) could not be carried through without it. This in turn affects the party and its dynamics.

do have a vital relation to another common feature of all contemporary societies, namely, the increasing amount of general literacy.[20] To this literacy must be added (in Russia, Italy, Germany, and other countries where totalitarian societies have arisen within the context of the Christian tradition) the fact that Christianity has tended to establish a broad predilection for convictional certainty.[21] But probably more important than either is the "democratic" antecedents of these totalitarian societies. Marx and Engels saw themselves as constituting the vanguard of the democratic movement of their day, and Stalin talked of the Soviet totalitarian society as the "perfect democracy" with evident conviction.[22] However, not only Marx and Engels, but Mussolini and Hitler organized parties with a program intended for mass appeal, designed to win as many adherents as possible.[23] It would never have occurred to the absolute monarchs of seventeenth- and eighteenth-century Europe to stoop so low, nor would the Roman Emperors have considered such an undertaking as politically significant. They appealed to the masses against senatorial privilege from time to time, but an organized and ideologically homogeneous party was "inconceivable." There was, to be sure, a party of the Medicis in Florence,[24] but this was in the days of flourishing factions contesting for power with each other — in other words, during a period resembling in some limited ways

[20] In this connection the rate of literacy in Japan as contrasted with China used to seem significant, but would not seem to be similarly striking now. However, in our view the question as to whether China actually is a totalitarian dictatorship cannot be answered satisfactorily at the present time. No doubt the Chinese Communists are a totalitarian movement; but whether they will succeed in organizing China along totalitarian lines remains to be seen. If they do, the effect will probably entail the rapid reduction of illiteracy, as has happened in the Soviet Union in conjunction with the forward march of totalitarianism.

[21] The objection that China does not fit this pattern — see comment of Robinson below, pp. 81–82 — should not only be considered in the light of what is said in the previous footnote, but also in relation to the fact that the totalitarian developments in China are closely associated with the reception of these Western ideas. Sun Yat Sen's *Three Principles of the People*, probably the most influential book of modern China, provides ample evidence for this aspect of the matter.

[22] See especially Stalin's great speech in the election of February 1946.

[23] Konrad Heiden, in *Der Führer*, has given the most elaborate account to date, to which Alan Bullock's *Hitler* adds little. Very revealing, even as a title, is the book by E. Czech-Jochberg, entitled *Hitler — Eine Deutsche Bewegung* (1930).

[24] From this our modern word state is in part derived, as the Medici party was called *il stato*. In the north, the estate of the king provided another source.

democratic conditions. But the carefully organized single mass
party, complete with program and ideology, is a distinct peculiarity
of the totalitarian societies of our time. The tie to its Christian and
democratic antecedents may gradually weaken — there are signs
that both the ideology and the party in Soviet totalitarian society
are declining in importance [25] — but there is some room for doubt
as to whether a totalitarian society could survive their destruction.

The foregoing may lend itself to the misinterpretation that democracy, Christianity, or technology had, in the author's view,
"caused" totalitarianism. No proposition of the kind is intended.
All that is meant is that it could only have arisen in the kind of
context created by Christianity, democracy, and modern technology. But it seems basically unsound to pick out of past intellectual
history some one or several exponents or supposed exponents of
some aspect of totalitarian views — for instance, of an authoritarian
society, be it Plato or Thomas Aquinas, Hobbes or Rousseau, Hegel
or Carlyle — and hold him "responsible" for the totalitarian movements or societies by claiming that he was a totalitarian.[26] None of
those mentioned were, because none of them could be: the historically unique features of the totalitarian society were unknown to
them.[27] Usually, it is quite easy to show that the particular thinker
would, on his own terms, have turned with disgust and indignation
upon these latter-day totalitarians, for a variety of reasons inherent
in his system. The peculiar moral obtuseness of contemporary totalitarian societies which has been stressed as *the* distinguishing feature
of these societies (we think, wrongly),[28] manifesting itself in violence on an unprecedented scale, is demonstrably entirely alien
to the thinkers we have named. They are all ardent rationalists, if
not moralists, whereas the totalitarians of today are indifferent to
such considerations because theirs is essentially an engineering ap-

[25] See, regarding this aspect, footnote 11 above.
[26] Concerning the abuse of the words "authority" and "authoritarian," see below
pp. 274–275.
[27] See J. L. Talmon, *Totalitarian Democracy*; W. M. McGovern, *From Luther to
Hitler* (1941); and Aurel Kolnai, *The War Against the West* (1938).
[28] It is not a distinguishing feature of these totalitarian societies, because such moral
obtuseness has been recurrent in the history of human government. As far as amorality
is concerned, Nero and Cesare Borgia yield little to contemporary dictators; indeed,
their amorality seems more thoroughgoing, since they do not camouflage it by relating
it to a presumably moral end, such as the Communist world society.

proach to society. They solve problems in a manner which they believe to be "scientific," while at the same time denying the importance of freedom and more especially freedom of inquiry, of teaching and learning, the essential conditions of scientific truth.

Closely related to these issues of novelty and conceptual distinctiveness is the as yet unresolved problem of succession in totalitarian regimes. This issue has recently been high-lighted by the death of Stalin. Most of the comments revealed as in a flash the hopeless noncomprehension of the totalitarian reality, as men gravely disputed about the successor to Stalin as if he had been occupying a legally or traditionally defined office, such as the King of France, or even the Tsars of Russia. In fact, the problem of succession in government has to date not been solved in any totalitarian society. This is a most important shortcoming, in view of the millennial importance of succession. Constitutional democracy and hereditary monarchy, oriental despotism with its deification of the ruler as well as its ancient tribal antecedents — they all revolve around this issue of succession. Tyranny has perennially been weak on this score, as Aristotle noted, and as the history of the two Napoleons suggests. Maybe, totalitarian societies will discover a means to cope with the problem. The vast array of documentary evidence we now have about fascism does not contain any really viable scheme for succession. The obstacles to evolving one are formidable. The building up of concentrated veneration for the one "father of the people" or "leader," which approximates and at times exceeds what the deifiers of kings used to do, obviously must create a vacuum the moment this unique person has gone "the way of all flesh." How the then controller of the machinery of communication can be brought to shift, and shift dramatically, to a new man who only yesterday was his equal and maybe competitor seems perplexing. Equally puzzling appears the question of what will be done by him who controls the terror apparatus.[29]

The sharp delineation of what distinguishes the past from the present in thought as well as action should not be mistaken, of

[29] It may be recalled in this connection that Bodin, even though he seeks to give the sovereign very broad authority, declares the laws of succession inviolable. While it is incorrect to call these "constitutional laws," as has at times been done, it is clear that Bodin assumed that such a succession would be regulated by law. In a totalitarian dictatorship, such regulation is inconceivable.

course, for a denial of significant links. One does not have to mistake Hobbes for a totalitarian in order to recognize the connection between his failure to understand the vital role of religion and of intermediary groups in a well-ordered commonwealth and the totalitarians' comparable blindness in these matters. The road of Western thought runs from Luther to Lincoln, as it does from Luther to Hitler; the seamless web of history is woven of many intertwined strands, and totalitarianism, for all its uniqueness, does not spring from the head of any ideologue or demagogue without antecedents. But these antecedents did not "cause" the phenomenon, and there was nothing inevitable about Hitler or Stalin. The totalitarian societies are basically alike, and they are historically unique; but why they are what they are we do not know.[30] Like everything genuinely novel in history, whether good or bad, whether beautiful or ugly, totalitarianism remains wrapped in the womb of creation. Hence only the genuinely creative answer will do effective service in supplanting and superseding it. The future, if there is one, will be a future beyond Communism and fascism, not some neo-ism of recent or more ancient prescription.

4. Social Prophylaxis as a Form of Soviet Terror

JERZY G. GLIKSMAN

Terror, as a governmental technique of coercive totalitarian control, expresses itself in the Soviet Union in manifold forms. Certain specific judicial and extrajudicial penal practices and the

[30] That is why the dispute over the origins of totalitarianism is at once so sharp and so inconclusive; e.g., between Eric Voegelin, "The Origins of Totalitarianism" and Hannah Arendt's reply, *The Review of Politics*, xv, 68ff. Miss Arendt wisely remarks that her book is not really a study of the origins, but when she says that it "gives an historical account of the elements which crystallized into totalitarianism," she overstates the case for her remarkable book; for it deals only with *some* of the elements, and they did not "crystallize," but were molded and used by the creators of totalitarianism. In her recent contribution to *Offener Horizont — Festschrift fuer Karl Jaspers* (1953), entitled "Ideologie und Terror," she rightly stresses the novelty and the creative aspect. In this connection, the observation may be in order that it is a Bergsonian and romantic prejudice to view all creation as somehow "good," and hence to overlook the "procreation in sin" and the possibility of fashioning the ugly which is wholly new. Man finds himself in a situation and he brings to his response such creative resources as are in him, both for good and evil.

methods of social prophylaxis with regard to actual or potential
political nonconformity are among the most significant aspects of
Soviet terror. They will be the subject of this paper, which is based
on the study of Soviet sources, eye-witness reports, and personal observations by the author in the Soviet Union in 1935 and again in
the years 1939–1942. Space limitations have governed the scope of
this paper.

To terrorize, in the penal sense, means to instill intense fear of
punishment. And yet our modern penal system, based on the principle of special and general prevention and aimed at deterring people
from illegal acts through fear of punishment for noncompliance, is
not defined as terror. This is not only because the *degree* of fear is
less than under a system of terror. It is because the area of fear is
strictly limited, owing to the fact that the law itself is limited. "Due
process of law" guarantees the elimination of arbitrariness, the precise definition of punishable acts ("rule of certainty"), and last but
not least, the principle of repression of actual offenders only as the
base of the whole system.

The variegated criminological doctrines of the democratic West
concerned with the prevention of crime may influence the mode and
degree of punishment to be applied or the educational or social reforms to be introduced, but, with the sole exception of war emergency or of preventive hospitalization of psycho-pathological cases,
penal procedure is initiated only upon the commission of a specific
offense by the individual. Under such circumstances only a small
fraction of society may find itself in a state of "intense fear."

The Soviet penal system has different criteria of criminal acts
from those accepted in the West, and Soviet repressive measures go
far beyond the limitations inherent in all the above stated principles.
The arm of Soviet punitive apparatus endeavors to reach not only
all real offenders but also the probable and doubtful ones, and even
— as a measure of social prophylaxis — the potential ones.

In analyzing the motivation of the Soviet repressive system, it is
possible to assume that from a purely theoretical standpoint Soviet
penologists would ideally prefer to find a scheme which would re-
press only those who are really disloyal (in the broadest sense) or
can with certainty be expected to become so in the future, provided

that such a scheme were infallible. Since such an ideal scheme is
humanly impossible, a social and moral choice had to be made. The
alternatives were (1) a system under which some people would take
advantage of the existing gaps, evade the grip of the penal machinery, and be able to carry out their illegal or simply nonconformist
acts; and (2) a system, calculated to preclude any possible noncompliance, of such rigid repression that the sacrifice of innocent people
becomes inevitable.[1]

The Bolsheviks, faithful to their general philosophy and tradition
and determined to preserve their minority dictatorship, irrespective
of the human element to be sacrificed in the process, opted almost
at the very beginning of their regime in favor of a far flung rigidity.
In order to avoid the risks attendant on exonerating dubious cases,
they adopted, in fact if not in theory, the principle of *in dubio contra
reum* (when in doubt turn against the accused); and, more significantly, they introduced the system of elimination of all potential
deviators.[2]

The term "prophylaxis" is used to define this policy because of
the analogy with the field of medicine, where protective measures
are applied to guard physical organisms from a possible future disease. In social prophylaxis, as practiced in the Soviet Union, the state
authorities, anticipating future developments, attempt to eliminate
or render harmless all groups of people among whom a social or
political conflagration might possibly develop. This Soviet pattern
of preventive action against "socially dangerous" elements has developed undoubtedly under the influence of the doctrines of Lombroso, Ferri, and Garofalo, and especially Ferri's theory of social defense and preventive measures has been applied *ad absurdum*. The
Italian criminologists of the anthropological and sociological schools
have been wholly and very definitely condemned in the Soviet

[1] Emile Durkheim believes that crimes committed by the fringe of society taking
advantage of democratic freedoms is the price that must be paid in order to insure
progress and the free evolution of our culture and social institutions. Crime is an
inevitable incident of social evolution.

[2] The rationalization of such a policy can be traced back to Lenin: "which is
better: to put in prison several tens or hundreds of instigators, *guilty or not guilty*,
[acting] consciously or unconsciously, or to lose thousands of Red Army men and
workers? The first is better" (V. I. Lenin, *Sochinenya* [Works; Moscow, 1935], XXIV,
241; italics supplied).

Union. Yet one cannot help comparing the search for definite stigmata in detection of criminals, that had misled Lombroso into dependency on physical characteristics, with the rigid Soviet criteria of predetermining the "socially dangerous" categories — a system which seems no more compatible with Marxism than the theories of the anthropological school.

The implementation of Soviet penal terror is multiple: there are the criminal code and the courts; there is legislation placing extensive investigative and punitive powers in the hands of the administrative organs; and, finally, there is a practice of handling great masses of people by *de facto* measures of deportation on special but not isolated occasions. All three forms give very little or no protection of the individual against arbitrary action by State officials.

Relatively the most moderate legal instruments of Soviet terror are the Criminal Code and the Courts. Soviet doctrine and Soviet practice admittedly recognize as prerequisites for social control a normally functioning judiciary and certain stable juridical principles. The educational role of the law as practiced in the courts is also considered a necessary complement to the system of persuasive control by propaganda.

In the Soviet court certain procedural safeguards are indeed observed: the hearings are public, the defendant has the right to be present in court, to have counsel, to defend himself, to introduce evidence, to appeal to a higher court, and so on. The Soviet standard of these safeguards is, of course, very different from that of the West, especially in all cases with the slightest real or illusory political taint. In practice inattention to the rights of the defendants and violation of the procedural rules are widespread; but there is also a tendency emanating from the Soviet Supreme Court to rectify the most blatant abuses, to correct numerous faulty proceedings and to reverse the most erroneous verdicts of the lower courts.

And yet, the Soviet court may remain, at least in its daily routine practice, fairly close to perfect legality (by Soviet standards) and still have sufficient latitude in action to prevent the escape from the penal dragnet even of the defendant whose guilt may be doubtful and against whom the evidence may be not entirely conclusive. *Nullum crimen sine poena* (no offense should remain unpunished) is the main imperative. Specific rules of the Soviet Criminal Code broaden its jurisdiction so as to encompass a substantial part of the marginal cases.

The Soviet Criminal Code allows, for instance, a very broad interpretation of the concept of punishable preparation of the crime (". . . seeking out and adapting means, bringing about conditions. . ." Article 19); it does not observe the rule denying retroactive effect to the penal law (*lex retro non agit*); it leaves the application of the statute of limitation in "counterrevolutionary" crimes to the discretion of the court (Article 14, notes 1 and 2); it allows criminal responsibility by analogy, for socially dangerous acts (Article 16), which is contrary to the perennial juridical rule that there is no crime except by legal definition (*nullum crimen, nulla poena sine lege*). The definition of a "socially dangerous act" (Article 6) is very broad and the definitions of the specific crimes are often phrased vaguely, so as to permit the broadest interpretation.[3] The articles of the code devoted to the "counterrevolutionary" crimes are formulated in an especially comprehensive way, so as to include, for instance, even actions tending toward "weakening" of the power of the government (Article 58[4]).

But the judiciary apparatus, even equipped with the specific features mentioned above, has by far, and at all times, failed to satisfy all the needs of the regime in the realm of repressive policy. This was neither because the law could not be made to serve without

[3] For example, economic sabotage (Art. 58[7] and 58[14]) had been interpreted by the Soviet Supreme Court in 1928 as including acts committed with "eventual treacherous intentions," so that even negligence was subject to punishment as an intentional "counterrevolutionary" act. It was probably the harm done to Soviet economy by the excesses in the application of this interpretation that moved the Supreme Court to reverse its instruction in 1938, although this did not entirely stop the abuses in practice.

[4] Some hesitation could be, however, observed in this matter. Krylenko and Pashukanis prepared, in 1930, a draft for a new criminal code, which would allow the courts to sentence "socially dangerous" persons. This draft was rejected. Article 7 of the Criminal Code now in force allows the courts to sentence people "dangerous" because of their connections or past activity. The courts also had the right to condemn to exile and banishment (*ssylka* and *vysylka*) "socially dangerous" persons even in cases when they were acquitted in court of the charge of commission of a specified crime (Art. 22 of the "Basic Principles of USSR Criminal Legislation"). It was only in 1946 that the Supreme Court of the USSR stated that the above-mentioned articles of the law "should be considered as having lost their power." It seems, however, that the role of the courts in applying the method of social prophylaxis has never been of great importance.

reserve the objectives of the regime, nor because the courts were not a sufficiently compliant tool. The constitutional independence of the Soviet judges is illusory to the same degree as other political and civil rights. The judiciary apparatus is admittedly but one more means of political power. The courts are an organic part of the administration, and though they differ in the method of performance, their objectives are basically identical with those of the entire government machinery, including even the watch over the fulfillment of the current party line.

And yet under the rule of distribution of functions, which replaced in the Soviet Union the principle of separation of powers, the courts, with their encumbrance of legal restraints, were assigned a particular limited task, to deal with defendants against whom there was a specific accusation, and — by Soviet standards — sufficient evidence to warrant public hearings.

The courts were, however, considered inadequate to apply the prophylactic measures and to deal effectively with people merely suspected of political offenses or of nonconformity, and *a fortiori* to serve as instruments of the extended mass operations aimed at the elimination of potential offenders or deviationists.[4] Even technically, the courts, with their time-consuming formalities and decorum, would hardly be able to cope with the great masses of people that the Soviet coercive system elects to encompass. Therefore, partly for the sake of expediency but also for other reasons, purely administrative penal procedures and *de facto* police actions have expanded, since the early days of the October Revolution, to a proportion that overshadows and surpasses by far the legitimate judiciary activity, and have become as stable and permanent a feature of the Soviet scene as the courts themselves.

Despite all the variegations, the line of development in this respect since the days of the Cheka is a consistent one. At the present stage of development the MVD (Ministry of Internal Affairs) is legally invested with the function of investigating all crimes and with the right to impose banishment, exile, or confinement in a labor camp up to five years, through a Special Council (*Ossoboye Soveshchanye* — in short, "OSSO").[5] If any rules of procedure bind

[5] The Statute of July 10, 1934, establishing the OSSO, is very explicit in this regard, and yet the author of this paper met in the Soviet Union in the years 1939–

the OSSO, they have never been officially revealed. The decisions of the OSSO are made *in camera*, in the absence of the accused, solely on the basis of the investigative material of the MVD. There is no appeal from the OSSO verdicts to a higher authority.

The official criteria which guide the MVD in deciding whether a case, after its investigation is completed, should be directed through the channels of the courts, or should be disposed of by the OSSO, were never revealed. It is, however, clear in the light of our previous analysis that the cases where there is no specific accusation or no sufficient evidence, as well as cases where there is only a general, unspecified suspicion of potential future deviation from the obligatory standards of behavior, would be presented to the OSSO. This rule does not necessarily, however, exclude the fact that some cases which would formally qualify for a judicial trial, may also for certain reasons (e.g., for the sake of secrecy, an unusually large number of cases, and so forth) be submitted by a decision of the MVD to its own OSSO.

Whenever there is a specific charge to refer to, the verdicts of the OSSO usually mention the corresponding article of the Criminal Code that has allegedly been violated by the arrested person.[6] In cases when the object of the penal measure is only a potential offender and no specific definition of a crime can be applied to him, he is characterized by a special formula, namely "SOE" (*sotsyalno-opasny elementy*, socially dangerous elements).[7] Although the use of this formula may be to a great extent arbitrary, there are certain objective characteristics of an individual that determine his classification as SOE. (These characteristics are very similar to those determining whole categories of people classed as suspect or dangerous, and are discussed later.)

Even the cursory procedures of the OSSO are not applied, and probably would be technically very difficult to apply, in the case of

---

1942 numerous people sentenced by the OSSO to *eight* years of confinement in the camps.

[6] According to eye-witness reports there were also verdicts of the OSSO stating that the defendant was condemned for "suspicion of espionage" ("p. sh." = *podozrenye shpionazha*).

[7] The OSSO deals also with cases of professional criminals, classed usually as *sotsyalno vrednye elementy* (socially harmful elements), but this is outside the scope of this paper.

mass deportations. In the period of dekulakization,[8] for instance, or later in the great purge of the thirties, when millions of people were involved, most of the sentencing was probably done by the central or local *troyki* (committees of three), consisting of one representative each of the secret police, the Party, and the state administration. In the period of mass deportations in Eastern Poland and the Baltic states (in 1939–1941 and after World War II) an even more wholesale procedure was applied. Orders from the central authorities of the NKVD (later MVD and MGB) with detailed lists of categories of people to be deported were dispatched to the local authorities and served as a basis for these large-scale operations.

It may be added that often all three methods of penal persecution were used simultaneously: some people were given the privilege of a court trial, some cases were transferred to the OSSO and most of the people concerned were deported in the just mentioned *de facto* operations. It must also be added that while in the courts all kinds of sentences were pronounced, in the OSSO it was practically always one of the three possibilities: three, five, or eight years of confinement in labor camps. Most of the people deported without any sentencing were exiled into "special" or penal settlements, usually for life.

The system of social prophylaxis as practiced in the Soviet Union may seem as arbitrary as the practice that prevailed during the Reign of Terror, when in the application of the law of 1793 against suspects, anyone recognized as such by the authorities was a suspect. Some observers of the Soviet scene assert that since all real, crystallized opposition against the regime had been wiped out in the thirties, the continuation of terror has no more rational basis and the categories of people against whom it is directed are meaningless and chosen at random.

In fact, however, it is possible to detect some of the criteria used by the Soviet authorities in identifying the groups against which at one time or another the repressive apparatus was directed. These quasi-objective criteria are mobile, changing with the development on the domestic and international scene and with the zigzags of the party line. This system of group selection, whimsical as it may

[8] The OSSO did not yet exist at that time.

seem on the surface, does respond to a certain logic and undoubtedly contains rational elements, as the whole Soviet system of terror is to a great extent a rational instrument for the maintenance of the regime and for coercion of the population by intimidation into conformity. No doubt this rationality is of a purely technical or instrumental nature. It is what Karl Mannheim might call "functional rationality," a rationality designed to serve definite pragmatic objectives of the rulers, but still a rationality — despite one's obviously negative value judgment about such a rationality and the objectives it serves.

These objectives — the elimination of possibly all actual and potential disloyalty and nonconformity — can be attained with the optimum result for the rulers only when the limits and scope of the preventive action are so defined as not to disrupt excessively the economic and social life of the country, and not to lead people to shirk responsibility or cease effective contributions to the state. Such limits are very difficult to define and even more difficult to observe in practice. Besides periods in Soviet history when the whole country was going overboard, excesses on the local level are a rather permanent phenomenon.

And yet, the system of Soviet social prophylaxis as a whole is based on a logical anticipation of possible events and on a study of symptoms and characteristics that would indicate whether the degree of disloyal attitude or behavior that already exists or might be expected in the future, from at least some of the members of a given group, would warrant, according to the current needs of the rulers, preventive action with respect to this group. In all such mass actions no attention is paid to the fact that the repression also affects necessarily people completely innocent and to whom even potential guilt, by the standards of the authorities themselves, cannot be attributed. This does not preclude, however, the possibility of exceptions with regard to all those whom the authorities deem necessary for expediency's sake to exempt from repression despite their formal classification in the doomed category.

As an illustration, on the basis of the available facts of the penal history of the Soviet Union, an attempt will be made to define and analyze some of the main groups and categories of people against whom preventive punitive mass procedures were leveled.

1. *Social status and origin.* The stigma of undesirable social status and social origin played an especially important role in the first two decades of the existence of the Soviet regime. "Bad" social status or origin [9] was a serious handicap in all aspects of Soviet life (education, food-rationing, etc.) and an aggravating circumstance in all, even the smallest, conflicts with the authorities, especially with all organs of the penal system.[10] It was also a sufficient reason for repression per se.

This attitude was considered consistent with the doctrinal Marxist approach. (Man's ideas are conditioned by his economic status.) It is also a psychologically plausible assumption that people who lost their possessions or their social position because of the changes introduced by the new order, would be inclined, more than others, to harbor negative feelings toward the regime.

The broadest single penal operation based on social status, and the best known, was the so-called "liquidation of the kulaks as a class." It must be born in mind that most of the kulaks did actually oppose the collectivization policy of the government, and some of them did fight against it by violent means. Those who yielded did so with manifest reluctance. A short-range action, to clear the field for expediting the collectivization of agriculture was combined here with a prophylactic measure to eliminate malcontents — ergo potential offenders.

It may be added that on the other hand it was not always the real social status that determined the official "class" of a person and his fate, it was sometimes also his attitude toward current Soviet policy. Even a poor peasant could be equated with the kulaks, as their "ally," if he were opposed to the collectivization.[11]

2. *Political affiliation.* People who had been affiliated, even loosely, with any non-Bolshevik political movement or ideology were fairly well cleaned out in the first decade after the Revolution. Deviationists from the "general line" of the Party and members or even sympathizers of various "oppositions" were dealt with in the great

---

[9] This group included mainly the well-to-do and middle classes, the clergy, the former officers of the Tsarist army, and the former officials of the old regime.

[10] For example, in a certain period kulaks could even be punished in court for certain acts which were not considered offenses, if committed by other people.

[11] Resolution of the VIth Congress of the Soviets in 1931.

purges of the thirties. Because of our almost virtual ignorance of the actual present internal relations in the leadership of the Soviet Communist Party, which are hidden behind a monolithic façade, it is difficult to predict who might be the future victims of the shifting party line.

It might well be added that at the root of the practice of elimination of all political nonconformists lies the realization that, under Soviet conditions, there is no place for legal political opposition and therefore no other possible logical outlet for divergent political opinions but "counterrevolutionary" acts. Terror in general and social prophylaxis in particular prevent such acts quite efficiently.

3. *Contacts with foreign countries.* People who had contacts with foreigners or with foreign countries constitute one of the most suspect categories. The regime's concern in this respect goes very far, to the extent of a real mania. Included are not only a considerable proportion of people who visited foreign countries, occupied official positions abroad or met with foreigners inside the Soviet Union, but also persons who corresponded with addressees abroad, who received relief parcels, and so forth. Though the Soviet authorities are no doubt aware that actual espionage through these channels would be rather exceptional, the policy of prophylaxis goes very far in this case. Because not all those actually guilty can be individually detected, the elimination from time to time of a considerable proportion of people who are suspect merely because they belong to this category is considered the safest way for state security.

It should be added that there are also other reasons for repression of this category, such as the apprehension that these people might have been "contaminated with Western ideas," or that they might, even unconsciously, counter the official information line about the life in the West. Hence, a desire to discourage the population at large from sustaining foreign contacts.

4. *Ethnic groups.* A major criterion that may determine classification in the "dangerous" category is an ethnic one. Here belong (among the established incidents) several waves of deportations of the Ukrainians and of entire groups from among the Moslem peoples of Central Asia, the deportations of the Soviet Poles (1936–1938) and of the Soviet Jews from the Ukraine and Byelorussia (1950–1951). In the above cases one kind of "nationalism" or another

among the population could be at the root of the penal action, but the scope of the action always went far beyond even those suspect of any deviation.

Especially striking examples of far-reaching prevention based on an ethnic criterion are the cases of the Volga Germans, the Crimean Tartars, and the Chechen-Ingush. These three peoples' Autonomous Republics were abolished, the first one in 1941 under the charge that "tens of thousands" of its inhabitants were "*preparing*" to sabotage Soviet defense, and the other two in 1946 under the charge that during the German occupation "the main mass of people" in these areas were disloyal. The mass deportations affected only Chechens, Crimean Tartars, and Volga Germans (and evidently most of them), despite the fact that all three Republics had a mixed population.

The ethnic factor played only a secondary role, however, in the mass arrests and deportations in the areas added to the Soviet territory since 1939, especially in Eastern Poland and the Baltic States.[12] The Soviet penal operations in those territories were similar — *mutatis mutandis* — to the repressive measures applied in the Soviet Union itself in the first decade after the Bolshevik coup. The tempo was naturally much accelerated and the techniques much more perfect. But the general pattern and the social and political strata affected were very similar.

It is very probable that among the populations of Eastern Poland and of the Baltic countries, there were at the time groups who did intend to resist the occupying power. There is also no doubt that the hostile attitude of a large part of the population toward the new authorities created fertile ground for oppositionist ideas and a possible reservoir of rebels. It is also plausible to assume that a great part of the potentially disloyal elements actually belonged to the arrested categories. All the above considerations made the preventive wholesale arrests and deportations rational in the eyes of the authorities.

5. *Family ties.* Family or friendship ties, or even sometimes only

[12] With regard to the situation in Eastern Poland in 1939–41 it might seem that in two instances the ethnic factor did play a dominant role: in the deportation of Polish *osadniks* (settlers, veterans of World War I) and in the deportation of hundreds of thousands of Jewish refugees from territories occupied by the Nazis. But even in these two cases the apparently dominating ethnic factor was complementary only.

acquaintanceship, with people repressed for offenses with a political taint, are the characteristics of the most stable category of people affected by preventive administrative arrests, a category complementary to and a function of all the other.[13] There are probably two factors taken into consideration by the Soviet authorities in this case: a possibility that a relative or a friend may be an associate in action or at least may share the opinions of the arrested person (a typical example of guilt by association), and a belief that people who lost their close relatives or friends through penal action of the regime, may become bitter and even inimical. In its extreme form, this kind of reasoning may lead to an absurd snowballing, as it did in periods of special tensions (e.g., the great purges). But even when excesses are curbed, this is the group that furnishes the greatest proportion of people with fear and guilt complexes.

Terror in the Soviet Union expresses itself in varied forms: in the institutionalized arbitrariness of the administration and its ruthlessness; in the absence of civil rights; in complete thought-control; in the all-penetrating activities of the secret police; in the system of mutual denunciation and mutual spying; in the extremely severe and extensive penal retributions; in the harshness prevailing in the places of confinement; et cetera. The method of social prophylaxis is but one of these forms, though of a specially vast significance.

The belief that terror in a totalitarian regime is in principle an aim in itself seems, at least with regard to the Soviet system, erroneous. The MVD apparatus, tending to perpetuate and expand its own power, has undoubtedly a vested interest in terror per se, but for the authoritative Soviet ideologists and leaders terror appears as an indispensable tool to achieve specific aims, in fact *all* their aims, in all fields of human endeavor.

The effectiveness of Soviet terror cannot be denied, especially when one has to bear in mind that the system is to a certain extent self-defeating, because it induces people to conceal their real propensities and to hide the indications of belonging to the "doomed" categories, which makes the task of the secret police even more difficult. Moreover, it is an inherent feature of terror that its edge becomes

---

[13] In case of desertion abroad, adult family members of the offender are made punishable in court by the Criminal Code (Art. 58 1–V).

blunt with time, unless the degree of terror continuously increases, and then, so great may become the degree of despair that the intended result is missed. There are some symptoms showing that a measure of fatalism might have developed already among the Soviet people.

To counteract these phenomena the Soviet rulers apply a scheme of alternating periods of great intensity of terror, when the limits of social prophylaxis are the broadest, with periods of relative relaxation. This method keeps the population in a state of a certain hope for a "quiet life." At the same time this method, combined with functional rationality and a certain flexibility of the preventive repressions, gives the individual a feeling that doom is not .inevitable, that he does have an alternative in his life, and a justifiable reason to believe that his own behavior might help him escape persecution.[14] Without such an alternative there would be insufficient incentive for compliance with all the wishes of the regime, even among the ideologically faithful.

Those aware that some features of their biographies are or might in the future be considered condemnable will energetically endeavor to compensate for their ominous status by manifesting extra zeal in fulfilling their duties and in showing their unlimited fidelity and obedience to the regime. But the largest strata of the Soviet population will be pushed into submissiveness by the terror applied to others and by the hope that the "right" attitude on their part might help them to evade possible group or individual classification as "socially dangerous." All, nevertheless, realize well that no measures of precaution can provide real security, create a sound basis for peace of mind or permit relaxation.

The Soviet playwright Alexander Afinogenyev, in his well-known play *Fear*, put into the mouth of one of his characters, Professor Borodin, the following words: "The milk-woman is afraid that her cow will be confiscated; the peasant is afraid of compulsory collectivization; the Soviet worker is afraid of the endless purgings; the Party worker is afraid that he will be accused of deviations; the scientific worker is afraid that he will be accused of idealism; the technical worker is afraid that he will be accused of sabotage. We

[14] An extreme example when there was practically no alternative is the fate of the Jews under Hitler in the war years.

live in an epoch of great fear. Fear compels talented intellectuals to renounce their mothers, to fake their social origin, to wangle their way into high positions. . . Fear stalks everyone. Man becomes suspicious — shut in — dishonest — careless —and unprincipled. No one attempts anything without an outcry, without having his name inscribed on a blackboard, without the threat of arrest and exile."

In this way Soviet terror manages to destroy the desire for any nonconformity and influences decisively the mental state and the behavior pattern of the whole population.

DISCUSSION

Mr. Bertram Wolfe: We have heard two sharply different approaches to the phenomenon with which our Conference is to deal. Mr. Friedrich insists upon the uniqueness of the totalitarian syndrome, whereas Mr. Timasheff urges us to view totalitarianism as a variant upon the older phenomena of despotism and dictatorship.

This problem, of course, is basic to all historiography; the historian must assume both continuity and uniqueness. But one can admit, from case to case, differing degrees of emphasis upon the one or the other, and in the present context I side with Mr. Friedrich.

Aristotle once asserted discrimination is the beginning of all wisdom. That which distinguishes totalitarianism, it seems to me, is rooted in the word *total*. All cultures have had their ideologies, but the ideology in a totalitarian society is deliberately total — that is, it embraces and prescribes for every aspect of human life. Similarly, every modern society has involved a "state," but the totalitarian state is designedly total, in that it becomes coëxtensive with the society itself.

This totality is unique to our age. Luckily for us all, only a few societies have "gone totalitarian" in the total sense, but we must recognize that a latent tendency to totalitarianism exists in all modern states, not excepting the United States today. This is the distinguishing characteristic of our age.

Mr. Karl Deutsch: We seem to teeter on the verge of a semantic pitfall. Mr. Wolfe agrees with Mr. Friedrich as against Mr. Timasheff, but nevertheless he employs the word "state," which Friedrich eschews. Now is the category "state" applicable to totalitarian regimes, or is it not?

Mr. Carl Friedrich: For reasons stated in my paper, I think it is not applicable.

Mr. George Denicke: The issue between Mr. Friedrich and Mr. Timasheff I was privileged to discuss with Rudolf Hilferding in Paris in 1938–39. He held (and I agreed) that totalitarianism is *sui generis*. Each occurrence can be described, but no adequate general concept can be defined.

I would, however, point to one common feature of all three members — Russia, Italy, and Germany — of the species. It happens that I was a witness to the early stages of all three systems, and I was struck each time by the element of extreme *voluntarism*. Goebbels once averred that *"Nationalsozialismus ist keine Weltanschauung, sondern eine Willensrichtung."* And Mussolini, in the early days of the Fascist movement, announced *"Ich will regieren. Das ist mein Programm."* This trait, I should argue, should be added to Mr. Friedrich's list of five: the totalitarian movement is a voluntaristic movement. From the very first there is a compelling and controlling will to power.

Mr. Paul Kecskemeti: I speak to Mr. Gliksman's paper. It is an error, I think, to focus on the prophylactic function of terror. Its action is not purely such. It is directed not against offenders, or even possible future offenders, but against the entire populace.

We must recognize that terror is not merely a deterrent. There certainly is a deterrent function, whose crux is the prevention of any group's "bargaining" with the regime in order to attain its own self-centered objectives — no "price" can be placed on coöperation. The terror insures that only unorganized and formless pressures can be brought to bear.

But terror has an essential positive purpose as well: It induces people to compete in demonstrating their loyalty. Everyone feels it necessary to prove that he is at least as loyal as the next man, if not more so.

Miss Hannah Arendt: My agreement with almost all of Mr. Friedrich's statements comes, I believe, from a more general and fundamental agreement with his "presupposition that *ta politika* are decisive for the patterning of any society" and "that . . . political science is the highest or most important science." Seen in the light of political science, his thesis that "totalitarian society is historically unique and *sui generis*" can only mean that totalitarian domination constitutes a novel form of government. This conclusion seems inevitable; yet it is extremely daring. For throughout our history there have been few forms of government, all of them already known to and described by the ancients. It seems so unlikely that we of all people should be confronted with a novel form of government.

This doubt, which certainly is legitimate, has given rise to certain descriptions of totalitarianism, usually couched in psychological or sociological terms, in which totalitarian government appears as some more radical form of something already well known. It is indeed true that the novelty of totalitarian government reveals itself clearly only if one considers its political institutions and modes of action. I would therefore be a little reluctant to use the term "totalitarian society" as freely as Mr. Friedrich. Totalitarian domination, if fully developed, is destructive of "society" strictly speaking, from its higher forms in interest groups down to its elementary level of family units.

I agree with Mr. Friedrich that we can understand the essence of this new form of government only by an analysis which insists on making distinctions. To the distinctive traits contained in his paper I should like to add two more: *First*, it seems to be a general feature of both Bolshevik and Nazi government that the army loses its position as the chief executive arm of government, and all the honors which went with it, to the police. This is an important shift of power, which was curiously foreshadowed perhaps in the eclipse of the army in the modern republics, particularly in the Third Republic which for more than thirty years expected a *coup d'état* from the side of the violently anti-Republican general staff of the French army, which never materialized. Only a similar loss of "will to power" can explain how in Germany the attempted military dictatorship of General Schleicher, backed by the presidency of a field marshal, lasted exactly four weeks. It is interesting that from the beginning Hitler was not so much interested in winning the Reichswehr and securing the monopoly of the means of violence as he was intent on building up the police and police troops (the SS) under a nonmilitary commander (Himmler). The eclipse of Roehm, the organizer of the SA and a military man, in favor of Himmler had already begun in 1929. The development, as we all know, ended in the forties when Himmler as chief of the SS and the police, was virtually the commander in chief of the armed forces. The trial of Tukhachevsky marked the same development in Soviet Russia; the Red Army then lost its position within the government's power machine and was put under the surveillance and virtually the command of the police.

My *second* point bears on a distinction between totalitarian governments and the movements, Communist, Nazi, or Fascist, which lead up to them. If we say that these movements are totalitarian, we credit them, to a certain degree, with the wisdom of hindsight; they never can be fully totalitarian in the pre-power stage. In this stage, they still share many characteristics with revolutionary movements and with those "above-parties groups" which were so significant for Continental party politics between the two wars. Some of them, for instance the Fascist movements of Italy and Spain, never developed into totalitarian government, but became one-party dictatorships. When it comes to judging the present different Communist parties or violent leftist or rightist movements throughout the world, one may find it useful to distinguish between those which are fully totalitarian, for instance completely under the control of Moscow, and those which are not.

One of the chief distinctions between totalitarian movements and groups which aim at the overthrow of government in some other fashion seems to be the following: revolutionary groups have a long tradition of constituting themselves as secret societies and using conspiratory methods. They do not pretend, however, that the government they want to overthrow is itself such a conspiracy. The totalitarian movements act in a different manner: they establish themselves openly and pretend that their opponents are members of a conspiracy. In order to combat this conspiracy, they pretend, they must use conspiratory methods. They establish a counterconspiracy in broad daylight. The conspiratory methods which they introduce are the methods of the secret police whose close connection with the methods of secret societies has often been demonstrated. The danger is that precisely because they function in broad daylight they are in a position to introduce these methods into society at large. They act in exactly the same manner as the secret police all through the nineteenth and the beginning of the twentieth century since they start from the same assumption and justify their existence with the existence of a secret conspiracy. That these methods of the secret police, as well as the organizational structure of secret societies, can be used by mass movements (and without keeping anything secret) is one of the most revealing aspects of modern politics. In brief, I should like to propose to call every movement totalitarian that pretends to fight, not the enemies of a class or a nation or the policies of a government, but a conspiracy such as the Elders of Zion, the Trotskyites, Wall Street, and so forth. Typical totalitarian thinking creeps into a free society, as when, for instance, the old fight against the New and Fair Deals by the Republican Party was perverted by certain people who pretended that a conspiratory clique existed within the United States government with power to influence United States policy.

I wish to respond finally to Mr. Friedrich's strictures, at the end of his paper, on those who stress totalitarianism's "peculiar moral obtuseness" as a distinguishing feature of totalitarian domination. His remarks may well have been addressed to me and my writings, yet I do not believe that I am wrong in finding this is one of those basic distinctions with which we both are concerned. The point, however, is not the use of violence per se, not even on an unprecedented scale, but that "totalitarian indifference" to moral considerations is actually based upon a reversal of all our legal and moral concepts, which ultimately rest on the commandment, "Thou shalt not kill." Against this, totalitarian "morals" preaches almost openly the precept: Thou shalt kill! The assumption, which can be seen very clearly in Himmler's speeches to the SS generals in Eastern Occupied Territories, is that this precept is as difficult to follow as its opposite. In other words, the peculiarity of totalitarian crimes is that they are committed for different reasons and in a different framework which has a "morality" of its own. The morality is contained in the ideology, or rather in what totalitarianism has made of the respective ideologies which it inherited from the past. I therefore would not agree with Mr. Friedrich that "both the ideology and the party in Soviet totalitarian society are declining in importance."

Mr. Gliksman's paper, with its insistence upon the prophylactic function of terror, the differentiation between the different courts of law, *de facto* administrative imprisonment, and special tribunals for mass deportations, seems to me very valuable as far as it goes. I am inclined to think that it does not take sufficient account of the later stages of totalitarian terror or distinguish sufficiently between the measures taken during the "revolutionary" period of the regime, when it is confronted with real enemies, and the mass liquidation which comes when all opposition has already been silenced. The distinctive characteristic of totalitarian terror is that it is not only, and not even primarily, concerned with known or suspected opponents, but that it "punishes" independently of any subjective guilt for "objective" reasons. Both accuser and victim know that the victim is not only innocent, but that his "crimes" could never have been committed. The selection of the victims shifts from suspects (for instance, members of the propertied classes in Russia, members of the socialist parties in Germany), that is, "possible criminals," to the possible or even "necessary crime" which lies in the course of history or nature (the liquidation of the peasants in 1930 in Russia because History shows that a peasant class develops as soon as peasants become proprietors of the land, that these small proprietors are the first beginnings of capitalism, and so on; or, Nature shows that the Jews or mentally ill persons or people afflicted with heart and lung diseases are parasites on the healthy bodies of the nations). The concentration camps are filled eventually with a majority of people who are innocent from every point of view. Guilt, no matter how interpreted, is no longer a criterion at all. The only criterion is the scientifically forecast course of history itself, according to which certain crimes are necessary and for which therefore "criminals" must be found.

Mr. Albert Lauterbach: I too agree in general with Mr. Friedrich, but I think he narrows his case too much. Both he and Mr. Timasheff concentrate entirely on political institutions and relationships. Once one turns (as our Conference will at a later session) to the psychological aspects of totalitarianism, the case for an assumption of uniqueness becomes far more conclusive. These systems differ from all others in imposing upon society, as a matter of public policy, a standardized perceptual scheme and a favored personality type.

These considerations lead me to a further remark. Mr. Friedrich writes in his paper of the "Communist challenge" as an essential element in the rise of fascist movements, and Miss Arendt has just spoken of the "counterconspiracy" aspect. One must beware of mistaking images for reality here: the point is not necessarily that there *is* a conspiracy to be countered, but rather that people are induced to *perceive* one, and to fear it. The Communists in the Germany of 1932 were probably not a genuine danger, but they were widely believed to be one.

In Europe today, similarly, the popularity of the Communism in Italy and France is perhaps based on a perceived and feared, but not necessarily a real, danger of resurgent fascism. Conversely, the Gaullist movement in France may be feeding on an unrealistic fear of Communism.

We have much to learn about the psychological aspects of totalitarianism. Are the Nazi and Soviet cases closely similar in these respects, or are there significant differences? Can we apply their similarities (or their differences) to the analysis of any attitudes in the United States today? Is there an American version of the totalitarian state of mind? All these are important questions to explore.

Mr. Michael Karpovich: In the final paragraph of his paper, Mr. Friedrich mentions Christianity, democracy, and technology as the necessary historical pre-conditions of totalitarianism. The reference to the first of these pre-conditions somewhat puzzles me, and I must therefore ask for clarification. Certainly "a predilection for convictional certainty" is not characteristic of Christianity alone; the other great world religions have it too. In fact, Christianity is probably less hospitable than the other religions to this predilection, because of its many basic dualisms. With respect to politics, in particular, Christianity lays great stress on the gulf between Caesar and God, a doctrine which should make it rather sharply opposed to totalitarian tendencies. Mr. Friedrich on the other hand minimizes the importance of the influence of thinkers in past centuries. But surely Rousseau has been exploited by later theorists who in turn have prepared the way for the totalitarian ideologies. In the specific instance of Russia, one can argue that Soviet leaders from Lenin to Zhdanov were psychologically predisposed to thought control by means of their reading in those Russian authors of the 1860's who denied the autonomy of culture with respect to politics.

Mr. Friedrich: I rather expected criticism on this point. I certainly do not argue that Christianity "created" totalitarianism. But I do believe that Christianity, democracy, and technology, together, created the necessary conditions or "context" for the totalitarian phenomenon.

I would add, further, that Christianity, especially its Protestant branches, has laid greater stress on credal certainty than any other of the great religions. Mohammedanism comes close, but not very close.

Much the same may be said of the philosophical "schools" so characteristic of the Western Christian societies. There is an aggressive rigidity in pragmatism, Hegelianism, existentialism, and the like, which is hardly unconnected with the credal rationality of which I have spoken. It is all a part of a general climate which today is secularized but whose origins are theological.

Mr. Gerold T. Robinson: Even with the addenda just advanced, I cannot agree that Mr. Friedrich's three-fold causal scheme fits the Russian case. The Soviet Union is the most totalitarian of all societies, but Tsarist Russia was hardly a democratized or a technologized society. Furthermore, Russian Orthodoxy is, among the major branches of Christianity, specifically the most mystical, non-intellectual, and credally immature. Autocracy, not democracy, provided much of the pre-Revolutionary political experience of Russia, and the totalitarianism of the Soviet regime was culturally foreshadowed in the collectivism of the church and the village in Imperial days. This was not the Marxist collectivism of an urban industrial proletariat, since that group was small in backward Russia, but a more primitive collectivism of the peasantry and the church which infused Russian thought, art, and literature. It is no accident that the "individual" in the great Russian novels is not the rugged, independent individual who deliberately and joyfully transcends his group ties, but the lonely, lost man who is individualistic in that he is out of touch with his group, his society, and his culture. In assessing the background of Russian totalitarianism, would it not be sound to emphasize autocracy rather than democracy, primitive collectivism rather than technological development, and the mystical Christianity of the East rather than the more rational Christianity of the West?

And do not most of these considerations apply currently to China also? In its pre-totalitarian phase, Chinese culture was neither Christian nor democratic nor technologized.

Mr. Friedrich: I entirely accept the facts as Mr. Robinson has put them. Perhaps our difficulty arises from my use of the term "context." Marx and Engels were certainly the products of a Western context, Christian and democratic and technological. (I should myself argue that Lenin and Trotsky, as tactical theorists, were too.) I would concur with Mr. Robinson in saying that totalitarianism would not have come to either Russia or China from the preëxisting circumstances of those cultures alone. The fact is that totalitarianism was imposed upon these cultures subsequent to its definition in a Christian, democratic, and technological context.

Mr. Boris Mirkine-Guétzévitch: I welcome Mr. Gliksman's emphasis upon the uniqueness of totalitarian terror. My own field is the French Revolution, and it is clear that the Terror then was much different from the twentieth-century type. The great majority of those who were put to death in 1793 and early 1794 were probably enemies of the regime or spies for foreign powers, or gave reasonable grounds for such suspicions. Only late in 1794 did the victims become unknowns who were perhaps utterly innocent.

But the real difference lies in the attitude toward terror. The French revolutionaries did not justify it per se (Marat is the only exception, and he was ill), whereas the totalitarians do. I can remember seeing an article in a Cheka journal which admitted that terror did not fit in a bourgeois society, but argued that it was fully consonant with a Marxist one.

Mr. George F. Kennan: I should like to add a few remarks to Miss Arendt's reflections on the place of the secret police. I agree that their significance is seldom appreciated.

One fact is worth notice. In Russia, both before the Revolution and since, and in Germany both before and after the Nazis came to power, the secret police (in Germany, the Nazi precursors) were in close alliance with the criminal underworld. Or perhaps more accurately, there was coöperation between the secret police and a demi-world not quite criminal in its complexion. The rulers in totalitarian societies, at least in the first generation, are themselves products of this demi-world; they have had intimate connections with it, and they continue to rely upon it.

In general, I would ask the Conference members not to concentrate too heavily on what totalitarianism in some abstract sense *is*, to the exclusion of concern with what it is *becoming*. Totalitarianism is dynamic: it does not stand still. Let me advance some illustrations of my meaning.

Once the movement has seized power, the nature and the function of the party is changed. The rank-and-file members fade out as politically relevant strata; the party as a whole becomes a glorified *Beamtenbund*. It is an organized means of getting a job, not an inspirational force.

Again, I would revert to Miss Arendt's remarks on the secret police. They gain ascendancy not merely over the army, but over the party too. The totalitarian "state" — if there is such a thing — seems to me to consist in the top party clique plus the secret police apparatus.

The central policy question, of course, is the future, Where is all this leading? I see signs, in Soviet Russia, of a rigidifying of the regime. Stalin in the thirties deliberately tried to prevent the formation of stable loyalty-groups by constantly moving personnel around. Hence also the purges. Since 1947, however, the higher echelons have been highly stable, the terror has slackened off relative to the 1930's or to the years of World War II, and the higher strata seem to be able to give their children a distinctive sort of up-bringing and education. The explanation for all this lies, I think, in Stalin's anticipation of the problem of succession, which has become real with today's newspaper headlines. If these tendencies should survive whatever difficulties Stalin's death may entail, I think we may see a stable regime of wealth and privilege which may move in the direction of oligarchical despotism and may, perhaps, lose some of its totalitarian aspects.

Mr. Franklin H. Littell: Mr. Friedrich's thesis of the uniqueness of modern totalitarianism is sometimes challenged by pointing to primitive cultures, which are certainly totalitarian in a real sense. But there is a difference which protects the Friedrich argument from successful challenge on these grounds. The primitive civilizations seem to have had no alternative to their kind of totalitarianism, whereas the twentieth-century varieties did have alternatives.

Perhaps I, as a theologian, might add some words on the contributions of Christianity. I think again that Mr. Friedrich is basically correct in emphasizing "credal rationality," but I would add another dimension. Christianity, in Russia, in Italy, and in Germany alike, had lost its sense of mission. The organized churches no longer had a dynamism, and the eschatological *esprit* which they failed to provide was supplied by the totalitarian movements. In this sense, the Christian churches are peculiarly responsible: they left the vacuum into which the totalitarians stepped. May I close with a query: can totalitarianism develop in a society with active, free, and dynamic churches?

Mr. Gliksman: I have no real disagreement with Mr. Kecskemeti's remarks on my paper. Certainly the terror is addressed to the maintenance of conformity in the entire population, and I did indicate this fact in the last part of my paper. But its scope extends only to a part of that population, and I was mainly concerned with the process by which the part is chosen.

I do, however, disagree to a certain extent with Miss Arendt. The question is not one of innocence or guilt, suspicion or lack of it. It is rather a question of whether or not there are rationally meaningful categories of those directly affected by terror. I think there are, from the Soviet point of view, and the one I would stress is that of the "pre-suspects," i.e., potential offenders who are exiled or imprisoned as whole ethnic or social groups because there are "rational" reasons to believe that they might, sometime in the future, become "dangerous" in the Soviet sense of that word. This happened for instance, to the inhabitants of the Volga German Republic during World War II, and to the Jews along the Western border in 1950–51, not because they were guilty or suspect, but because there might someday be reason to consider them "socially dangerous."

Mr. Timasheff: There is no real collision between Mr. Friedrich and myself. I am quite willing to say that the "state" disappears, so long as he will agree that its disappearance is a result of extension to the point where it absorbs all of society. I do feel that definition of totalitarianism by juxtaposition of traits, rather than by reference to one basic component, is misleading, for different analysts will combine different traits.

PART THREE

Totalitarianism and Ideology

■

5. The Totalitarian Mystique: Some Impressions of the Dynamics of Totalitarian Society

ALEX INKELES

Two broad approaches bulk large in the efforts made to understand modern totalitarianism. Perhaps most prominent, certainly most extensive, are those analyses which assign a central role to such formal ideologies as Marxism-Leninism. A rather different approach holds that modern totalitarianism may be understood primarily in terms of the drive for absolute power. The difference between the action of the modern totalitarian and that of earlier seekers after power is generally seen by those taking this position as lying in the thoroughness and effectiveness of the technical means of control both necessary to and possible for the ruler of a modern industrial society. This paper seeks to add another explanatory principle to these, on the grounds that there are important dimensions of totalitarian social organization which cannot adequately be explained solely in terms of formal ideology and power seeking, used either separately or jointly as explanatory principles. In addition, this paper seeks to extend our grasp of totalitarianism by concentrating on totalitarian society, which has been relatively neglected, rather than on totalitarian politics, which have previously been the prime focus of analysis. To these ends I present below a series of what appear to me general characteristics of the totalitarian elites' approach to society, as well as several illustrations of the pattern of *social* action which is manifested by them when they come to power.

Specifically, it is posited here that the totalitarian leader is a particular type of individual in that he is characterized by a distinc-

tive approach to problems of social organization. This approach is
assumed to manifest itself regardless of the particular content of the
totalitarian's formal ideology — although it may be that only certain kinds of formal ideology will appeal to him. This element of
the totalitarian "character" is not conceived of as replacing the power
drive, but rather as distinguishing the totalitarian from other individuals who also seek power, even absolute power.

I have used the term "mystique" to represent the combination of
elements which make up the totalitarian's distinctive approach to
social organization. Although the several elements which constitute
this orientation are individually discussed below, a word of explanation about the general term "mystique" is in order here. The term
is used to express the idea that the totalitarian, despite extensive
rationalization of his position through the citation of purported
biological or historical fact, is convinced that he has *directly* perceived some immanent law of social development. This law is seen
as relatively overriding, and its implication as bound eventually to
be manifested. Consequently, the totalitarian's knowledge of the
law is seen by him both as dictating necessary action on his part,
and as guaranteeing the "correctness" of that action. Further, although the point is not developed in this paper, I believe that only a
certain psychological type is likely to have such conceptions. To my
mind this common psychological characteristic accounts for a significant amount of the similarity in the pattern and tone of totalitarian action programs, even when this action starts from different
formal ideological premises and occurs in radically different socio-
cultural environments. In other words, the totalitarian mystique is
presented not as a quality of the totalitarian society, but as a quality
of the totalitarian *leader* who imposes his conception on the society
in which he comes to power.

Thus the mystique posited in this paper is not meant to replace
formal ideology or power seeking as bases for explaining totalitarianism, nor is it meant to stand above them as having a "higher" explanatory potential. Like them it has its limitations as an explanatory
principle, and in my opinion could not alone adequately explain
the facts of totalitarian social organization. The concept of the totalitarian mystique is offered simply as a supplement to explanations
based on the role of ideology and of power seeking, and it is the

central focus in this paper only because I feel it to have been neglected. The task of assessing the relative importance of formal ideology, power seeking, and the mystique in the development and functioning of totalitarian social structures is beyond the scope of this paper. I must, therefore, limit myself to the comment that I assume the mystique to have its greatest importance and widest influence in the early decades of the establishment of a totalitarian society, and to operate largely as a "residue," although an important one, in the actions of the "second generation" of totalitarian leaders.

The principles and characteristics presented here are aspects of an ideal type in the sense in which Max Weber used the term. Consequently, although the model which underlies the ideal type is the Soviet social system, I will proceed largely without reference to many of the specific and distinctive institutional features of Soviet society. Indeed, the central aim of this statement is to suggest a mode of analysis which can encompass totalitarian systems as divergent in their concrete institutional structure as the Communist and Nazi systems, which most closely approximate the ideal type; Fascist Italy, which only imperfectly approximated it; and Franco Spain, which fits the model in only a few crucial respects.

It should perhaps go without saying that the principles and operating characteristics of totalitarian social organization presented here are highly tentative. Further, they are not meant to be in any sense complete or exhaustive, but are selected as simply illustrative of the results given by the general mode of analysis adopted here.

SOME BASIC PRINCIPLES OF TOTALITARIAN SOCIAL ORGANIZATION

1. *The Principle of the Precedence of the Totalitarian Mystique*

It is proposed here that the most distinctive and basic determinant governing the structuring and operation of totalitarian society is the principle that certain essentially mystically derived, relatively abstract goals and imperatives must stand above and take precedence over considerations of human welfare, of personal and group interest, comfort, and gratification, and of stable and calculable patterns of social relations. This orientation is usually characterized as the principle of "the subordination of the individual to the state." While that statement goes far in exposing the central feature of totalitarianism, it fails to deal with several important dimensions of the problem.

Totalitarianism does not merely subordinate the *individual* to "the state," but it also, indeed preëminently, subordinates human *associations*, the organizations and institutions which man creates to meet his social needs. Neglect of the prime importance that totalitarianism gives to the subordination of institutions as such, may lead to neglect of some of the most important structural features of totalitarian social organization. Traditional liberalism, because of its emphasis on the individual, his rights and needs, naturally tends to see first in totalitarianism its direct impact on the individual, in particular his subordination to state purposes. But totalitarianism, in contrast to liberalism and pluralism, leaps over the individual to give full recognition and weight to the role of social institutions in the structure and functioning of society. It recognizes that one of the important aspects of social organization in the large-scale society is that the individual is related to the total social system primarily through the institutional networks in which he is enmeshed. And it has therefore given special and primary emphasis to the subordination of the traditional human associations, the organizations and institutions, of which the individual is a member. This becomes the *chief* tool for its ultimate subordination of the individual to the state. Totalitarianism recognizes that so long as certain of its crucial membership units are not themselves subordinated to the demands of the central authority, the individual himself may to that degree be immune to full subordination.

The second difficulty I would like to note in the formula that defines totalitarianism as a system in which the individual is subordinated to the state lies in its emphasis on "the state." To stop at this point is to assume that it is indeed the state in and of itself which is the ultimate goal toward which the totalitarian is oriented. Further, since the final concern of the state is with power, there is a tendency in contemporary political analysis to assume rather facilely that the prime interest of the totalitarian is in *power* per se. It should not be forgotten that in the last analysis all participants in politics are interested in power, yet many are far from totalitarians. Indeed, although those who are interested in power as an ultimate end may become dictators, not all dictators are totalitarians.

The significant question, of course, is "power for what?" It is in the *ends* for which he seeks power that the crucial characteristic of the totalitarian emerges.

I submit that it is not power in and of itself which motivates the totalitarian, but power sought for some specific "higher purpose." In other words, the totalitarian sees the state as predominantly an instrument of another purpose, a mere vessel which he gives content. It is precisely this which makes him so great a threat to established institutions and freedom — that he has no real respect for the state as such, for the state as an institution with legitimacy and purpose in and of itself. Paradoxically, it is rather the non-totalitarian who accepts the state as sufficient unto its own purpose of governing, of allocating authority, and of regulating relations among men. The characteristic of the totalitarian is that he sees the state as an institution with no right to existence in itself, but rather as a mere tool serving the attainment of some higher goal which is above the state. It is essentially the imperatives of this higher law which spell the doom of "the rule of law."

Invariably this higher goal involves some mystique, some principle above man, some force that responds to laws of its own and that merely requires the state as the instrument through which it may work out its inner imperatives. The mystique may be the dialectal laws of history and of social development for the Marxist, the destiny of the nation and race for the Hitlerian, or the ideal of the true Christian society for Franco. In each case the totalitarian fortifies himself with — indeed loses himself in — this mystique. It is the fulfillment of the higher law, the mystical imperative, which he sees himself placed on earth to achieve. The state is of course the most obvious and indeed indispensable instrument for effecting this purpose. But in the last analysis what dominates the totalitarian is his compulsion to make man and social development conform to the dictates of his particular perception of higher law. It is not the state as such he values, nor its power per se, but the use he can put them to in order to make man conform to the dictates of the higher law. The totalitarian subordinates not only the individual — in the end he subverts the state itself.

This is not to say that the totalitarian may not in time become so involved in the state as the instrument of his mission that state power becomes an "autonomous" goal. Neither is it to deny that given sufficient time men come into leadership in totalitarian societies whose main training and preoccupation has been with the state as an instrument of power per se and as an end in itself. But it is submitted here that in both of these cases the original dedication to a mystical goal will continue to exercise substantial influence, and an understanding of the behavior of the totalitarian leader will not be fully accessible if it neglects to account for this principle.

I recognize that this view runs counter to many, perhaps most, current interpretations of modern totalitarianism. I suspect it will be particularly objected to because it does not make full allowance for the cynical manipulative propensities of totalitarian rulers. Lest there be serious misunderstanding, therefore, permit me to stress that I do not minimize the cynicism and the manipulativeness of totalitarians. Indeed I suspect the world has never seen cynicism and manipulation to surpass theirs. The questions are what makes them cynical and what are they cynical about? The mystique dictates their morality, indeed it stands above ordinary human morality and places its adherent outside the demands normally to be made of a man and leader. Hence the totalitarian may be cynical about and manipulate "law," "loyalty," "truth," "honesty," and so on. For as long as he manipulates these in the service of the mystique, his action is beyond question — it is law, truth, honesty, loyalty, unto itself.

In our efforts to understand the behavior of the totalitarian we have become so disillusioned from his evident and obvious disregard for "principle," as we commonly understand it, that we have been driven to the theory that the mainspring of his behavior is raw, immoral power seeking by whatever means are available. But the man who is interested in power only as an end in itself can be counted on to make predominantly rational calculations about the balance of forces as they affect his chances to secure and hold power. He therefore can, to some extent, be controlled and manipulated by the action of others within a total power field. The lasting and profound danger to our liberty and freedom, I submit, lies in the fact that the full-blown totalitarian such as Lenin, Hitler, or Stalin is *not* interested in power alone. Frequently he appears to respond first to the imperative of his mystique, and the mystique is by nature arational. It does not defer to the rational calculus of power. Indeed its threat lies in the fact that it may drive the totalitarian leader to run risks in response to the demands of a higher law, of a mystical calculus which seeks to break through the earth-bound rational calculus of power.

Such an orientation is, unfortunately, much less subject to control and manipulation from without through a mere shifting of the balance within the total world field of forces. Therein lies the permanent threat of totalitarianism to world peace. There is no threat to others greater than the pursuit by rational means of an essentially irrational goal — it is just this combination on the level of the individual personality which makes the psychopath so dangerous. Magnified to the nth degree as a pattern of state policy, it is dangerous beyond measure.

2. *The Principle of Monolithic Social Organization*

One branch of modern sociology and anthropology is characterized by its emphasis on structural-functional analysis. This assumes that the discrete institutions and institutional complexes in any society are intimately interrelated and interdependent, so that the structure and operation of any given institutional pattern has important implications for other institutions and for the structure as a whole. In brief, society is seen as an institutional *system*. It is rather striking that without giving explicit formulation to this concept, totalitarian movements and leaders reflect a similar set of assumptions.

Our image of the totalitarian leader as motivated primarily by the desire for power has tended to encourage us to neglect what the totalitarian leader *does* with his power by way of remaking the society he comes to control. The weight given to the principle of power alone as an end in itself has also frequently caused us either facilely to assume the preservation of power as the prime motivation for almost every major program of social change undertaken by the totalitarian dictator, or to attribute many of the actions of the dictator to caprice, to paranoia, or some similar deviant personality manifestation in the dictator. Much of this "residual category" type of explanation can be avoided if there is full recognition of the extent to which the dictator and his lieutenants in modern totalitarian society are oriented to the assumption that every element of the social system, no matter how minor, has implications for the structure as a whole. It is this assumption which prompts the close examination of *every* institution, *every* pattern of behavior, to test its relevance for the whole.

Clearly, if the subordination of the individual cannot be complete without the subordination of his associations, then it follows further that *absolute* subordination of the individual requires absolute subordination of *all* the human associations which form the web of society. But it is not on these grounds alone that the totalitarian exempts no organization from being measured against his Procrustean rule. The mystique implies a plan of the good society. It provides a single metric for all forms of human organization. The totalitarian rejects outright the principle which inheres in the formula "render unto Caesar the things which are Caesar's." He accepts no distinction between the sacred and the profane, the public and the private, in social life. The demands of the mystique determine what decision shall be taken in regard to any particular institution, but all institutions are equally subject to review.

Take, for example, the attack on the family and the church in the early decades of Soviet rule. What rational balance sheet of power would have led a group of leaders who were concerned first and foremost with preserving their power to attempt that particular diversion of energy with its obvious consequences of social resentment and popular hostility? Surely this cannot be understood unless we see the extent to which the Soviet leaders had a mental image of the society their particular mystique demanded be created, an image in which traditional "bourgeois" family life and widespread religious belief and practice were seen as inadmissible because they did not fit the pattern of the future society to which "history" was giving birth. To them it was axiomatic that the "new man" of this society, the rational, socially motivated, scientific man of the future, could not be expected ever to arise were he to be raised in the atmosphere of the traditional family and in the presence of the other worldly values of religion.

This is not to deny that the regime did not also see a direct challenge to the new authority in the parents' influence on their children in the old family structure. Similarly, it must be recognized that the Church had a substantial amount of real control over people's loyalties and actions. But it can hardly be argued that the Soviet leaders were ignorant of the probable impact on their own power which would result from attacking these institutions, *relative* to the probable effects of a *laissez faire* attitude. For the totalitarian there is a design, and everything which exists must serve a function in fulfilling this design. The totalitarian is a social teleologist. But this is teleology stood upon its head, because the design inheres not in what is, but in what must be brought to exist. Not the calculus of power alone, therefore, but equally the Communist totalitarian's opposition to any suggestion of pluralism in society, and his devotion to the mystique of the planned and integrated monolithic society, must be considered for a full understanding of these early action programs of the Soviet leaders.

3. *The Principle of Elite Leadership*

We generally think of totalitarian leadership in terms of the principle of dictatorship — that is, absolute one-man rule based on the ability to seize and hold power without regard to traditional right, popular concensus, or the rule of law. We tend to look on the men immediately around this dictatorial leader as essentially henchmen utilized by him for his purpose of controlling the society, and motivated on their part by the desire to secure the share in power which he offers them. We are prone, further, to think that the totalitarian dictator looks on the organization or party which he builds and heads as a simple and necessary instrument for effecting his rule. In brief, as far as *political* organization is concerned, we incline to equate the totalitarian dictator with the non-totalitarian dictator.

As in the case of the formula for totalitarian society as one subordinating the individual to the state, there is a great deal of validity in this characterization. But this description of the totalitarian dictator equally neglects to emphasize certain essential dimensions of the situation which I believe may be an aid in attaining fuller understanding of totalitarian society.

Consider again our first-stated principle of the subordination of men and their associations to a mystical general social law. One may fruitfully view the dictatorial leader as the man who sees himself as the essential *instrument* of the particular mystique to which he is addicted. He conceives of himself as having been placed on earth for the specific purpose of seeing that the imperatives of the mystique are met, and considers that his life lacks meaning unless he conse-crates himself to that purpose. Thus Hitler is, from this point of view, seen as regarding himself as destined by fate (a theme that runs through his autobiography) to secure the fulfillment of the historic destiny of the German race, and Lenin as viewing his life as unfulfilled unless he served as the midwife of history in assuring the revolutionary birth of the new Communist society.

On the basis of this assumption, the lieutenants of the dictator may be seen in a new light, for there emerge requirements for these positions which go beyond mere adaptability to the dictator's power goals. Two such requirements are most prominent.

First, the cohorts of the dictator are obliged themselves to have a substantial awareness of and commitment to the mystical com-mandments. Unless they do they cannot be expected to serve effi-ciently in the cause of working out the destiny dictated by fate, history, the laws of social development, or the imperatives of "Chris-tian" civilization. The orders given to those high in command and responsibility cannot be more than general directives, which they must know how to implement. Large amounts of initiative are inevi-tably left to them no matter how centralized the structure of author-ity. If then they are to act "meaningfully," "correctly," they must understand the general purposes and direction of the total program. They must understand the mystical law.

Second, the totalitarian dictator's cohorts must be above the usual demands of the human spirit in this world. Most important, they must be above the things of this world in their ability to turn a deaf ear to the groans of their fellow men. Their consecration is not to man, but to the mystical law which they seek to fulfill. If they be moved by the hopes, the fears, and especially the pains of their fellow men, or be slowed in the execution of duty by the hatred of those fellow men, then they lack the qualities essential in a disciple of the leader. The sufferings of ordinary human beings are but temptations designed to deflect the elect from the pursuit of the true goal. Note the statement of Stalin: "The Party is no true Party if it limits its activities to *a mere registration of the suffering* and thoughts of the proletarian masses . . . if it cannot rise superior to

the transient interests of the proletariat." Thus the totalitarian, following Ulysses, lashes himself to the mast of his mystique and
stops his sailors' ears with wax against the cries of the popular sirens,
lest the ship of the revolution be swept up in the current of decadent
bourgeois sentimentality and founder on the rock of compromise.

As with the lieutenants so with the rank and file of the movement,
even if in lesser degree. It is not enough that they be willing soldiers
who carry out orders precisely. They too must have some understanding of the mystique, some vision, however simple, of the overriding law of which they are the instrument. And like the leaders,
they too must be able to resist the human pressures of their fellow
men, to stop their ears to their cries, to "push on the masses from
without." They must excel not so much in their propensity for
self-sacrifice as in their ability to remain unblenched at the sacrifice
of those all around them. No one is wholly, fully, one with the
party and its cause until he in fact or in reasonable facsimile has
smashed against a wall the head of a baby of racially inferior stock
or denounced a close comrade to the secret police. Such unholy acts
of consecration are the most important rites of passage into full
status in the totalitarian movement. One wonders, further, whether
or not this demand of the mystique does not figure prominently
as an element in the logic of the purges, for so often their victims
seem to be sacrificed not so much for what they have done as for what
they have not done. They are cast out not for bashing in the wrong
heads, but for not bashing in enough heads. They are tried not so
much for acting incorrectly, but for inaction which is taken as a sign
of waning devotion and doubt in the mystique. The terror is most
merciless with those of its agents who have blanched at the execution of the mystical imperative.

4. The Principle of Contamination

The preceding section has already hinted at the last of the general
principles I shall discuss: the principle of inner contamination, or
what might be termed the virus theory of social pathology. It is a
characteristic of totalitarian leaders that they see every social movement as having within it the seeds of its own destruction, and that
they are ridden by fear that within their own movement and social
organization there is such a potentially destructive foreign body

which must be wholly and violently expunged — it is not enough to build antibodies against it — lest it cripple its host society from within. For Hitler it was the Jews and all other forms of "race mixture," whether of blood, of physical contact, or of ideas, which he saw as opening up the possibility of the disintegration of his particular mystical structure. For the Soviet Bolshevik it is the taint of capitalist thought remnants, or of various forms of "deviation." And I suppose that for Franco it is any sign of "socialism" or "anti-clericalism."

When the inner taint is "discovered," there is no solution but to cut out the infected part root and branch, to destroy the tainted carrier himself lest he soon infect all. Furthermore, the taint may be manifested not only in people, but by institutional forms, ideas, and systems of ideas. Once the taint is recognized in them, the threat of contamination of the whole organism requires the absolute elimination of these types of carrier as well. By its nature, however, this taint, this cancer which can in no time spread to the whole organism and precipitate its breakup and decay, is not wholly specific and concrete. It has a specific and concrete original source in most cases, but it is not limited to that specific source. Jewishness, bourgeois-capitalist sentiments, lack of "vigilance," atheist or protestant heresies, may appear anywhere in the total social organism. Even the healthiest and greatest may some day be discovered to be tainted.

Here again one is led to consideration of the phenomenon of the totalitarian purge, which seems to be underlain by and to derive its intensity from essentially irrational compulsion. The terror may be an instrument of power designed to stimulate fear, and through fear obedience, in the common people. But the *purge* under Hitler as under Stalin struck mainly at the faithful, indeed in large measure at the inner circle and those immediately concentric to it. Is not the threat of contamination all the more anxiety-provoking the closer to home the dreaded taint is thought to be found?

SOME OPERATING CHARACTERISTICS OF TOTALITARIAN SOCIAL ORGANIZATION

We turn now to a consideration of some illustrative patterns of social action which characterize the implementation of totalitarian

goals in the society in which the totalitarian leader and his organization have seized power. Although these action patterns may be
directly derived from the general principles already described, no
systematic effort to relate them will be attempted. Further, it is
hoped that for the purposes of the present discussion they will be
considered each as standing on its own merits relative to the general
principles and to the other patterns.

1. *The Subversion of Independent Associations and Loci of Power*

Among the earliest actions of the totalitarian in command of
state power there seems always to be the effort to destroy or convert
to new purposes all existing independent associations and other
potential loci of socio-political and economic power. The most
prominent of these are other political parties, certain ethnic or socio-
economic class groups, and selected major economic organizations,
but regularly attention is also given to trade unions, universities,
professional associations, national recreational associations such as
those for sport, and certain religious organizations or sects. Furthermore, although these are the more massive and prominent
human associations, the list is not limited to these. Rather it will
extend as far as those small and intimate, universally present associations, the family and the friendship group.

Almost without fail each and all will at least be subjected to examination and evaluation. Some will be destroyed outright, others
will be "remade" in a new mold, still others will be freshly created
to meet the needs of the totalitarian leaders. Which ones are marked
for any given course of action will, of course, vary with the totalitarian movement, its program, proclivities, and sensitivities, as determined by its particular mystique. But when the examination is
complete, only those associations will remain which fit the required
pattern, or can be made to fit. The rest will be ruthlessly expunged,
and where necessary their membership will likewise be destroyed
or dispersed.

Why is this pattern so widespread and the program of action so
thorough and drastic? If we take the dissolution of all political
parties save that of the totalitarian leader, or the subversion of the
trade unions into instruments of state policy, the explanation seems
obvious enough. The totalitarian leader seeks for power, indeed

for absolute power, and hence he cannot permit the existence of any group with which he must in any sense "share" power. Further, the totalitarian leader is characterized by fear, hence he must seek out and destroy or emasculate real or potential challengers to his power. But as one moves away from the obvious power-potential associations like political parties and trade unions to the universities and the sports clubs, and still further to the family, the theory of power as the wellspring of action cannot fully satisfy the demands of the situation. Indeed one may even doubt how adequately the theory of power alone explains even the destruction of other political parties and the subversion of the trade unions. Is not some essential element missing?

I would suggest that the subversion of the independent association is governed not alone, nor indeed primarily, by considerations of power, but rather by the demands of the totalitarian mystique. The mystique is a higher law, a universal principle, an incontrovertible truth. Further, it is the essence of the totalitarian orientation that it assumes one truth, one law, one interest, and hence only one program. How then shall there be independent political parties? Parties stand for programs, they express political truths, they represent interests. To permit more than one political party, that one which is the expression of the mystique, is to admit the existence of other truths which require other programs, other interests which belie the central and only valid interest. To tolerate these expressions signifies lack of faith in the absolute law, indeed a direct challenge to it. It is to sanction blasphemy.

In addition the mystique implies a plan, a model of the true society, a blueprint for the working out of the principles of the mystical law. Hence, for each association there is a place and a function in the society of the future, and a role to be played in bringing that society into being. All that are permitted to live must assume their appropriate place and begin to exercise their function. All those for which there is no place or function are dross to be cast off. And the principle of contamination comes into operation here, for if there be associations for which there is no place or function, clearly they were not *meant* to be and are in some sense evil. Being evil they may infect the rest of the system, taint and contaminate. Hence those institutions which have been in the Marxist sense "outlived," must be expunged, cut out root and all like the cancerous growths which they are.

2. *The Nationalization of Affect*

The totalitarian society is not spartan in its orientation to human emotion and feeling. It does not seek to suppress the expression of affect. Love and hate, desire and ambition, all have their place. But the totalitarian society permits the expression of affect only for specific purposes and in the last analysis only for one purpose, the purpose of meeting the requirements of the mystique and of insuring the working out of the basic law of society.

It is only "private," personal emotion, particularly sadness and depression, that is frowned upon and indeed suspected. Frowned upon because man has only so much emotional energy, and what he expends for private ends he does not have to contribute toward working out the imperatives of the mystique. Thus, when Lenin indicates his opposition to sexual excess he does so not on moral grounds nor on the basis of some principle like that of the golden mean, but rather because this energy could be better applied to fighting the battles of the revolution! You do not have children for the pleasure they give you, but so that Hitler and Mussolini may have more workers and soldiers to effect the high purposes for which they were put on the earth. Friendship is not important for the gratification it gives, but because comrades may join forces in carrying out the greater task of all.

3. *The Communalization of Communication*

The means of mass communication are an obvious instrument of power in modern society, and their immediate seizure and monopolization by the totalitarian movement which has assumed command should require no special comment. But it is perhaps a neglected fact that the exclusive concern of the ever-present and ironically named ministry of information is not with the transmission of orders, instructions, and other communications intimately relating to the exercise of power. Rather it is to an amazing degree engaged in the business of disseminating and inculcating the articles of faith, in spreading abroad the mystique and seeking to win allegiance to it. It concentrates not so much on commanding obedience to orders, as on winning converts, strengthening the faith and consecration of the common man to the sacred goals — or at least to the humble part assigned him in the program for achieving those goals. The Soviet press spreads the common man's Marxism-Leninism-Stalinism and features the elaborate iconography of its saints. Hitler's press devoted itself to the task of making convinced racists of the last German, consecrating all to the greater glory and fulfillment of the *Herrenvolk*.

But perhaps more important than what totalitarianism does to mass communication is what it does to private communication. Mass communication receives a new content, but remains mass, whereas private communication is transformed and ceases to be private. No matter what the context, on the street talking to a stranger or in the intimacy of one's home, one must say only the right thing. And one must say it as publicly as possible. Private communication becomes suspect, for to speak privately implies the desire to speak without being overheard by others. And the wish not to be overheard suggests that one is saying forbidden things — for if they were not forbidden, blasphemous things, would you not be proud to say them aloud for all to hear? In the end, even silence becomes suspect, for it may mean an unwillingness to reiterate the catechism which the mystique requires all to intone, and hence mark one out as an alien, a non-believer, and a potential source of contamination. Thus, private communication becomes public communication, and along with mass communication is subverted to fulfilling the imperatives of the mystique. Communication is communalized.

4. The "Statification" of the Arts

In thinking of the common totalitarian incursion into art we usually recognize that everywhere the totalitarian classifies art into two broadly defined groups of the acceptable and the unacceptable. Any given piece of art is defined as good or bad in so far as it is German or racially mixed art, bourgeois idealistic art or socialist realism, decadent or progressive, and so on. But what makes it so? The actual characteristics of "good" art, whatever the precise label, tend to be much the same in all modern totalitarian societies regardless of differences in the specific content of the mystique.

Such art must be concrete rather than abstract, directly representational, "wholesome" rather than dealing with "unpleasant" subjects, light in color rather than dark in shade and tone, "social" rather than predominantly "private" in subject matter, and "cheerful" rather than somber or "depressing."

These characteristics of the totalitarian orientation to art are widely recognized and have been frequently commented on. The policy is usually explained on much the same grounds as the totalitarian's seizure and subversion of the media of mass communication. According to this theory, art is simply another instrument used by the totalitarian to affect his absolute rule. It is reduced by the totalitarian to propaganda, for it is only as propaganda that art becomes a useful instrument of power much like the media of mass communication. Further, according to this theory, since art is treated primarily as an instrument of communication, a means for mobilizing people to serve the purposes of the state, it must be understandable to those being communicated with. Hence, it is reduced to the level of taste of the common man.

While I do not challenge this formulation, I would like here again to attempt to go beyond it. I submit that the degradation of the arts under totalitarianism has only a tenuous connection with matters of taste and is not predominantly due to the effort to insure communicability.

That this is the case is all too apparent in the Soviet Union, where it appears that however simple in taste the officially approved plays and novels are, they do *not* appeal to the tastes of the average Soviet reader — who indeed seems to avoid official art and to prefer to snatch such reading from the classics as he can get. Furthermore, I do not think that what is officially approved necessarily has too much to do with the taste of the elite either. Although I cannot support this, I have the distinct impression that Andrei Zhdanov, the arbiter of Soviet literature during his lifetime, had no more "taste" for the novels he approved and praised than for those he rejected and excoriated during the literary purges. Indeed the essence of the totalitarian approach to art is that taste, including the taste of the totalitarian leader, is *irrelevant* to its evaluation. He praises not what he likes aesthetically, but what he approves as serving his mystique. Consider for a moment Mr. Zhdanov's infamous commentary on the Leningrad writers. The writer, said Mr. Zhdanov, is "on the forward line of the ideological front," and a successful work of art "may be compared with a battle won or with a great victory on the economic front." The significance of a work of art derives from its status "as a means of bringing about social reform." In Mr. Zhdanov's diatribe there is hardly a word said about taste, good or bad.

But if the business of art is not to satisfy tastes, what then is its function? Its function is to serve the mystique. Literature must express the mystique, it must show what will be when the totalitarian's particular image of the "good society" has come to pass. Thus, Mr. Zhdanov notes that just as the feudal and later the bourgeois period of full flowering "could create art and literature that asserted the establishment of the new order and sang its praises," just so "it goes without saying that our [Soviet] literature . . . must reflect the new socialist order that represents the embodiment of all that is best in the history of human civilization culture."

This gives a new meaning to the representational character normally attributed to totalitarian art. Such art is not obliged to be, as it is so often thought to be, representational in the sense that photography is representational. For photography represents what was in the past or what is now; it shows things as they are. Photography may, of course, be used to distort true images. But even the best tricks of photography cannot accomplish the task which Zhdanov assigns to art, namely "to show our people not only as they are today but to glance into their future *and to show them as they shall be tomorrow.*" In addition, photography cannot tell you what "not" to be, yet Soviet literature "while disclosing his future . . . must at the same time show our people what they should *not* be like, we must scourge the survivals of yesterday . . . " Thus, the arts for the totalitarian are not really representational, photographic, realistic. Paradoxically enough they are the essence of the symbolic. But they symbolize only what is yet to be. They must expose the future and show a glimpse of what the mystique holds in store, what the kingdom of heaven on earth will look like when the totalitarian leader has finally fulfilled his glorious mission.

Further, the totalitarian leader is not prepared to rest here. Unlike the ordinary dictator he is unwilling to ignore the existence of "bad" art so long as he can be assured of getting enough of the "good" art. On the contrary, the totalitarian seeks the elimination, the physical destruction of the bad art, no matter how much of the good art he can get and no matter how limited the circulation of the bad art. Indeed, it is not enough to say that he does not encourage the bad art. He actually proscribes not merely its circulation but its very *creation*. Even when the artist produces it in the privacy of his studio, for his own eyes alone, indeed even if he destroys it soon after its creation, the artist may not produce bad art. Why is this so? Is this too to be understood as simply another example of the extremity and absoluteness of the totalitarian's thirst for power? I think not.

Art, being expressive, is linked to affect. If it is produced privately for private viewing, it violates the principles of the nationalization of affect and the communalization of communication. The expression of the artist which is undertaken primarily for private reasons is equated with that sexual energy which Lenin could not bear to see lost to the greater glory and advancement of the higher cause, to the working out of the mystical law of social development. Such expression, by virtue of being private, is, in addition, suspect. No less than in the case of conversation, the fact of its being private hints that it is a-communal, and more likely that it is anti-communal; else why should the artist seek to hide it? Finally, the war on private art is determined by the more general principle of contamination. Private art, by definition corrupt art because it does not serve the cause, holds out by its mere existence the threat that it will infect and contaminate other art. It poses a double threat, for it may sneak into the public art of the artists who create it, and it may be seen by others and contaminate their taste for the acceptable public art.

5. *The Institutionalization of Anxiety*

The terror is probably the most revolting and dehumanizing feature of totalitarianism, and it wins this dubious distinction from a field of by no means mild competitors from the Augean stable of totalitarianism. It is therefore right and proper that it should have received so much attention, and that we should have tried so hard to understand it. Yet even in this most discussed field there is an important dimension of the problem which from the point of view of social structure we have perhaps given inadequate attention. Our discussions of the terror tend to focus primarily on its methods as directly applied to its physical victims, and to the victims themselves. In human terms these are of course the aspects of the terror which most urgently command our attention. But have we not in our disgust for the terrorist and our compassion for his immediate victim neglected to give adequate attention to the important functions which terror performs for the totalitarian social order in its effects on those fortunate enough never to become immediate victims?

Terror is tremendously important in an immediate and practical way to the totalitarian for handling those who are a problem for him, or who he believes could potentially become problems. The latter are those who come under the formula of prophylactic arrest, which Mr. Gliksman discusses in his contribution to this symposium. But prophylaxis through arrest is only one dimension of the prophylactic function of terror. Attention must be given to the importance of the prophylactic virtues of terror in dealing with the *non*-arrested.

I am suggesting that the terror is as important for handling those whom the regime regards as relatively solid citizens as it is for dealing with those whom the totalitarian wishes to eliminate or put out of circulation for varying periods. In other words terror is a means for institutionalizing and channeling anxiety. Its purpose is to create in every man a deep sense of insecurity. This insecurity is not merely fear, a state in which the expectation of harm has a specific referent, but rather is anxiety in the technical sense. That is, the individual who anticipates being harmed does not really know for what he will be harmed, but merely has a vague feeling that he will indeed be harmed because of "something" he may have done or not done.

Anxiety, if properly harnessed and given focus, can be a powerful force. The regime seeks to create in every man the nagging fear that he may have done something wrong, that he may have left something undone, that he may have said some impermissible thing. It is an important part of the pattern that he be unable ever to find out with certainty whether he actually did err or not, or if he did, exactly what it was that he did wrong. In this light the studied caprice of the terror in its impact on its actual victims may be seen in a new light. The non-victim, looking at the actual victim, can never find out why the victim was victimized, because there are different and contradictory reasons for different victims, or *there may have been no reason at all.*

The non-victim thus becomes the prisoner of a vague uncertainty which nags him. It is this nagging uncertainty in the non-victim which the terror seeks to create. For it is a powerful force in making every man doubly watch his every step. It is prophylactic in the extreme. It will make the citizen properly compulsive about saying the correct things in public and saying them loud for all to hear, or, almost as good, it will teach them to say nothing in public. It will wake him in the middle of the night to go back to his office to do his sums over again, to redraw his blueprint and then redraw it again, to edit and then edit again the article he is writing, to check and then recheck and then check his machine again. Anxiety demands relief, and compulsive reiteration of action is one of the most common human patterns for the handling of anxiety. It is this compulsive conformity which the totalitarian regime wants. It gets it as a derived benefit from the influence of the terror on the non-victim, who puzzles over the reasons for the treatment of the victim. Anxiety has been institutionalized.

SUMMARY AND CONCLUSION

Much of what I have presented here by way of impressions of totalitarian social organization — such as the comments on the terror and on monolithism — is widely accepted, although I do hope that it gives a somewhat fresh formulation to well-established analyses of totalitarianism. In contrast, the emphasis on the totalitarian mystique, and particularly my insistence on its pervasive role in shaping patterns of totalitarian social organization, will probably have a more critical and perhaps hostile reception. For this interpretation runs too strongly counter to our current emphasis on the raw power seeking of the modern totalitarian. I hope, therefore, that I have made it abundantly clear that I do not minimize the importance of the unprincipled drive for power in the modern

totalitarian. And, of course, much remains to be done in exploring
the intimate interrelations between the totalitarian's drive to fulfill
his mystique and his drive to power, a task which unfortunately
lies outside the scope of this article. I hope, as well, that it is clear
that I assume the role of the mystique to be most prominent only
in certain types of totalitarian movement, and even in these most
influential only during the early stages of totalitarian social development before the stabilization and bureaucratization of the social
order has fully set in. Here again, much remains to be done in
studying the cultural forces, the social setting, and the personality
factors which give rise to such mystiques, as well as in assessing
the forces which act to weaken the hold of the mystique on its
adherents.

My plea is simply that we not stop our analysis with the power
theory. There would be cause to urge this, however comfortable
we might feel with the theory, because our obligations as scholars
and scientists require us to continue the pursuit of knowledge and
the refinement of theory. But in addition I for one am not completely
comfortable with the power theory. It seems to me to groan under
the weight of the explanations which rest solely on it, and yet to
provide no base on which to rest the explanation of many features
of totalitarianism which cannot be fully understood in terms of
the power drive alone. It is my suggestion that we look at the
totalitarian as the captive as well as the manipulator of a mystical
theory of social development.

6. The Protestant Churches and Totalitarianism (Germany 1933–1945)

FRANKLIN H. LITTELL

Three delimitations of this paper are immediately stated,
for reasons of clarity in handling a very large and involved subject.
In the first place, although the problem of the care and cure of souls
is the most acute aspect of church life under Nazism or Communism, this matter has recently been discussed in a professional
paper by the present writer, and it is unnecessary to travel again the

same path.[1] Second, the more general lines of the relation of the
German churches to Nazism have been rather thoroughly exploited,
although there is good reason to feel that further research on the
ground by a competent professional staff would bring forth additional information.[2] Third, this paper will make no attempt to assess

[1] F. H. Littell, "Pastoral Care under Totalitarianism," a paper read at the Annual
Meeting of the Commission on Religion and Health of the National Council of
Churches (Columbia University, November 12, 1952); reprints available at the
Commission office.

[2] It would be well if, before correspondence and records are scattered and the
principals departed from the scene, a team of social and political scientists could make
a study of certain basic issues (parallel to the concerns of the Strategic Bombing
Survey and the Psychological Warfare units): (1) How did internal structure affect
the ability to resist; i.e., did a church with a more democratic pattern (lay officers,
decentralization of power toward the local parish) prove better or less able to resist
than one highly centralized? (2) At what points did the confessing churches stand
for humane and democratic traditions, and where was their resistance primarily ecclesiastical? (3) What factors (i.e., traditional relation between altar and throne) weakened and what strengthened the churches' influence as centers of resistance? (4) At
what points was the traditional Land Church pattern abandoned (that is, did the
Confessing Church become temporarily a "free church") to effect resistance? (5) What
part did dogmatic formulation play in capitulation (for instance, the traditional
Lutheran position on Romans 13) or resistance (e.g., in the power of the dialectic
theology of Karl Barth)? Was this an historical accident, or is there a more general
lesson to be learned? (6) To what extent did the witness of the BK martyrs provide
a control element and disciplinary function in strengthening general antipathy to
the policy of *Reichsbischof* Müller and the *Deutsche Christen*? (Are martyrs "useful"?
If so, how and at what point early or late?) (7) What is the significance of the fact
that major resistance centered in the old Prussian Union? Is it to be attributed to
strong leadership, tight ecclesiastical machinery, theological orientation (e.g., Calvinist
influence), or is there another factor related to the general "legitimist" resentment
against Hitler and his parents? (What is the connection of the resisting Churches with
the conservative opposition in the Prussian Army officer caste, etc.?)

These questions and others of like direction are of great significance to social and
political scientists, and of obvious importance to persons in the Church or in government who want to correctly assess the resistance potential of religious bodies to contemporary totalitarianism. Those involved in such general strategic discussions will
want to consider, in addition to such primary material as is made available, such
excellent studies or compendia as these: Joachim Beckmann, *Kirchliches Jahrbuch,
1933-44* (Gütersloh: Bertelsmann Verlag, 1948); Stewart W. Herman, *It's Your
Souls We Want* (New York: Harper, 1942); Heinrich Hermelink, *Kirche im Kampf*:
*Dokumente des Widerstands und des Aufbaus in der Evangelischen Kirche Deutsch-
lands von 1933 bis 1945* (Stuttgart and Tübingen: Rainer Wunderlich Verlag, 1950);
W. Jannasch, *Hat die Kirche Geschwiegen?* (Frankfurt: St. Michael-Verlag, n.d.);
Walter Kuenneth, *Der grosse Abfall* (Hamburg: Fritz Wittig Verlag, 1947); Henry
Smith Leiper, *The Church-State Struggle in Germany*, No. 21, "Friends of Europe"
Publications (London, 1935); Rugh Martin, *et al.*, *Christian Counter-Attack, Europe's
Churches Against Nazism* (London: SCM Press, 1943); Wilhelm Niemoller, *Kampf*

the Roman Catholic record during the period treated, although I believe that any attempt to understand postwar Germany will give considerable attention to comparisons and contrasts between the Evangelical and Catholic situations under Hitler and under the occupying powers. This is a neglected factor in most current discussions, yet basic to comprehending the roles of Niemöller, Heinemann, Dibelius, Held, Iwand, and others upon whose activities and influence so much now depends.[3]

The burden of this paper will be to review a matter too little considered outside the theological faculties, yet of basic significance to an understanding of the capacity of religious bodies to resist totalitarianism: *the role of dogmatic formulas in laying the grounds for and developing a disciplined community of opposition.* This field, a happy hunting ground for professional theologians for some years, deserves more serious attention from social and political scientists than it has yet received. The problem may be bluntly introduced by quoting from one of Hitler's most gallant and persistent opponents on the Continent:

The liberal theology in Germany and in her orbit utterly failed. It was willing to compromise on the essential points of divine law and of "the law of nature"; to dispose of the Old Testament and to accept the law of the Nordic race instead; and to replace the "Jewish" law of the Old Testament by the autonomous law of each race and nation respectively. It had made all the necessary preparation for the "Germanization of Christianity" and for a racial Church.[4]

These are harsh words. But they are no more harsh than the parallel judgment of a distinguished British scholar:

The Protestant Churches also welcomed Hitler. They had steadily been losing ground in the Germany of the Weimar Republic. The Liberal Theology had done much to disintegrate the theological integrity of

---

und Zeugnis der bekennende Kirche (Bielefeld: Ludwig Bechauf Verlag, 1948); Wilhelm Niesel, *Der Weg der Bekennenden Kirche* (Zürich: Gotthelf Verlag, 1947); Frederik Torm, *Kirkens Kamp: Jyskland under Krigen* (Copenhagen: H. Hirschsprungs Forlag, 1945).

[3] Cf. F. H. Littell, " 'Why Don't They Understand Us?' — A Report on Germany," XII *Christianity and Crisis* (1952) 14:106–110.

[4] Joseph L. Hromadka, *Dawn and Resurrection* (Richmond, Virginia: Madrus House, 1945), p. 102.

the Protestant Churches. Activity in the field of social reform was taking the place of witness to the Gospel of Redemption. And there were those who were willing to fill the void created by their own disbelief by political enthusiasms — enthusiasm for Socialism, or, in the situation of 1933, for National Socialism. It was from these people that the so-called "German Christians" emerged.

And yet the Protestant Churches were not as weak as they seemed. There were within them strong conservative elements, loyal to the theologies of the Reformation: while, in the dialectical theology, there had emerged a new, post-liberal re-statement of the theology of the Reformation. It was particularly out of this post-liberal reaffirmation of the Gospel that the Confessional Church was born. The very exaggerations of this theology were a source of strength. They made possible a radicalism of dogmatic statement that would hardly have been possible within, what we in England would regard as, a more balanced presentation of the Christian Gospel.[5]

In what respect did the nineteenth-century liberal theology of Schleiermacher, Ritschl, and Harnack fail the church in the middle twentieth century? How were even the exaggerations of the Crisis Theology a source of strength to the centers of resistance?

No net for the feet of the unwary was ever more cleverly laid than that hidden in the twenty-fourth article of the NSDAP platform:

We demand the freedom of all religious confessions in the state, in so far as they do not imperil its stability or offend against the ethical and moral senses of the German race. The Party, as such, adopts the standpoint of a positive Christianity, without binding itself confessionally to a particular creed.

Certain content-laden word-symbols stand out: "freedom" (*plus*), "a positive Christianity" (*plus*), "binding . . . confessionally" (*negative*). Here is an obvious appeal to the spiritualizers, the individualists, the emancipated — the "third type" which Ernst Troeltsch mentioned in the *Soziallehren*, so common in the latter years of the Enlightenment and so resentful of the "offense" and "sectarianism" of fixed belief:

[5] J. O. Cobham, "The Significance of the Barmen Declaration for the Oecumenical Church," in a pamphlet of that title, No. 5, New Series of *Theology Occasional Papers* (SPCK, 1943), London, pp. 30–44, 35.

. . . that third sociological type of Christian thought, which does not
depend, like the Church, upon the institutions, nor like the sect on the
liberal interpretation of the Law of God in the Bible, but which is an
individualism which freely combines Christian ideas with all kinds of
other elements, and which is entirely unrecognized, or else exists along
side of the Church and assumes its necessity for the mass of mankind.

Full of the sense that today it still does represent the highest ethical
ideals of humanity, it is still unable easily to formulate for itself the
unwritten social programme which the Gospel contains, nor to apply it
clearly to the conditions which oppose it. Gradually, in the Modern
World of educated people, the third type has come to predominate. This
means, then, that all that is left is voluntary association with the like-
minded people, which is equally remote both from Church and sect.[6]

The millennial age prophesied by Joachim of Fiore,[7] when Church
and World should become one in the power of the Spirit, when the
divisiveness of ecclesiastical institutions and dogma should wither
away, was realized for many in the passionate *Blut und Volk* of
the Thousand Years of the Third Reich.

What was this "positive Christianity" of which a totalitarian
party approved? What were the characteristics which made it
appealing to so many sections of German Christendom? (We are
not dealing here with the passive nonresistance of the Lutheran
leadership which remained reluctantly obedient to state policy, nor
with the so-called "Intact Churches" who walked a difficult path
between resistance and capitulation, but rather with the convinced
Deutsche Christen.)

1. It was grounded in a thorough acceptance of the most radical
interpretations of textual critics of the Bible and practitioners of
the comparative method in the study of religions. This led readily
to placing an equal value (*Gleichwertung*) upon all religious myths.
This fact is evident not only in continual attacks on "Christian
priestcraft" and "sectarian dogmatics" in popular circles, such as
*Amheiligen Quell Deutscher Kraft: Ludendorffs Halbmonats-
schrift*, but in tracts and monographs by professors and alumni of

[6] Ernst Troeltsch, *The Social Teachings of the Christian Churches* (New York:
Macmillan, 1931), I, 378, 381. Cf. Walter Köhler, *Ernst Troeltsch* (Tübingen: J. C. B.
Mohr, 1941), pp. 269f.
[7] F. H. Littell, *The Anabaptist View of the Church* (Philadelphia: American Society of Church History, 1952), pp. 55f.

the leading theological and related faculties.[8] An interesting illustration of this point is the book by Professor Wilhelm Vollrath of Erlangen: *Houston Stewart Chamberlain und seine Theologie.*[9] Under this unlikely title the author demonstrates Chamberlain's dependence on Renan, Wellhausen, and other liberal critics; armed with such references, and making a practical use of scientific knowledge,[10] he was able to reduce the Jewish mythology and folklore of the Old Testament to its proper insignificance, defend an instrumentalist interpretation of the function of the Aryan Jesus of Nazareth, separate the simple teachings of Jesus (best understood, according to Chamberlain, by those good German mystics Eckhart, Tauler, and Böhme) from the accumulated priestcraft and dogmatics of the Christian churches. In Karl Dworski's *Die Entdeckung eines arischen Evangeliums*[11] Jesus is shown to be not a Jew but of Persian extraction, and a frontal attack is made on all systematic theology which has but obscured the simple Aryan truth which he taught. The author of a popular *Deutsche Christen* attack on the Confessing Church, Friedrich Murawski, leans heavily upon the radical speculations of such as Professor Lietzmann of Berlin and numerous scholarly articles of liberal persuasion in the second edition of the five-volume *Die Religion in Geschichte und Gegenwart.*[12] His rejection of the Biblical World view is a revealing repudiation of myths, legends, folklore, fairy tales:

The theological judgment is unanimous and no longer to be put aside. And there remains open only the question: Why is there still taught in the German schools as "history" that which the theologians themselves term "lore" and "fairy tales"? What significance should *Jewish* mythological stories have for *Germans?*

When the overwhelming majority of the teachers of the Church repudiate the whole evaluation of the historicity of the Bible as free inven-

[8] An interesting exercise for any suffering from illusions is to read the record of the theological professors in Max Weinrich, *Hitler's Professors* (New York: Yiddish Scientific Institute — Yivo, 1946), pp. 263f. The pastors did better, with the worst percentage of implicated leadership in Thuringia (15%) still in striking contrast to the records of teachers, doctors, jurists, government officials, etc. (75–85%).

[9] Erlangen: Palm & Enke, 1937.

[10] *Ibid.*, pp. 58f.

[11] Stuttgart: Tazzelwurm Verlag, 1939.

[12] Tübingen: J. C. B. Mohr, 1927–1931.

tion, when they don't pause once before the concepts of the founders of the churches, when they announce the very focus of church life to be untrue, when according to their demonstration the Bible is nothing other than a book of folklore — shouldn't the German man of the twentieth century decisively renounce the myths of Asia Minor and the Jewish Church for himself and his children, in order to choose *his own* myth, which is a part of *his* blood, *his* world-view, *his* feeling for life: The Myth of the Twentieth Century? [13]

At one time it was hotly debated whether there could be traced through the underbrush a road leading from Luther to Hitler. However this may be, there is a rather plain path through the maze from Schleiermacher to the *Deutsche Christen*, via Ritschl and Harnack.

2. The "positive Christianity" of the NSDAP was "nonsectarian" (*Entkonfessionalisiert*). At first "confessionless," in the true tradition of the Spiritualizers,[14] it came to accept an ideology and discipline dictated by the state. Stewart W. Herman has analyzed this situation rather carefully in his *The Rebirth of the German Church*. The Church of Bremen, for example, was one of those swiftly corrupted, and its operative charter (1924) opened with the words, "The doctrine of the Bremen Church is free . . . " The Thüringian Christians were the first who were Nazified, and when they published their Church Book upon Hitler's accession the Old Testament was dropped and the New Testament rewritten as a "National Testament," "from which the resurrection and ascension of Jesus as well as the miracle of his birth, were eliminated."[15] One of the focal points of conflict, as it is today in the East Zone of Germany under the Communists, was the Nazi determination to secularize the schools. Here a recent book by Bishop Dibelius is relevant. Summarizing experience with the Nazis and Communists, and even with totalitarian tendencies among the Social Democrats, he finds that the political ideologies claim to want to "de-confessionalize" the schools; what they actually want is to replace Christian faith with another creed. "Responsibility for the children is not a

---

[13] *Die politische Kirche und ihre biblischen "Urkunden"* (2nd ed.; Berlin: Theodor Fritsch Verlag, n.d.), pp. 15, 95.

[14] Littell, *The Anabaptist View*, pp. 34f.

[15] London: SCM Press, 1946. Chapter i.

question between the parents and the Minister of Education, but between the parents and God."[16]

The *Deutsche Christen* attacked the Confessing Church as a "Donatist heresy" with an independent law and sociology, political and religious thought, profoundly un-Lutheran in its insistence on the integrity of the church order, furthering sabotage and restlessness among the people. In a *Gautagung* held at Bochum, March 31 –April 1, 1936, the following points were made: "The State expects from the Evangelical Church (a) at least an organizational unity, (b) abandonment of the confessional struggle, (c) recognition of the biological aims of the Party and the State." The extent to which the former champions of a "nonsectarian" and spiritualizing point of view had come to embrace an ideological discipline given by the state and a new dispensation dictated by the Party, was evident in their criticisms of the confessing church (*Bekennende Kirche*):

The first Barmen thesis makes it difficult to properly esteem the coming of the Third Reich as the Work of God.

The law-giving of the Third Reich aimed at sustaining and purifying the people is not viewed in its connection with divine revelation.

The power of the State to create discipline, also over the Church, is not recognized.[17]

3. The resisting church, with the exception of defense of the Jews and protection of defectives (for example, in the epilepsy center at

[16] Otto Dibelius, *Grenzen des Staates* (Göttingen: In Furche-Verlag, 1949), p. 85. One is immediately struck by the deeply personal and pastoral nature of the problem, only hinted when stated as a conflict of systems. Bishop Hahn of Saxony (East Zone), in May 1950, summarized the school issue between the Church and the Communists: "It is becoming continually more evident that education in the school has a wholly secular trend, which stands in open contradiction to the Church's freedom to propagate the Gospel, guaranteed under the Constitution. In several cases of conspicuous non-observance of this right, the Ministry of Education accepted the Church's protest. In most cases, however, protests cannot be made, because in the event of a dispute arising one would have to depend heavily on the testimony of school children. It is rather a matter of an alien spirit, which the children sense, without being able to do much about it. Baptized children are growing up in a world in which, despite the efforts of catechists and preachers, they are inwardly ground to pieces." Quoted, p. 445, in "The Protestant Church in Germany," VII *The World Today* (October 1951) 10:439–449, by "C.C.W."

[17] *Die Deutsche Christen in Abwehr und Aufbau* (Münster: Buchdruckerei Balve, 1936), pp. 6, 9.

Bethel bei Bielefeld), seems to have taken its stand on ground which was narrowly churchly and theological rather than general and humane. This seems to be true, although very early in 1933 Church leaders issued warnings against idolatry of the state, against the new political *Schwärmerei*, and proclaimed that a just state needs and requires the corrective critique of the true church.[18] The first open resistance, led by Professor Karl Barth at the University of Bonn and Pastor Martin Niemöller at Barmen Synod (May 28, 1934), was at any level far in advance of the educated conscience in England and America. With firm grounding in the Bible and the theology of the Reformers, a stand was taken at Barmen, Dahlem, Steglitz, Augsburg, and succeeding synods, against anti-Semitism, against forced introduction of the *Führerprinzip* into the Church, against illegal imprisonments and the subversion of an objective justice, against abuse of minority peoples, against the "new revelation" claimed to be embodied in the Third Reich; later actions dealt with sterilization and murder of defectives, refusal to pray for a Hitler victory, and so forth. Within the ramparts of this theological fortress young men were educated for the ministry in bootleg seminaries, pastors expelled by the Nazis were supported by free collections, and a leadership of integrity maintained to take control of the church organizations after the collapse by a group which could only testify by the boldness of hope in 1935: "We *will not abandon this our Church and become a 'free church'; we are the Church*."[19] There are many illustrations of the level of courage required for opposition, and none more impressive than the martyrdom of some thousands of Churchmen for their part in the July 20 attempt on Hitler's life — an act not properly told or assessed as yet in this country, which took some of the noblest of the young Christian leaders, including Dietrich Bonhoeffer, Elisabeth (the sister of Reinhold) von Thadden, and Peter York von Wartenburg.[20] More representative would be the pastoral letter following the

[18] W. Jannasch, *Hat die Kirche Geschwiegen?* (Frankfurt: St. Michael-Verlag, n.d.), pp. 8–9.

[19] *Im Reiche dieses König hat man das Recht lieb (Psalm 99:4)* (Tübingen-Stuttgart: Furche-Verlag, K. G., 1946), No. II, *Zeugnisse der Bekennende Kirche*, p. 23. Address of Dr. Ehlers at the Third Bekenntnissynode, Augsburg, June 4–6, 1935.

[20] Cf. Allen Dulles, *Germany's Underground* (New York: Macmillan, 1947).

Steglitz Synod of the Old Prussian Union (March 4–5, 1935), a critique of the "New Religion" with its breach of the First Commandment, for reading which nearly 500 pastors went to jail. Referring to the "New Religion," the Church said among other things:

1. In it the world view of race and *Volk* becomes a myth. In it *Blood and Race, Peoplehood, Honor and Freedom become an idol.*

2. The belief in an *"eternal Germany"* which this New Religion furthers is put in place of belief in the *eternal Kingdom* of our Lord and Savior *Jesus Christ.*

3. *This superstition* creates its own God according to human vision and manner. In it man honors, justifies and saves himself. Such *idolatry* has nothing to do with positive Christianity. It is *Antichristentum.*[21]

Theological harshness was not alone a mark of the Confessing Church in Germany. This dour and intransigent unwillingness to compromise also marked the resisting Church in the Netherlands, where leaders of the Reformed Church such as Dr. W. A. Visser t'Hooft (General Secretary of the World's Student Christian Federation and subsequently of the World Council of Churches) and Professor Henrik Kraemer (author of *The Christian Message in a Non-Christian World*) were influential. In 1941 a comprehensive statement of thirteen articles, "What We Believe, and What We Do Not Believe," was drawn up and circulated against the ideology of the German Army of Occupation and its Dutch adherents. Representative paragraphs are these:

. . . *we believe* that he who is hostile to Israel turns against the God of Israel . . .

Therefore, we regard anti-semitism as something far more serious than an inhuman race ideology. We regard it as one of the most stubborn and deadly forms of rebellion against the holy and merciful God Whose Name we confess.

Moreover, we do *not* believe that the sovereignty of our rightful Lord extends only over our souls, so that some other domination, be it State, Nation, leader, can claim unlimited dominion over our bodies. Obedience to our Savior, Jesus Christ, takes precedence over every other

[21] Jannasch, *Hat die Kirche Geschwiegen?* p. 15.

obedience, even before every other lawful obedience, such as parents and civic authorities.

. . . we do *not* believe but *reject* as one of the gravest errors of this time that each nation or national group or race represents a particular thought of God and that the spirit of Jesus will take a different form in each one.

We *reject* as anti-Christian doctrine that all things must be subordinated to the welfare of the nation, and where the doctrine is taught that the interests of the State determine what is right and what is wrong, then we hold this to be the destruction of righteousness and the sanctioning of all iniquity . . .[22]

It seems a fair summary that the resisting churches, in several branches, were characterized by theological intransigence and an open hostility to any attempt to weaken their ideological discipline through syncretism, harmonism, denial of a historical revelation, speculative exegesis or philosophy, or appeal to popular feeling.

(If this be true, it is an important test to apply to churches in other situations. What do we know of the theology of the church in North Korea? in China? in East Germany? in Russia itself?)

There is a final factor, not unrelated to ideological questions, to which Professor Helmut Thielicke of Tübingen has called attention:

Many serious observers therefore believe that the surprising decline of the sects during the Nazi regime — at least among Protestants — may have been due to the fact that the closely knit groups of the Confessing Church produced a large measure of group feeling and therefore competed with the sects.[23]

There is good historic and theological reason for saying that, insofar as the Confessing Church did acquire a strengthened "we-feeling" (*Wirgefühl*) and take on the order of a disciplined community, it approximated the pattern of a free church rather than the traditional promiscuity of a state-church or land-church. It is not irrelevant to note that the mentor of the resistance, Karl Barth,

[22] J. H. Boas, *Resistance of the Churches in the Netherlands* (New York: The Netherlands Information Bureau, 1944), Booklet No. 13, pp. 82ff. Cf. a parallel study of resistance in the Norwegian Church: Bjarre Höye and Trygve Ager, *The Fight of the Norwegian Church Against Nazism* (New York: Macmillan, 1943). Also on the church struggle: Gunnar Westin, *The Protestant Church in Germany and Sweden* (Oxford: Oxford University Press, 1945).

[23] "Religion in Germany," 260, *The Annals of the American Academy of Political and Social Science* (November 1948) 144–154, 148.

has recently exercised the church by criticizing infant baptism and championing Believers' Baptism — a classical symbol of the free-church position. But this is to lead us into another question: Whether free churches or establishments are best equipped to maintain their integrity and witness in the face of totalitarianism. This is a vital matter, and students of the record of the Confessing Church in the Third Reich are often led to speculate on it, but it would require another paper.

In this necessarily brief review of the place of disciplined ideology in resistance to totalitarianism I am not unaware that I have used phrases and concepts which are not common discourse among social scientists. But a basic lesson to be learned from review of the experience of the Bekennende Kirche and useful in understanding the latent potential of various communities, is in appreciation of "the thoughts that wound from behind" (to use Kierkegaard's fine phrase). It is our wont, in planning psychological warfare in defense of free society, to call upon all groups for open declaration in support of democratic objectives *as such*. It may well be that those whose ultimate loyalty is elsewhere, who are not prepared to accredit divine sanction to the German *Volk* (or "the American way of life"), are yet as a consequence of their own ideological and practical discipline necessarily among the most sturdy opponents of all *Gleichschaltung*.[24]

And it is in the thrust "to make everything alike" that the totalitarian state has run a-foul of the universalism of the Christian churches, and will continue to do so whenever there are faithful men to stand up and be counted for the sake of the Lord of History.

7. Totalitarianism as Political Religion

WALDEMAR GURIAN

Words widely used today often were unknown yesterday. The term "totalitarianism" is a striking example of this fact. True,

---

[24] Cf. Ernst Cassirer, *The Myth of the State* (New Haven: Yale University Press, 1946), p. 275. Also Otto Kirchheimer, "In Quest of Sovereignty," VI *The Journal of Politics* (May 1944) 2: 139–176.

Hegel occasionally mentions the word "total" but no particular attention was paid to that. Totalitarianism became a widely used expression only after Mussolini's article on Fascism; this article proclaimed the totalitarian character of the state as master and end of life and society. A little later Ernst Juenger's study on the total mobilization popularized the term in Germany. Goebbels liked to employ it in 1933, in order to justify the coördination of groups and associations with the Nazi party — he had to impress those German professors and intellectuals who with Carl Schmitt had proclaimed the "turn to totalitarianism." But the Nazis emphasized, differently from the Fascists, that not the state, but the movement — of course, the Nazi movement as expressing the true will of the people and the racial elite — was the determining center of totalitarianism: "The movement gives orders to the state," was a popular slogan of the first years of Hitler's rule; and Carl Schmitt tried to prove that Hegel, the glorifier of the state and the civil service, was now dead. The totalitarian Nazi movement, the expression of the "people," used the state as its instrument. Nazi "philosophers" feared that, by ascribing totalitarianism to the state, reactionary elites and civil servants would be favored; they were for the totalitarian unlimited power of the movement and its leader. As the Nazi jurist, E. R. Huber, put it: The will of the Führer is the will of the people.

The term "totalitarianism," which started its triumphal march through our time in Italy and was taken over in Germany, has never been accepted by the regime which today is regarded as the survival of totalitarianism in its most powerful form. For obvious reasons: the representatives of the Soviet regime do not care to appear on the side of Fascism and Nazism as belonging to the front of totalitarianism. The ruling Soviet party does not officially pretend to be a ruling elite separated from the masses, destined to lead and dominate them; it is simply their true consciousness, their *avant-garde*. And even today, after the withering away of the state, announced in Lenin's *State and Revolution* (1917), has been postponed to a future very far away, beyond all human calculation, and after the strong almighty Soviet state has been accepted as the decisive fact of the present, the belief is not abandoned that the state will disappear. But this belief has become a utopian promise completely overshadowed by the political regime as it exists today. Therefore, it can be said that despite the rejection of the name "totalitarianism," the USSR has become the purest embodiment of totalitarianism, for in Germany it did not have time to last long enough. Hannah Arendt has correctly remarked that there it developed fully only in the last period of World War II; and it remained more or less restrained and limited by non-totalitarian forces in Italy where Mussolini did not abolish the monarchy and made his peace with the Church.

These observations about totalitarianism in the three regimes which are commonly described as totalitarian compel us to discuss the question: What is totalitarianism? After all, in order to avoid confusion it is necessary to show why totalitarianism exists precisely in that regime which refuses to regard itself as totalitarian and why it existed only in a very impure form in that political system whose leader proudly regarded himself as its originator.

Totalitarianism is often not distinguished from absolutism. Under absolutism all regimes without parties or elected representative bodies are subsumed. True — in the tradition of Montesquieu — a distinction is made between monarchies where the absolute power of the monarch is checked by groups and institutions based on traditional rights and the acceptance of laws, that is, of a constitution which gives form to the political and social life on the one hand, and on the other hand the despotism where the arbitrary whims of the ruler may determine everything. Totalitarianism appears then as a modern despotism. A power-hungry group achieves power — using demagogic means and deception of the masses as the tyrants in old Greece did. Thereafter it employs all means to maintain and expand its unlimited and unchecked power. These means are particularly terrifying and efficient in our time because of technical progress and inventions which permit swift concentration and application of power and manipulation as well as production of public opinion. There are no truly representative subleaders, there are no independent social groups (Montesquieu's intermediary powers), no traditional rights, no historical contributions and merits which can check the modern absolute totalitarian rulers; it must be emphasized that the totalitarian system differs from old fashioned despotism and autocracy in its use of economic and technological pressures and manifestations of so-called public opinion. The totalitarian tyrannies of our time do not appeal to the "divine right," but they claim to represent the true will of the masses and of the people. They like to characterize themselves as representing the "real country" against legalistic fictions of democracies which destroy the unity of the people and paralyze it by parties, the instruments of parasitic and egoistic particular interests. They present themselves as "true" democracies because, for instance, only the communistic party (which allegedly is identical with the working productive masses) exists; whereas all exploiters and their representatives are suppressed.

But it seems to me that this identification of despotic absolutism, authoritarianism, antidemocratic political philosophies with totalitarianism, this tracing of the lines from Luther to Hitler, from tsarist autocracy to Lenin and Stalin, does not tell the whole story. In any case it overlooks a decisive and peculiar feature of totalitarianism. This feature strangely enough can be traced with the help of Montesquieu, though obviously this great son of the 17th and 18th centuries did not know the totalitarian regimes of the 20th century. Montesquieu remarks that religion works as a check in despotic regimes which do not have any institutional or traditional checks against the arbitrary actions of the despot. An essential feature of totalitarianism consists in the disappearance of this factual, though neither legal nor institutional, limiting power of religious habits and customs. On the contrary, energies and forces which formerly had their outlet and expression in religion, limiting the old despotic ruler, are now driving forces behind and in the new despotic regimes of the 20th century. The totalitarian ideologies replace and supersede religion.

Therefore it may be said that the various forms of totalitarianism — Nazism and Soviet Communism — are politico-social secularized religions, characteristic of our epoch. The totalitarian movements and their power replace God and religious institutions such as the Church; the leaders are deified; the public mass-meetings are regarded and celebrated as sacred actions; the history of the movement becomes a holy history of the advance of salvation, which the enemies and betrayers try to prevent in the same way as the devil tries to undermine and destroy the work of those who are in the service of the City of God. There are not only sacred formulas and rituals, there are also dogmatic beliefs, claims to absolute obedience and damnation of heretics in the name of absolute truth which is authoritatively determined by those leading the movement. The doctrine may impose certain slogans and formulas — racism for the Nazis; class war, anti-capitalism for the Bolsheviks — but just the unlimited and uncontrollable right of interpretation and re-interpretation by the leadership gives to totalitarian politics its flexibility. It is Lenin himself who rejected those Marxists who were dogmatists accepting the letter of the master; this attitude permitted the acceptance of policies (for power-political reasons) which were regarded — as were Lenin's agrarian policies of 1917 — as non- and anti-Marxian.

Of course, the totalitarian movements are *secularized* religions. They do not have beliefs in a transcendent reality beyond this world, beyond political power and social order. God is openly denied as an expression of the immaturity of men, who create Him in order to explain the things which cannot yet be explained because of the lack of scientific knowledge; men need too in this phase of history an opium in order to escape from an unbearable and unintelligible reality. That is the Soviet view. For the Nazis, God is a myth, a symbol of vital forces, of the will to power of the racial elite and its soul. Transcendent beliefs are changed into immanent ones — even if the traditional terminology is maintained as in the anti-Communist varieties of totalitarianism, which try to avoid an open clash with traditional religions.

But despite this open or hidden totalitarian basic hostility to religion it is legitimate to characterize the totalitarian movements as secularized politico-social religions. The objection that there can be no religion where there is no belief in God, and where transcendence is swallowed up by immanence, seems to me only a terminological one. Of course, we may use the term ideocracy, introduced by the Russian Eurasian school, in order to satisfy those who are reluctant to connect the venerable name of religion with the totalitarian movements, with their cynical manipulations, incredible platitudes, and revolting horrors. The ideocracy would then mean what has been described as secularized socio-political religion.

The ideocratic or pseudo-religious character of totalitarianism must obviously result in conflicts with traditional religious groups. These groups are challenged because their claims limit the complete domination of society by the totalitarian movement. But their existence may be temporarily accepted for practical reasons because their immediate liquidation would be unwise, even impossible, since the necessary degree of social maturity has not yet been reached; therefore, it is advisable to appear friendly to religion and hostile to atheism.

Marx rejected Bakunin's attempt to wipe out the belief in God by decree; social conditions must be changed slowly, by a long process, before the education of mankind to atheism is completed. According to Nazi "philosophy," religious groups may lose their independent dignity while maintaining an external existence — as such Christian bodies would do — which, as Hitler's philosopher, Alfred Rosenberg, hoped, could be transformed into chapels of the one racial Church expressing the racial myth of the twentieth century. The "Church" of this racial myth can be served in many particular chapels, Hitler's philosopher said. What matters is the replacement of the central role of old religion by the totalitarian ideology. This ideology requires that political power must be the center of life, for everyone, for all groups, including religious ones.

Therefore, the conflicts of totalitarianism with churches are of a quite different character from the fights between civil and secular authorities in the old authoritarian states. There the rulers claimed to control the visible manifestations and organizations of religion; but they did not pretend to replace religious beliefs or make the articles of moral consequences of religion dependent upon their service for the political all-embracing power. Even such views on religion as those of Hobbes, who regarded it as an irrational superstition, necessary in order to satisfy human curiosity, to be controlled by the sovereign in order to prevent opposition against him by priests, ministers, and others — even this kind of extreme Erastianism, which makes the church into a kind of propaganda department of the state, is quite different from totalitarianism. Hobbes does not make absolute political power a religion; he is simply interested in preventing, first, opposition to the sovereign, whose authority must be undivided and unlimited in order to make the existence, welfare, and progress of individuals and society possible.

Secondly, he demands that the sovereign should utilize and control religion as an important social and psychological force. Hobbes may call his sovereign Leviathan a mortal God, but he is not the creator of this God, whose overwhelming artificial power makes the realization of social order possible. The sovereign is the sword for the enforcement of covenants, based on the laws of nature, the convention under which violent death can be eluded and a profitable life conducted.

The totalitarian movements establish a power which seeks to produce, control, and direct everything. The world shrinks; only the totalitarian power and its activities matter. Such shrinking of the world can sometimes be claimed only in order to *appear* almighty: this was the case in the Italian Fascist totalitarianism. The Fascist movement was limited by recognition of the state: The maintenance of the monarchy and the peace treaty with the Church through the Lateran Pact with the Concordat do not, of course, mean that Mussolini was a believing Catholic. He was an agnostic who regarded the Church as a national institution and who was too skeptical to take his totalitarian doctrinal claims seriously. Italian totalitarianism was a political oratorical technique, but despite all formulas it was not a new faith designed to replace the old one. The will to power was not necessarily connected with the ideology.

In the pure forms of totalitarianism — which are not only an expression of methods by which the "new prince" of Machiavelli must operate in the world of the twentieth century — the ideology is the driving force (and not primarily oratory) determining the reality of the movement.

The formal structure of the ideology can be filled with various contents and permits great flexibility. But it would be a decisive error to conclude that therefore the ideology — Marxism and Leninism on the one hand, the racial *Weltanschauung* of the Fuehrer on the other hand, — is unimportant, only a cover-up of a drive for power and control without sense of limits and moderation, as required by existing conditions and power relations.

What is the formal structure of the totalitarian ideocracy or sociopolitical religion? Essential is the belief; there are laws of necessary social development, economic or biological ones. After many fights the good forces will win out; the right order will be established.

The victory of these good forces is dependent upon elites who represent either groups of natural superiority or those by whom the true interest of the masses become conscious. The domination of these groups is necessary for the world salvation; indeed it is the world's salvation.

This domination cannot be a limited one; it must embrace the whole of life and society. It must determine all realms of individual and social existence. There can be no private life outside. Passive acceptance is insufficient. Enthusiastic, active acclamation and support are necessary, or men must serve as malleable material in order to show the superiority and the unlimited power of the rulers.

This absolute total domination — which is the expression of the totalitarian creed that everything is a moment in that necessary development, known and accomplished by the totalitarian leaders — can be compared with the activity of engineers. These have to adopt the kind of machines which they use to the environment and to the type of fuel available. The totalitarian masters must know what are the power conditions at the moment, what social switches are the best for control of society. If the totalitarian masters are in a ruling position, then they start to build up their machinery for total domination. Their power must be organized in such a way that it appears unassailable and omnipresent. There seems to be no other alternative left than submission and public acceptance. Each individual must appear and regard himself as an isolated helpless atom whose movements are dominated by the totalitarian masters; their power machinery is based on the pillars of the belief in their own world mission, the monopoly of propaganda and production of public opinion and a systematic terror which at the same time is surprising and crushing in its manifestations. All that must result in the attempt to replace reality by the official ideology. The doctrine enforced by the totalitarian power determines the reality; enemies, betrayers, evil contaminating forces are constantly created. There seems to be no other aim and purpose than the existence of totalitarian power and its leadership. Totalitarian terror — this must be emphasized — is not primarily directed against real or even potential enemies; it is directed against those who are declared to be enemies; what is real, is determined by the declaration of the totalitarian masters, and of course, corresponding *facts* must and can easily be found; for the masters cannot err, though they may correct errors of subleaders.

The contents of the ideocratic belief can, as in the case of Nazism, be the revolt against decadent evil forces and the restoration of a healthy order where the domination is exercised by the master race, the movement which represents it, and the leader who is its perfect embodiment. Then the support of traditional-minded groups opposing modern democratic society with its atomization, intellectualist planning, and artificial groups is exploited. Or, as in Communism, a development toward a utopia without domination, with perfect planning and equality, is announced as the necessary accomplishment of the future which will result from the dictatorship, the ruthless rule of the group knowing the real will and interest of the masses. Whereas Hitler's totalitarian system subordinated all traditions and their groups to its own power — after appearing first as their rescuer and restorer — the abstract totalitarianism of Communism opposed first state and all authority, but then moved in the direction of accepting as permanent the total domination by a group and a leader whose orders are expressions of the necessary laws of development. Nazism turned against the traditional ruling classes — Hitler tried to crush them in the last stages of his regime after he had made them completely his instruments, as the behavior of the generals showed. For Stalin the Great Russian people and their domination became identical with socialism and the victory of world revolution.

The enthusiasm of the first initial periods evaporates but that does not matter as long as the totalitarian regime has the power to impose its orders and to demonstrate its strength which apparently does not know limits; for even potential opposition is "liquidated" or reduced to impotent lack of cohesion and organization. Tests for the almighty power of the totalitarian system are recurrently appearing in the constant fight against internal or external enemies; purges, crises, and wars are necessary for the totalitarian regime as giving opportunities to prove and to increase their own power. Purges of most reputed subleaders show that nobody is indispensable or secure, that no traditional claims and merits impose caution and respect. The loyal servant can simply be declared to be a traitor, if that seems useful to the master, and everyone — including the

victim by his public confessions — participates in the choir of condemnation of the unmasked criminals. Aggressions, unexpected ad-
ventures, are proofs of the invincible and superhuman qualities of
the regime. Their successful outcome shows that God's blessing is
on Hitler's side or that the Soviet policies correspond to the necessary laws of socio-historical development. The attempt must constantly be made to demonstrate that the totalitarian regime by its
power creates the reality and that it is therefore the "wave of the
future."

The totalitarian ideology is the deification of a power system —
the power system directed by that group which came into being as
its creator and claims to act as its realizer. Therefore, it is on the
one hand a system which pretends to answer all questions and to
solve all problems by its doctrine; on the other hand, it is very
flexible, for it can be adapted to all situations according to the decisions and the interests of the ruling elite. Unauthorized criticism
of details and rational arguments against the general line are without effect; they appear simply as expressions of evil and ignorant
forces unable to see the whole truth. The individual must sacrifice
himself to the collective dynamic. The imperfect present is justified
by the coming perfect future, that of the classless society or of the
Third Reich. Scientific and "ethical" justifications are used to express the necessity of the totalitarian politics and demonstrate its
superiority.

The totalitarian ideology becomes at the end a purely formal one.
Under Stalin the belief in the withering away of the state is transferred to a realm practically beyond human history, but it continues
to be most important. It justifies eternal dynamism, it makes all
actions of the totalitarian regime appear as necessary and corresponding to the unity and logic of a system. The ideology becomes
an eschatology which is accepted because the belief in it is enforced
and expressed by power and organization; it continues to keep the
regime in existence, for it remains a symbol of its power and its
all-embracing, all-permeating character. It justifies even, as Lenin
emphasized, pauses and retreats; for in the long run the totalitarian
system must win.

The totalitarian society would dissolve into a chaos if it could not
be kept together by the artificial totalitarian doctrine whose domina-

tion corresponds not only to the laws of society and history, but fulfills the mission which is above all challenges. It does not matter that this mission results in the maintenance of the imperfect present with the unbearable totalitarian domination. The ideocracy becomes the justification of the most ruthless power having its own perpetuation and expansion as aim. The immanentism is completed — the claims for the future order serve only for the absolute domination of today. All political questions become technical questions — individuals and collectives become material for the application and increase of power. The ideocracy is the ideology for the continuation of the present rule by a group which has established a system of absolute domination by terror, organization, manipulation, and propaganda.

DISCUSSION

Mr. Louis Nemzer: I think that Mr. Inkeles' emphasis on "mystique" is needed, but I think he carries it to the point of over-emphasis. If we look at the process of policy formulation in totalitarian systems, it is clear that the mystique is less important than the other two determinants, which are the techniques for controlling the society and the efficiency of the society thus controlled.

Whatever the functional importance of the mystique may be, I should like to point out a further component of it. In the writings of Lenin and Stalin, there is an evident compulsion to play the role of God by creating a new sort of man. Zhdanov, in 1934, quoted Lenin on this aspect: "We must be engineers of the human soul."

Mr. Carl Friedrich: I would lean toward Mr. Inkeles, rather than Mr. Nemzer. Whether one calls it "ideology," as I do, or "mystique," as Mr. Inkeles does, makes little difference, but whatever term we use I would insist that this element comes first, and is more important than social control or social efficiency.

Mr. Alexander Gerschenkron: I wonder if there is really a dichotomy between power and mystique, as Mr. Inkeles seems to assert? Does this juxtaposition get us anywhere? Doesn't each shape and serve the other?

Ideology (or "mystique") clearly has two functions: a role as a determinant of policy decisions, and a role in shaping the propaganda which makes the policies acceptable. These roles shift in relative importance over time. In the early stages of the movement, ideology serves primarily to aid in decision-making, whereas its function in the matured totalitarian system is that of vindicating decisions in propaganda. And, as the movement attains power and must make new sorts of decisions, the ideology must become more heterogeneous and amorphous in order to justify them all. This development is illustrated by Soviet policy and ideology on the structure of the family.

I challenge another juxtaposition, too. I think the distinction between "rational" and "irrational" factors in the ideology is false, for the simple reason that a policy may be rational from the standpoint of one part of the ideology and irrational from the standpoint of another part of the same ideology. The later the historical stage, the more complicated the ideology, and the more probable is this kind of ambiguity.

Mr. Friedrich: We seem to be turning again to our methodological problem. Must one pick out a single dominant factor to define a phenomenon, as Mr. Inkeles and Mr. Timasheff have claimed? Or must one insist upon a set of interconnected traits — a syndrome rather than a motif?

Mr. N. S. Timasheff: Mr. Inkeles' paper is a most interesting union of Weberian typological analysis with the structural-functional approach. I would like to point out that the sets of traits advanced this morning by Mr. Inkeles and Mr. Gurian do not coincide, although they are intended to characterize the same phenomena. I would argue, in response to Mr. Friedrich, that such "trait-sets" must be made up of traits which are functionally related one to another. In other words, there must be a central theme. Choosing such a theme is a matter of trial and error, and we should always bear in mind the possibility that the theme may change over a period of time.

The ideology is important at all stages, but its specific significance may be altered. I would rephrase Mr. Gerschenkron's remarks on this point by saying that the ideology, in the early years of a totalitarian movement, provides the ends which must be served, whereas those same "ends" later become "means" of buttressing the position of the totalitarian state. In the Soviet Union at the present time, for example, the crucial problem is that of political power rather than Marxian economics, and the ideological status of the latter is used to assist in resolving the former.

Changes in the function of the totalitarian ideology can also be illustrated by considering its relations with religion. The ideology is itself a kind of religion and no totalitarian rulers can, in theory, permit two competing religions to exist side-by-side. The Soviets therefore initially attempted to destroy the Orthodox faith, but later altered their policy to one of compromise. Stalin took this step after reading Napoleon's remark that "it is better to have the Church serving us than opposing us." We must remember that the Orthodox Church is the most conservative of all Christian denominations. It has never had a Reformation, and its higher clergy, as recently as the Conference of 1948, decided all issues along the most conservative lines. The Soviet leaders welcome this tendency for they consider it an anti-Western force.

Today, fifty-three million Roman Catholics live under Soviet totalitarianism in the satellite countries. There too, we seem to have some accommodation going on. Some prelates are supporting some official statements, opportunistic priests have cropped up, and the national churches are being cultivated by the governments.

It is clear to me that the degree of terror under the Russian regime is greater than it ever was under the Nazis. We are therefore deluding ourselves if we look for an independent Church either above or under ground.

Mr. Paul Lehman: I am afraid that discussions of anything as complicated as totalitarianism cannot avoid over-simplification, and I fear even more that searching for a typology compounds the danger. Typology tends to ignore growth, and therefore to lead us away from the developmental aspects of totalitarianism. We must not overlook the cultural context out of which this phenomenon emerges. We must look to the soil as well as the plant.

In the case of totalitarianism, the soil is *Christian*. Here I would agree whole-heartedly with Mr. Friedrich's remarks of yesterday afternoon in replying to Mr. Karpovich and Mr. Robinson. But I would go on to insist that the soil is Christian after a kind of secularization which has not eliminated the demand for an eschatology. Although our Western culture has been deeply secularized since the eighteenth century, we still feel ourselves responsible for the human world, and we still share a need for an understanding of history. And, as Mr. Friedrich has pointed out, we cannot understand totalitarianism unless we view it as a new kind of attempt to meet these ultimately Christian demands.

This line of analysis would lead into a consideration of rational Christian dogmatics as contrasted to the irrational totalitarian mystique. I think we must work out between the poles of the rationalistic individualism of the enlightenment and irrationalistic totalitarianism a new kind of ideology, or mystique, which will be stronger than the former as an anti-totalitarian force.

I might add a few words with respect to the situation in the Soviet Union. Lenin, I sometimes think, may have made a great blunder in taking Marxism to Russia. The Russians have much space and much time: they can wait. This, I think, together with the tradition of "Byzantine messianism," may give birth to forces which will engulf Soviet totalitarianism and transform it. The Baptist Church in Russia is making great strides in expanding its membership, and the Orthodox clergy are now preaching to the people — something which they have not done for centuries.

Mr. David Riesman: We know very little about the Soviet Union, for the basic reason that we cannot "get at" it. This raises a perplexing methodological issue: how does one go about the study of a historical phenomenon which is not accessible? Clearly we must work indirectly. For Soviet totalitarianism in general, the Nazi documents, now becoming available in great quantity, are the most obvious indirect approach.

But, for the nature of "mystiques" and their staying power, there are other indirect devices. Any complex society contains sects whose own ideologies conflict more or less radically with that of the culture as a whole. In Germany, for example, we can study the experience of Jehovah's Witnesses in the Nazi period, and in the United States there is the same group as well as the Mormons and other religious minorities. My colleague Professor Everett Hughes has been studying for some years the way sects tend to become churches in this country; for instance, several of his students are now engaged in a study of a "Church of God" seminary in Indiana, which began as a theological training-ground and is moving towards the formula of a liberal-arts college; likewise, some students of his and mine have been examining the Negro "Holiness" Church as it tends to become both more worldly and more theological.

I should say that two factors determine the ability of the ideology of a sect to survive beyond the life-spans of its founders. These seem to be its measures to reward and to intimidate the young. The most effective test for new initiates is perhaps that of Jehovah's Witnesses, a movement which requires its recruits to undertake the conversion of their own families and to withstand the ridicule which this effort involves.

There may be a significant difference here between the Nazi situation and the Soviet one. Germany in the twenties was already an urbanized and industrialized nation, with centers of small-scale nucleation already present. In these circumstances, sects have ready-made structural roots. Russia in 1917, on the other hand, was a more diffuse culture, lacking such potential sectarian nuclei.

Miss Hannah Arendt: Two questions, is seems to me, underlie the discussion this morning: First, what is an ideology? and second, what happens to it in a totalitarian system? This assumes that ideologies by themselves are not necessarily totalitarian and that totalitarian domination changes the ideologies it uses. In Mr. Gurian's presentation, the totalitarian change would lie in a formalization ("The totalitarian ideology becomes a purely formal one") and transformation of ideologies into "ideocracies." With this I roughly agree, but would like to add a few remarks.

Long before any totalitarian ruler used them, ideologies aimed at total explanation, as Mr. Gurian stressed, by the application of a single idea to the various realms of reality. They usually explained not reality as it *is*, but its movement; even those that applied a "natural" idea, such as race, were more interested in explaining the course of the world than the world itself (Gobineau). In all instances, however, these ideologies had specific contents and well defined, though usually utopian, aims, such as as the survival or domination of the Aryan race or the emancipation of the proletariat as the only class whose interests coincided with the interests of mankind.

In the totalitarian use of these ideologies, a peculiar shift of emphasis took place. Ideologies became strictly the *logic of an idea*: the idea was no longer applied to a given reality, but a logical process was developed from the chief "idea," which became a kind of logical premise. This premise, to be sure, was not self-evident; but totalitarianism in power could change reality to such an extent that the premise could practically achieve the dignity of the self-evident. Hitler's ice-cold reasoning, Stalin's strictly logical argumentation, became more important than the original content. This logical process moreover seemed to fit very well with the pseudo-scientific belief in the Laws of History or of Nature, both of which are first of all laws of movement.

For these reasons, I think that if we have to rename totalitarianism, the word "logocracy" would be better than "ideocracy." There is no longer any rule of an "idea," no matter how perverted it may be, but of the logical process itself which is deduced from the "idea" as its logical premise. For the same reasons, I cannot accept Mr. Inkeles' term of a "mystique" implied in totalitarianism. This word was used originally by certain French nationalists and had a very clear meaning there; they saw indeed in the nation some mystical body. All the connotations which go with this term are entirely absent from the totalitarian use of ideologies. Only if one looks at the movements from the outside can they appear to have an aura of "mystique"; but this impression, which in some instances is consciously created for propaganda purposes, has its limited use only for the uninitiated.

Mr. Bertram Wolfe: I prefer "ideology" to "mystique," and I would characterize a totalitarian ideology as one which has these five features: (1) it is monistic; (2) it is all-inclusive; (3) it is exclusive — it is *allein selig machend*; (4) it is psychologically exhaustive, in that it demands total passion and total engagement; (5) it contains an imminent eschatology. And, in each of these aspects the ideology develops — it has a history.

The imminent eschatology is perhaps best illustrated, for the Soviet ideology, by Lenin's remark of 1917, in which every word counts: "The State will begin to wither away immediately." But with time this notion disappeared. Stalin insisted that enemies existed even within the best of all societies after it had endured for twenty-five years.

Soviet ideology included another element in the early days which disappeared later on. The original Soviet theory required a complete break with the past. But the past soon took its revenge and the leaders reconciled the movement with the worst features of it. The best features were still rejected.

In Stalinism only a few elements of the early ideology remain in full force, but these are of central significance. The Soviet citizen is taught to believe that his own system is the wave of the future, that it alone can sanctify and bless (the *allein-selig-machend* aspect), that capitalism is decadent and its collapse inevitable. He therefore believes that time is on his side. This conclusion perhaps helps to explain both the appearance of moderation, as in Stalin, and the utter intransigence and disbelief in any genuine or really lasting compromise.

Mr. Waldemar Gurian: The Communist ideology is more complex and less consistent than some of the discussion might lead one to believe. From the very beginning — certainly in Marx, and even as far back as Hegel — there have been both a utopian eschatology and an insistence that it will evolve only gradually. This, after all, was the burden of Marx's argument with Bakunin. When the Soviets emphasize the utopian element, they heighten the revolutionary implications; when they stress the evolutionary aspect, they bring forth the problem of stabilizing power. I don't agree with Mr. Wolfe's interpretation of Lenin as a sure utopian in 1917. He was then also a realist, though he repeated the pronouncements of Bebel about the classless society of the future, which would be good realized.

As the years wore on, the realist power-oriented side of the Soviet ideology came more and more to predominate over the utopian side. We have now reached the stage where the future utopia is invoked as a means of supporting, and making even more absolute, the present power of the ruling group.

I think Mr. Inkeles' term "mystique" should be avoided. It is filled with associations from the history of ideas which do not bear at all on Mr. Inkeles' purposes — Péguy, for example, used it with a totally different meaning.

Mr. Riesman's suggestion that we study sects is very interesting. It would be very difficult, however, to analyze Russian sects under the Soviet system, for the records, in so far as they existed at all, have almost certainly been destroyed. In the first years, the regime sup-

ported the sects as a device for weakening the Orthodox Church,
but they soon discovered that the disorganized sects were harder to
control than the Church would be. They therefore reversed the
policy and opposed the sects.

Mr. Franklin Littell: Every modern society is in danger of totalitarianism. We therefore have a duty to prevent it, and one preventive measure is the development of ideologies which the totalitarian
one cannot defeat and replace. In this effort the churches have a
major role, and fulfilling it adequately is their responsibility both to
man and to God.

Mr. Inkeles: I do not suggest — and my paper does not say —
that the mystique is an adequate explanatory principle taken alone.
I don't think there are such single-factor explanations. I merely
thought of it as a neglected dimension of totalitarianism worthy of
more careful analysis.

I must dissent from the many efforts to deal with "ideology" and
"mystique" as synonyms, and to pick and choose between them.
There are two different phenomena here, I think, and I don't want
to be understood as believing that the "mystique," as I define it,
is the "ideology" under another name. It isn't. An ideology is a
rationalization of the total situation and of the individual's relation
to it. A mystique isn't rational or irrational: it is a personal revelation which transcends such considerations. For this reason I disagree
basically with Mr. Lehman, for I don't see how you can work out
an "ideology" which lies "between" such completely diverse things.
Unfortunately, I don't have time to argue this point here.

The basic difference between Western liberal society and totalitarianism is that the former is ideologically pluralistic. There are
lots of ideologies in a liberal society; in a totalitarian society only
one is permitted.

Some of those who took part in the discussion have referred to
the fact that my paper is not historical. I agree. I have deliberately
centered my study on the early period of the totalitarian movement.
This procedure is rooted in the assumption that study of the child
is one way to understand the man.

In conclusion, let me return for a moment to this matter of the
difference between ideology and mystique. Miss Arendt has said
that an ideology includes laws. I don't think so. An ideology is a

set of attitudes or perhaps better of positions, toward the world. The mystique, on the other hand, is a law — but the law comes from an a-rational — not irrational — revelation. It states a binding ultimate end which cannot be proved. This end may be rationally achieved, but it is *not* rationally perceived.

PART FOUR

Psychological Aspects of Totalitarianism

■

8. The Bolshevik Attitude Toward Science

RAYMOND BAUER

I shall attempt to discuss only a small segment of the arc of topics that are embraced under the subject of the intellectual in totalitarian society — namely, a few dimensions of the attitudes toward science held in one totalitarian society: the Soviet Union. My discussion is based largely on the history of one science that I know in some detail — psychology — but I have tried to use the insights gained from this source as a basis for understanding some central general aspects of the system. The focus of my presentation will be partially on the question of the role of ideas in the Soviet system. Therefore, it will overlap to some extent the topic of the place of ideology in totalitarian society, which is being considered by another section of this conference.

The Bolshevik attitude toward science is of peculiar interest because it bristles with so many real or seeming paradoxes. Marxism-Leninism (and if you choose, you may add the names of Engels and Stalin) is extolled as "science," and "based on scientific principles," yet science is much interfered with. Bolshevik leaders assert that they are historical materialists, yet they give an extraordinary importance to the role of words and ideas in history. They are, in a special sense, rationalists; but they have less than average respect for empirical data. These paradoxes, whether actual or seeming, reflect basic differences in attitudes toward intellectual activity between Western liberal societies and at least this one totalitarian society, the Soviet Union and its satellite countries, where this pattern is now being imposed.

The justification for this essay is that it may illuminate the general characteristics of totalitarianism and at the same time reveal some of the distinctive aspects of Bolshevism. It is my impression that in certain of its essentials the attitudes toward science and intellectual activity which are generally held in the Soviet Union reflect fundamental differences between it and other totalitarian societies. I leave the final judgment on that point to those members of the Conference who are competent authorities on these other totalitarian societies.

TOTALITARIANISM AND THE INTELLECTUAL

Totalitarian society is *rationalized* in the sense that the basic principle which lies behind totalitarianism is that the component elements of the social order — be they men or institutions — shall be rationally coördinated to the attainment of the goals of the State.

The world of the intellectual, however, comprises a semi-independent social order with its own system of values, sanctions, rewards, and needs. As such it threatens the "totalness" of a totalitarian society. Traditional problem areas develop in science which may be of strategic importance for the long-run development of the discipline or may simply represent topics which are inherently interesting and rewarding to study. The international community of scientists sets up its own criteria for awarding prestige and status. As a result, scientists devote a considerable portion of their efforts to "theoretical" work, which may seem to an outsider (such as a politician concerned with economic planning) to have no practical importance, or at best to have practical implications only in the long run. Furthermore, a characteristic of intellectual activity in both the arts and the sciences is that it generates independent ideas.

Thus, the scientist poses two problems for the totalitarian leader. By virtue of his allegiance to a relatively independent community which cuts across national boundaries and has its own set of demands and pressures (even within national boundaries), the efforts of the scientist may be channeled in "inefficient" directions — "inefficient" being defined in terms of the needs of the totalitarian state. Second, the scientist may prove to be the locus for the generation of independent ideas which may challenge the existing ideology. As a result, totalitarian intervention in science must have two prongs: act control and thought control. A point that will be made throughout this paper is that because of the close relationship between act and thought in Bolshevik thinking, these two types of control are perhaps less differentiated than they might be in other totalitarian societies.

THE BOLSHEVIK RATIONALE FOR INTERVENTION IN SCIENCE

A distinctive aspect of Bolshevism is the highly elaborate ideological rationalization which has been evolved to justify and implement a closely coördinated program of act and thought control in the sciences. For the Bolshevik, thought and act, idea and practical consequence, are so closely linked that the distinction between act and thought is almost an artificial one. Probably more than any group of men in modern times the Bolsheviks have laid stress on the pragmatic consequences of ideas.

These are highly general assertions, however. We had best proceed, at first, from a more limited base, with a consideration of the Bolshevik rationale for intervention in science. This doctrine was inherent in Lenin's writings, but evolved in full form in the late twenties and early thirties, the period in which Soviet society became "totalitarianized." It was developed for the specific purpose of providing a rational justification for the suppression of deviant ideas and the coördination of all activities to serve the program of the Party. A consideration of this doctrine is important for three reasons. It illustrates the highly intellectualized approach of the Bolsheviks to so anti-intellectual an act as intervention in science. It spells out the argument whereby they arrive at a pragmatic approach to scientific truth. Finally, it exemplifies the highly instrumental attitude they hold toward ideas.

Soviet ideologists constantly inveigh against pragmatism. Yet there is no question that the Bolsheviks have a highly pragmatic attitude toward scientific truth — complicated by the circumstance that they are simultaneously representational realists in their epistemology. Without going into the historical circumstances under which this doctrine evolved, and the previous ideological commitments which colored each successive stage of its evolution,[1] the main

---

[1] This history is gone into in some detail in Raymond A. Bauer, *The New Man in Soviet Psychology* (Harvard University Press, 1952), chaps. ii, iii, and vii.

outlines of the position are as follows: Every scientific theory is affected by the social order in which the scientist works. Yet, there is absolute and knowable truth. However, at any one time we can only approximate this absolute truth since our consciousness is affected by the social order in which we live. In the meanwhile, society is advancing in an evolutionary scheme in which successively more "advanced" classes come to domination. The more advanced the class, the less it clouds the consciousness of its members and therefore the more closely they can approximate absolute truth in their theorizing.

Up to this point, we have only a theory of the sociology of knowledge, but it is given its pragmatic twist from here on. The proletariat, it is argued, is the most advanced class in society, and the Communist Party (Bolshevik) is the most advanced segment of the proletariat. Since every theory reflects *and serves* the interests of that social class in which it originates, that theory which serves the interests of the Party is closest to the truth. Therefore, the test of the truth of a theory is to ask the question whether or not it serves the interests of the Party. It may be added that the logic of this doctrine is perhaps even tighter than indicated. Since the Party is the source of truth, and there can be only one truth, any theory or fact not consonant with the program and proclamations of the Party is, *ipso facto*, false.

This highly elaborate argument is the "theoretical" justification of the principle of *partinost*. *Partinost* means literally "Partyness" but it can only be adequately translated by some such cumbersome phrase as "partisan vigilance in the interest of the Party." Another phrase which is applied to this doctrine is "the Leninist theory of reflection." This latter phrase refers to Lenin's activist conception of epistemology which asserts that we know the world only by acting on it, and that the ultimate test of knowledge is our ability to act with practical effectiveness.

Clearly, by Western standards this is full-blown pragmatism. Yet Bolshevik theorists regard pragmatism as heresy. The postulation that there *is* an ultimate truth and that the interests of the Party, as the vanguard of the most advanced social class in history is the touchstone of truth, distinguishes the Leninist theory of reflection or *partinost* from the unanchored relativism of Western bourgeois idealist pragmatists. This distinction, parenthetically, must be maintained, since Lenin's main theoretical work (*Materialism and Empiriocriticism*) was an attack on Machian positivism. After all, ideological consistency, or at least the appearance of consistency, is highly valued.

Having fashioned this highly rationalized justification for political pragmatism in the field of intellectual activity, the Party attacked various scientific theories on this basis as early as 1931–32. In the field of psychology both theories and empirical findings have been labelled counterrevolutionary because of their practical and ideological implications.

Objectivity, so much valued in Western science, became a term of abuse. Certain conclusions based on statistical studies were referred to as "arithmetical tailism" [2] with a terrible panic in the face of objective facts without *partinost*.[3]

This principle of *partinost* or "Leninist theory of reflection" offers a basis for evaluating scientific theories on the basis of their political acceptability. An additional set of "principles" is required to keep the scientist's nose to the grindstone — to keep him from fleeing practical, applied work in order to concentrate on theoretical problems.

Under pressure of such intervention there is a strong tendency for the scientist to find in theoretical work a refuge from the world of politics. This is a version of what he calls "internal emigration," [4]

[2] "Tailism" is the Lenist term for passively hanging on to the tail of history rather than taking initiative in shaping it.

[3] Anon. (Resolutions on the Question of the Status of Things on the Defectological Front), *Pedologia*, 1931, p. 106.

[4] One Soviet intellectual described the internal emigration in these terms: "It enabled Soviet scientists to withdraw from the everyday hardships of the Soviet life into their solitudes of inner emigration where they worked on their problems, trying not to notice the terror which swept the country. However, it was not possible to keep away from the terror and Soviet reality completely. The spirit of the Soviet Union made itself felt everywhere — in the crowded apartments with noisy children, in the overcrowded streetcars and buses, where our buttons were torn off, in the movies, etc. This spirit seldom penetrated the quiet room of a scientist. Sometimes the secretary of the local party committee dropped in and inquired about the latest developments. He said: 'Oh, you are studying ants? Well, who is interested in ants nowadays? Better study the 4th chapter of the brief history!' The scientist usually didn't pay any attention to such small talk and kept on working" (Personal Interview).

a flight away from politicized areas of life. For the regime, this is "formalism," occupation with theoretical problems having no practical use.

The Western reader is most familiar with the charge of "formalism" in the arts; prominent composers in particular have been criticized for writing music which meets the approval of their artistic colleagues but which does not serve the social task outlined for them by the Party. The same phenomenon takes place, however, in the sciences. In many disciplines there is a constant campaign to keep scientists from fleeing into work of abstruse theoretical importance that directs their energies away from problems of an applied nature. To a great extent, the point of the Lysenko controversy in genetics was to direct the efforts of geneticists away from theoretical research toward practical problems such as plant breeding. There is, naturally, an elaborate ideological argument for the subordination of abstract theoretical work to more practical research.

The "theoretical" rationale on the basis of which applied science is pushed at the expense of theoretical science is the "dialectical principle of the unity of form and content." This principle is one of the basic premises of dialectical materialism, and shows up as a methodological tenet in many areas of intellectual life. It says, in essence, that the nature of the whole of an organized phenomenon cannot be reduced to the sum of its parts, but it is, to a great extent, determined by these parts.[5] This is to say, that you cannot understand any phenomenon unless you understand also its component parts, and that this alone is not sufficient. You must understand also those characteristics of the phenomenon that come from the structured relationship of the parts. Furthermore, the same "part," in a given context, exhibits different characteristics. A favorite area for the exemplification of these principles is the psychology of perception. There it can be demonstrated that the modification of a unit within a picture affects the perception of the whole, and that a similar unit is perceived differently if it is presented in different contexts.

From the principle of the unity of form and content it is argued that theory cannot be developed abstractly from practice. To do so is to be guilty of formalism. A theory must be developed "in unity

[5] This portion of the argument will be very familiar to the Western intellectual. It is the old argument of the mechanist *vs.* the wholest.

with" and fashioned for the practical problems with which it is intended to deal.

Furthermore, following from the Leninist theory of reflection, we acquire knowledge through acting purposefully on the real world. Thus, we get the principle of "the unity of theory and practice," and the doctrine that "practice must lead theory."

Perhaps the doctrine of the unity of theory and practice may be regarded as but a variant on the pragmatic test of scientific truth. In my opinion, however, it adds a new element. Not only is truth to be evaluated by its usefulness "to the Party," but it is maintained that work on applied problems is the best means for developing theory, for arriving at truth. We get from this both a pragmatic theory of verification and a "practical" theory for acquisition of knowledge.

The principle of the unity of theory and practice is the basis on which educational psychologists have been criticized for treating their field of study as "applied psychology," that is, as an area of application to which are brought general principles of psychology developed in the laboratory, or Lord knows where. The correct approach, they have been told, is to take the problems of education as a point of departure and let theory develop out of their efforts to solve these problems. The former approach is formalism and "the divorce of theory from practice."

THE REACTION OF THE SCIENTIST, AND THE EFFECT ON SCIENCE

This paper is concerned with the Bolshevik attitude toward science, and not with the effect of the Soviet regime on science and the scientist. Nevertheless, it is necessary to discuss briefly the impact of this policy on the work of the scientist.

The Bolshevik leaders, in recent decades, have been increasingly concerned with the optimum coördination of the efforts of science with the over-all efforts of the state. This trend became marked during the period of the First Five Year Plan and has accelerated ever since. But it must not be assumed that the Bolshevik regime has been entirely successful in its effort to "totalitarianize" science. It is obvious from both the official Soviet press and the reports of refugee scientists that this "totalitarian" policy is somewhat less than total.

Working in an atmosphere of political control is unquestionably difficult for the scientist, and to a very significant degree his work is impeded (judged by our standards of scientific progress). Certain social sciences, such as sociology and psychology, have been virtually emasculated. Economics was "Marxified" from the beginning, but seems to be quite sound in certain limited technical areas. Physics and mathematics — by the consensus of competent Western observers — are generally first-rate. This does not mean that they have not been subject to political interference. They have indeed. It is true that the Bolshevik leaders have shown respect for these disciplines because of their practical importance. But this does not mean that the leadership has in all instances seen as practical all that the physicist and mathematician do. Within the last few years, mathematicians, for example, have had to defend their use of mathematical logic (pure formalism, by many Bolshevik criteria), on the grounds that it was essential for the construction of calculating machines required in the development of atomic weapons. And refugee scientists testify that before the war nuclear physicists themselves had difficulty persuading Party officials that their field of study merited the investment of scarce resources in expensive equipment. Always the touchstone of practicality is applied, and the verdict of the bureaucrat is not always identical with that of the scientist himself. However, the variation in the extent of interference and damage is so great between disciplines that no general statement can ever serve to characterize the status of all Soviet science — even if we had the very crudest of metrics with which to judge such progress.

Three factors act to offset the negative impact of political interference. First of all, the extent of interference is less than complete, partly because equal attention cannot be paid to all facets of Soviet life simultaneously and partly because the Party line is so broad in some problem areas that it has little practical consequence. Second, the Soviet intellectual has developed techniques of maneuvering within the framework of control. Close acquaintanceship with any one of the Soviet sciences over a period of time makes it very apparent that a considerable number of scientists have learned how to justify their activities in terms of the established ideological line. Aside from assisting their own careers, they have (on occasion) pro-

tected large areas of intellectual activity from potentially very substantial damage.

Finally, political interference per se is not always so disastrous
as we might expect. Never, to my knowledge, has this interference
been based primarily on particularly sound scientific grounds, even
though many of the complaints, if phrased in non-Marxian terms,
might sound familiar to us. Nevertheless, the programs or methodological positions imposed are on some occasions fairly salutary and
permit respectable scientific work, at least within limited areas of
a science. I have in mind here particularly the effect of the "dialectical" position on research by soviet psychologists in the field of
sensation and perception. I think that most Western researchers
would find that the theoretical stand taken by Soviet psychologists
as early as 1938 — on the basis of a new political line laid down by
the Central Committee — is strikingly similar to that which has
become dominant in American psychology in the last five to seven
years.

I am not arguing, as is sometimes maintained, that Bolshevik interference in science is justified on a sound scientific basis. It would,
indeed, be very hard to find such an incident. All that I am maintaining is that the methodological positions which are imposed are
seldom entirely unsophisticated, are sometimes *very* sophisticated
even though unfounded scientifically, and sometimes even facilitate
fruitful scientific work.

Unquestionably, science and all intellectual activities are in the
long run dealt a death blow by political interference, but the nature
and extent of the damage done is much more complicated than
Western writers ordinarily assume.

However, this is a digression. I wish only to make clear here
that I am taking no stand on the impact of the Bolshevik attitude
toward science on the work of the scientist. We are concerned not
with the success of the leaders in enforcing their policy nor with the
effects of this policy, but with the mode of thought which this
policy reflects.

PRACTICAL USEFULNESS AND IDEOLOGICAL CONSISTENCY

The preceding three sections have indicated the high degree of
ideological rationalization that has accompanied Soviet interven-

tion in science. Interpretation of Soviet intervention in science and the arts by Western authorities has usually taken one of two lines. It is maintained, on the one hand, that such intervention is a blind imposition of dogma, and on the other, that it represents a complete disregard for ideas and ideology in the interests of immediate practical utility. Both these interpretations miss the essential point of the relation of ideas to action in the Soviet system.

To some extent, the impression that Soviet intervention in the arts and sciences represents blind imposition of dogma stems from a failure to understand the highly instrumental approach to ideas which Soviet leaders take. It is true that consistency of ideology is highly valued — as the proponents of the "blind imposition" interpretation maintain implicitly. But much of what looks like far-fetched dogmatism is usually far-reaching pragmatism. This point of view of the preceding sections is that what may have looked like pedantic quibblings on highly abstruse topics were actually deliberate rationalizations for interference in the arts and sciences. Illustrations could be multiplied far beyond the point of satiation of even the most skeptical reader. The philosophical controversy of the late twenties, for example, was actually an attempt to redefine man's place in history in order to furnish a theoretical bulwark for the Stalinist Five Year Plans. The Lysenko controversy in genetics was, in part, designed to direct the research of geneticists to more practical problems, and, in part, to reaffirm man's ability to determine his own destiny, and thereby reaffirm the ability of Soviet man to overcome all obstacles (a bit of flattery the end result of which is to justify burdening the citizen with superhuman obligations commensurate with his postulated superhuman abilities). The necessary thing to remember is that Bolshevik pragmatism, coupled with a value on ideological consistency, often leads to a preoccupation with basic premises that seem at first glance far removed from practical problems. Therefore, deviant ideas must be suppressed and orthodox ones enforced, because deviant ideas will inevitably lead to undesirable actions. We have returned once more to a consideration of the close relationship between ideas and acts in the thinking of the Bolsheviks.

My contention that even the most abstruse of Bolshevik dogmatic assertions have a practical intent need not invite the simplistic explanation in the opposite direction — that such policies are "sheer expediency." The mere fact that such elaborate rationalizations are fabricated for intervention in intellectual activity is in itself a sufficient demonstration of the fact that on some levels the Soviet elite take ideology seriously. There is considerable evidence that ideology does play an important role in the Bolshevik attitude toward science, even though, as I shall argue later, "practicality," broadly defined, seems always to take precedence in the long run.

Ideology can be conceived as playing a role in the action of the Soviet elite in two ways, as a system of ideas to which they are personally committed, or as a set of circumstances essentially external to them to which they must pay attention and which they must manipulate in the pursuance of practical goals. For the purposes of this discussion, it is not necessary to inquire into the extent to which Soviet leaders actually "believe" much of their ideology. Unquestionably there are tenets which they believe and some which they do not believe. For the moment, however, I am contending only that they take ideology seriously as a set of external circumstances. This stand is taken without prejudice to the possibility that they may believe some or all of what they say.

The evidence that ideology is taken seriously by the Soviet elite lies in the persistent attempts which are made to maintain the *appearance* of ideological consistency. I offer only one example, again for illustration rather than for demonstration.

Determinism was one of the salient premises of Marxism, and in interpreting man's behavior the "Marxist" point of view has generally been that what man did was a function of his inheritance and his environment, that he was not responsible for his behavior in the sense that moralists have held. This point of view has been stood completely on its head in the course of Soviet history. Present-day Stalinist ideology holds man completely responsible for his behavior, as has any philosophy in history but (and this is what is crucial) *the principle of determinism has nevertheless been retained*. This has been accomplished, of course, only by highly sophisticated rationalization.[6]

⁶ One of the difficulties of such a discussion is that the writer sometimes finds himself in the position where it might be assumed that he was taking a stand on more than he really intends to. I do not mean to comment on the merit of the

Even though basic policy may change direction, the orthodoxy of this policy must always be established. There are a number of propositions in present-day Soviet ideology whose primary functions are the symbolic one of affirming the orthodoxy of Stalinism. Determinism is one of them. Materialism is another. So far as I can see, the retention of these terms is essential to establish the legitimacy of present-day Soviet policies and ideas. When a new policy line is evolved in any area it thus becomes necessary to establish its orthodoxy by referring and relating it to these and other premises of Marxism-Leninism-Stalinism.

The comparison between Communism and religion has been made repeatedly. In these comparisons the linkage has ordinarily been based on the psychological function of belief for the individual. The mere fact of the intense competition between Communism and religion in many areas of the world in itself gives some credence to this contention.

In making this point, however, writers have rather consistently missed one other of at least equal importance, and that is the similarity between Bolshevik ideology and orthodox religious theology. In those instances in which the comparison between Bolshevik ideology and theology has been made, it has usually been made from the point of view of "blind dogmatism" as discussed above, but I have already stated my grounds for rejecting this view. In any theology there are certain premises which are based on faith. The suggestion that such premises be subject to empirical test is regarded as either idiocy or heresy. Once these premises are accepted the rest of the structure of the theology follows rationally from them. Undoubtedly, there are instances in which we suspect that theological systems have been modified, stretched, or rationalized to permit accommodation to pressing practical needs. But, in the long run, the major doctrinal premises tend to remain relatively stable and are the fixed reference points around which the structure of the theology develops.

----

philosophical position which Soviet writers take on the question of freedom and determinism. It impresses me as not being substantially better or worse than that of a number of other positions with which I am acquainted. All I am concerned with is its *intent*, and on this score I am contending that the philosophical position was evolved deliberately to meet a particular need.

This relationship of practical need to doctrine in religious orthodoxy is exactly the reverse of what obtains in Bolshevik ideology. The fixed reference points of Soviet ideology are the action programs of the Party at any given moment in time. The main *doctrinal* tenets of Bolshevik ideology are those general principles of Marxism-Leninism which the proponents of the "blind dogmatism" approach see as projected rigidly onto events. Whereas in an ordinary religious orthodoxy these would be, as stated above, the most stable elements, in Bolshevik ideology substantive[7] doctrinal tenets are always considered expendable to the demands of the action program of the Party. If necessary the basic statements of Marx, Engels, Lenin, and even Stalin are altered. But, when such alterations are made, argument and/or citation of appropriate textual quotations are used to preserve the air of continuity and consistency. The orthodoxy of the new policy must be established.[8]

If we remember the characteristically instrumental attitude toward ideas which the Bolsheviks hold, then it can safely be said that the seriousness with which Soviet leaders regard ideas is without precedent in recent history. What other leader of a modern

[7] It is necessary, at this point, to distinguish between *substantive* and *supporting* tenets. There are certain doctrinal tenets in Soviet ideology which serve to support the legitimacy of the Party as the executor and interpreter of Marxism-Leninism. The principle of "the leading role of the Party" is one such tenet. Obviously, if such tenets were revised then the whole basis on which the Party can revise other tenets would collapse, and in general they are unexpendable. There are likewise some other tenets which are statements of the conditions under which the Party can stay in power. To revise these on the basis of expediency would also be self-defeating.

[8] As anyone would quickly guess, such transitions are not always entirely smooth. In the recent linguistics controversy, a Comrade Kholopov complained plaintively to Stalin: "From your article . . . I understand that a new language can *never* be formed, while before your article I was firmly convinced that, according to your speech before the 19th Party Conference, under Communism languages fuse into one general [language]." Stalin replied to the comrade in terms like these: "Comrade Kholopov . . . considers it necessary to discard one of these formulas as erroneous and to catch hold of the other as correct for all times and countries; but precisely what formula to catch hold of, he does not know. The result is something akin to an impasse. Comrade Kholopov did not think of the fact that both formulas can be correct, each for its own time.

"This is always the case with exegetes and Talmudists, who, probing into the essence of matter, quite formally, without relevance to those historical conditions with which the quotations deal, inevitably fall into an intolerable position" (*The Soviet Linguistic Controversy*, translated by Murra, Hankin, and Holling [King's Crown Press, 1951], p. 97).

state would issue over his name documents such as Stalin's letters on linguistics or his recent criticism of the economist Vossnesensky? It matters not whether Stalin himself wrote these and other similar documents. What is crucial is that in the Soviet way of thinking this is considered the proper manner whereby the chief of state announces and effects a change of policy, and that the chief of state is expected to have opinions on such technical topics.

Wherein is the resolution between this seeming paradox of rationalism and intellectualism and distaste for or distrust of free intellectual inquiry and empirical data? I think that we can understand it if we regard it as traditional Western rationalism accompanied by an ambivalent attitude toward empiricism. Rationalism and empiricism have come to be so closely linked in the minds of Western thinkers since the nineteenth century that we tend to regard them as a unity. We sometimes forget that Descartes too was a rationalist, but that his thinking proceeded from "self-evident" premises rather than from sensory data. What seems to have happened to Soviet ideology is that the rationalism which was introduced with Marxism has remained as a dominant value in the Soviet system, one which plays an essential role not only in the ideology but also in principles of social, political, and economic organization; but empiricism has atrophied over time as Marxist doctrine has come more and more to be an adjunct to the Party's action programs. Facts which might lead to conclusions that conflict with the Party's program are an annoyance to the man of action. Freedom of intellectual inquiry may produce ideas which disrupt the orthodox ideology. The result is a profound ambivalence of the Soviet leaders toward both ideas and data — the two commodities with which the intellectual habitually deals. This does not mean that the Bolshevik rejects empirical data completely, but merely that he will override and reject it when it conflicts with his action program. All in all, he likes to have his position supported by empirical findings. There are areas of Soviet psychology, for example, where for more than a decade psychologists have been constantly urged to prove the official line by empirical research. But, alas, no one has devised a research technique which will provide the necessary data to demonstrate that the Soviet order actually produces the traits of character which the Party line ascribes to the New Soviet Man.

SUMMARY

Because our topic is complex and the treatment short, I have some-times jumped from topic to topic in a rather abrupt fashion. Let me try to state in summary fashion what the main contentions of this paper are.

The Bolsheviks interfere drastically in both the work and the ideas of the scientist, but this interference is in itself accomplished in a highly intellectualized fashion. I have described this as traditional Western rationalism, accompanied by an ambivalent attitude toward empiricism. We find simultaneously in the Bolshevik a strong em-phasis on practicality and a paradoxical concern with ideas. This is due to the fact that he sees a very close relationship between ideas and action.

Ideas, however, are valued as instruments for action, rather than for their own sake. For this reason, the Westerner uninitiated in Bolshevism is frequently confused by the doctrinal statements of Soviet leaders. He seeks to understand such statements in terms of their explicit content rather than in terms of their *intent* in a concrete historical situation. Thus an investigator who arrived at an opposite conclusion would be accused of "lack of Party vigilance." It is true that the tradition of rationalism that has been inherited from nineteenth-century philosophy via Marxism is reflected in a strong value placed on ideological consistency. This consistency, however, is secondary to the demands of action — specifically the demands of the political program of the Party. The result is an attempt to main-tain the appearance of ideological consistency which manifests it-self in very elaborate essays — some more successful than others — to rationalize the relationship of action to ideology.

Suppose we were to pose to the Bolshevik directly the question of which comes first: ideological consistency or practical policy? He would answer typically that we have posed a false problem, that the two are inseparable. But, in point of fact, a study of the develop-ment of Soviet policy toward science shows clearly that practicality takes the lead and ideology follows after; not, however, without playing a very real role in the formulation of practical policies.

It is this particular concern of the Bolshevik for the role of ideas in action and his highly rationalized approach to practical problems that I believe distinguishes Soviet totalitarianism from the other totalitarian systems. Nazism and Fascism seem to have been almost unequivocally anti-rational and anti-intellectual. In Bolshevism, rationalism and intellectualism remain as values inherited along with the main body of Marxism. But forces endemic in totalitarianism — fear of independent loci of ideas, impatience with facts that stand in the way of action, belief that the elite leadership already has the "Truth" — produce a simultaneous hostility to these values.

9. Wholeness and Totality — A Psychiatric Contribution

ERIK H. ERIKSON

A glance at the list of the participants in this Conference narrows the area within which I can contribute a statement to that of childhood. All men begin as children: does this commonly shared fact contribute significantly to what is universal in totalitarianism? Since I am primarily a clinician, I must also draw of psychopathology for suggestions concerning some of the puzzling features in the emergence of a totalitarian orientation.

I

Works on history, society, and morality usually contain little reference in the text, and none in the index, to the simple fact that all individuals are born of mothers; that everybody was once a child; that people and peoples begin in their nurseries; and that society consists of individuals in the process of developing from children into parents. To most scholars, childhood seems to belong to the field of social work rather than to that of social science, to the aspirations of do-gooders rather than to those of thinkers. Yet man is characterized by a long biological childhood, and civilization tends to make psychological childhood ever longer, because man must have time to learn how to learn; all his high specialization and all his intricate capabilities of coördination and reflection are contingent upon his prolonged dependence. And only as a dependent does man develop conscience, that dependence on himself which makes him, in turn, dependable; for only when thoroughly dependable with regard to a number of fundamental values can he become independent and teach and develop tradition. But this dependability carries within it the ambiguity of its roots in a slow developmental process which leads from extreme helplessness to a high sense of freedom.

Modern anthropology, following suggestions derived from psychopathology, is studying the ways in which societies "intuitively" develop child-training systems designed not only to keep the small individual alive and well but also to insure, through him and in him, a continuation of tradition and a preservation of his society's uniqueness. But it is becoming equally clear that the polarity Adult–Child is the first in the inventory of existential oppositions (Male–Female being the second) which makes man exploitable and induces him to exploit. The child's proclivity for feeling powerless, deserted, ashamed, and guilty in relation to those on whom he depends is universally utilized to the point of exploitation. The result is that adult man remains irrationally preoccupied with anxieties and suspicions which center in such questions as who is bigger or better and who can do what to whom. The contribution of man's extended childhood to the development of his capabilities and to his capacity for sympathy and faith is well known, but often too exclusively known: it is necessary to acquire deeper insight into the earliest consequences of the potential exploitation of childhood. By psychological exploitation I mean the misuse of a divided function in such a way that one of the partners is impaired in the development of his potentialities — with the result that impotent rage is stored up where energy should be free for productive transformation.

To those who accept all this it must seem reasonable enough, then, that childhood should be represented at this conference on totalitarianism, so that we may begin to do away with this "oversight" concerning the fateful importance of childhood. Yet it must be said that this oversight does not seem to be an accidental one, and therefore not one so easily corrected. Psychoanalysis has amply demonstrated the fact that the individual develops an amnesia concerning crucial childhood experiences; there is good reason to suspect that this individual amnesia is paralleled by a universal blind spot in the interpretation of history, a tendency to overlook the fateful function of childhood in the fabric of society. Maybe moral man, and rational man, having fought so hard to make man's moral and reasonable image absolute and irreversible, refuses to see how each man must begin with the beginning and thus, ever again, develop the potentiality for undoing human accomplishments with infantile compulsions and irrational impulsions. It is as if we were dealing here with a deep-seated superstition that rational and practical man would lose his single-minded stamina if he ever turned back to meet the Medusa of childhood anxiety face to face again. Here a formidable "personal equation" imposes itself on all attempts to put the fact of childhood in its proper perspective. Yet, if man would understand this fact, maybe he could manage to become less childish in some respects and remain more childlike in others.

It is probably a result of the long undisputed existence of the universal blind spot discussed here that the sudden emergence in our time of insights into the relationship of childhood, neurosis, and personality in human life have tended to develop another, a compensatory loss of perspective: I mean the tendency on the part of psychologists and psychopathologists to explain societal phenomena (such as totalitarianism) by equating them with specific infantile or adolescent stages, with mental disturbances, or with particular "character structures" (personal or national). From the personological approach, suggestive generalizations have emerged, for example, in regard to certain analogies between patterns of child rearing, ways of conceptualizing the world, and inclinations toward political creeds. This approach, however, has contributed little to the all-important question, namely, under what conditions the energy invested in given patterns of thought and action becomes available for relevant political indoctrination and for effective mass action. The second, psychopathological approach in turn has led to insights, some of which will be presented in the bulk of this paper; yet, it has weakened its case by diagnostic name-calling, designating peoples and people actively or passively involved in totalitarian revolutions as either pathological or immature human beings. Man can be many things on many levels, and history does not always permit him that unification of defined creed, conscious attitude, and pragmatic action which we in the Protestant world have come to demand of a "balanced" or at any rate a "logical" human being.

What follows, then, is not an attempt at fixing the origin or cause of totalitarianism in the fact of childhood or in particular forms of childhood; nor shall I treat it as a transient affliction or localized epidemic. I begin with the assumption that totalitarianism is based on universal human potentialities and is thus related to all the aspects of human nature, wholesome and pathological, adult and infantile, individual and societal. Totalitarianism has often been a near reality: it has merely waited for "its" historical moment. The properties of this moment (for example, the advance of technology) will undoubtedly be discussed in other papers, which, I assume, will also deal in detail with historical factors of which I am not unmindful, although I must neglect them: I mean the varieties of conditions which give rise to the idea of the total state as a fanatic anticipation, which realize it in well-timed revolutionary acts, and which maintain it through the realities of power and terror. Only such historical perspective can give the proper measure of the different degrees and kinds of ideological involvement on the part of the many types that make up a totalitarian state: fanatic apostles and the shrewd revolutionaries; lonely leaders and oligarchic cliques; obedient bureaucrats and efficient managers, soldiers, engineers; sincere believers and sadistic exploiters; willing followers, apathetic toilers, and paralyzed opponents; unnerved victims and bewildered would-be and could-be victims.

The means at my disposal in my present work permit me to attempt a contribution only to one of the more basic, and yet often less tangible, factors in all of these historical stages and individual functions, namely, the psychological prerequisites of a totalitarian ideology.

II

I can now return to my initial question and try to focus on that something in the nature of childhood which may throw light on man's inclination, under certain conditions, to undergo what the Germans call *Umschaltung* and *Gleichschaltung*, that sudden total realignment and, as it were, co-alignment which accompanies conversion to the totalitarian conviction that the state may and must have absolute power over the minds as well as the lives and the fortunes of its citizens.

We discern in normal and abnormal histories, and in occasional transitory states not commonly considered psychopathological, sudden transitions from a balanced "wholeness" of experience and behavior to states of feeling and acting "totally." The most dramatic examples of such total realignment are, of course, to be found on the borderline of pathology. As one young man said to me, smilingly, in looking back on his tendency to withdraw: "I was a majority of One" — by which he meant that, having chosen to be totally alone, he was the universe, and thus more than mankind. A young woman spoke, in the same vein, of her "right to oneliness." Yet such solipsism is neither restricted to pathology nor to adult life. Already early in childhood a child's healthy alternation between waking or sleeping, for example, may suddenly turn into a total avoidance of sleep or an overall sleepiness; a child's happy alternation between sociability and aloneness may turn into an anxious or furious insistence on his mother's total presence or a blank refusal to show awareness of her proximity: many a mother is deeply disturbed when she notices, at her return from a sudden but not so lengthy absence, that her small child has blandly "forgotten" her. Total dependence or total independence may, temporarily or lastingly, become states which are not amenable to normal degrees of alternation; or total goodness or badness may suddenly appear as states seemingly beyond reach of parents who may actually prefer a child who is reasonably good but by all means also a little bad. Such total realignments occur as transitory phases at significant stages of infantile development; they remain a potentiality in the adult, and they may accompany the outbreak of a mental disturbance.

As for the co-alignment with an object, or a person, we are all familiar with the small child's fetishes, which, sometimes in the form of bedraggled dolls, become the subject of his elder's disdain and yet remain his total and exclusive token of security and comfort. Later, violent loves and hates and sudden conversions and aversions share with the child's fetishism and fears such factors as the exclusive focusing of a set of (friendly or unfriendly) affects on one person or idea; the primitivization of all affects thus focused; and a utopian (or cataclysmic) expectation of a total gain or a total loss to come from this focus.

Finally we may point to a well-known example of a split of such original unification: In the change that comes over married couples who have decided on a divorce, the sudden transformation of what seemed a reasonably wholesome twoness into two totalities can be rather awesome (as one soon finds out if he tries to remain friends with both).

While such realignments may seem to appear suddenly, they develop slowly. Only uncommonly aware and brave people know about themselves what psychoanalysis reveals in others, and particularly in patients — namely, how strong and systematic are man's *proclivities and potentialities for total realignments*, often barely hidden behind one-sided predilections and convictions, and how much energy is employed in inner defenses against a threatening total reorientation in which black may turn into white and vice versa. Only the affect released in sudden conversions and in sudden aversions testifies to the quantity of this energy. Equally revealing is the much described and much deplored, yet therapeutically useful, tendency of even the most enlightened and best informed patients of psychiatry to develop a "transference" and to become, as it were, violently dependent on their therapists — and this either with predominantly positive or negative feelings: a sobering demonstration of the tendency for totalization which ill fits the intellectual contempt for fellow humans dependent on cosmologies and deities, monarchies and ideologies. At any rate, we have learned to understand such realignments as readjustments on a more primitive level, made necessary by increased anxieties, especially of infantile origin, and called forth by acute life crises. To mark them as pathological and thus as "bad" helps neither to understand nor to overcome them: to chart a purposeful course of action toward them, one must understand their inner rationale, their psycho-logic.

In giving these examples, I have used the terms "wholeness" and "totality." Both mean entireness; yet let me underscore their differences. Wholeness seems to connote an assembly of parts, even quite diversified parts, that enter into fruitful association and organization. This concept is most strikingly expressed in such terms as wholeheartedness, wholemindedness, wholesomeness, and the like. As a *Gestalt*, then, wholeness emphasizes a sound, organic, progressive mutuality between diversified functions and parts within an entirety, the boundaries of which are open and fluent. Totality, on the contrary, evokes a *Gestalt* in which an absolute boundary is emphasized: given a certain arbitrary delineation, nothing that belongs inside must be left outside, nothing that must be outside can be tolerated inside. A totality is as absolutely inclusive as it is utterly exclusive: whether or not the category-to-be-made-absolute is a logical one, and whether or not the parts really have, so to speak, a yearning for one another.

It is, then, the psychological need for a totality without further choice or alternation, even if it implies the abandonment of a much desired wholeness, which I would invite you to consider. To say it with one sentence: When the human being, because of accidental or developmental shifts, loses an essential wholeness, he restructures himself and the world by taking recourse to what we may call *totalism*. It would be wise to abstain from considering this a merely regressive or infantile mechanism. It is an alternate, if more primitive, way of dealing with experience, and thus has, at least in transitory states, a certain adjustment and survival value. It belongs to normal psychology. Any possible psychiatric inquiry is restricted to these questions: Can the transient means of emergency adjustment be prevented from becoming fixed ends? Can totalism reverse itself when the emergency is over? Can its elements be resynthesized in a wholeness which is then possible?

In the individual it is the "inner institution" called by Freud the "ego" which has the task of mastering experience and of guiding action in such a way that a certain wholesome synthesis is, ever again, created between the diverse and conflicting stages and aspects of life — between immediate impressions and associated memories, between impelling wishes and compelling demands, between the most private and the most public aspects of existence. To do its job, the ego develops modes of synthesis as well as screening methods and mechanisms of defense. As it matures through the constant interaction of maturational forces and environmental influences, a certain duality develops between higher levels of integration (which permit a greater tolerance of tension and of diversity) and lower levels of integration where totalities and conformities must help to preserve a sense of security. The study of those fusions and defusions which — on the individual level — make for a successful wholeness or an attempted totality thus belongs to the realm of psychoanalytic ego-psychology. Here I can do no more than point to this field of study.[1]

III

The ego's beginnings are difficult to assess. But as far as we know it emerges gradually out of a stage when "wholeness" is a matter of physiological equilibration, maintained through the mutuality between the baby's need to get and the mother's need to give. The mother, of course, is not only a parturient creature but also a member of a family and society. She, in turn, must feel a certain wholesome relation between her biological role and the values of her community. Only thus can she communicate to the baby, in the unmistakable language of somatic communication, that the baby may trust her, the world — and himself. Only a "whole" society can vouchsafe to the infant (through the mother) an inner conviction that all the diffuse somatic experiences (from the first search for breath to the disruptions of the teething stage) and all the confusing social cues of early life can be balanced by a sense of continuity and sameness which gradually unites the inner and outer worlds. The ontological source of faith and hope which thus emerges I have called a Sense of Basic Trust: it is the first and basic wholeness, for it seems to imply that the inside and the outside can be experienced as an interrelated goodness. Basic Mistrust, then, is the sum of all those diffuse experiences which are not somehow successfully balanced by the experience of integration. One cannot know what happens in a baby, but overwhelming clinical evidence indicates that early mistrust is accompanied by an experience of "total" rage, with fantasies of the total domination of the sources of pleasure and provision; and that such fantasies, and such rages, live on in the individual and are revived in extreme states and situations.

In fact, every basic conflict of childhood lives on, in some form, in the adult. The earliest steps are preserved in the deepest layers. Every tired human being may regress temporarily to partial mistrust whenever the world of his expectations has been shaken to the core. Yet social institutions seem to provide the individual with

[1] See the papers of H. Hartman, E. Kris, D. Rapaport, and others in D. Rapaport, *The Organization and Pathology of Thought* (New York: Columbia University Press, 1951).

continuing collective reassurances in regard to such anxieties as have accrued from the step-and-layers of his infantile past. There can be no question but that it is organized religion which systematizes and socializes the first and deepest conflict in life: it combines the dim images of each individual's "pre-historic" providers into collective images of superhuman providers; it makes comprehensible the vague subject matter contained in Basic Mistrust by giving it a metaphysical reality in the form of tangible Evil; and it offers to man by way of rituals a periodic collective restitution of that Basic Trust which in mature adults ripens to a combination of faith and realism. In prayer man assures a superhuman power that (in spite of everything) he has remained trustworthy, and asks for a sign that he now may also continue to trust his deity. In primitive life, which deals with one segment of nature and develops a collective magic, the Supernatural Providers of food and fortune are often treated as though they were angry if not malicious parents who needed to be appeased by prayer and self-torture. Higher forms of religion and ritual equally clearly address themselves to the nostalgic remnant in each individual of his expulsion from the paradise of wholeness which once gave liberal provision, but which, alas, was lost, leaving forever an undefinable sense of evil division, potential malevolence, and deep nostalgia. Religion restores, at regular intervals and through rituals significantly connected with the important crises of the life cycle and the turning points of the yearly cycle, a new sense of wholeness, of things rebound. But, as is the case with all such endeavors, that which was to be banished beyond the periphery is apt to reappear in the center. Much cruel, cold, and exclusive totalness has dominated some phases of the history of religion. One may well ask in what way the idea of a Universe totally embraced by One God and his dogma prepared mankind for the idea of One State as well as for that of One Mankind: for there can be no doubt but that, in periods of transition, a total realignment can insure progress to an eventual greater wholeness, as well as a fixation on totalistic means.

Today no derision on the part of the careless unbeliever and no punitive fervor on the part of the dogmatist can deny the staggering fact that much of mankind finds itself without a living religion such as gave wholeness of existence to the tool-man in his productive dealings with nature and to the trading man in his gainful exchange of goods in an expanding world market. How deeply worried self-made man is in his need to feel safe in his man-made world can be seen from the deep inroad which an unconscious identification with the machine (comparable to the magic identification of primitive man with his principal prey) has made on the Western concept of human nature in general and on a kind of automatized and depersonalized child training in particular. The desperate need to function smoothly and cleanly, without friction, sputtering, or smoke, has attached itself to the ideas of personal "happiness," of governmental perfection, and even of "salvation." Sometimes one feels a strange totalism creeping up in those naïve initiators who expect a new wholeness to come from the process of technological development in and by itself, just as in times not so distant the millennium was to emerge from the unfailing wisdom of nature, from the mysterious self-balance of the market, or from the inner sanctity of wealth. Machines, of course, can be made more attractive and more comfortable as they become more practical; the question is where that deep sense of specific goodness will come from which man needs in his relation to his principal source and technique of production, in order to permit himself to be human in a reasonably familiar universe. Unanswered, this need will continue to increase a deep and widespread basic mistrust which, in areas overcome with all too sudden changes in historical and economic perspective, contributes to a readiness for a totalitarian and authoritarian delusion of wholeness, ready-made with one leader at the head of one party, one ideology giving a simple rationale to all of nature and of history, one categorical enemy of production to be destroyed by one centralized agency of justice — and the steady diversion to outer enemies of the impotent rage stored up within.

It must be remembered here, however, that at least one of the systems which we call totalitarianism, Soviet Communism, was born from an ideology which envisages beyond all revolutions a final wholeness of a society, freed from the interference of an armed state and of the class structure which necessitated it. In this vision, the total revolution and the totalitarian superstate is only a state-to-end-all-states: it will abolish itself by "becoming dormant," leaving in the final wholeness of a stateless democracy nothing to be administered except "things . . . and processes of production." This Conference will undoubtedly discuss the question of the degree to which the totalitarian means and methods have already become irreversibly rigid in the now already aging center of this utopian undertaking. In the meantime, however, we must not lose sight of those young peoples (and their young people) on the periphery of both the Soviet world and ours, who are in need of a common belief in this period of common technological change.

IV

I shall not outline here the implications of each of the successive childhood stages for the ideology of totalitarianism. The original alternative of a "whole" solution in the form of Basic Trust and a total solution in the form of Basic Mistrust, which we related to the matter of Faith, is followed on each step by analogous alternatives, each, in turn, related to one of the basic human institutions.[2] Only in passing do I wish to make reference here to that aspect of infantile development which in the psychoanalytic literature on totalitarianism has received the greatest, if not an exclusive, emphasis: I mean that infantile period (around the age of five) when the child gets ready to develop not only a more goal-directed and rebellious initiative, but also a more organized conscience. The wholesome child of three or four enjoys an unsurpassed sense of autonomous wholeness which leads to great dreams of glory and achievement, and if preserved, outbalances a sense of doubt and a sense of shame. It is then that the child suddenly faces episodes of fear and guilt, evidences of a more organized conscience, an inner governor who has quietly assumed a central position and who, now that the little human being has learned to enjoy the wholeness of being a separate being and to envisage excessive conquests ("Oedipus Complex"), tries to divide him against himself.

The guardian of conscience is, according to Freud, the "superego," which is superimposed on the ego like an inner governor, or one might say, an inner governor-general, who now represents the outer

[2] To enumerate those which will not be discussed here: there is the Sense of Autonomy vs. the Sense of Shame and the Sense of Doubt (related to ideas of Justice); there is the Sense of Initiative vs. the Sense of Guilt (related to the Ethos of Production); and the Sense of Workmanship vs. the Sense of Inferiority (related to Techniques of Production).

authorities, limiting the goals as well as the means of initiative.
One could develop this analogy. While originally imposed by a
foreign king, this governor-general now makes himself independent,
using native troops (and their methods) to combat native insur-
rection. The superego thus comes to reflect not only the sternness
of the demands and limitations imposed, but also the relative crude-
ness of the infantile stage during which they were imposed. Thus
human conscience, even while serving common ideals, retains a certain primitivity. Historically, a relationship has been emphasized
between the Father God of the Western World, the absolute power
of crowned heads, the absolute power of fathers over their children,
on the one hand, and on the other, the cruelly categoric attitude employed by a strict conscience against the self, which is thus exposed
to irrational guilt feelings and to "moral masochism." There seems
no doubt but that the Judo-Christian and feudal world has exploited man's proclivity for guilt. Psychologically, however, an assumption of a direct ratio of outer and inner pressure would be too
simple. For, to spoil a child, or even be merely "tolerant" with him,
does not necessarily make his conscience more considerate of himself; only a combination of true tolerance (born of maturity) and
of firmness (born of integrated ethics) can guide an infantile process
which otherwise, on one way or another, becomes one of the main
sources of human exploitation.

This inner split, then, is the second great inducement (separation
from the mother was the first) to "total" solutions in life which are
based on the simple and yet so fateful proposition that nothing is
more unbearable than the vague tension of guiltiness. In transitory
states, or in lasting personality formations, individuals often try
to overcome this vagueness by becoming totally good or totally bad
— solutions which betray their totalistic nature in that the totally
"good" may learn to be cruelly stern *ad majorem Dei gloriam*, while
the totally "bad" may develop quite rigid loyalties to leaders and
cliques. It is obvious that authoritarian propaganda addresses itself
to this conflict by inviting man, collectively and unashamedly, to
project total badness on whatever inner or outer "enemy" can be
created by state decree and appointed as totally subhuman and ver-
minlike; while the obedient adherent may feel totally good as a
member of a nation, a race, or a class blessed by history.

I shall now proceed from this relatively better-known fact to considerations pertaining to the end of childhood and to what seems to me the third, and more immediately political, crisis of wholeness.

v

Young people must become whole people in their own right, and this during a developmental stage characterized by a diversity of changes in physical growth, in genital maturation, and in social awareness. The wholeness to be achieved at this stage I have called a Sense of Inner Identity.[3] The young person, in order to experience wholeness, must feel a progressive continuity between that which he has come to be during the long years of childhood and that which he promises to become in the anticipated future; between that which he conceives himself to be and that which he perceives others to see in him and to expect of him. Individually speaking, identity includes, but is more than the sum of, all the successive identifications of those earlier years when the child wanted to be, and often was forced to become, like the people he depended on. Identity is a unique product, which now meets a crisis to be solved only in new identifications with age-mates and with leader figures outside of the family. The adolescent search for a new and yet a reliable identity can perhaps best be seen in the persistent endeavor to define, to overdefine, and to redefine oneself and each other in often ruthless comparison; while the search for reliable alignments can be seen in the restless testing of the newest in possibilities and the oldest in values. Where the resulting self-definition, for personal or for collective reasons, becomes too difficult, a Sense of Role-Diffusion results: the youth counterpoints rather than synthesizes his sexual, ethnic, occupational, and typological alternatives and is often driven to decide definitely and totally for one side or the other.

Here society has the function of guiding and narrowing the individual's choices. Primitive societies have always taken this function most seriously; their puberty rites replace a horror of undefinedness (dramatized by rituals) with a defined sacrifice and a sacred

---

[3] The following parallels parts of my paper "On the Sense of Inner Identity," in *Health and Human Relations* (a Report of the International Conference at Hiddesen, Germany; to be published by the Blakiston Company, New York).

badge. Advancing civilization has found other more spiritual means of "confirming" the right life plan. Yet youth has always found ways of reviving more primitive "initiations" to membership in exclusive cliques, gangs, or fraternities. In America, where youth on the whole is free of primitive traditionalism, of punitive paternalism, and of standardization through state measures, nevertheless a spontaneous self-standardization has developed which makes seemingly senseless and constantly changing styles of clothing and ways of gesturing and speaking absolutely mandatory for "insiders." For the most part this is good-natured business, full of mutual support of an "other-directed" kind, but occasionally cruel to non-conformists and of course quite unmindful of the tradition of individualism which it pretends to extol.

Let me once more refer to individual pathology. The necessity of finding, at least temporarily, a total stamp and standard at this time is so great that youth often prefers to find and to adopt a *negative identity* rather than none at all. In further pursuit of the old solution of total badness, a youth sometimes prefers to be nothing, and that totally, to remaining a contradictory bundle of identity fragments. Even in individual disturbances usually called prepsychotic or psychopathic or otherwise diagnosed in line with adult psychopathology, an almost willful *Umschaltung* to a negative identity (and its roots in past and present) can be studied. On a somewhat larger scale, an analogous turn toward a negative identity prevails in the delinquent (addictive, homosexual) youth of our large cities, where conditions of economic, ethnic, and religious marginality provide poor bases for any kind of positive identity. If such "negative identities" are accepted as a youth's "natural" and final identity by teachers, by judges, and by psychiatrists, he not infrequently invests his pride as well as his need for total orientation in becoming exactly what the careless community expects him to become. Similarly, many young Americans from marginal and authoritarian backgrounds find temporary refuge in radical groups in which an otherwise unmanageable rebellion-and-diffusion receives the stamp of universal righteousness within a black-and-white ideology. Some, of course, "mean it"; but many are merely drifting into such association.

It must be realized, then, that only a firm sense of inner identity marks the end of youth and is a condition for further and truly individual maturation. In outbalancing the inner remnants of the original inequalities of childhood (and in outbalancing the dominance of the "superego") a positive sense of identity permits the individual to forego irrational self-repudiation (the total prejudice against themselves which characterizes severe neurotics) as well as an irrational hate of otherness. Such identity, however, depends on the support which the young individual receives from the collective sense of identity characterizing the social groups significant to him: his class, his nation, his culture.[4] Where historical and technological developments severely encroach upon deeply rooted or strongly emerging identities (i.e., agrarian, feudal, patrician) on a large scale, youth feels endangered, individually and collectively, whereupon it becomes ready to support doctrines offering a total immersion in a synthetic identity (extreme nationalism, racism, or class consciousness) and a collective condemnation of a totally stereotyped enemy of the new identity. The fear of loss of identity which fosters such indoctrination contributes significantly to that mixture of righteousness and criminality which, under totalitarian conditions, becomes available for organized terror and for the establishment of major industries of extermination. Since conditions undermining a sense of identity also fixate older individuals on adolescent alternatives, a great number of adults fall in line or are paralyzed in their resistance. My final suggestion, then, is that the study of this third major crisis of wholeness, at the very end of childhood and youth, reveals an additional potentiality for totalism which seems to be of significance in the emergence of new collective identities in our time. Totalitarian regimes everywhere emphasize that youth *is* the wave of the future; and this in countries where youth is left high and dry by the ebbing wave of

---

[4] It will be seen that in individuals as well as in groups I prefer to speak of a "sense of identity" rather than of a "character structure" or "basic character." In nations, too, our clinical concepts would lead me to concentrate on the conditions and experiences which heighten or endanger a national sense of identity, rather than on a static national character. A clinical introduction to this subject is offered in my book, *Childhood and Society.* Here it is important to remember that each identity cultivates its own sense of freedom — wherefore a people rarely understands what makes other peoples feel free. This fact is amply exploited by totalitarian propaganda and underestimated in the Western world.

the past. A better understanding of this may help us to offer alternatives of guidance and support, instead of our present inclination to
disdain or to forbid, in feeble attempts to out-totalize the totalitarians. This Conference, I hope, will provide the occasion to discuss what happens to youth when totalitarian ideologies come to be
taken for granted, perish, or are revived.

To have the courage of one's diversity is a sign of wholeness, in
individuals and in civilizations. In our civilization, it is not easy
to discern whether or not, and in what respects, wider and firmer
identities promise to meet all the diversities, dissonances, and rela-
tivities which emerge as we ourselves evolve a new world-image —
an image which encompasses all of mankind and extends to the very
core of matter as well as of mind. As we orient ourselves, we may
well reassess more planfully the resources of wholeness, as well as
the mechanisms of totalism which are reborn with each generation.

10. Environmental Controls and the Impoverishment of Thought

ELSE FRENKEL-BRUNSWIK

THE ROLE OF PSYCHOLOGY IN THE STUDY OF TOTALITARIANISM

It is conceivable that in the study of certain social and political movements, especially the more matter-of-fact or rational
ones, psychology will have little to say. Thus psychology may not
play an obvious or prominent role in the explanation of the formation and structure of the American Constitution. But in the eluci-
dation of inherently compensatory and distortive social systems such
as totalitarian the picture could not be made complete without
the aid of psychology.

To be sure, totalitarianism originates in the structure of society
as a whole and this structure is shaped in the ultimate analysis by
historical, economic, and political forces. Since all these factors depend on psychological process for their mediation it is obvious that
psychological dynamics may play into the resulting course of events.
Especially as soon as we shift our view from the origin of political
institutions to the manner of their functioning, and particularly to

the influence they exert upon the cognitive and social behavior of the individuals and groups that make up the concrete instruments of their execution, it becomes clear that totalitarianism, almost by definition, undertakes to permeate and to indoctrinate every area of individual or collective life. An inquiry into the complete cycle must therefore consider both the structure of the social institutions and the different ways in which the political and social organization is experienced by, and incorporated within, the individual.[1]

Although in authoritarian systems promises concerning economic and social amelioration seem to play an outstanding role, there are strong reasons to believe that it is not these promises which exercise the most potent psychological appeal. For those who have fallen within the grasp of totalitarianism, rational argument is overshadowed by the image of an all-powerful, superhuman leader whose aura of strength, superiority, and glory afford surcease from feelings of isolation, frustration, and helplessness and whose doctrines provide an absolute and all-embracing answer to the conflicts and confusions of life and relief from the burdens of self-determination. These solutions, presented in a dogmatic, apodictic, and often inarticulate and unintelligible way, are formulated for the explicit purpose of by-passing the processes of reasonable consideration and of finding their mark in those emotional and instinctual processes which prompt to precipitant action. Reason, deliberation, and a many-sided orientation toward objects, situations, or toward life itself then appear as irrelevant and thus as morbid. Beyond and above material advantages offered, there is provided a style of thought and of life, a systematic outlook, an ideology.

This ideology delineates not only the required political attitudes but implies by force of psychological necessity the attitudes toward authority in general, and the conceptions of family, of work, of sex roles; [2] upon some scrutiny it seems that there hardly remains a corner of thought or activity that completely escapes its reach.

[1] For the function of psychology in the study of political movements see also Else Frenkel-Brunswik, "Interaction of Psychological and Sociological Factors in Political Behavior," *American Political Science Review*, XLVI (1952).

[2] The function of ideology in totalitarian systems has been emphasized by most students of totalitarianism. See especially Erich Fromm, *Escape from Freedom* (New York: Farrar and Rinehart, 1941), and Karl Mannheim, *Ideology and Utopia* (New York: Harcourt-Brace, 1949).

Here, again, we must call upon historic, economic, and political factors to explain the conditions under which people are rendered helpless and develop a longing for total surrender and a craving for absolute and definite solutions. The same factors may provide an explanation of why certain groups within a population, as for instance the lower middle-class in Germany, are especially susceptible to totalitarian ideology. The marginality of this group and the discrepancy between its social aspirations and its actual socio-economic position have been frequently mentioned in this context. But looking beyond the socio-economic factors concerned, it is psychology which is instrumental in discerning the particular psychic needs to which totalitarian ideology appeals and in identifying the strong emotive reactions which lead to a partially voluntary renunciation not only of critical faculties but in the end of self-interest as well, and to a readiness for self-sacrifice or even for self-destruction.

Although the ideology as such also must be conceived as originating in the total structure and history of a given society, it is its psychological function which provides an explanation of why dictators are able to elicit spontaneous and genuine followings over and above the adherence they ever could achieve by compulsion, and why those who follow do not become disillusioned in the face of material promises which are never fulfilled. We may perhaps expand psychologically upon the frequently used phrase that the function of totalitarianism is comparable to that of a religion.[3] Totalitarianism seems to create the illusion that merely embracing its ideology confers a kind of magical participation in the source of all power and thus provides absolute salvation and protection.[4] The analysis of magical thinking with its characteristic confusions of subject and reality and of reality and symbol has been one of the prime concerns of recent psychology, especially in areas bordering on anthropological and evolutionary or developmental considerations.[5] Only by re-

[3] See especially Sigmund Neumann, *Permanent Revolution: the Total State in a World at War* (New York: Harper, 1942).

[4] The propensity toward magic thinking and superstition in individuals susceptible to totalitarianism has been empirically demonstrated. See T. W. Adorno, Else Frenkel-Brunswik, Daniel J. Levinson, and R. Nevitt Sanford, *The Authoritarian Personality* (New York: Harper, 1950), and Else Frenkel-Brunswik, "A Study of Prejudice in Children," *Human Relations*, I (1948).

[5] Heinz Werner, *Comparative Psychology of Mental Development* (rev. ed.; Chicago: Follett, 1948).

course to magic involvement can we hope to account for the fact that individual freedom is cheerfully relinquished by many and that the most contradictory statements — such as the Nazi's promise of socialism to the masses and their promise to industry that capitalism would be saved — are taken in stride. The function of the ideology more than compensates for the lack of a realistic program. This is one of the reasons why fascistic movements must depend as much as they do on elaborate ideologies.

This system of ideas as expressed in an ideology is not, as Marx would have it, merely a superstructure or an epiphenomenon; it is the formative force which molds and shapes into total subjection those whom it touches. These ideologies not only appeal skillfully to the so-called higher moral forces by their reference to glory, superiority, honor, and other virtues: they also provide outlets and give permission for the release of "lower" needs, especially aggression, under the pretext of subordinating these needs to the exercise of moral indignation. Though it is of course beyond doubt that opportunistic reasons are of considerable significance in the totalitarian appeal, especially as far as adequate instrumentality and adequate means-end relationships are concerned, much of the behavior, especially on the part of the genuinely enthusiastic branch of the followership, must be viewed as irrational.[6] In the face of the concrete psychological evidence which is continually accumulating, and some of which is to be surveyed below, it would be extremely difficult to shut one's eyes to the fact that irrationality, distortion of perception, and the projections of hostility and of other thwarted tendencies enter the social and political scene as a major component, In turn this irrationality, although more prominent under certain specified historical and socio-economic conditions, cannot be explained within the framework of these conditions alone but must be viewed, in addition, from a psychological point of view.

In the present paper an attempt is made to throw light on the psychological mechanisms by which the totalitarian outlook is transmitted and the role it plays in the adjustment balance of the individual. Our findings show a parallelism between the social and political organization of totalitarianism and the structure and functioning of

[6] The quality of irrationality has been stressed by many investigators of totalitarianism. See especially Fromm, *Escape*, and Mannheim, *Ideology*.

individuals who are susceptible to this ideology. Thus we will find
in statistical samples of such individuals a more or less pronounced
preponderance of mechanization, standardization, stereotypy, dehumanization of social contacts, piece-meal functioning, rigidity, intolerance of ambiguity and a need for absolutes, lack of individuation and spontaneity, a self-deceptive profession of exalted ideals,
and a combination of over-realism with bizarre and magic thinking
as well as of "irrationality with manipulative opportunism." [7] All
these are features inherent in the system of totalitarian ideologies.
Not only do we find statistically significant relationships between
political attitudes and personality makeup, but our understanding of
social and political beliefs and of religious and ethical ideologies is
deepened when these factors are woven into the matrix of the total
individual. That these attitudes are also woven into the pattern of
society is more widely stressed and is more generally accepted than
are the relationships of these attitudes to the seemingly more remote
intimate aspects of our lives.[8] The time seems to have come to establish a proper balance by stressing personality structure along with
social behavior as important links in the societal network. An analysis of the psychological processes involved will increase our understanding and possible control of totalitarianism, as long as we remain aware that this avenue of approach is by no means the only
one and that totalitarianism, like every social movement, is multi-
determined. This fact, however, does not require that every single
investigator deal with and control all the factors involved. Such a
quest for completeness would be but an invitation to dilettantism.

Since the eradication of independent and critical judgment lies at
the very core of totalitarianism, we shall concentrate on this theme.
But we hope at the same time to throw light on other psychological
aspects of totalitarianism. We shall draw on the resources of academic psychology, with its emphasis on perception and cognition
and the adaptive processes in general, as well as on those of social
psychology, with its emphasis on social attitudes and their relationship to social institutions, and last but not least on those of depth

[7] See the present writer's paper on "Interaction of Psychological and Sociological
Factors," p. 45.

[8] Harold D. Lasswell, *Psychopathology and Politics* (Chicago, 1930), should be
singled out as a pioneer study in relating political attitudes to personal life histories.

psychology, which has sharpened our eyes to the underlying pattern of the emotive and instinctual life and has helped us to differentiate the "official" façade from the "dynamic" realities of social behavior.

In order to expand our knowledge concerning distortive interference with thought processes, our group at the University of California undertook to study the cognitive approach of a sample of children and adolescents (age ten years and older) growing up in American homes.[9] We proceeded through direct observation and by experiment, using as our subjects those who had previously been found to have either a relatively extreme democratic or a relatively extreme totalitarian outlook. The susceptibility to totalitarian ideas turned out to be correlated with the outlook of, and the home regime exercised by, the parents, who had been interviewed separately from the children. These data were collected during and shortly after the last war. Many of the parents selected on the basis of their susceptibility to totalitarian ideas expressed more or less veiled sympathies for the existing dictatorships in Germany or Italy, or at least they made some attempts to vindicate these regimes.

Choice of the approach via personality is especially called for when objective social structure is taken for granted as a common background for an investigation aiming primarily at the finding of differences in the appeal various aspects of one and the same civilization—here the American—exert upon varying personalities. In a society as complex as ours, we find contradictory social institutions and political currents. Psychological factors must be called in to help explain selectivity and choice between alternative ideologies. Although our studies are concerned with American samples, the universality of the authoritarian personality type will emerge by the comparison of our findings with the views of the leading Nazi

[9] Brief surveys of the plan and of some of the major results of the project involved, the California Study of Social Discrimination in Youth, were given by the present writer in "A Study of Prejudice in Children," and in "Patterns of Social and Cognitive Outlook in Children and Parents," *American Journal of Orthopsychiatry*, XXI (1951). This project is part of the activities of the Institute of Child Welfare of the University of California. The separate project on *The Authoritarian Personality*, cited above, had dealt with adult subjects only and did not involve a study of the conception of social roles at the ideological level, of purely cognitive processes, nor did it involve a direct observation of the subjects' families. The present paper concentrates on the aspects just listed.

psychologist, E. R. Jaensch, who explicitly extolled rigidity, lack of adaptability, and anti-intellectualism — all features which develop in the wake of totalitarianism and which we too found prominently displayed in individuals in this country who are susceptible to totalitarian ideas.

For a number of years my students and I collected materials on perception, reasoning, and imagination and related them to the types of upbringing to which our subjects were exposed. The intimidating, punitive, and paralyzing influence of an overdisciplined, totalitarian, home atmosphere seems to have effects upon the thinking and creativity of the growing child analogous to those which are apparent under totalitarian social and political regimes. We came to realize that situations encountered within the family unit and the special destinies of early experiences stemming from these situations contribute in large measure to the way social institutions are experienced, integrated, and selectively responded to. This may be especially true in countries where such choices are actually open to the individual. A consideration of the responses to threats in childhood seems to reveal much about the ways in which people react to threats in adult life, though such intensive experiences in later life are undoubtedly in themselves capable of superseding both earlier influences and the individual predispositions to a certain extent. It seems that external pressures of a traumatic character, be they past or be they presently imposed, are likely not only to bring authoritarian personalities to the fore but to reinforce authoritarian trends in individuals who otherwise would remain democratic-minded.

Our finding that harsh discipline at home inhibits and paralyzes the thought processes of growing children does not necessarily imply a direct or exclusive causal relationship between family structure and the rise of totalitarianism. Although in Germany a long history of authoritarian regimes is mirrored in, and undoubtedly reinforced by, authoritarian family and school structures, totalitarianism may well arise in countries with more permissive family atmospheres. Anxiety-inducing social and political situations such as economic depression or war can bring to the fore irrational elements and feelings of helplessness, and thus create susceptibility to totalitarianism regardless of how democratic the family situation might have been.

What we mainly want to achieve by reference to the family atmosphere of our authoritarian subjects is to demonstrate in slow-motion the effects of threats upon thinking and thus to understand better the analogous processes in the social and political area.

SUBMISSION TO AUTHORITY, DOGMA AND CONVENTION

Before we proceed to a more detailed discussion of the thought patterns, in the cognitive area proper, of the individuals susceptible to totalitarian ideas, let us sketch briefly the way in which preconceived and stereotypical categorizations determined by authority, dogma, and convention permeate their general social outlook. The materials reveal a hierarchical rather than equalitarian conception of human relationships characterized primarily by an admiration for the strong and contempt for the weak. There is a tendency for total, unquestioning, albeit ambivalent, surrender to every manner of authority — be it a political leader, a superior in business or army, a teacher, a parent, or, as we will see, even a perceptual stimulus. The same rigid and compulsive conformity is exercised toward socially accepted standards of behavior — even though the standards may sometimes be unwritten and those of a small "ingroup" — and this conformity is accompanied by an unrealistic and punitive condemnation of those who deviate from such norms.

This compulsive conformity with its all-or-none character differs in several ways from genuine and constructive conformity. First, it is excessive since it compensates for feelings of marginality and the attendant fear of becoming an outcast, and since it often serves the function of covering up the resentment — unconscious as this resentment may be — toward the social system as a whole. The lack of a genuine incorporation of the values of society accounts for the rigidity of the conformity; at the same time it accounts for a certain unreliability, the readiness to shift allegiance altogether to other authorities and other standards. The adherence to the letter rather than to the spirit of the social institutions, which further characterizes the compulsive conformist, issues from his distortion and simplification of the system of norms and commands in the direction of what one may call unidimensional interpretation.

Along the lines just listed the ingroup is glorified while the outgroup is rejected *in toto*. External criteria rather than intrinsic values are prevalent in these dichotomies. In order to be able to maintain the image of oneself and of one's ingroup as strong and at the same time as virtuous, fear, weakness, passivity, and aggressive feelings against authoritative ingroup figures are repressed. Lack of insight and differentiation in the emotional area result in the impoverishment of interpersonal relations and to projection of the unaccepted tendencies into the environment. Thus the other ones — and especially outgroups — are apt to be seen not only as basically weak and impotent but also as immoral, hostile, and depraved, and as imbued, therefore, with all the secondary power and strength such forces of darkness may be able to impart. In the wake of this there follows an attempt to compensate for the ensuing general distrust of people and pervasive cynicism by an overcredulity towards a few chosen leaders.

In the evaluation of the self [10] the authoritarian person is prone to emphasize such morally overpitched traits as "will power" and an iron determination in overcoming the handicaps and vicissitudes of a struggle for existence, the hardships of which are perceived in the image of unmitigated brutality. Energy, decisiveness, "ruggedness," and "toughness" tend to be particularly prominent in the ego-ideal of the men in this group. There is evidence in our material that the display of a rough masculine façade serves to a considerable extent as a compensation for a basic self-contempt and intimidatedness and for the ensuing tendency toward passivity and dependence.

The ostentatious stress which, according to the findings in *The Authoritarian Personality*, is placed by the ethnocentric person upon sincerity, honesty, courage, and self-control, along with his tendency toward self-glorification, must be evaluated in the light of certain earlier results based on a comparison of verbally espoused ideals with actual behavior.[11] It was found that emphasis on favorable traits, of the type just mentioned, in one's "official" self-image or self-ideal tends to go with objective weakness rather than strength in the particular area concerned. One of the most significant findings concern-

[10] For more extensive discussion of the attitude toward the self, toward sex roles, and toward parents and other figures of authority see the present writer's chapters x, xi, and xii in *The Authoritarian Personality*, and the material on adolescents referred to above, note 9.

[11] See also Else Frenkel-Brunswik, "Mechanisms of Self-Deception," *Journal Social Psychology*, X (1939).

ing the authoritarian personality is the fact that the explicit self-image is in exactly the same contradiction to the one revealed by a more objective evaluation by the expert as had been found in the earlier study just referred to.

In line with repressions and the lack of insight we also find in authoritarian individuals a break in the experienced continuity between childhood-self and present-self. Subjects in this group tend to display a reluctance to make spontaneous reference to their lives as developmental units. They also tend to refrain from going into judicious socio-psychological explanations of the self as well as of others or of society in general.

The stereotypical approach to social and ethical challenges with all its inherent inhibitions carries over into such related, more specific areas as the conception of sex roles, parental roles, and so forth. At least on the surface there is an emphasis on aggression and "toughness" and a disparagement of tenderness and softness ("sissiness") in the masculine ideal, and an emphasis on submissiveness, docility, and "sweetness" in the feminine ideal professed by the authoritarian of either sex. The possibility of trespassing from one syndrome to the other is explicitly excluded. Rigid defenses are erected against cross-sexual tendencies, leading to a "rigid and exaggerated conception of masculinity and femininity" [12] at the ideological level, albeit with frequent break-throughs of these repressed tendencies on the action level.

There is rigid categorization in terms of clearly delineated norms even if this should imply the acceptance of restrictions and disadvantages for one's own sex group.

Aside from strength vs. weakness, virtue vs. vice, badness vs. goodness, masculinity vs. femininity, such dichotomies involve cleanliness vs. dirtiness and a host of other pairs of opposites vaguely related to the basic juxtapositions. In each case the cleavage between the opposite attributes tends to be considered mutually exclusive, absolute, natural and eternal. In this manner, there is a general tendency toward prejudgments on the basis of rigid set or dogma.

[12] See the present writer's "A Study of Prejudice in Children," p. 299; on the same page the reader will find verbatim passages from the protocols of authoritarian and democratic-minded adolescents concerning their notions of masculine and feminine ideals.

Such an approach does not provide sufficient space for an independent variability or evaluation of facts nor for learning to use one's own experiences. It is in this manner that human relations become shallow and externalized.

In the individual children whom we have studied the total outlook, just described, seems to a very appreciable extent to have its root in the home. However, as mentioned above, we do not imply that this is the only or the decisive source of such attitudes; it is necessary to keep in mind that social conditions and institutions have a direct bearing on the family structure. Second, political institutions influence personality formation directly, especially if they are forcefully imposed with the help of all-inclusive ideologies as is the case in totalitarian regimes. In this context we must not forget that although at the action level Hitler may have contributed to the weakening of the family by placing loyalty to the state over loyalty to the family, at the ideological level he made use of the family as a potential instrument in the execution of totalitarianism by advocating as a model of a man one who is a good soldier-father and as an ideal woman one who fulfills her child-rearing functions.

It is primarily the fact that the home discipline in authoritarian homes is experienced as overwhelming, unintelligible and arbitrary, demanding at the same time total surrender, which makes for a parallelism with totalitarian political and social organizations. The parallel becomes even more evident if we consider that the child, by virtue of his objective weakness and dependence, is entirely at the mercy of the parental authorities and must find some way to cope with this situation. In our study we found that parents in the authoritarian group frequently feel threatened in their social and economic status, and that they try to counteract their feelings of marginality by an archaic and frequently unverbalized need for importance. It is noteworthy that what seems to matter is not so much the actual status on the socio-economic ladder nor the objective marginality within a certain class that seems decisive in this respect; but rather the subjective way these conditions are exeperienced and allowed to build up to certain vaguely conceived aspirations. Recent data further suggest that the status-concern of individuals susceptible to totalitarianism is quite different from a realistic attempt to improve their position by concerted effort and adequate means-goal instrumentality. More often, we find their aspirations to take the form of an unspecific expectation of being helped by sudden changes in the external situation or by an imaginary person who is strong and powerful.

Authoritarian disciplinary rules seem to have their chief origin in this vaguely anticipatory yet inefficient state of social unrest on the part of the parents rather than in the developmental needs of the child. The parents expect the child to learn quickly certain external, rigid, and superficial rules and social taboos. At the same time they are impatient, demanding a quick execution of commands which leaves no time for finer discriminations and in the end creates an atmosphere comparable to acute physical danger. The rules to be enforced are largely nonfunctional caricatures of our social institutions based on a misunderstanding of their ultimate intent; in many ways one may even speak of a defiance of culture by external conformity. In any case, the rules are bound to be beyond the scope and understanding of the child. Compelling the child to obey the rules which he is thus unable to internalize may be considered as one of the major interferences with the development of a clear-cut personal identity. The authoritarian form of discipline is thus "ego-destructive" in that it prevents the development of self-reliance and independence. The child, being stripped of his individuality, is made to feel weak, helpless, worthless, or even depraved.

Parents and parental figures, such as teachers or other authorities, acquire a threatening, distant, and forbidding quality. Disciplining, controlling, and keeping one in line is considered to be their major role. A systematic inquiry into the children's conceptions of ideal parents has shown that authoritarian children tend to consider strictness and harshness as some of the prime attributes of ideal parents. Next to this, another desirable quality of the ideal parent stressed by children in this group is that of delivering material goods. By contrast, the more democratic-minded children are given to stress primarily companionship, understanding, and demonstration of love as the function of ideal parents.

It seems to be largely fear and dependency which discourage the child in the authoritarian home from conscious criticism and which lead to an unquestioning acceptance of punishment and to an identification with the punishing authority. This identification often goes as far as an ostentatious glorification of the parents. As we have learned from psychoanalysis, however, repressions of hostility cannot be achieved without at least creating emotional ambivalence. Thus the same children who seem most unquestioningly to accept parental authority have frequently been found to harbor an underlying resentment and to feel victimized without being fully aware of this fact. The existing surface conformity without genuine integration expresses itself in a stereotypical approach devoid of genuine affect. The description of the parents elicited by interview questions is characterized by the use of exaggerated clichés rather than by expressions of genuine feelings. The range of responses is rather narrow and without the variations commonly found in descriptions of real people. Only the more palpable, crude, and concrete aspects are mentioned.

The rigidification of the child's personality originally induced by the stress on self-negating submission and on the repression of nonacceptable tendencies not only leads to stereotypy; eventually the inherent pattern of conflict may result in a more or less open break between the different layers of personality, and in a loss of control of instinctual tendencies by the individual. This contrasts rather sharply with the greater fluidity of transition and intercommunication between the different personality strata which is typical of the child in the more permissive home. This is not to say that we necessarily find a minimum of guidance and direction in the homes of those of our children and adolescents who exhibit the syndrome of liberalism of personality structure and social outlook most markedly. On the contrary, guidance is essential, especially when it is combined with acceptance and understanding and thus strengthens the moral functions of the children and helps them to overcome their impulses toward selfishness and aggression.

PATTERNS OF PERCEPTION AND THOUGHT; INTOLERANCE OF AMBIGUITY

The emotional makeup and the rigidity of defense, lack of insight, and narrowness of the ego of the authoritarian personality as just described carries over even into the purely cognitive domain. Here too, ready-made clichés tend to take the place of realistic spontaneous reactions. This is one of the findings of experiments on perception, memory, and thinking in liberal and authoritarian children [13] which have been conducted with the purpose of investigating the pervasiveness of ways of functioning within the authoritarian personality. The shift from the social and emotional to the cognitive area has the added advantage of removing us from the controversial social issues under consideration. So long as we remain under the potential spell of certain preconceived notions, the evaluation of what is reality-adequate or reality-inadequate may be difficult. The fascist may accuse the liberal, and the liberal the fascist, of distorting reality.

In one of the experiments a story — conceived as a clear-cut piece of reality — was presented to children of distinctly authoritarian and of distinctly liberal outlook. The story began with the portrayal of a number of different children and proceeded to a description of their behavior toward a newcomer in terms of aggressiveness *vs.* protectiveness. In retelling the story, authoritarian children tended toward a restriction of scope by concentrating on certain single phrases and details; or else they tended to stray away from the original altogether so that in extreme cases there was almost no relation to the material presented. In other words, there was either a clinging to the original elements with little freedom and distance — a "stimulus-boundness" in the sense of the psychiatrist, Kurt Goldstein [14] — or else a farreaching neglect of the stimulus in favor of purely subjective fantasies. In this manner a rigid, cautious, segmentary approach seems to go well with one that is disintegrated and chaotic. One and the same child sometimes manifests both patterns in alternation or in all kinds of bizarre combinations. Both of these ways of responding result in an avoidance of uncertainty, one by fixation to, and the other by breaking away from, the given realities.

Another result of this experiment was that the authoritarian children tended to recall a higher ratio of undesirable over desirable

[13] Concerning the problems and results discussed in this section see Else Frenkel-Brunswik, "Intolerance of Ambiguity as an Emotional and Perceptual Personality Variable," *Journal of Personality*, XVIII (1949).

[14] Kurt Goldstein, "The Significance of Psychological Research in Schizophrenia," in S. S. Tomkins (ed.), *Contemporary Psychopathology* (Harvard University Press, 1943). See also Kurt Goldstein and Martin Scheerer, "Abstract and Concrete Behavior," *Psychol. Monog.*, LIII (1941), no. 239.

features in the characters involved. This result is in line with another of our empirical findings, that is, a general overemphasis on negative, hostile, and catastrophic features in stories given by authoritarian-minded subjects in responses to indirect, so-called "projective" tests involving "thematic apperceptions" of still pictures.[15]

In democratic-minded children the average ratio of undesirable to desirable features recalled was closer to the ratio in the original story than was the case in authoritarian children, indicating greater faithfulness to the "reality" presented. In addition there is some tendency toward remembering the friendly features better than the unfriendly ones. This is in line with other evidence from liberal subjects revealing the operation of a mechanism of "denial" of aggression and violence, that is, a certain naïveté or ostrich policy toward evil.

Some of the trends reported above become especially apparent in an experiment on perception. When presented with pictures of familiar objects and then with similar but ambiguous or unfamiliar stimuli, authoritarian children tended to cling to the name of the original object and in other ways to respond but slowly to the changing of the stimuli. There was a marked reluctance to give up what had seemed certain, and a tendency not to see what did not harmonize with the first set, as well as a shying away from transitional solutions. Once broken, this rigid perseveration was usually followed either by a spell of haphazard, reckless guessing or by a complete blockage. Situations possessing inherent uncertainties or otherwise lacking in firmness seem thus bewildering and disturbing to the authoritarian child even if there is no particular emotional involvement. In most of the other verbal productions there is a similar pattern of either restrictiveness or flow of sterile rumination. Assumptions once made, even though proved faulty and out of keeping with reality, tend to be repeated over and over and not to be corrected in the face of new evidence.

The conclusion suggests itself that all this constitutes an effort to counteract, in the cognitive sphere, the excessive underlying emotional ambivalence induced by environmental overcontrol. The re-

[15] For a description of the Thematic Apperception Test see H. A. Murray and workers at the Harvard Psychological Clinic, *Explorations in Personality* (New York: Oxford University Press, 1938), pp. 530–545.

sulting syndrome I have proposed to call "intolerance of ambiguity." A rigid cognitive superstructure in which everything opaque and complex is avoided as much as possible is superimposed upon the conflict-ridden emotional under-structure. In effect, this merely duplicates slavery to authority rather than remedying it. Now there is slavery not only to the authority of the other person; there also is slavery to the authority of the stimulus. In other words, the attitude toward a perceptual stimulus or a cognitive task mirrors the attitude toward authority.

The following aspects of intolerance of ambiguity may be specified: tendency toward unqualified black-white and either-or solutions, oversimplified dichotomizing, stereotypy, perseveration and mechanical repetition of sets and of faulty hypotheses, premature "closure" and preference for symmetry, regularity, and definiteness in the sense of "good" (or *prägnant*) form as defined by Gestalt psychology,[16] achieved either by diffuse globality or by overemphasis on concrete detail; compartmentalization, piecemeal approach, stimulus-boundness; quest for unqualified certainty as accomplished by pedantic narrowing of meanings, by stress on familiarity, by inaccessibility to new experience, or by a segmentary randomness and an absolutizing of those aspects of reality which have been preserved; satisfaction with subjective yet unimaginative, overconcrete or overgeneralized solutions. Totalitarian propaganda takes advantage of this syndrome by the use of vague generalities combined with reference to unessential concrete detail. The opposite attitude, "tolerance of ambiguity," embraces the many-sidedness, complexity, and differentiation which is an essential aspect of the creative process; it has nothing to do with confusion or inarticulate vagueness, in fact, it is in diametrical opposition to these latter features.

The fact that specific manifestations of intolerance of ambiguity tend to reoccur within an individual in contexts seemingly far removed from each other is best brought out by a synoptic analysis of corresponding segments in the protocols of individual cases. Thus, one of the boy subjects in our study showed a great deal of conformity and compliance toward parents and authorities with an occasional breaking through of fits of rage and explosive aggression. This was reflected in the various perceptual and thinking experiments by a generally cautious, restricted, and conservative

[16] Kurt Koffka, *Principles of Gestalt Psychology* (New York: Harcourt Brace, 1935).

attitude toward the stimulus with an occasional shift toward dis-integrated, random behavior when the strain of coping with the task became too great. Other case studies reveal that some of the authoritarian children perform well on some relatively simple or routine perceptual and cognitive tasks — on tasks which do not require imagination or freedom from stimulus-boundness — in spite of the fact that there are signs of rigidity in their performance; here we are reminded of the frequently noted technological abilities of the Nazis.

The subtle but profound distortion of reality in the course of the elimination of ambiguities is in the last analysis precipitated by the fact that stereotypical categorizations can never do justice to all the possible aspects of reality. So long as a culture provides socially accepted outlets for suppressed impulses, smooth functioning and fair adjustment can be achieved within the given framework. But the adjustment of the authoritarian-minded person depends on conditions that are comparatively narrowly circumscribed. Whenever differentiation and adaptability to change are required, this adjustment will run the risk of breaking down. Basically, therefore, the various forms of rigidity and of avoidance of ambiguity, directed as they are toward a simplified mastery of the environment, turn out to be maladaptive in the end.

Dramatized, concrete, and at the same time global, diffuse, and undifferentiated types of thinking are, of course, characteristic of certain early developmental stages as such. However, the atmosphere of the home and the more specific expectations of the parents regarding the child's behavior determine whether such primitive reactions become fixated, or whether progress toward higher developmental stages can take place. For the latter course, a reduction of fear, greater relaxation, acceptance of and tolerance for insecurity and weakness in and by the child are necessary. Realism, originality and imaginative cognitive penetration presuppose some such advance in general psychological maturity.

CLOSENESS OF OPPOSITES AS A PRINCIPLE OF PERSONALITY ORGANIZATION

In spite of the rather consistent recurrence of common elements in various areas, there is no obvious or simple "unity of style" in the authoritarian personality. This is due at least in part to the many repressions and to the break between the conscious and unconscious levels as discovered and explored by depth psychology.[17] In the sense of the above brief exposition, the authoritarian person has been found to combine within himself rigid perseverative behavior with an overfluid, haphazard, disintegrated, random approach; compulsive overcaution with the tendency toward impulsive shortcuts to action; chaos and confusion with orderly oversimplification in terms of black-white solutions and stereotypy; isolation with fusion; lack of differentiation with the mixing of elements which do not belong together; extreme concreteness with extreme generality; cynicism with gullibility; over-realism with irrationality; self-glorification with self-contempt; submission to powerful authorities with resentment against them; and stress on masculinity with a tendency toward feminine passivity.

The seeming paradox given by these coëxistences is resolved when one considers the fact, hinted at previously in this paper, that a personality thrown out of balance in one direction usually requires counterbalancing in the opposite direction. Elsewhere I have spoken of the "closeness of opposites" as an essential feature of authoritarian personality organization. Indeed, the authoritarian personality may be characterized as consistently inconsistent, or as consistently self-conflicting. In elaborating on intolerance of ambiguity it became evident that lack of distance and too much distance to culture, parents, and other stimulus configurations are more closely related to each other than is either of these opposites to what may be termed "medium distance" from these environmental realities. The non-authoritarian personality avoids undue reduction of existing complexities and retains balance by maintaining a flexible type of conformity and order. A kind of self-reconciled consistency is thus achieved which manages the inconsistencies of reality at the conscious level rather than allowing them to invade the unconscious and to be lived out by devious means of tension-reduction and by displacement of aggression upon substitute targets.

Although most of our authoritarian adolescents tend to follow the self-conflicting pattern described above, we are able to distinguish subvarieties in whom one or the other side prevails. In one there

[17] Sigmund Freud, "Instincts and Their Vicissitudes" (1915). In *Collected Papers*, vol. IV (London: Hogarth, 1925).

is a prevalence of control, rigidity, caution, and order as far as overt
behavior is concerned, while the chaotic side becomes manifest only
under stress; in the other there is a predominance of chaos, fusion,
and impulsive action while the ideal of control and rigid order remains to a large extent confined to the symbolic level of consciously
accepted values.

EXPLICIT ESPOUSAL OF RIGIDITY IN THE NAZI PERSONALITY IDEAL

While to us the authoritarian pattern of personality seemed impoverished and closed to new experiences, many of the features
which from the standpoint of adjustment to physical or social realities must be described as negative were listed among the desirable
attributes of an ideal type of personality by E. R. Jaensch of Marburg.
Jaensch is probably the most articulate and brilliant exponent of the
Nazi ideology so far as professional psychological contributions to
this field are concerned. He was the Hitler-appointed permanent
President of the German Psychological Association until his death
in 1940. He formulated a comprehensive valuative personality typology on the thousands of pages he published during the last years
of his life. An analysis of his writings reveals some important aspects
of the most markedly fascistic version of German thinking. Exposure of his self-contradictions and rectification of his errors is important in view of the fact that his writings carry a great deal of
sweep and persuasive power, hardly diminished by the endless
repetitions and confusions with which they are encumbered. His misuse and distortion of basic categories and facts, his subtle mixture
of insight and confabulation will continue to have a great appeal to
a frame of mind by no means dead with the military defeat of
Nazism. Jaensch's most comprehensive publications on the subject
bear the following characteristic title, in translation: "The Antitype:
Psychological-Anthropological Foundations of German Cultural Philosophy Based on What We Must Overcome." [18] This antitype
(*Gegentypus*) is seen as the enemy of the national German movement and the incorporation of all that is evil.

The antitype is characterized primarily by tendencies toward
loosening (*Auflockerung*) and dissolving (*Auflösung*; hence also
the term "lytic type"). The antitype is also called the S-type since

[18] Erich Jaensch, *Der Gegentypus* (Leipzig: Barth, 1938).

he allegedly often manifests synesthesia, the well-known phenomenon of color-hearing or tone-seeing. Jaensch sees in this latter phenomenon a lack of clear-cut and rigid evaluation of, and submission to, the stimulus on the part of the perceptual response.

Passages from Jaensch's *Der Gegentypus*, presented in my own literal translation, will illustrate his notions of the antitype. It should be stressed at this point that Jaensch is notorious for his neglect of even the most elementary principles of statistical scrutiny. Many of his statements concerning interrelationships of traits are downright incorrect, while others are merely unsubstantiated.

We begin with a quotation referring to perception:

His spatial perceptions are unstable, loosened up, even dissolved. Normally the objects of the external world are given to the psychophysical organism of man in a univocally determined spatial order. (Each object in the external world creates an image on the retina of our eye . . . To the points of the retina correspond firmly and univocally determined locations in visual space or, as this is usually expressed, the spatial values of the retina are fixed.) This fixed — more precisely we should say relatively fixed — coördination between its stimulus configuration and perceptual Gestalt is disrupted in the case of the S-type (p. 37).

In this quotation, Jaensch considers his ideal German type as giving unambiguous reactions to stimuli, a feature which he confuses with receptiveness and precision. This desideratum of a one-to-one relationship between stimulus and response directly contradicts the findings of modern psychology, especially those of the so-called Gestalt psychology, which experimentally demonstrated the universal multiple determination of our perceptual responses by a variety of factors, some of them constellational and some attitudinal or temporal. It is for the stress on spontaneous perceptual "restructuring" and on its crucial role in problem-solving and in scientific or artistic creativity that Jaensch has declared the orientation of Gestalt psychology to be "morbid." The glorification of rigid stimulus-response relationships by Jaensch and his assertion of their predominance in the ideal Nazi type fits well with the fact that what we have called intolerance of ambiguity is predominant in our authoritarian children.

Rigid control, perseveration, and avoidance of differences also are

an integral part of Jaensch's ideal of discipline. To him, one of the
most gratifying experiences is the feeling of "equality of palpable,
physical characteristics . . . [wearing a] uniform, marching in
step and column" (p. 337). The antitype is criticized for his aspira-
tion to some measure of being different in developing his individuality.

All this ties in with a questionable notion of maculinity. As we have
found in our authoritarian subjects, emphasis on an exaggerated
ideal of "toughness" goes with repression and rejection of feminine
traits in men, and with contempt for women. There is hardly any
mention of women in the presentation of Jaensch; when there is,
usually some affinity between women and the antitype is construed.
According to Jaensch, the struggle between firmness and lack of
firmness, between stability and what he calls "lability," is identical
with the struggle between the masculine and its opposite, disparag-
ingly labeled the "effeminate."

All-important to Jaensch is the evaluation of the antitype as to
his aptitude for military service, considered by him one of the highest
values:

The pronounced lytic type is . . . an "anti-type" not only from the
standpoint of our German national movement but also from that of
military psychology. He is the one of whom the army must beware most,
the extremely unsoldierly type. . . . Since he lacks all firmness the lytic
type is always more or less unvirile . . . far removed from a heroic
conception of life (pp. 38ff.).

The intellect, as such, is considered a nonvirile element in this
latter sense. The antitype is said to have an inclination toward the
playful, aesthetic and intellectual. We have actually found this inclination to be present in our liberal-minded subjects but have found
little reason for looking askance at it. Again, Jaensch confuses two
essentially disparate and incompatible features, the looseness of arbitrary license, on the one hand, and the loosening of rigid fixations
that defines genuine mastery of the stimulus at the level of essentials,
on the other. So he comes to think that "liberalism" of any kind —
"liberalism of knowledge, of perception, of art, etc." (p. 44) — is
identical with a libertine lack of firmness and stability of the personality. And he assumes liberalism — along with "adaptability" in

general (see below) — to be degenerative, immoral, and dangerous for society.

Prominent in Jaensch's version of anti-intraceptiveness and anti-intellectualism is his attitude toward scientific theorizing. Theory is seen by Jaensch not in its positive function as a detour to better understanding of reality but rather as a subjectivistic leading-away from reality. (It is possible to trace such overemphasis on nearness to reality to an underlying tendency to escape from reality.) Concerning the particular case of relativity theory in physics Jaensch has this to say:

The struggle conducted by the physicists Lenard and Stark in an attempt to dislodge the theory of Einstein by establishing a more concretely oriented "German Physics" can be understood only from this point of view. It is the struggle for consideration of reality in natural science and against the . . . inclination to dissolve all reality into theory (pp. 46, 49).

It will be remembered that more recently Soviet writers have attacked Einstein from an antitheoretical standpoint very similar to that of the Nazis, accusing him of an "idealistic" orientation in his physics.

Systematic espousal of rigid environmental controls by totalitarian regimes thus seems not only to stifle imagination and to prevent the acquisition of the theoretical skills so necessary for the comprehension of reality but even to lead to glorification of this defect and to its being turned into a propagandistic weapon. In tricks of this kind lie one of the seeds of self-destruction inherent in totalitarian systems.

The way in which intolerance of ambiguity and anti-intellectualism tie in with racial theory is revealingly illustrated by the following quotation from Jaensch. In the case of racial mixture,

nature has to leave . . . everything uncertain and in suspense. . . . The individual at birth may be endowed with nothing fixed and certain, just with the uncertainty, indeterminability, and changeability which will enable him to adjust to each of the various conditions of life . . . The opposite is true if an individual possesses only ancestors who from time immemorial have lived in the North German space and within its population . . . The characteristics necessary for this life therefore may be safely placed in his cradle as innate, fixed, and univocally determined features (pp. 230ff.).

Jaensch further states that in the case of blood-mixture, which he considers an "abnormal state of affairs," adaptability must be increased since "the entire conduct of life and the total existence is entrusted to intelligence alone"; and he adds condemningly that "among all the higher mental functions intelligence is the most flexible and adaptable." In discussing adaptability, Jaensch further points out that the antitype, when engaged in psychology and anthropology, is prone to think in terms of environment, education, intellectual influences, and reason while his ideal type will refer to such factors as blood, soil, and heredity.

The Jews are considered the purest though by no means the only representative of the S-type, and this Jaensch attempts to relate to racial mixture:

> According to Hans F. K. Gunther, the Jews do not constitute a primary race but rather a highly complex racial mixture. This may be taken as an explanation for the fact that they tend so much toward the dissolving type, and that they play such an outstanding role in the development of a dissolution culture (p. 22).

Racial pollution is connected in the mind of Jaensch with physical pollution by germs: "Already in studying adults we were impressed by the fact that bodily illness, especially tuberculosis, is found most frequently in the group representing the S-type" (p. 22). Fear of germs and of spread of contagious disease has in our California material been found to be a prominent preoccupation of the authoritarian personality syndrome. According to psychoanalytic theory, the idea of pollution and contamination with germs is related to sexual thoughts. And indeed Jaensch somewhat fantastically, proceeds to say:

> Since some kind of a connection between tuberculosis and schizophrenia is established on the basis of the development and the symptomatology of the two diseases, and since, on the other hand, the connection between schizophrenia and and an affliction of the genital sphere seems highly probable, it seems to follow that we should pay more attention than hitherto to the hidden effects of camouflaged tuberculosis, infections

(and mixed infections) in the genital sphere when approaching the problem of schizophrenia (p. 460).

Our above considerations are by no means limited to Jaensch. It is well-known that Hitler thought of blood-mixture as the sole cause of the decline and death of cultures. Equally well-known is the exaggerated fear of syphilis — "syphilidophobia" as labeled in psychiatry — in the writings of the leading Nazis, and the connection they see between this infection and sexual intercourse between what they consider different races. Like Hitler, Jaensch thinks of the Nazi movement as "a biological movement, a recuperative movement, with the purpose of guiding humanity or at least our own people out of the vestibule of the psychiatric clinic" (p. 461).

Jaensch's programatic quest for firmness, for absence of ambiguity, and for definiteness is in strange contrast with the fact that his own writings are endless, full of needless repetitions, speculative intricacies, and bizarre if sometimes shrewd and subtle observations. It seems that Jaensch is struggling for a way out of his own and his culture's unbearable complexity. Reportedly Jaensch was well aware of the presence of "antitypical" features in himself; apparently it is the projections of these features which he fights in his image of the antitype.

In his conceptions of mental health as being mainly a matter of vitality and physical vigor Jaensch somewhat resembles Nietzsche whom he often quotes as his master. It is interesting to note that he joins forces with Nietzsche, another sick man, when he says: "The struggle against the hollowed-out and diseased Christianity (of the antitype) . . . was at the climax of this unfortunate epoch already carried on by Nietzsche . . . Today we shall carry it on by action" (p. 511).

Just as in our empirical findings on authoritarian children, the stimulus-boundness ascribed by Jaensch to his ideal German personality type all too soon reveals its affinity to confusion, chaos, and to a missing-out on essential aspects of reality-adaptation. The Nazi tendencies to expansion were unrealistic, to say the least, and so was their gross distortion of the personality of the enemy, as, for example, their view of the American as unsoldierly and effeminate. In this manner the refusal to face masculinity-femininity conflicts or other alleged or real difficulties or shortcomings in oneself turns out to lead to a personalized, "projective" view of other nationalities and of the outside world, resulting in a general distortion of reality and eventually in self-destruction.

SOCIAL AND POLITICAL OUTLOOK

The political irradiations of the personality pattern as found in the authoritarian individual and as idealized by Jaensch are grave. The feeling of unworthiness and the resulting anxiety implanted into the individual in an authoritarian atmosphere prevent him from squarely facing his weaknesses, shortcomings, and conflicts, and prompt him to project into his social environment — that is, to "externalize" — what he considers "evil." Evil then is fought outside rather than inside. There is, as we have seen, a striving for compensatory feelings of superiority as afforded by the condemnation of others, especially of outgroups. Images of social groups are thus dramatized and conceived as either altogether good or altogether bad, and social realities appear as oversimplified and excessively clear-cut structures.

Under an authoritarian regime — may this be a state or the home — the hostilities against the given authority must be repressed and the helplessness of the individual is exploited. This fact must be considered a strong reinforcing agent for the "anti-weakness attitude" which in our material was found to be a further attribute of the authoritarian presonality and an accompaniment of his positive if superficial identification with the strong. Sympathy for the weak cannot develop where there is ingrained fear of weakness and where the weak furnishes the only practical target of aggression. It is this same fear which makes for a shying away from responsibility and from the facing of one's own guilt, for the rejection of individuals, groups and nations different from oneself, and for magic expectations of, and magic dependence on, strong leaders and "fate." Blind trust in the potency of fate frequently leads to the development of elaborate systems of superstition. It is primarily the "strength" of the leader and the fact of force in general which reaches the authoritarian individual. He pays very little attention to the political program as such but follows the lure of a few slogans incorporating the dichotomies discussed above in the context of intolerance of ambiguity. Such persons could not possibly at the same time be accessible to democratic values.

The authoritarian person may sometimes be kept in check by authorities, who take over for them the regulatory functions of conscience and reality testing. This need for permanent reinforcement tends to persist and is likely to become an entrenched state of affairs. The preferred authority is the one who promises most in terms of material goods, who offers an ideology as a means of orientation and self-confidence, and who grants permission for more or less unbridled release of the suppressed hostile tendencies in certain specified directions. It is in this manner that the combination of over-realism and irrationality finds its expression in the political scene.

Since, as we have seen, there is ample underlying resentment against authorities on the part of the authoritarian-minded follower, we find a tendency toward easy exchange of such authorities. The combination of surface conformity with lack of internalization and integration explains the apparently paradoxical fact that we often find the rigid conformist flooded by repressed unsublimated and unmodified tendencies which threaten the brittle and tenuously maintained superstructure. Out of anxiety this individual adheres to the familiar and unquestioningly accepts the customs of his society; out of the same anxiety, however, he readily turns against this very society, the values of which he has never espoused with more than a divided heart. This is but one of the vicious circles inherent in a personalization of the social and political scene.

Under an authoritarian regime, the conception of society must become as unpsychological and ahistorical as is that of one's own life. Since continuities can be perceived only when there are no repressive breaks and no taboos on the application of freely searching social or psychological concepts and theories, the authoritarian individual tends to expain individual actions or social events in terms of incidental factors or of superstitution and magic forces.

The feelings of social and economic marginality which we found to be predominant in the home atmosphere of our authoritarian subjects suggests a further parallel between certain results of our studies and the rise of facism, especially the rise of Nazism in Germany.

Another comparison may be based on the fact that differentiation, articulation, spontaneity and autonomy are in an authoritarian home or state taken away not only from the individual; these characteristics are also lost so far as the organization of society as a whole is concerned. Both the individual and the society in which he lives are transformed into an amorphous aggregate with a superimposed strong leadership.[19] In our California studies we have tried to supply details on the impoverishment of the individual personality that forms the counterpart to the impoverishment of the social institutions under authoritarian rule. Under this aspect it is primarily the lack of integration and individuation which compels the authoritarian individual to use all kinds of stereotypes, clichés, and ideologies as crutches and substitutes for personal opinion and as an antidote against underlying confusion.

THE ROLE OF REASON

In spite of the great hopes which the eighteenth and nineteenth centuries placed upon reason and progress, we are faced today with an eruption of the irrational and with a skepticism concerning reason and science. In part, the abandonment of the critical and independent faculties of man is voluntary. Were the expectations concerning the dynamic force of reason unrealistic? Has the rational approach been overrated and did modern civilization nourish an illusion? Is mankind governed, perhaps, by altogether different forces? I think these questions must partially be answered in the affirmative. It is certainly true that in the era of Enlightenment an overly simple conception of human motivation was entertained. We have learned from Freud that the unconscious and irrational factors are of great importance in the formation of personality. We know today that they also influence the social and political attitudes, at least of some individuals. Under irrational factors Freud includes tendencies toward destruction and excessive dependence along with derivatives of infantile sex attitudes, such as Oedipal residues, especially if unconscious and displaced; further included are magic, archaic, and primitive patterns of thought and action. Over and above these irrational factors which are rooted in the history of the

---

[19] Emil Lederer, *State of the Masses* (New York: Norton, 1940).

individual, Freud[20] as well as some sociologists, among them LeBon[21] and Mannheim, have stressed the irrational factors which derive from the participation in groups. Total identification with the masses and the collective often leads to the renunciation of individual responsibility, to a reduction of intellectual ability, to an increase of cruelty, and a lack of moderation. Unless some measure of individuation is achieved, there can be no constructive group membership.

Both Durkheim and Weber have emphasized that the foundation of society lies in fundamentally nonrational moral or religious qualities. In contrast with the irrational factors just mentioned Durkheim[22] stresses such factors as respect for normative rules and moral obligation. Although Weber[23] elaborated on the rationalism of Western civilization, he was much concerned with the problem of the nonrational meaning of life; he made the well-known assumption that within Protestantism religious feelings, interests and experiences have led from the preoccupation with salvation to an ascetic puritanism and the emphasis on exemplary earthly life based on work, self-reliance, rational planning, and virtue. It was also Weber who predicted that there will be a reaction to the rationalism of the nineteenth century. Pareto, Sorel, and Nietzsche thought they had to abandon — with varying degrees of despair — the hopes that the masses will be open to reason.

Freud, on the other hand, while far from underestimating the power of irrational tendencies, was not discouraged. He never relented in supporting the struggle for greater awareness and mastery of the unconscious. His famous saying that the voice of the intellect, "though low, does not stop until it is heard," is one of the many expressions of his belief that some day reason will prevail. Further relevant in this context is the realization that for the establishment of genuinely ethical behavior it is not enough to make the instincts

[20] Sigmund Freud, *Group Psychology and the Analysis of the Ego* (translated by J. Strachey (New York, 1949).

[21] Gustave LeBon, *The Crowd: A Study of the Popular Mind* (1895). Translation, London: Unwin, 1920.

[22] Emile Durkheim, *The Rules of Sociological Method*, translation, edited by G. E. C. Catlin (Glencoe, Illinois: Free Press, 1950).

[23] Max Weber, *The Protestant Ethic and the Spirit of Capitalism* (New York: Scribner, 1930).

conscious and integrated so as to render them modifiable. Ethical behavior can be achieved only if both the so-called id-tendencies and the frequently overlooked, likewise unconscious sadistic, primitive, and unadaptable superego-tendencies, clothed as they are in moralism and the condemnation and exclusion of others, are replaced by more reasonable moral judgments.

In some respects the authoritarian children of our study were found to display a severity of moral standards reminiscent of the primitive superego tendencies just referred to. Thus, in answering the question of what type of punishment should be imposed for different types of misdemeanor, children in this group tended to demand cruel and extreme retaliation for the slightest infractions. We know today that sheer repression and denial of evil does not assure its being overcome and that such devices are detrimental rather than constructive for genuinely socialized behavior. The avoidance of conscious guilt-feelings and of related kinds of suffering is achieved by projection of the unaccepted impulses onto others, especially outgroups, and by unquestioning loyalty to a questionable ideal or leader on whom the moral demands of the conscience are projected and at whose disposal the individual has placed himself. The authoritarian individual does not generaly succeed in making the maturational step from repressive fear of authority to an internalized social conscience. It is the repressed, latent forces which are most likely to be projected onto the political and social scene. Especially in the authoritarian personality, rational control extends to a relatively small sector of the personality only and the repressed impulses lurk close to the surface, ready to break through at any appropriate occasion. Totalitarianism and its political and social propaganda machinery attempt to appeal primarily to these impulses, reinforcing them at the same time. In order to effectively counteract the potential chaos resulting form these impulses, such slogans as that of Goebbels, "cleanliness and orderliness are the foundation of life," were at the same time promoted.

For the clarification of the interplay of impulses and their eventual mastery we owe much to psychoanalysis with its stress on the importance of awareness, integration, rationality, coöperativeness, and maturity. However, psychoanalysis has often been misunderstood; by virtue of such misunderstanding it has contributed, along with other theoretical systems, to a swinging of the pendulum from the traditional blind faith and belief in reason to an overextended relativism and tendency toward unmasking of motives. A number of misunderstandings have arisen through the widespread tacit notion that if something is bad, its opposite must be good. Thus, the idea has been promoted in many homes and in some educational systems and political circles that in order to avoid authoritarianism, all authority must be forsworn. Against this ultramodern view it must be held that total permissiveness would verge upon anarchy. Respect for the authority of outstanding individuals and institutions is an essential aspect of a healthy society. It does not as such lead to total surrender to, nor to an absolutistic glorification of, the given leaders. This is especially true if leadership is limited to specialized fields or to special functions.

We must further stress that rationality does not imply amorality and freedom from obligation. On the contrary, genuine ethical behavior involves a comprehension of the issues involved, a facing of all uncertainties, conflicts and one's own guilt, and a readiness to accept the anguish involved in such an open confrontation. Irrationality and the tendency toward destruction of self and of others, on the other hand, are often combined with a short-range over-realism and an orientation toward immediate material benefits.

Furthermore, the avoidance of the quest for certainty does not imply cynicism and morbid doubt. On the contrary, in the authoritarian personality the need for absolutes turns out to be combined with basic disbelief and general distrust. In this sense the obvious function of the philosophical outlook which at the present time dominates Germany in general, and her philosophy and psychology in particular, that is, existentialism, is that of emphasizing — to a generation plagued by the deepest doubts about the value of living — the worthwhileness of anything that exists by virtue of the sheer fact of its existence. Nazi rigidity and intolerance of ambiguity has here given way, in a remarkably close succession of opposites, to the extreme relativism which is at the core of existentialism.

Many modern writers seem resigned to the fact that only what is irrational, absolute, and dogmatic can really incite people and motivate them to action, whereas the rational, many-sided approach is seen as inherently inhibitory and as leading to a barren and sterile conception of life. Against this we must hold that virility of a nation does not seem to be grounded in blind fanaticism, militant aggressiveness, and short-cuts to action. The "official" optimism often characteristic of such an outlook disguises only thinly an underlying despair. Our findings show that individuals who are more open to reason and facts are in general those who have a more differentiated internal life and deeper and more reliable — though often relatively calm — emotions. They are also those who, although less fanatic and less compulsive, show more consistency, conviction, and dedication in their principles and ideals. But the fact remains that the extreme and obvious positions lend themselves more readily to verbal formulation and thus give the false impression of solving some of the eternal perplexities. Very concrete as well as very general formulations can be put into the service of such definite and unqualified statements. In the task of a positive formation of democratic outlook and values, we must face the difficulties intrinsic in the complexities, ambiguities, flexibilities, and less fetching logicalities of the social realities.

Examples of apodictic and nonrational systems are given by both the race doctrine of Nazi Germany and the dialectical materialism of Soviet Russia. Though the two differ in the particulars of their bizarreness, both offer an essentially unscientific, metaphysical, all-inclusive *Weltanschauung* which has the appearance of definiteness, but is unrelated to fact. There is empirical evidence that individuals susceptible to totalitarianism manifest more disturbance in their empirical and rational thinking than they do in the area of pure logic; furthermore, metaphysical systems do not prevent the acquisition of technological skills which constitute a domain by themselves. However, totalitarian states stifle free inquiry not only in the social sciences and in psychology, but even in physics, at least so far as theory construction is concerned. We have witnessed this in the reaction to Einstein on the part of both Nazi Germany and Soviet Russia. An interesting problem is posed by the question how long a society can exist in which there is a certain mastery of technology but in which the social, political, and human outlook is impoverished to the point of dogmatic and distortive schemes.

Different countries vary thus to some degree in their readiness to tolerate ambiguity. As we have seen, this readiness relates not only to the structure of social and political institutions, but is also expressed in the philosophical and psychological outlook. For America, a long-range optimism seems justified to this writer. On the one hand, it must be granted that there are probable reinforcers of the authoritarian personality pattern in our culture. Among them we may list the following as the most important: presence of external threats; cultural emphasis on success and power; the necessity of proving oneself, if by no other means than by establishing social distance to those who are allegedly lower on the social scale; increasing standardization; increasing unintelligibility of poltical and social forces; presence of a powerful propaganda machinery used to manipulate public opinion; increasing difficulties in a genuine identification with society, resulting from the anonymity of big organizations and the ensuing isolation of the individual; some tendency toward a short-cut to action, toward externalization, and toward avoidance of introspection and contemplation. But it seems that these reinforcers of authoritarianism are more than counterbalanced by a long list of powerful reinforcers of tolerance for ambiguity and for liberalism in general: the democratic political tradition with its many-power check-and-balance system; the tradition of a pragmatic philosophy which, in contrast to the German philosophical tradition, is undogmatic and antimetaphysical; the general preference for scientific and rational explanations; the relative weakness of the tendencies toward oversystematization and fanaticism; the American "melting pot" ideal; the democratic tradition with its protective attitude toward the weak; the emphasis on individualism; the equalitarian relationships between children and parents, and between pupils and teachers; the readiness to criticize governmental as well as parental authorities; the increased choices offered by technological progress; the rising attempts to understand the social and economic processes in their inconsistencies and irrationalities; and the readiness and ability to accept tentativeness, conflict, and suspense.

The struggle between these opposing forces characterizes not only our civilization as a whole, but every single individual. How this struggle will end and which of these opposing trends will be victorious does by no means hinge solely on the number of mature and rational individuals, but on the interplay of political, social, and psychological phenomena in their entirety.

11. Ideological Compliance as a Social-Psychological Process

MARIE JAHODA AND STUART W. COOK

One of the most frightening aspects of totalitarian regimes is their apparent power to elicit widespread compliance with the ideologies they advocate. The hopeful assumption that individuals under such regimes feel and act as Galileo did — paying lip service to the official creed while at the stake but reaffirming their true beliefs when not in immediate danger — seems to be justified only with regard to a selected few. The naïve optimism based on the assumption that "it can't happen here" because the people will not stand for it was proved wrong in several European countries. And the qualified optimism which holds that, owing to differences in that vague entity "national character," totalitarianism may find popular support in some nations but not in others has lost its plausibility in the light of recent history. When people as different in culture and tradition as the Italians, Russians, Germans, Spaniards, Austrians, Chinese, and Czechs apparently comply in vast numbers with their totalitarian regimes, the hope that the "national character" of any given country will protect it against the totalitarian danger becomes shaky indeed.

We know from historical experience during the last three decades the role which physical terror plays in destroying both established and incipient democratic institutions. But even under the worst of the totalitarian regimes, the people outside the prisons and concentration camps far outnumber those inside. It seems clear that many — perhaps most — of these people are subjugated through influences other than the direct threat of physical violence. We do not have full knowledge of this process. We do know, however, that such people are broken in spirit so that they comply without reservation with the new order. The Nazi period has provided a term for this process, *Gleichschaltung*, and a name for those who excel in it, the Quislings. We shall call this process ideological compliance. The effort to understand it in psychological terms and to identify the conditions under which it waxes or wanes is the subject of this paper.

IDEOLOGICAL COMPLIANCE IN THE CURRENT AMERICAN
CLIMATE OF THOUGHT

There are some who maintain that ideological compliance is the direct and inevitable consequence of totalitarian institutions. Under the dictatorship of one party with complete suppression of the opposition, with a monopoly on sources of information and indoctrination, with secret police and concentration camps — under these conditions, and only under these conditions, they maintain, ideological compliance appears. It is, of course, true that totalitarian institutions do give rise to this process. But it is a misleading simplification to regard ideological compliance as a phenomenon appearing in political dictatorships only. Indeed, we are about to demonstrate that it is not uncommon in this country whose democratic institutions are intact. Whether the intensification of the process in a democratic country carries an inherent threat to its democratic institutions or whether these institutions will ultimately reduce the process to manageable proportions is an interesting speculation — in which, however, we need not engage at this moment.

In an exploratory study among federal employees of professional rank conducted in the fall of 1951,[1] we analyzed the voluntary restrictions which such employees have adopted, beyond the obvious and imposed restrictions inherent in the conditions of federal employment. These restrictions include: reading matter ("I have sometimes wanted to see a copy of the *Daily Worker* but now would not be caught within a mile of one"); ownership of books ("The bookshelves of some of my friends have changed"); subscription to periodicals ("I buy the *Nation* from a newsstand; there is no sense in being on their subscription list"); membership and activity in voluntary organizations ("I dropped out of the American Veterans Committee; it isn't on the list but it may get there"); talking about controversial subjects or holding unorthodox views ("A person should not be radical, he should not get into arguments on religion, he should not be extreme in his views on atomic theory, but he should also have ample freedom of thought . . . I would be careful of my conversation on religion and politics"). With this conformity in one's

[1] Marie Jahoda and Stuart W. Cook, "Security Measures and Freedom of Thought," *Yale Law Journal*, LXI, no. 3 (March 1952).

own behavior goes a growing intolerance of the nonconformist and a growing suspicion that others who show less compliance than one's self may actually be dangerous spies.

It should be emphasized that none of these restrictions has any bearing on the country's security, or for that matter, any relation to the conduct of the executive orders on loyalty and security provisions for government employees. Yet many federal employees conform to such self-imposed restrictions as though to do otherwise would be prevented by physical force.

However passionately we may oppose the doctrines of Communism, it is a far cry from the initial decision to prevent Communists from holding jobs in which they might endanger national security to present actions which include, for example, demanding non-Communist oaths from public-housing tenants and judging the acceptability of performers in the entertainment world in terms of their political beliefs. These are punitive measures completely unrelated to the security of the country. Nevertheless, there are indications that many people are as ready to comply with these latest actions as they were to endorse the earlier and far different decision.

A PSYCHOLOGICAL MODEL FOR THE PROCESS OF COMPLIANCE

Ideological compliance of the kind now found among federal employees and conformity requirements such as those just mentioned are certainly not within the scope of the traditional ideas of American democracy as expressed in the great national documents of the country. How, then, are we to understand our present trend toward increased conformity?

In a recently published series of experiments, completely outside the sphere of social thought and controversy, Solomon Asch has created a simple model of the psychological process with which we are concerned.[2] His basic experiments involved groups of seven to nine individuals, all college students. The experimental performance

[2] Solomon E. Asch, *Social Psychology* (New York: Prentice-Hall, 1952), esp. pp. 450–484, and Solomon E. Asch, "Effects of Group Pressure upon the Modification and Distortion of Judgments," in *Readings in Social Psychology*, edited by Swanson, Newcomb, and Hartley (New York: Henry Holt, 1952). We hope that Mr. Asch will agree with our interpretation of his work, but he should not, of course, be held responsible for it.

involves the comparative judgment of the length of lines; each subject in the group announces his judgment aloud so that all others hear his decision. The task in itself is unambiguous and easy, and the students are able to make the correct choice with monotonous uniformity. The coöperation of all but one of the students is enlisted; they are told that the experiment does not concern perception, as it might appear, but the influence of group processes on the judgment of an individual. They are instructed to make correct judgments in the first two trials, but incorrect judgments in seven of the following trials. After this instruction the naïve subject, unaware of the preceding group meeting, joins the group and takes the last seat left empty for him. Asch describes very vividly the impression an outsider would form of this unsuspecting individual from observing his behavior during the experiment. The outsider would

begin to single out this individual as somehow different from the rest of the group and this impression would grow stronger as the experiment proceeded. After the first one or two disagreements he would note certain changes in the manner and posture of this person. He would see a look a perplexity and bewilderment come over this subject's face at the contradicting judgments of the entire group. Often he becomes more active; he fidgets in his seat and changes the position of his head to look at the lines from different angles. He may turn around and whisper to his neighbor seriously or smile sheepishly. He may suddenly stand up to look more closely at the card. At other times he may become especially quiet and immobile.

Altogether, thirty-one naïve subjects were exposed to this situation, Of these, 58 per cent "yielded" on two or more of the trials and concurred in the incorrect judgment being announced by the instructed subjects.

One of the most interesting parts of the study followed the experimental trials. The experimenter engaged in a discussion with the group by first asking for spontaneous comments; in most cases the unsuspecting subject commented first. The discussion revolved around the question of how the disagreements could be understood. The subject was asked who he thought was right, how confident he was of his judgment, whether in a matter of practical consequence he would stand by his own judgment or that of the group, how he felt an outsider would judge, and so on. At the end of the discussion the subject was informed of the true nature of the experiment.

It is the content of these discussions which provides a simplified psychological model for the process of ideological compliance. No single subject, Asch reports, disregarded the group judgment, regardless of whether or not he finally concurred with the majority. All were puzzled, confused, embarrassed, and often full of self-doubt. Virtually all localized the source of disagreement in themselves. The following verbatim remarks from the discussions illustrate the state of mind in which the subjects found themselves.

Subjects who did not yield to the majority:

"To me it seems I am right but my reason tells me I am wrong because I doubt that so many people could be wrong and I alone right."

"I began to doubt my vision."

"Even though in your mind you know you are right, you wonder why everybody else thinks differently. I was doubting myself and was puzzled."

"Despite everything there was a lurking fear that in some way I did not understand I might be wrong; fear of exposing myself as being inferior in some way. It is more pleasant if one is really in agreement."

"I don't deny that at times I had the feeling to heck with it, I'll go along with the rest."

"[If this were a practical situation] I'd probably take the judgment of the people here. I'd figure my judgment was faulty."

Subject who yielded to the majority:

"I did not want to be apart from the group; I did not want to look like a fool . . . Scientifically speaking I was acting improperly, but my feeling of not wanting to contradict the group overcame me. Then I resolved to answer correctly. Then, when they continued to disagree, I felt an antagonism to the group."

Several subjects explained that they did not answer in accordance with their perception "because this would interfere with the purpose of the experiment." One staunchly maintained that his perception actually changed and that he never responded contrary to what he saw, for "that would have defeated the purpose of the experiment . . . If I am asked to give an honest answer, I'll give an honest answer."

Asch introduced a number of variations into his basic experiment. First, he experimented with two persons only, one a naïve and one an instructed subject. Although under these circumstances the naïve subject did not shift to the incorrect judgment, he nevertheless lost his unquestioned confidence in his perceptions. As one subject said, "I think I was right but I wouldn't say 100 per cent." Asch then experimented with two naïve subjects versus an instructed majority. The compliance effect under these conditions was greatly weakened though not entirely eliminated.

In the next variation, Asch reversed his original experiment, putting in a naïve group only one subject instructed to give the wrong answers. In this variation the first dissenting judgment was greeted with incredulity. On subsequent trials smiles and comments appeared, until the whole group was swept by uncontrollable laughter, which even the experimenter in the full knowledge of the situation could not resist. The discussion in this group yielded comments as: "I felt the person was attempting a stupid joke at which I was annoyed. Then I felt a pitying contempt." "The disagreement seemed either deliberate (dishonest) or else an abnormality in perception . . . I felt annoyed." These "natural" reactions of the majority toward the lone dissenter are, of course, much more extreme than those of Asch's instructed majorities, a fact which suggests that however startling his findings may seem, Asch nevertheless may be understating the full scope of the compliance effect.

Next, Asch instructed one group member to give correct answers in support of the unsuspecting subject for the first half of the experiment but then to join the majority in their incorrect statements. Having first had and then lost a supporter apparently restores the compliance effect to its full force. Later, Asch varied the time sequence by having the supporter appear only toward the end of the experiment. The appearance of a partner reduces the level of yielding but does not eliminate it completely. Asch also experimented with the size of the majority and discovered that a majority of three was sufficient to produce compliance with the same frequency as larger groups.

A further variation of the experiment confronted eleven naïve subjects with nine instructed subjects. Here the emotional response was completely different. Asch describes the behavior of this group

Marie Jahoda and Stuart W. Cook

as follows: "The bulk of the comments were attempts to explain the cleavage in terms of relatively objective factors such as optical ability and misunderstanding of the instructions. The reactions of the naïve group changed from outright repudiation to a more respectful attitude as the ranks of the opposition increased."

Let us now make explicit what these experiments demonstrate. Individuals show an almost universal tendency to seek accord with groups to which they are in some way related. For Asch's subjects this tendency took several forms. Many, though not renouncing their own judgments, struggled throughout to find some way to reconcile their disagreement with the group in order to escape the discomfort which the disagreement evoked. Other subjects disregarded their own correct judgments and reported instead the judgment expressed by the group majority. They arrived at these erroneous responses in different ways: some became uncertain of their judgments and shifted to the group judgment because they had lost self-confidence; some, though remaining convinced of their judgments, shifted because they could no longer bear their isolation from the group; and at least a few found accord with the group by coming actually to see the line lengths in the incorrect manner which the instructed subjects were reporting. We can safely assume that more would have behaved as did these latter individuals had the judgment concerned a less objective and clear-cut issue.[3]

The underlying motive in this tendency to seek accord with the group is our need for social approval by those whom we value — for the feeling that we and our actions are accepted by our families, our social groups, our co-workers, and so forth. It is, of course, of considerable importance to develop this need during the process of socialization in childhood. Upon its presence in sufficient strength depends society's ability to induce in its members that amount of compliance to rules and regulations without which social institutions would quickly deteriorate. As a matter of fact, so strong is this need (and the resulting tendency to seek accord with the group) in all of us that it may justify the reverse of our original question. Instead of asking, "Why compliance?" it may be more to the point to ask, "Why noncompliance?"

[3] Asch indicates that he has actually demonstrated this experimentally, though he has not yet reported on it in detail.

A partial answer to this question is indicated by the Asch experiments. The subjects who did not yield to the majority judgments made statements of the following kind: "I believe what I see . . . inasmuch as I saw the lines I will believe that I am right until I am proved wrong." The confidence in and reliance upon the evidence of one's senses, as it is expressed in these words, is as a rule a characteristic attribute of the act of perceiving. Even beyond the area of perception, of course, self-confidence and self-reliance are fundamental psychological necessities. Without some degree of confidence in one's perceptions, thoughts, and beliefs, it would be impossible to cope with the continuously changing demands of the environment. The degree of such self-confidence varies, of course, from person to person. Where it is strong it represents a potent force counteracting the tendency to comply.

A second answer suggested by the experiments, not unrelated to the first, is that the tendency to compliance may be reduced by insight into the psychological process at work. One subject who had not yielded but who had been so deeply bewildered that he asked, "Is there anything wrong with me?" reacted to the explanation with deep relief: "Now I feel triumphant . . . this is unlike any experience I have had in my life — I'll never forget it as long as I live." The denouement made the yielders, too, realize — though in a less gratifying way — their susceptibility to group opinion. This is indicated by the shame they experienced about having answered as they did. What all the subjects learned in a dramatic way was that even in matters in which they may be completely correct they should expect to experience a strong inclination to shift their positions when majority opinion runs against them.

In addition, as Asch also demonstrated, compliance can be reduced by situational factors. If the dissenter is supported by even one other person, he is much more likely to withstand the tendency to yield to the group than if he stands alone. If the matter at hand were a fist fight, the influence of a partner would be too obvious to mention; it goes without saying that two are stronger than one. But in perceptual judgments and in other intellectual functions the presence of a supporter serves another purpose. It establishes in the subject the realization that he is not "queer," different from everyone else and hence suspect to himself. In other words, such external support helps to restore self-confidence. In keeping with this interpretation of the partner's function are the results obtained when that partner "deserts" the unsuspecting subject half-way through the experiment. Contrary to Asch's first expectation that the subject would have learned by then to oppose a majority and persist in giving correct answers, yielding reached its full force as measured in the basic experiment. The crucial experience here seems to be again the "aloneness" of the individual which undermines self-confidence.

While pointing up these principles which apply more or less uniformly to all subjects, the Asch experiments also make it clear that people differ from one another in their readiness to comply under identical circumstances. From one point of view this is the most suggestive of Asch's discoveries, since it holds out the hope of finding the factors accounting for such differences. Once understood, such factors might be utilized in efforts to reduce compliance tendencies in areas of life where they are undesirable. Unfortunately, Asch himself has so far said little on this point. We shall return to it later in our discussion.

AN ANALYSIS OF CURRENT DEVELOPMENTS

As we examine current phenomena of ideological compliance, in terms of the principles demonstrated by the Asch experiments, we should remember that these experiments concern a situation in which the conflict between the individual's own judgment and the verdict of the group is clear and open. Asch himself believes that "the majority effect grows stronger as the situation diminishes in clarity." When social or political issues are involved rather than the judgment of length of lines, most people will be less sure of their positions than were Asch's subjects, and hence even more ready to yield to group influence. This is apparently what we find on the part of those ready compliers both in totalitarian nations and among federal employees in Washington, neither of whom have been persecuted for the beliefs they hold or the practices they follow. Both groups, in their desire to escape the disapproval of their neighbors, supervisors, or co-workers, adopt those ideas and actions for which, they believe, approval will be forthcoming.

Among the professional employees of government whom we interviewed in Washington, this conformity, as we noted earlier, involved changes in choice of reading matter, in the type of book or magazine purchased, in the type of organization affiliated with, in topics discussed and in views expressed. As was the case with the subjects in the Asch experiments, the individuals reporting these changes have come to them in different ways. Some report that they have become uncertain and confused about their original value system. One, for example, said: "I have changed. My values in the past were democracy, peace, socialism in that order. Now I am all confused about socialism. Maybe it is wrong for this country. I don't know any more." Others indicate that while their values may not be affected they are changing their behavior because of possible criticism from their friends and neighbors: "At one time I might have gone to unsegregated places without thinking but now I am much more aware of the political import of such an action; and I am much more conscious than before of what my neighbors might think about the people I entertain and the books on my shelf." Another said: "Why lead with your chin? If things are definitely labelled I see no point in getting involved with them. If Communists like apple pie and I do, I see no reason why I should stop eating it. But I would." Still others report that they have actually changed: "I feel that in the last two years there have been changes in my thinking about with whom to associate and what to read. This hasn't been deliberate but when I look back it is noticeable to me."

Another development encountered in the Washington interviews can also be understood by reference to our model. Although a number of the people we interviewed had not modified their views in response to the conformity pressures which they experienced, they usually gave evidence of the discomfort, tension, low morale, and so on, reported by the nonyielders in the Asch experiments. "I'd take any job outside," one of them said, "though my conscience is clear" — implying that the atmosphere of suspicion had taken the satisfaction out of his work. Another one said: "When people talk of things which might have political connotations, they have a tendency to look around to make sure they are not overheard. I've been amazed and shocked to see myself do this."

In these interviews it is the *degree* of change in compliance during the last few years which raises the most challenging problem. The tolerated range of deviant behavior has been narrowed; compliance has become the rule on an increasing number of concrete matters. Similar changes have been reported, of course, among other segments of the population; for example, among college students, news commentators, teachers. Nor is the phenomenon a new one; at other points in our history we have seen parallel upswings in ideological compliance, sometimes of a political and sometimes of a religious nature.

A change in the degree of ideological compliance can be the result of an increase in conformity pressures, on the one hand, and of an increase in people's readiness to comply, on the other. In actual fact these two elements often cannot be separated. For to the extent that increased pressure produces greater compliance, those who observe this response in others will experience it as a form of conformity pressure. In no totalitarian country is it necessary to have the secret police search every household. If the neighbors of one whose premises have been searched note his heightened fear and extreme compliance, they will be affected by this almost as if they themselves had been exposed to the harrowing experience. In the following discussion we shall attempt to analyze several social and psychological factors which affect conformity pressures and compliance tendencies at the present time.

The Experience of External Threat

A threat to the group from some outside source is generally regarded by either a group majority or the power figures in it as requiring an intensification of pressures on deviant members to conform. In response to the threat the group moves to insure greater unity for fear that deviant or marginal members may weaken its capacity to meet the potential danger. This in turn leads to closer scrutiny of such members and to less tolerance of atypical ideas and behavior. In other words, the external threat leads to a heightened concern with its possible internal counterpart.

The fear of an enemy from within is a permanent concern of totalitarian regimes. The methods they have developed to protect themselves against this potential danger implement point for point the principles which Asch has shown to operate in producing compliance. Individual independence and self-reliance counteract, as we have seen, the universal tendency to comply. They have been eradicated in totalitarian countries; the party line replaces individual judgments. Even the scientist may be told what the outcome of his reaserch has to be. Similarly, since the existence of a supporter for deviant views also counteracts compliance, all opposition is eliminated. Not even the anonymous supporter is permitted; all "secret" elections result in unanimous expressions of compliance. The failure of a supporter, as we know, also weakens resistance. The self-accusing confessions at purge trials highlight such loss of support, leaving the potential dissenter in the population at large with a heightened need to comply.

The recent purges in Czechoslovakia provide a striking illustration of the use of these methods. In *Commentary*, January 1953, Peter Meyer describes Rudolf Slansky's answer to the question why he committed his crimes:

> In reply to this question Slansky gave an outline of his origins and political past. He said he came from a bourgeois family of a rich village merchant and this had influenced his "personal traits and character." In 1921 he joined the Communist party still burdened with "petty bourgieos opinions, which I never abandoned. This prevented me from becoming a real Communist. Therefore I did not act as a Communist, and I did not fulfill honorably the duties arising from my membership in the Communist party."

Those who had regarded Slansky as their supporter now know from his own words that he has endorsed the party's judgment without qualification, that he was a treacherous supporter even in the past. They will be less likely in the future to dissent from whatever the party line prescribes.

Under the impact of possible external danger a democracy, too, becomes increasingly concerned about potential enemies from within. The present international situation which is experienced as a threat to our national security is undoubtedly one of the major factors responsible for extended conformity requirements in this country. Various steps have been taken by the government to improve our defenses against an external enemy should this become necessary. Other measures are directed at the identification and neutralization of possible internal enemies. The essential difficulty in these protective measures is the vagueness of the criteria for such identification. Is every Communist a potential spy or saboteur? Is every student

of Marx a danger to the security of the country? Is every member
of an organization which includes Communists to be distrusted?
How should the internal enemy be identified? By oath? By his reading habits? By views which are shared by Communists? By his
associations?

The answers to these questions are not easy. The Federal Bureau
of Investigation collects all information which might possibly be
relevant to the appraisal of individual cases. Since government
investigators are asking questions about membership in all kinds
of organizations, about political views and opinions on various social
problems, about interests and reading matter and other items of the
kind, the impression has been created that to credit somebody with
an active organizational life, with unorthodox or even only out-
spoken views on public affairs, with extensive reading habits, and
so forth, is a disservice to him. The thought naturally arises that if
such things are asked about, in the eyes of the government they
must be questionable. There is only a brief step from feeling that it
is not wise to describe one's friends in this way to the conclusion that
it is not wise to have such activities to one's own credit.

A variety of self-appointed individuals and groups have taken the
next step in the process. Though having no official connection with
the machinery through which national security is protected, and
perhaps not always motivated by a concern for national security,
they publicly call attention to the records of individuals who deviate
from their standards of acceptable behavior. What they emphasize
is quite similar to the areas checked upon by official investigators;
the important difference is that, whereas the official investigations are
confidential, the unofficial ones are broadcast as widely as possible.
Such publicity makes the pressure to conform, of course, much
stronger. One is in constant danger of public exposure as an individual associated with activities about which questions are asked.

The final increment is supplied by employers. Advertisers, business-
men, school authorities, movie producers, all hesitate to hire or retain
employees thus singled out, since this may offend some client,
customer, or patron. To the social pressure to conform is now added
the force of economic necessity.

Thus, as an unintended consequence of official efforts to identify
an internal enemy, the notion gets abroad that all matters on which

questions are asked are no longer tolerated. Through this chain of events the experience of an external threat leads to increased conformity requirements.

LACK OF KNOWLEDGE AS A FACTOR IN INAPPROPRIATE
REACTIONS TO THREAT

We know from observation and experiment that the experience of threat can give rise to very diverse responses: it can lead either to an organization of all resources for meeting the danger, or — and this seems to be the case when the threat is experienced as extraordinarily great — to a disorganized, haphazard, panicky, and self-defeating reaction. Anyone who has driven a car toward a group of hens on a country road is familiar with inappropriate reaction to threat. The hens lose their heads, first figuratively and because of this, often literally. In human beings the sense of extreme danger can create a similar lack of appropriateness in response, as the behavior in panics amply demonstrates. Current compliance behavior as we have described it so far represents an equally inappropriate reaction to the problem of safeguarding our national security.

One factor which encourages ideological compliance in the present situation is, undoubtedly, a lack of knowledge on the part of many people about the basic issues involved. Those who know little or nothing about the Communist Party, about the differences between democracy and Communism, about the practice of espionage and how to meet it, and so on, are prone to develop an oversimplified approach to the matter wherein all spies, dissenters, and deviants are merged into one undifferentiated category. In such an oversimplification the distinction which Sidney Hook makes between conspiracy and heresy is lost, as is also the differentiation between sensitive and nonsensitive jobs in the government. Likewise, the actual organizational separation between the Russian espionage apparatus and other activities of the Communist Party is overlooked, despite the testimony of Whittaker Chambers, who, in his eloquent description of his lonely life as a conspirator far from comforting contacts and friendships with party members, makes it abundantly clear that the majority of party members are completely unaware of the activities of the secret apparatus.

Perhaps the most glaring example of conformity behavior emerging from, but in function unrelated to, our increased concern for national security is provided by the widespread approval for the idea of administering a loyalty oath to all academic personnel. The relation between such behavior and knowledge of the issues involved is suggested by the responses of the federal employees whom we interviewed in Washington. When we asked them about their views on this matter, it emerged that those who had previously given evidence of their grasp of the problem, and especially of Communist doctrines and methods, tended to reject the idea of an oath as a meaningless gesture. "The Communists would be the first to sign it," one said; and another, "Do you think a spy will give himself away because he is under oath?" Those who were ignorant of the basic characteristics of Communism and democracy — and some of them prided themselves that they had never taken an interest in political ideas — tended to favor an oath. "We have to do everything we can against the Communists," was the justification of one who recommended an oath.

If such oversimplification is in fact as widespread as it appears, we may face the prospect of ideological compliance on a far greater scale than is now the case. Asch states that "the majority effect grows stronger as the situation diminishes in clarity." And he adds: "Concurrently . . . the disturbance of the subjects and the conflict-quality of the situation decrease markedly. The majority achieves its most pronounced effect when it acts most painlessly." Inherent in his remarks is not only a warning but a partial remedy. If lack of clarity about the issues permits more ready compliance, then greater clarity should have the opposite effect. What this implies is a need for an intensive educational campaign directed at developing such clarity in as many people as possible. This is not the place to outline in detail the nature of such a campaign; it must be sufficient to indicate our conviction that information adequate to the purpose can be communicated effectively through mass media and our expectation that as a result oversimplification should give way to a more differentiated view of the complex issues involved.

Personal Characteristics Affecting Resistance to Compliance

Even when faced with exactly the same objective situation, different people meet conformity pressures in different ways. In Asch's experiments some subjects yielded quickly to the majority, others only after longer periods of resistance, and still others not at all. In the loyalty oath controversy at the University of California, members of the faculty who initially opposed the proposed oath held out for differing amounts of time and showed generally wide variation in their resistance effort.

Comprehension of the compliance process would be considerably enhanced if the personal characteristics responsible for such individual differences were better understood. Of prime importance, undoubtedly, are characteristics associated with personality organization. Recent research has begun to focus on the relationship between conformity behavior and the so-called "authoritarian character structure." In a complementary approach, Nevitt Sanford has prepared a detailed analysis (as yet unpublished) of the role of personality factors in the California controversy. To review this work would take us beyond the limits set for this paper; the promise it holds for explaining the differences in reactions among people under conformity pressure should be emphasized, however, at least in passing.

A second significant group of characteristics are the individual's attitudes and values; particularly the values placed on independence of thought and defense of one's convictions, however unpopular. For some, such concepts have little meaning — if they are familiar at all. Others value them highly. That they play a role in the phenomenon we are analyzing was illustrated in our Washington interviews by comments such as, "You have to make a stand for the principle," and, "People should not give in to hysteria; everyone has the right to think what he wants, to read what he wants and to associate with whom he wants."

In addition to personality structure, the most likely origin of individual differences in such values is the training emphasis in home and school. Available for emphasis are several key traditions in American history which bear a close relation to values of independence and self-reliance in thought. When effectively taught, these traditions should lead to the acquisition of values which would heighten resistance to ideological compliance. It may well be that this opportunity has not been utilized to full advantage in recent years. Should this be true, correction of it through appropriate educational provisions would not be difficult.

It may be the case, on the other hand, that the fault lies not in the failure to develop these values in children but in the failure to keep them alive in adults. The two possibilities are not, of course, mutually exclusive; any effective attempt to strengthen values opposed to ideological compliance would require their reinforcement in adults as well as the intensification of their development in children. What is required to achieve such reinforcement is that when individuals take a stand against efforts to require conformity in political life or when they defend others for so doing, they should receive some public commendation for their acts; i.e., their actions motivated by these values should be rewarded. Not only is this most often not the case, but, in contrast, in the current atmosphere of increased conformity, the reverse, in the form of public disapproval, must often be expected. Such a reward would, of course, be less important for the person receiving it than for the community awarding it. Hence it would be most effective if given on a national scale, in a manner comparable to annual community awards for other achievements, to the person who has contributed most to strengthening the ideals of freedom of thought and independence of action in political life.

Whatever the specific step taken, some action in this direction seems indicated. Unless they are continuously revitalized, our traditional values opposed to ideological compliance might cease being a barrier to the acceptance of a totalitarian orientation in political behavior.

Situational Factors Affecting Resistance to Compliance

The existence of organizations dedicated to the preservation of civil liberties and academic freedom testifies to the general appreciation of the role of group support in resisting conformity pressures. The significance of such support was also noted by our Washington respondents, several of whom pointed to the crucial influence of support — or lack of it — from others. One said: "In my place I could fight an unjustified accusation, because I have confidence in the head of the department; he would support me. In other departments I would not be so sure." Some went so far as to say that unless they were sure of some support they would much rather leave their positions immediately than risk a fight which was lost before it started.

Additional understanding of these observations is provided by Asch's research. His findings made clear the *psychological significance* of social support. When opposing a unanimous majority, whether small or large, one is led to question the adequacy of one's own mental processes. The availability of even a single supporter restores self-confidence.

If these findings are generalizable, they suggest, for example, that the first protest voiced in the California incident was probably the crucial one, since it demonstrated to each potential dissenter that he had at least one ally. Conversely, they make clear the unfortunate error involved in the many instances in which potential resistance to compliance has been abandoned in the conviction that one objection would make no difference.

Our Washington study suggests that the manner in which such resistance is expressed is of crucial importance. Even those most out of sympathy with increasing restrictions may unwittingly contribute to the impression of widespread compliance by frequent criticism of the instances of compliance which come to their attention. In this way, they make known the failure to resist rather than the instances of successful resistance. This could be altered by the initiation of a program of public information devoted to the advertising of instances of successful resistance to conformity pressures. Hopefully, this information might constitute a source of social support to those who find none in their immediate environments.

A frequently described feature of totalitarian regimes upon which these research findings throw light is the practice of totally isolating a prisoner from whom a confession is being sought. This isolation makes it possible both to present a unanimous majority against the victim and to convince him that his former sources of social support no longer hold their earlier convictions — in short, to produce the impression that he stands, like Asch's subjects, entirely alone against the otherwise unanimous group.

Insight into the Compliance Process

Modern psychology has demonstrated that control often may be gained over one's behavior if the events leading to it are brought into consciousness. With this in mind, two related findings reported by Asch seem especially suggestive. The first of these has to do with the insight the subjects appeared to gain into the effects of group pressure during the discussion following the experiment. The second deals with the fact that subjects working with tasks less objective than perceptual judgments are less aware of a conflict between their positions and those of the majority and modify their own judgments more rapidly in the direction of the majority.

These findings suggest that the compliance process is often unconscious in nature. The question this raises, of course, concerns the possibility of weakening compliance tendencies through educational experiences aimed at developing insight into the process. Such a topic might be fitted into the "self-understanding" or "mental hygiene" courses currently offered in many high schools.

A NOTE ON THE OUTLOOK

In concluding this discussion of ideological compliance as a social-psychological process, it might well be asked whether or not the actions suggested at various points in the analysis hold sufficient promise to make it worth while to put them into effect. It is generally agreed that international tension is at the root of our current alarm about national loyalty and deviant political behavior. We have supported this position by identifying the experience of external threat to national security as the major source of the increase in conformity pressures. If this is true, does it not follow that little can be done to affect the course of events until the threat has passed and the tension been alleviated? Until that time comes — if it ever does — will not any less potent factor be quickly engulfed by the accelerating avalanche of conformity pressures and compliance?

Although in agreement with the diagnosis of the cause of the trouble, we cannot accept its implication that everything else is without significant effect. Our study of the problem has convinced us that forces are available which, if harnessed, would noticeably reduce community pressures for ideological conformity and noticeably increase individual resistance to ideological compliance. We have no way of assessing, of course, whether and to what extent these forces will be utilized. We are clear, however, that the outcome of this most recent engagement in the history of the struggle between conformity pressures and freedom of thought cannot be said to be already determined and beyond the influence of efforts as yet unmade. The importance of making such efforts lies in their goal: to demonstrate at home and abroad that, even in an atmosphere of danger, democracy preserves those freedoms which totalitarianism in its fear stamps out.

DISCUSSION

Mr. Leo Lowenthal: It is important that we not become the victims of a monolithic conception of the totalitarian ideology. There are large differences between the Stalinist and the Hitlerite ideologies, one of them being the fact that the former has a universal mailing list, so to speak, whereas the latter had only a very restricted one. Marxism and its later variants appeals to everyone; Nazis appealed only to the *Herrenvolk*. This means that it is possible for a Zionist to become a Communist, whereas it was impossible for a Jew to become a Nazi. In practice, this kind of conversion was and is very difficult within the Soviet Union, but its presence in the ideology strengthens the export value of that ideology. The Soviets have a free ride on the universalistic elements in the Judeo-Christian tradition; the Nazis were imprisoned in a paganistic particularism.

With respect to the specifically psychological aspects of totalitarianism, I submit that we must accept as demonstrably feasible the restructuring of human perception. This is achieved by the totalitarian regime to such a degree that it is almost a biological change in the sensory apparatus. People are made to perceive Jews as insects, capitalists as grossly fat men, and so forth.

Art in a totalitarian society becomes a part of the propaganda techniques, and is particularly useful in restructuring perceptions. In Western society since the Renaissance, the artist and the author have depicted the marginal members of society — the criminal, the prostitute, the *Lumpenproletariat* in general — as spokesmen for his own individualistic protests. No totalitarian regime can permit this. Totalitarian art has the function which Inkeles has summarized in his quotation from Zhdanov: "to show our people . . . as they shall be tomorrow." The marginal groups which exist in all complex societies may not even be touched upon.

Mr. Philipp Frank: I speak to Mr. Bauer's paper. I agree fully with his observation that the Russian regime has two attitudes toward science, one of which is technological and the other ideological. But

I would add that this is true of the situation of science in all societies, not just in the totalitarian ones. The degree of relative significance of the two aspects varies, but both are always present. Some features of scientific findings cannot be ignored — if a government wishes to build armaments it cannot repeal the laws of mechanics whatever their ideological implications may be. In other areas, science is not yet technologically so useful, and it is furthermore ideologically dangerous. This is why the totalitarians must oppress the social sciences.

I think one would find that the working scientist in the Soviet Union and in Nazi Germany pays the minimum necessary lip service to the official ideology, for he finds the stability of the regime to be socially useful. This attitude is not much different from that of Western scientists to the established churches and their philosophies. They are irrelevant to his work but he need not and usually does not actively oppose them.

Mr. Sigmund Neumann: My remarks this afternoon are addressed to the problems which have appeared in all of our sessions so far.

We face throughout our discussion the difficulty of definition. So far three viewpoints on the nature of totalitarianism have been represented: (1) What are its origins? (2) How does it function? (3) What are its effects on people? Any one-track definition which answers only one of these questions will lead us astray, and will contain dangerous implications for policy formulation.

I think we should view the origin of totalitarianism as a total crisis, in the medical sense of "crisis." This is not necessarily death's door, but it is a definitely dangerous clinical turning point. This is true on three levels, the international, the national, and the individual, and all three are closely interrelated. In analyzing the crisis on the last of these levels, I would spotlight late adolescence and early adulthood as the socially crucial formative period. An investigation along these lines might give us some clues to the differences between the Nazi and Soviet types of totalitarianism. The Nazi leaders were at this stage in life during the crisis of the First World War and its immediate aftermath, whereas the founders of the Soviet regime were young men in the old prewar, pre-crisis Tsarist society. We now have in Russia the first second-generation totalitarian regime that the world has seen — a regime most of whose leaders were young men during the Revolution and the early years of the Soviet system. This change may yield striking alterations in the ideology and in the institutional manifold.

Mr. Paul Kecskemeti: I wish to add some comments to two points in Mr. Bauer's paper. He has insisted upon the high appraisal of ideas in the Soviet ideology, and has asserted that this pro-intellectual bias in the Soviet ideology sharply differentiates it from its Nazi counterpart. I concede the validity of both conclusions as first approximations, but I wonder whether the Marxist ideology does not tend more and more, as time wears on, to approach by a different route an anti-intellectualism whose results are closely similar to those under the Nazi regime.

Marxism, unlike Nazism, purports to be a superscience. Hitler never pretended that National Socialism was a superscience from which all other scientific truth might be derived. The chief link between the Nazi ideology and science was the *Volksgemeinschaft* component of the former, to which all scientists were required to accommodate. It was specifically this loyalty of all wills to the community which epitomized the anti-intellectual, anti-rationalistic elements in Nazism.

Both ideologies, however, contain a rejection of objectivism, or as the Soviets term it, of "formalism." Because of the fact that independent scientific research is an activity disruptive of social unity, a totalitarian regime finds it necessary to insist that scientific labor shall be orientated as the ideology demands. The restrictions imposed on science in this manner must be greater in the Soviet Union than they were in Nazi Germany simply because the Marxist ideology is presented as a rather simple superscience to which complete conformity is exacted.

Mr. Adam Ulam: I would argue that Marxism is not important in Soviet Russia as a system of ideas. It is rather a label for those ideas which the immediate power situation demands and which the regime must justify. The preëminence of the power problem goes back at least to Lenin's *What Is to be Done?*, which exploited Marx's ideas in order to develop a tactic for seizing power. The same kind of exploitation has been going on ever since. Both lowering wages and raising wages may be described at different times as Marxist or un-Marxist, but Bukharin's "Enrichissez-vous" is permanently heretical.

We can conclude, I think, that theoretical Marxism is no longer an independent force in the Soviet ideology. It has become a frame of reference and a conveniently legitimate stockpile of ideas, but it is in no sense a binding bible.

Mr. Geroid Robinson: We have heard two characterizations of the Soviet ideology: That it is one which pretends to be completely scientific, and that it is essentially anti-intellectual and anti-rational. I should agree with those who hold the latter position. This dominant strain appeared very strongly, for example, in Lenin's *Materialism and Empirio-Criticism*, where he attacks the philosophical position of some of the greatest scientists of his time, and says flatly that ideas and hypotheses which conflict with the Leninist interpretation of Marx are simply wrong.

I should like to submit to Mr. Bauer and the other students of the psychological side of totalitarianism a problem which has long intrigued me. Is it possible to distinguish in the Soviet manipulations of human personalities an attempt to create two types, which we might call the "Soviet leader" on the one hand, and the "Soviet follower" on the other? If there is such a differentiation, how is this reconciled with the ultimate "withering away of the state" which the Soviet ideology promises? Is there any evidence of attempts in the Soviet Union to mold people so that they will be at home, in the future, in a free, stateless society? If there is any such attempt, how can they do this and still create the kind of personalities consonant with their present totalitarian, state-ridden society?

Mr. George Denicke: Some of the psychological features of totalitarian movements are fully visible to the naked eye. I can remember remarking the difference between German Catholic and Socialist youth groups, on the one hand, and the Nazi and Communist youth groups on the other hand in the late 1920's. The former groups were made up of strikingly more relaxed and more open sorts of young people; in the Nazi and Communist groups one could not miss a completely different disciplined aggressiveness.

I should like to address a query to those who study the roots of the desire to comply. The Asch experiments, it seems to me, are ambiguous, for they do not distinguish between "wanting to agree" and "wanting to belong." I shall not try to define the distinction, but I can illustrate it: the French are well known for their sociability (that is, they wish to belong), but they are also noted for their nonconformity (they also want to disagree).

Mr. Jerzy Gliksman: We must, I think, distinguish both the similarities and the differences between the Nazi and the Soviet ideologies and their effects on the psychology of those who live in the two systems. One important difference has already been touched upon by Mr. Lowenthal: the Nazi ideology had a restricted appeal, whereas the Communist one is universalistic.

On the other hand, we must realize that Nazism at one time had a majority of the German people behind it, something that has never been true of Communism in the Soviet Union. We should also understand that compliance can be of several sorts, something which Miss Jahoda seems to recognize when she advances evidence drawn from college students in one set of experiments and from federal civil servants in a second set of observations. Surely the "compliance" exacted in the second case is different, if only in its sanctions, from that of the first situation.

The minority nature of Communism means that compliance must be exacted, whereas for the majority Nazis it could be evoked. We have found from the defectees interviewed in Western Europe that while in the USSR they had rendered external conformity by means of lip service; it was pretense, not the genuine thing. There is clearly a sense of superiority which one can wring from adequate external compliance coupled with internal resistance to it; one feels superior to those who demand the conformity ("*Ketman*"). I should say that there is more internal psychological resistance to compliance in the Soviet Union than there was in Nazi Germany.

Mr. Paul Lehman: Perhaps it might be worth while to state what we are for, as well as examining what we are against. I submit that our objective is twofold: a society which commands the loyalties of its members without reducing them to subservience but rather guaranteeing them creativity, and a society which prevents loneliness and "floating" by giving its members a sense of responsible belonging. The totalitarian ideologies have succeeded by exploiting grave weaknesses at precisely these two points.

Religion, I believe, can help us here, primarily by providing a meaningful commitment combined with responsible self-criticism. Cochrane, in his *Christianity and Classical Culture*, has pointed out that classical civilization declined because it could not furnish a critical security. Stoicism made men the prisoners of insecurity, for it lacked the conception of Providence. Christianity, by means of the doctrine of Grace, made the insecurity creative.

Christianity has certainly molded minds which are uncritically subservient to dogma, but it has also yielded the type of ideology I am trying to describe. Tillich has argued that this is the kernel of Protestantism — individual commitment together with individual criticism and responsibility.

Mr. Franklin Littell: It has been argued, among others by Simon in a *Fortune* article in 1940, that totalitarian youth movements failed in the United States in the 1930's, for the reason that American youth movements typically try to close gaps between the generations, whereas totalitarian youth organizations attempt to exploit them. It seems to me that this is certainly true of Germany and the Nazis. The authoritarian structure of the German family, and the "two-track" German school system, had the effect of delaying adolescence for many young Germans. Thus it was possible for the Nazis to mobilize the feelings of resentful dependence and to undertake a "politics of adolescence" fiendishly adept at manipulating those age-groups. This is evidently also a mark of East Zone Communist strategy for using youth.

Mr. David Riesman: Again I would urge the study of small groups in the non-totalitarian countries as a means of learning more about the psychological aspects of mobilizing the young. In the United States today, for example, the closest psychological equivalents for the Stalinist youth groups of the thirties are the contemporary Zionist youth movements. These young people go far beyond the rather moderate Zionism of their parents, partly to distinguish themselves from their contemporaries and partly to excel their parents.

The general setting is also subject to change, of course. At the present time, the model school boy in this country is no longer the Tom Sawyer, Peck's-bad-boy-type, but rather the conformist who gets along well with teacher. A part of the background of this shift is the shift in teacher's conception of her own role. Nowadays she wants to be loved more than she wants to be successful in teaching Latin. Thus, student groups which want to establish their deviance from the "official" school culture may be pushed toward ideological extremes — quite a different situation from that of a generation ago.

Miss Arendt: I think that Mr. Bauer's assertion that there are close similarities between Leninism and pragmatism, that both act on the assumption that "we can know reality only by acting on it," is very much to the point. However, I would disagree that the same is true for the later totalitarian development. Totalitarianism is distinguished from pragmatism in that it no longer believes that reality as such can teach anything and, consequently, has lost the earlier Marxist respect for facts. Pragmatism, even in the Leninist version, still assumes with the tradition of occidental thought that reality reveals truth to man, although it asserts that not contemplation, but action is the proper truth-revealing attitude. The totalitarian attitude to reality assumes that I can change reality at any moment beyond recognition, that facts can be manipulated and that experience is irrelevant. For Stalin, Lenin's repeated admonition about the "stubbornness of facts" no longer makes sense. His attitude can best be expressed not by the early nihilistic "everything is permitted," but by the belief that "everything is possible." This belief rests on the assumption that everything that *is*, is in constant movement and that dialectic materialism has discovered the law of this movement. There is no longer any stable reality which could be "known," or which anybody would care to know. Pragmatism always assumes the validity of experience and "acts" accordingly; totalitarianism assumes only the validity of the law of a moving History of Nature. Whoever acts in accordance with this law no longer needs particular experiences.

The Asch experiments, upon which Miss Jahoda reports, are quite significant; but they do not appear to me to test ideological compliance. They rather show that people do not trust their sensory impressions when in a minority of one. And in this, I think, they are right. Perceptual and all other sensory impressions are constantly checked by each of us against those of our fellows. We need this control precisely because sensory experience is so particular that for smell and taste experiences we do not even have adequate words to share and communicate them. What we usually call "common sense" is a sort of sixth sense through which all our other sense experiences are made "common," fitted into the world which we have in common. In other words, if my sense experiences are contradicted by all other people present, I can conclude only that either something is wrong with my eyes or that I am insane.

The experiments, even though I do not think they prove what they intended to prove, have a certain bearing on political problems. They show indeed very clearly that people who are completely isolated, for instance in solitary confinement, not only lose their confidence in what they know and believe, but cannot even trust their senses any longer. Ideological compliance, I think, is difficult to test. It would be interesting to know how people behave in the same situation if some axiomatically accepted proposition like "two plus two equals four" is disputed. The difficulty is that in all such situations there is the possibility of a *reservatio mentalis* which can hardly be broken down in a short experiment, although I am inclined to conclude from our experiences with Nazi and Bolshevik domination that the mere pretense of compliance and the *reservatio mentalis* which goes with it cannot be kept indefinitely.

Mr. Bauer: There is much less difference of opinion between myself and those who commented on my paper than might at first sight appear. What I wanted to do was to scotch two contrary oversimplifications: first, that one need only read Marx and he will know how the men in the Kremlin think, and second, that the men in the Kremlin aren't Marxists at all — it's just a façade. The truth lies between these extremes.

The Soviet ideology clearly has a deep respect for ideas, including technologically necessary new ideas which postdate the Marxian classics. Thus mathematical logic has been vindicated in the USSR, for the reason that they can't build computing machines without it. But, together with this care for ideas, the Soviet ideology teaches that orthodoxy must be maintained. Thus it is anti-intellectualistic while simultaneously displaying a great involvement with ideas. On both counts, I think, Leninism is more insistent than Nazism ever was.

Mr. Erik Erikson: In the rise and the maintenance of totalitarian regimes, one most important consideration is the matter of what happens to which age-group at what time. So far as the young people are concerned, the distinguishing feature of totalitarianism is the spectacle of youth in uniform and on the march. In these systems the heaviest of stress is placed upon identity through conformity, and in all of them the parents come to play a diminishing role in the training of the young. Youth goes through a great crisis in life and looks for leadership outside of the family, and though they usually are not directly affected by political reality as such, their anxieties and enthusiasms can be manipulated by skillful political leaders.

Let me submit a further word on compliance and the Asch experiments. Miss Arendt is perfectly correct in insisting that they test only one's trust in his own sense impressions, but — and this is the important point — they test that trust in a context in which one has no reason to mistrust the veracity of one's fellows. This latter condition links such tests of trust in the senses up with social trust.

On the matter of guilt, I would suggest a distinction between pure "guilt," which requires a more or less autonomous conscience, and a sense of "shame," which does not. There is yet a further degree, which we might call "cynical mistrust," in which all professed standards become meaningless and irrelevant, with a gnawing feeling that one should be able to trust. This last I think pervaded much of German youth after the war.

There is an important psychological problem here: How far down the scale of guilt and then shame and then cynicism does a totalitarian regime dare to push human beings? When does it get to the point where cynical conformity corrodes effective loyalty?

Miss Else Frenkel-Brunswik: No one would argue that the Nazi and Soviet ideologies are identical, but perhaps their differences have been overemphasized this afternoon. On the point of anti-intellectualism, we can certainly note that both opposed free inquiry in the social sciences, and both were scornful of the relativity theories of Professor Einstein. In effect, both ideologies are "metaphysically materialistic," though this is more formally worked out in the Soviet case.

Miss Marie Jahoda: We recognize the distinction between perceptual and ideological compliance which Miss Arendt has pointed out. Experiments on the latter are now in progress. Perhaps we will find that for the great mass of a population there is no significant difference, for the reason that many people, having no inner convictions of their own, comply ideologically in much the same way as all of us comply perceptually.

PART FIVE

Totalitarianism and Intellectual Life

■

12. Science under Soviet Totalitarianism

H. J. MULLER

The politicians of the Iron Curtain countries, in their blighting attacks on several important branches of science, and especially in their complete destruction of genetics, have provided an amazing object lesson of the disaster which can befall science even in our time when one small group of men, arrogating to themselves all power, become convinced of the superiority of their judgments in all directions and, with the aid of modern physical and social techniques, succeed in subjecting all human activities, including science, to their own dictation.

The Communists would like the world to believe that these attacks are controversies within the walls of the house of science itself, but this is far from the truth. Considering the most instructive attack, that on genetics, it should be noted that neither Lysenko nor Present were really scientists, nor could they get any real scientists to join them until after the Communist Party made its official decision in their favor. These two men and their subordinates simply furnished a false scientific "front" for the Party, like the fronts it has in many other fields. They served as its tools, and although they were the best tools to be had for the purpose they were nevertheless such poor ones that many scientists could not take them seriously until too late — not that it would in the end have helped the scientists to have done so.

Of course Lysenko was genuinely opposed to genetics, or thought he was, although since he did not understand it he did not know what he was opposed to. It is true that he had attended an agricultural school, had considerable experience in raising plants, and had

even brought into use some methods of treatment, not original with
him, which under certain circumstances increase the yield. It was
this which furnished the basis for the build-up which the Party en-
gineered for him. But Lysenko's discussions of matters of theory are
on a puerile level. They would have gained no attention among scientists had Lysenko not gotten an artificial build-up and been given
the aid of Present. They can fool only the uninitiated in the subject,
and the fact that they were endorsed by the Party is a striking demonstration of how far away the Communist politicians are from the
influence of scientists and of scientific ways of thinking, despite their
claim that their own theories are scientific.

Lysenko and Present are a curious pair — Lysenko, the ignorant
fanatic, nursing a peculiar psychosis which makes him afraid of
water, and possessed of the fiery, irrational demagoguery of a Hitler;
Present, the suave professor of dialectical materialism, a scheming
sophist insincerely weaving a sticky web of high-sounding words
to confuse the unsophisticated, and to ensnare the scientist for de-
livery to the politician.

Present's conscious insincerity is well illustrated in an incident that
occurred during the debate on genetics held in December 1936 in
a huge auditorium in Moscow. He had asserted, in opposition to my
claim that the direction of mutation is in general independent of
the type of environment, that in certain experiments with wheat it
had been possible by means of a special treatment to cause 100 per
cent of the resulting offspring to contain a desired type of mutation.
When I challenged him to give the details of this, which he did only
reluctantly by being forced to admit one point after another, it
turned out that what had really happened was as follows: A great
lot of seed of spring wheat had been planted in a field under the conditions for winter wheat. As would be expected, nearly all died. One
seedling, however, managed to come through (as might also be
expected because of the natural variability of seeds, especially of
those used in the inaccurately conducted work of the Lysenko-ists).
And this one seedling transmitted to its offspring its ability to grow
under these same conditions (as might also be expected if it were a
hereditary deviant). Now the figure of one deviant, out of a total
population of one offspring, is of course 100 per cent. Therefore 100
per cent of the offspring had been mutants of the desired type, pro-

duced, according to Present, by the special treatment. No attention was called to the possibility that only this type could have survived, under the given conditions, and that there was therefore no evidence of any relation between the treatment and the origination of the variation. But all this, when pointed out, was lightly passed over by Present with a sneer, and the Party authorities present apparently thought no worse of him for it.

The Party, being in 1935 relatively new to this game of attacking science, proceeded with its assault gradually, and with much circumspection. With a persistent singleness of purpose, drawn out over some thirteen years, from 1935 to 1948, it pursued the policy of softening up the scientists' prestige, morale, and physical strength, by means of propaganda on all levels, staged public controversies, demotions, dismissals, dissolution of laboratories, alterations in teaching and research programs, exilings, and mysterious deaths. At the same time the Lysenko group were more and more pushed forward, and given the places of the geneticists. When at last, in 1948, all the geneticists of well-established reputations had been removed, and there were left to defend it only relative youngsters, weaklings, political compromisers, and some good biologists whose primary field was not genetics, the final controversy was staged, before a well-packed audience, and it was at last announced that the Party had officially decided in favor of Lysenko.

After that, there remained only the work of "cleaning up," of final eradication of all traces of genetic ideas from the curricula of schools, universities, and medical colleges; from textbooks, journals, and all publications, and from theoretical research centers and agricultural establishments. Not only did genetics as such have to be removed, but, since it is a very basic subject, having important bearings on the nature of life itself as well as on its evolution, there had to be a thoroughgoing reorientation and impoverishment of virtually all of biology, including such subjects as evolution, development, physiology, microbiology, anthropology, and psychology. In this process, the scientists themselves had been helpless victims. All those who remain have had to profess conformity, but to their great credit, there have been only a very few — notably the biochemist Oparin and the third-rate geneticist Noujdin — who have actively jumped on the Lysenko bandwagon.

It is important to note that the attack on genetics, started in the USSR, has been carried over in full force to all the satellite countries. I could cite cases from Poland, Czechoslovakia, Bulgaria, showing how the screws were tightened on scientists personally known to me, until genetics was squeezed out and the word "gene" could not even be mentioned. In Bulgaria the geneticist Kostoff, who had been Minister of Agriculture, is reported to have died (it is not stated how) during the very week that a genetics controversy was being conducted. Soon after the Communists took over in China, the ex-geneticist Noujdin arrived as a Lysenkoist emissary from the USSR (having previously coördinated East Berlin), and presently the process of "reëducation" was in full swing in the Chinese Universities. A few geneticists who were fortunate enough to get out before the Bamboo Curtain came all the way down have told the story. But within the entire Soviet world, and it is a large one, there is now no escape.

The charges made by the Communists against genetics and the geneticists are typical, and it is instructive to list them. Mendel was a Catholic abbé. Both for this reason and because the concept of the gene is subject to mathematical treatment, it is said that genetics is idealistic and formalistic, whereas statistical principles, according to Lysenko, do not apply to living things. At the same time, since Morgan was a mechanist, and since the genes are regarded as particles, subject to definite rules of behavior, genetics commits the sin of being mechanistic. Thus it is "idealist-mechanist" and hence anti-dialectical, just as some political traitors are accused of being "fascist-Trotskyist" and hence anti-Soviet.

Moreover, since genetics pictures the genes as being relatively stable, it is said that it does not permit of evolution. Since such changes as do occur in the gene are according to genetics not *directively* related to the types of environmental conditions under which they occur, genetics is said to deny the possibility of controlling evolution. Thus again it is said to be clerical in spirit, dealing with fancied eternals. Since according to dialectics everything in nature influences everything else we must infer that not only does the hereditary material influence the nature of the body which develops from the germ cells containing it but that, reciprocally, the characteristics of the body, even those acquired during its life as a result

of its nutrition, experiences, etc., influence the hereditary material
in its germ cells in some corresponding way, as Lamarck and others
before him had thought, and as genetics claims to have disproved.
Genetics is therefore considered as sabotaging one of the main
methods by which living things may be improved. In consequence,
it is charged, genetics has not yielded enough in the line of practical
results for agriculture, and has expended itself in formalisms.

It is said that, by laying stress on genes, which in fact do not exist,
geneticists try to exalt heredity as against environment. Thus they
are pictured as taking sides with the Nazis, Ku Kluxers, old-style
eugenists, and other racists, and as opposing the Communists' efforts
to abolish racial discrimination and to elevate the working classes.
Genetics, in other words, is reactionary and bourgeois. It is also foreign, since it originally developed outside of Russia, and was at the
turn of the century opposed by the Russian evolutionist Timiriazef,
then senile, and later by the Russian practical plant breeder Michurin,
an analogue of our Burbank.

There is no doubt that the Communists who stood behind the
attack on genetics, and this means primarily Stalin, believed most of
these charges. It remains to inquire into the psychological background which induced this belief. Stalin and the others of his hand-
picked group were not men who had training in or understanding of
the manner of thinking and the methods used in natural science. Despite some of the precepts of the dialectics they claimed to follow,
they tended to think in terms of all or none, A or not-A, black or
white. They were extremists, who were jealous of any method of
achieving progress but that very limited one which they had inherited from Marx, Engels, and Lenin. This involved the obtaining
of results directly by manipulation of the environment, and in it
the part played by heredity was hardly considered. Heredity, therefore, was virtually nonexistent. Those who claimed a place for it
must be, at heart, opponents of Communism, as was in fact so
frankly admitted by the Nazis and other racists. It should here be
noted that the racists made the same mistake as the Communists in
thinking of heredity and environment as mutually exclusive agents.
Only they chose the opposite horn of the supposed dilemma. In
fact, modern genetics recognizes the important influence of both
groups of factors at once, in proportions varying with the situation,

but this is too subtle a view for the official Communists, who regard it as an insincere evasion.

The theoretical view of the official Communists fits in with their wishful thinking in matters of practical results, or rather, it seems to them, within the limited range of their own thinking, that there is harmony between their theory and their practice. For those who believe in Lamarckism promise that by direct treatments they can get much improved varieties of wheat in only a couple of years, while the geneticists admit their methods will take them longer and will allow no such confident predictions. Similarly, as for man himself, the Lamarckians assert that the improvement of each generation, in regard to education, nutrition, and so on, will become impressed on their descendants through heredity, a result which would greatly magnify the achievements of today's Soviet leaders.

It is probable that in the case of Stalin there were also personal reasons for his wishing to deny the role of heredity in man. Among these may have been the facts (1) that he was a member of a rather undeveloped minority group which he did not wish to think genetically inferior, as racists would represent them, (2) that the status of his father, as a cobbler, was not very high even within that group, (3) that he himself had certain troublesome and unpleasant character traits which it would have been depressing to regard as having a genetic basis, and (4) that some of these traits were expressed conspicuously, with fewer relieving features, in his son Basil.

Despite the fact that the present Soviet leaders pride themselves in the thought that their thinking about genetics is straightforward and philosophically sound, it is not only contrary to the empirical evidence but it involves an inner contradiction which they hate to have the world know about. Their Lamarckian view that changes in the body, caused by environmental conditions and experience, influence the germ cells in a corresponding way necessarily implies that peoples who have lived under conditions that gave them very little opportunity for mental and physical development have become ever more inferior, in their heredity, to the peoples of better developed countries. It has been admitted to me that this is the official Stalinist view, but it is too embarrassingly like that of the Nazis for it to have been admitted to the world. Its sponsors counter it only by saying that after some generations of the well-being which Communism will bring to all peoples, they will become equal again in their hereditary basis. But it accounts for the fact that the Communists became unwilling to discuss matters of race or human genetics, and that the preparation of books, articles and discussions designed to refute the racist doctrines was halted on orders from above. In contrast to this, Western geneticists actively disputed with the Nazis on the ground (not conceded by the Communists) that the good heredity of the so-called underdeveloped peoples had been hidden by their poor environment, but had not really been affected by it.

It is interesting to note that the naïveté of thought and the wishful thinking above outlined was not present in the earlier Soviet leaders, such as Lenin, Trotsky, Bukharin, Kollantai, and Deborin. Even in the early days when these persons were in control, genetics, although still so new, was regarded by them as a legitimate and important subject, and persons working in the subject were accorded prestige and ample facilities. The accession of Stalin marks a distinct step downward intellectually, and that of Malenkov is continuing the descent. In view of this, it is tragic that the totalitarian leaders have such pretenses to being great theoreticians, and that they are so egotistical and shortsighted as to think themselves capable of deciding any question of principle in science or philosophy. There is not any doubt that, in Stalin's reign, it was he personally who decided that genetics was fallacious, and that it should be attacked. Similarly he himself intervened in other important cultural matters, ranging from which types of music and of architecture were good and which bad, to problems of linguistics, educational methods and physical science. Malenkov is now in a position to continue this blessed guidance from above, for which the victims always publicly thank their attackers.

Genetics, and many related lines of work and thought in biology, would be unable to recover in the Soviet countries in our generation, and probably not in two generations, even if it were decreed today that the attack on it had been a mistake. Even though the successful prosecution of any branch of science today requires many people, these usually include a few key people without whom it would fall behind. In genetics, this is illustrated by the fact that in England from about 1910 to 1930, because the few leading figures in genetics failed to accept the chromosome theory, and because several of the more important younger men died about the time of the First World War, there was comparative stagnation in the field until another generation grew up, while in France there was even more widespread and long-lasting decay in the subject, because of the attitude of the outstanding figures.

In the Soviet countries not only are all the key men in genetics gone, but even most of the young men. Such work as is being done on plant and animal breeding is done by ignorant Lysenkoists, since real geneticists could not force themselves to do that kind of mummery. Moreover, human heredity has become forbidden ground. Even the study of what is done in genetics abroad cannot be carried on, since the heretical journals would be banned except in the highest Communist circles, who are incapable of understanding them. The oncoming generation is not being taught the subject and has no access to it. It is not going to rediscover, under the present limitations on its directions of research, what it took all the rest of the world, under conditions of free communication, half a century to work out. But, even if it did, it would by that time be again a half century behind. We must also remember that it is not merely the words but the very concepts of genetics which are banned, and even its methods of investigation.

It might be held that the fallacies of the Lysenkoist doctrines will prove their own undoing, as the evidence accumulates of their failure to deliver the goods in a practical way. This becomes very improbable however because of the fact that Lysenko and his subordinates are not sufficiently scientific to do a properly controlled experiment, or to know how to use statistical evidence. The collective farmer, for example, may be handed out one vernalized lot of seed (that is, a lot specially treated by Lysenko), and one untreated lot, and told to grow both and compare them to see which is superior. He knows which the Lysenko seed is and which he is expected to find superior, and it is not difficult for him to bestow special care in the cultivation of that seed which he believes should be given the best attention. Moreover, biological results are subject to such fluctuations and vicissitudes anyway, that there is usually a handy alibi if things do not turn out as expected, especially if the conditions are not rigorously controlled.

But even when the failures begin to become too evident, it will probably be a long time before the higher leaders cease to make special excuses to explain them. For they are too far and deeply committed to undertake such a major reversal without great loss of face, both to themselves and to their subjects. It would be the same sort of thing as if Stalin had at last made overtures to Trotsky. And not only did Stalin himself commit himself in genetics, but Malenkov, even more than Stalin, has for years been an especial friend and admirer of Lysenko's, a fact which by the way does not speak highly for Malenkov's intelligence or ability to judge people. It is true that Lysenko could nevertheless be found guilty some time, and purged, but it would be harder for Malenkov to go back on Lysenko's doctrines than on his person, especially since this would also mean repudiating Stalin's endorsement of them. In any case, if and when that reversal happens, and whether it be sudden or protracted, such damage will already have been done to biology that it will take generations for Russia again to catch up with the Western world. At present, genetics is actually nonexistent in the USSR and the countries allied to it. It is dead.

Although the attacks in other fields of science have not been so devastating as in genetics, the direct interferences in the fields of psychology, chemistry, physics and some others must nevertheless have had important demoralizing effects. Moreover, the entire conduct of scientific work in the Soviet countries is conducive to demoralization of the scientists, quite apart form the direct interference with the principles of the sciences themselves. For one thing, the fact that the scientists must profess a belief in a set of principles and slogans of so-called dialectical materialism, as interpreted for them, often in a mystical way, by mediocre medieval-minded political philosophers, and must pretend to make their own science harmonize with these principles and slogans, is in itself repellent to most scientists. When in addition they must have their lines of work guided, and must confess to sins and errors which they do not themselves recognize, physical labor begins to look preferable. Added to this they are subjected to intrigues and pressures by their Party cells, and see others unfairly accused or glorified.

Two incidents which occurred in my own experience in scientific work in the USSR illustrate some of these difficulties of scientists.

There had been undue delay in the publication of a bibliography which I had compiled of a certain field of genetics. In connection with this, I was called in by the secretary of the Academy of Sciences — a man who belonged to the uppermost cell of the whole academy, with all its institutes. The time was early in 1937, shortly after the execution of my friend Agol, who had spent a year with me in Texas on a Rockefeller fellowship. "This is embarrassing," he said to me; "look at your bibliography. On the very first page you list many titles by the traitor Agol. Of course, since his name begins with *A* it had to be on the first page, but think of the impression it makes. And then, all through the bibliography, you have equally bad names, some with long lists of works, such as that of Dobzhansky, who never returned from his fellowship in America, and of Timoféeff-Ressovsky, who never returned from Germany. How can we publish such a list?"

"What would you do?" I asked.

"Simply omit those references."

"But then," I objected, "how can I call it a bibliography of this subject?"

"Then call it a list of the more important works," he said.

"But these," I said, "are among the very most important."

The matter was dropped but I smuggled the bibliography out and published it later when I was in Scotland.

On another occasion he asked me to give him a list of the fifteen scientists working in my department at the institute. "Now," said he, "put a check against the names of those who are Party members."

I checked the names of the three or four who were weakest scientifically, the members of the cell.

"We should like," he said, "to keep these people for you and get rid of all the rest. We will replace them all by good Party members."

I protested that the year plan and the five-year plan of scientific work, which our department had pledged itself to fulfill 100 per cent, and which required continuity of operation and expert knowledge, could not in that case be carried out. This caused him to desist, for the time being.

Another source of interference with the work of scientists is that they are required to make out projects long in advance, as in a factory, even in unexplored fields where no fixed long-range plans are reasonably possible. They must later show that these plans have been fulfilled completely. Unfortunately we in this country are to some extent copying this project- or program-system in science, although it has not yet reached anything like the lengths it has attained in the USSR. There, even though larger and larger numbers of people are being drawn into science, it is inevitable that the type of mind selected, and the type of experience gained in it, will lead more and more in the direction of submissive mediocrity, and will result in a mentality which, in matters of theory, can be readily fooled or tamed. This will mean the withering away of real science.

It is easy to throttle science. It is an extremely delicate organism, requiring very special conditions. These have seldom, in the world's long history, existed to a sufficient extent to allow it to live. Among these special conditions are freedom of thought, communication, and criticism, a tradition of adventure and adventurous thinking, a generally high standard of living and of education, a certain security and the comparative absence of distracting pressures, and the opportunity for experiencing some appreciation from one's colleagues.

Although Soviet science is bound eventually to wither unless the Soviet political system becomes greatly moderated, we should not let this conclusion lull us into the belief that the Soviets will soon cease to make important scientific advances or that their physical power will soon dwindle. It often takes a long time, decades or longer, before the progress or retrogression of one branch of science has conspicuous effects in another, and before the fruits of the more theoretical branches are seen in practical results. The Soviets have a tremendous scientific personnel, supplied with abundant facilities, and this personnel is under great pressure to produce practical results in lines which the leaders consider important. Let us not underestimate the practical danger of this for us. The fact that science under that system is subject to a long-range decay only makes this short-range danger for the whole world the more ominous. That is one reason why it is so important for people in the West to become aware of these facts.

The most important lesson from it all is that dictation by government or politics is in the long run fatal to the development of science. Its creative spirit cannot function adequately without freedom from outside interference in the drawing of conclusions, and in their communication, and in the choosing of lines of work. Unfortunately, however, so long as the Soviet system menaces us from the outside, we have to compromise to some extent even with our own freedoms, in order to remain physically strong enough to resist that system. This is the situation which Stalin and his successors are forcing upon us. It gives opportunity for the machinations of reactionaries in our own midst who, on the pretext of defending us against Soviet slavery, try to restrict our own freedoms after a pattern that savors of the very practices which we are opposed to. This is a procedure which tends to become self-increasing. We have therefore to walk a narrow, slippery path today, and to be ready to guard ourselves against falling into the chasms which yawn on both sides of this path.

13. Phases of the Conflict Between Totalitarianism and Science

GEORGE DE SANTILLANA

I

The earliest case of totalitarianism in science occurs not long after the beginning of science itself. It is to be found in Plato's ideal constitution. True, it remains in the realm of the imagination, along with that state itself. (Plato could not even bring about the burning of the books of Democritus, which he strongly advocated.) But since Plato's utopia has had a profound influence on later Christian thinking, the policy set down in the *Laws* should not be passed over lightly:

As to our younger generation and their wisdom, I cannot let them off when they do mischief. For do but mark the effect of their words: when you and I argue for the existence of the Gods, and produce the Sun, Moon, Stars, and Earth, claiming for them a divine being, if we would listen to the aforesaid philosophers we should say that they are earth and stones only, which can have no care at all of human affairs . . . They say that fire and water, and earth and air, all exist by nature and chance, and none of them by art, and that as to the bodies which come next in order, — earth, and sun, and moon, and stars, — they have been created by means of these absolutely inanimate existences . . . This is impiety, even when not accompanied by any wrongfulness in deeds

. . . The interpreter of the law shall proclaim to all impious persons that they must depart from their ways and go over to the pious. And to those who disobey, let the law about impiety be as follows: — If a man is guilty of any impiety, any one who happens to be present shall give information to the magistrates, in aid of the law; and let the magistrates who first receive the information bring him before the appointed court according to the law; and if a magistrate, after receiving information, refuses to act, he shall be tried for impiety at the instance of any one who is willing to vindicate the laws . . . Let those who have been made what they are only from want of understanding, and not from malice or an evil nature, be placed by the judge in the House of Reformation and ordered to suffer imprisonment during a period of not less than five years. And in the meantime let them have no intercourse with the other citizens, except with members of the Nocturnal Council, and with them let them converse with a view to the improvement of their soul's health. And when the time of their imprisonment has expired, if any of them be of sound mind let them be restored to sane company, but if not, and if he be condemned a second time, let him be punished with death.

II

The Catholic Church, once the "deposit of the faith" had been established, could not but proceed along the lines suggested by Plato. However, it did so with more than a grain of salt. What counted with the Inquisition was not a man's thought but his behavior: what was called the "sowing of tares." We shall therefore select a clear-cut and crucial episode, which turned out to be the final one: the trial of Galileo.

The earliest attacks on Galileo come not from the Church, but from the vested Aristotelian interests in the schools. It is they who about 1611 inject Holy Scripture into the argument, which on the part of lay scholars was a blow below the belt, and also something against the university rule of not giving church authorities a pretext for intruding into philosophical questions. But the discoveries of the telescope had shaken their position, and like many a politician before and after, these men preferred to aggravate the incoherence of public opinion in order to dissimulate their own.

Some Dominican preachers picked up the ball and launched the first public attack from the pulpit, followed by a secret and extremely slanderous denunciation to the Inquisition. Galileo protested to their superiors and received proper apologies. He was quite sure at this point that he had the theological authorities on his side, but he feared this move as one would fear today some "incipient Mc-Carthyism." He wrote serious theological letters to Rome showing that it would be disastrous to create a split between faith and science, and command people to believe what they could see was actually not so.

The chief theological authority at the time was Cardinal Bellarmino, a Jesuit (canonized in 1947). He reassured Galileo's friends by telling them that some directive might have to be issued about these new Copernican ideas, but merely as a matter of "orientation." They were of course permissible, but strictly as "mathematical hypotheses," it being well known that mathematics had nothing to do with physical reality. Physically, geocentrism stood, as Aristotle had proved long ago, and it would be very bad to challenge it on grounds which were bound to be insufficient, and thus create a useless scandal among pious souls who had been taught to believe that Joshua had stopped the sun.

It was only Galileo and a very few of his friends (these included Kepler, unfortunately a Protestant) who could see the real situation: that the new astronomy, born of the telescope, and the new physics, born of dynamics, were on the point of effecting a junction which would invalidate the old cosmology as a whole. Galileo rushed to Rome, was assured that there was nothing against him, but was not even able to present his case to the authorities. Aristotelian learning and ecclesiastical doctrine joined in a solid front against him. Bellarmino himself, a man of legal training like his colleagues, was quite unable to get a glimpse of the new point of view. For him, there was the whole deposit of the faith to be protected, and with it the already well-tested philosophical foundations.[1] He felt this was no time, after the Protestant crisis and the Council of Trent, to bring in "novelties," born of these "Florentine minds which are too subtle and curious and can persuade themselves and others of almost anything."

[1] This, incidentally, is a point that has been made again by the Pope recently. He said that the deposit of the faith was by one half accrued tradition. These words were meant — and understood — as a protection of freedom within the Church. The same doctrine, however, works also for the protection of obsolescence.

Galileo has been even too amply justified in history. What civilization remembers is the tragic urgency of his letters, as he saw the irrevocable happening before he had time to convince anybody. He wanted to prevent an official pronouncement, or at least to stave it off. But we must also remember that he was as yet in no condition to present an airtight case. He did not have a complete and coherent "natural philosophy" to replace the old one — in fact, we don't have it either; we have simply compelled the intellectual world to drop that requirement and take science for what it is, an organized thought in flux which delivers enormous confirmations in terms of power over nature.

What Galileo could "deliver" in those terms was still quite limited — it was the discoveries of the telescope, and they were big enough for a shock effect on public opinion; but it was hard to follow them up with a coherent presentation, in terms of a science yet incomplete and very hard to understand anyway: dynamics. As it stood, his presentation was cogent enough to give pause, but it was also full of holes: for instance, he insisted that the heavens obeyed the laws of physics as we can discover them on earth, but the facts were still there: stars in heaven turn around forever, whereas stones fall. This gap, in the absence of Newtonian gravitation, was only very partially filled by his views on inertia. He still had to have recourse to epicyles, which make no physical sense and never had, as the Aristotelians rightly remarked.

It is of the essence of scientific imagination to go ahead on an important trail and leave certain problems to take care of themselves. To the conservative side, it seemed simply a new version of "the house that the Pythagoreans are forever trying to build on sand."

The crucial position, at that point, was that of the Jesuit astronomers who were Bellarmino's experts. They were consulted and dodged this issue. Part of their attitude may be due to the Tychonic system, which gave hopes (at least to such as wanted to hope) that the difficulties of Ptolemy might be solved without such a subversion; most of it, it would appear, was due to the obedience ingrained in their system, which made them follow *perinde ac si cadaver* the instructions of their general, Acquaviva, never to do anything that might shake the official teaching.

The *Ratio Studiorum* of Acquaviva was a carefully designed

directive, which allowed selections from the classics only for rhetorical education, and kept to Cicero, the safe and prudent corporation lawyer, as the mainstay of education. Nothing is so safe as we would like to believe, and one cannot help remembering a quip of Bernard Groethuysen, that it was Cicero and Plutarch that made the French Revolution. But in 1600, the choice had its grounds. Of the two rival innovating currents of the Renaissance, naturalism and humanism, the Jesuit educators had decided that humanism was the safer, with its quieting vision of a *plenitudo temporum*, and had provided their own dehydrated version of it. Science, of course, was admitted, on the side, as a means of power (we need only think of the Jesuits in China) but it had to be kept under control by careful compartmentation into genres and specialties; any philosophical implications were kept out of it and reassigned to official doctrine.[2]

Thus, when Bellarmino asked his experts for guidance, he simply received the echo of his own thoughts. Philosophy has to be a coherent and closed whole. This new thing was no philosophy. Moreover it shook the faith in Scriptural truth at the wrong moment.

Would a great philosophical consultant like Bonaventure or Aquinas have decided the same way? It is open to doubt. But Bellarmino and his colleagues were essentially legal minds. Such minds go by precedent, practical interests, weighted "opinions." Also, Bellarmino knew best what an incredibly disparate assemblage of ideas, notions, beliefs, and sentiments he had kept together in a lifetime of struggle. Once he allowed ideas to start moving, he could no longer feel responsible for the outcome. *Sint ut sunt, aut non sint.*

It must be admitted that our statesmen, legal minds too, would be baffled by Galileo's proofs. If they did not have scientific consultants, and a blind respect for science instilled into them since their childhood, they would react the same way. John Donne had wanted Copernicus and Machiavelli haled before the Judge of Hell, as "innovators" who had upset the world. Church statesmen, to whom science was still an ornament of the mind, may be excused for wondering whether those "novelties" about the heavens would be all to the good of the spiritual order it was their duty to uphold.

[2] This directive is still in force today. When Professor Wiener was invited to lecture on cybernetics in Spain in 1950, he was told to stick to the mathematical and physical side and keep clear of any physiological and philosophical implications.

In recent months, we have had two significant developments out of this classic position. Pope Pius XII has officially endorsed scientific speculation, even to the most "temerarious" of cosmological attempts. At the same time (in his message to the Austrian Katholikentag in September 1952) he has taken a strong reactionary position with respect to property, which almost amounts to a withdrawal of *Rerum Novarum*.[3] The motives remain the same. Science, in his opinion, is no longer a danger, especially in the higher reaches, where its difficulties with physical reality seem to make it again amenable to spiritual guidance; whereas socialism is the course which requires a check. It is relatively safe to practice science, but one cannot join socialism without being dragged along.

This does not imply that Bellarmino's course was entirely correct according to precedent. In the opinion of many of his advisers, the new philosophical problems were of such a nature as made it best to leave them to themselves until an Ecumenical Council should decide.

The previous legislative decisions came from the Council of Trent: "Petulant minds must be restrained from interpreting Scripture against the authority of tradition, in matters that belong to faith and morals." This was aimed at the fundamentalist reformers, not at all at mathematicians, and in fact Copernicus had been left unmolested. Thus the judiciary might well have felt some doubts before committing itself to what was really a "fundamentalist" decision alien to the spirit of Rome. It was "conciliar business," as Descartes was to write with cold Gallican sense, to reconsider the whole issue.

But Bellarmino was of the anti-conciliar persuasion. He decided the thing should be settled by administrative decree. He never even had the book of Copernicus formally examined, notwithstanding Galileo's pressing request that it should at least be read. In fact, Galileo fancied himself as a "friend of the court" but was considered a patient under observation. Obviously, Bellarmino was semi-consciously frightened by the whole intellectual issue. He fell back on his Inquisitorial policy for an estimate of the situation. They gave him a couple of garbled quotes from one of the initial *agents*

[3] It is mainly against *Mitbestimmung*, but it goes further in reacting against the idea of property as a "social function," which had gradually established itself in Catholic theory, and states that the right to property must be defended "in all its forms."

provocateurs, Caccini, as "the Copernican doctrine." These were processed, "qualified," and officially condemned by Decree of the Index on March 5, 1616.

Galileo was treated courteously throughout, but the battle had been lost.

The more celebrated second phase is really only a corollary of the 1616 prohibition. In 1623 Urban VIII Barberini ascended the pontifical throne. He was a protector of the arts and sciences and a personal adviser of Galileo. This looked like a most auspicious conjunction, and Galileo hastened to Rome where he was most favorably received. His early hopes of an official reversal were indeed frustrated; but he was encouraged by the Pope to write a dialogue contrasting the traditional with the Copernican cosmology. The Pope put only one condition: that he leave the conclusion "hypothetical," for it would never do to "constrain God Almighty within the limits of our particular imaginations." Therefore, the explicit conclusion was to be that even if the new world scheme might appear to us as dictated by mathematical necessity, "God may well have achieved his ends in many, aye in infinite other ways which would be unthinkable for us." Galileo followed the instructions to the letter. When the *Dialogue on the World Systems* came out, there would be no doubt that the saving clause at the end was only a formal concession. But the license's instructions from Rome were equally formal: "The author must add the reasons from divine omnipotence dictated to him by His Holiness, which must quiet the intellect, even if it were impossible to get away from the Pythagorean doctrine otherwise." The conditions having been complied with, the book was licensed and published. But it had no sooner come out than the Jesuits were able to show that this was no mere ingenious theory, but a demolition charge planted by an expert engineer. The whole of traditional doctrine, they said, was threatened with collapse, and this one work might do more damage than Luther and Calvin put together. Strictly speaking, they were right. The Pope realized that he had been outwitted, and in rage had Galileo summoned before the Tribunal of the Inquisition.

Tradition has made of Galileo the unworldly prophet of pure science who is suddenly attacked by the forces of superstition. This is much too simple. Galileo was a man of consummate tact and worldly experience, and he knew he was playing a close game. But then how could he commit such a grievous miscalculation? He had always been able to write rings around the censors. It would have been easy for him to end the *Dialogue* by having his Aristotelian bring forward, let us say, an elaborate Tychonic conclusion, and having the others agree with some pious phrases about the uncertainties of science. That was the best that the Jesuit Riccioli could invent in 1657, when he undertook the official refutation of the *Dialogue*. It would have made the authorities look foolish, and he and his friends might have sat back to enjoy the joke. He had not done it, because he wanted to persuade. Living in a highly formal civilization, he had understood the compliance clause to be a juridical formality. He was not playing a game against the authorities, he really wanted to convert them while saving their face, and he wanted to protect the authority of Scripture and to save its interpreters from a blunder, thus averting a major historical disaster. He trusted the Pope would realize this in time. He had followed the rules, he expected the others to do the same. And in fact, when the storm broke, he did not cower like a man who has tried to "pull a fast one" and has been unmasked, but he wanted to fight it out then and there. The Grand Duke of Tuscany was on his side, and requested the appointment of a mixed commission to investigate the matter. If anyone was to be punished, it was clearly the licensers. But the storm had broken, sweeping all safeguards before it.

Galileo had been mistaken not because he was a progressive, *but because he was a conservative*. The strange paradox of the drama lies in this, that the Church was facing at last what it had tried in vain to shape through the late Middle Ages, the orthodox natural philosopher. In Galileo's thinking there is nowhere to be detected the cold sneer of Valla, or the impenetrable aloofness of Leonardo, or the cynical dodge of the "double truth" used by Pomponazzi and the Averroists, or the adventurous fantasies of Pico, or Campanella, or Telesio. He really believes that there must be a concordance between God's word and God's works. He is thinking and acting as a consultant of the theologians in natural philosophy, and relies on the ancient freedoms of Catholic and Conciliar Christianity in which he has been brought up. As he himself wrote later: "In this matter of introducing novelties; and who ever heard that minds created

free by God should submit to someone else's dictation, that the incompetent should be set up as a judge over the expert? . . . These
are the things which bring about the ruin of states and the subversion of commonwealths."

It might be objected that prohibitions had always existed and that
he knew it, but he knew best that administrative prohibitions are
not dogmatic pronouncements *ex cathedra*. They are subject to
reversal, under the pressure of discreet and respectful opinion. And
in fact the anti-Copernican decree was reversed in 1757. But the
mechanism of change had been devised for very slow chances inside
a stable body of opinion. It was not geared for the tempo of modern
science — nor for its demonstrative certainties. The Earth at that
time, at least according to certain "grave opinions," was allowed an
"imperceptible motion." If it had gained only one mile of speed a
year, like any correct social reality, in less than two centuries it would
have been revolving comfortably in its orbit. In that sense, it may be
said that it is the Church authorities, and not Galileo, who were the
first bewildered victims of the impact of science. They had come into
collision with an unsuspected entity in a state of unsuspected
acceleration.

It would have been the part of wisdom for the authorities to follow
precedent and not to commit themselves on physical issues. But the
Church had been caught between wind and water by the new
developments. The Protestant crisis — or rather the hot and cold war
that followed — had led it to table theological and philosophical
revisions and to concentrate on propaganda, indoctrination, and
salesmanship, on rhetoric and revivalism, on political pressure,
panegyric, social psychology, style, display, literary elegance — on
everything that would allow it to control man's actions in the surest
and quickest way. This had been the work of the Jesuits, and in
fact it was the Jesuits who perceived the danger of the *Dialogue* to
their system of teaching, and prevailed on the Pope to bring Galileo
to trial.

This involved forcing the law, for the work had been licensed
and the most that could be done was to prohibit its sale, pending
correction. But a document was conveniently discovered in the file,
an injunction of the Inquisition in 1616, which forbade Galileo
personally to "discuss in any way" the Copernican system. All the

intrinsic evidence goes to show that this document is a forgery, and a carefully planted one.[4] But it was badly needed. Out of this the authorities were able to bring Galileo to trial, and then to trap him into statements which could be construed as "suspect or heresy." Galileo had felt secure not without justification, because he could not imagine that the Pope would go back on his word, and that the Inquisition would then fabricate documents against him. But reason of state prevailed.

Thus, what looks in the larger context like the conflict of the new social classes and the power of science with obsolete orthodoxy, becomes very different in the specific context. Here it is Galileo, like Copernicus and Cardinal Schoenberg before him, who is the conservative. He stands on the old freedoms and customs. Against him, the Church of the Counter Reformation is the "pilot project" of the modern totalitarian state and stands for the streamlined and the new in executive efficiency.

III

As a third phase, we might take Auguste Comte's positivistic authoritarianism. This again, like Plato's *Laws*, remains in the realm of theory. But it is nonetheless significant.

The experience of the French Revolution had driven Comte, a believer in "modern science," toward a revival of absolute orthodoxy. His motto is, "*L'ordre pour base, le progres comme but.*" In the name of progress and the integrated society the supreme science is going to be sociology, and all the other sciences are tyrannically subject to it. They are, in fact, totally *gleichgeschaltet*. No more telescopes or spectroscopes, not even microscopes. No reëxamination of already established simple laws. Nothing but what is going to be "directly useful to society." The list of forbidden topics is half a page long. Among them is the calculus of probabilities, an "outdated aberration." We shall meet again with this feature later in our discussion.

Comte hoped to get the Jesuits on his side, and with their help, to replace the Pope. When he saw that it did not work, he wrote letters to the Tsar and to the Sultan, asking them to help him

---

[4] The proof of this will be given in a forthcoming book by the author on *The Crime of Galileo.*

create a new philosophical papacy. But those potentates apparently had been softened up by liberalism; they did not even answer.

Such were Comte's endeavors around 1848, and there was method in that madness.

IV

We come now to the modern form of absolutism in knowledge. The scientific tragedy of Lysenkoism has been so amply illustrated, that it is perhaps needless to go again into its unfolding from 1935 to 1948.

We shall only quote two statements which characterize the whole situation. One of them is by G. Platonov, the average Soviet biologist of 1951:

The main and decisive force which has brought about the victory of Michurin's doctrine has been the Communist Party . . . The classics of Marxism-Leninism, Marx, Engles [*sic*], Lenin, and Stalin have not only created the philosophy of dialectical materialism, or the abiding principles of which the Michurinist biology is developing, but have given a series of clear instructions about the direction in which Darwin's evolution theory should be developed, and which aspects of this theory should be discarded in building the truly materialistic biology.

The other is a recantation by a prominent biologist in 1948:

My appearance of two days ago, when the Party's Central Committee marked the dividing ridge which separates the two movements in biological science, was unworthy of a Soviet scientist and member of the Communist Party.

I admit that I took an erroneous stand. Yesterday's remarkable speech of Academician Lobanov, his phrase, addressed directly to me, "We are not on the same path with you" (and I regard P. P. Lobanov as a great statesman) — these words upset me greatly. His speech threw me into confusion. A sleepless night helped me think over my behavior . . . I will fight, and sometimes I am very capable at it, for the Michurinist biological science.

I am a responsible individual because I am in the Committee for the Stalin Awards, in the Council of Ministers and in the Expert Commission for the awarding of higher scientific degrees. Thus, I think that I have a moral duty to be an honest Michurinist, to be an upright Soviet biologist!

The first quote represents roughly the position of Jesuits like Scheiner, who took the orthodox stand while knowing better, in 1633. The second is a close paraphrase of Galileo's statements before the Tribunal of the Holy Inquisition.

Such is the picture. It has given rise on this side to immense amounts of self-congratulation and condemnation, but I have not found much in the way of an etiological study. This is possibly because it is felt to be unsafe ground. After all, certain things belong to our time in general, as Hitler prophesied. The Iron Curtain is more of a mirror than a screen, and the Lysenko episode only a vexatious grotesque reflection of many politicians' secret thoughts. A certain type of American Legionnaire is not very different from Lysenko. Both are lower-middle-class phenomena, both are selling their services as trouble-shooters in case the system proves to have a weak spot.

In the absence of authoritative analyses, I shall try to reconstruct as best I can the motivations underlying the crisis in genetics.

Marxism claims "scientific objectiveness." In fact, Bogdanov had written: "Marxism contains in itself the denial of any eternal truth." Thus, Marxism in its cognitive attitude, far from being as rigid as Comtean positivism, ought to be as progressive and liberal as Professor Dewey himself.

It recognizes, however (like Comte), an intellectual danger, and that is relativism. A doctrine bent on action, it needs definite objective reality on which the transforming action is to take place. Lenin admitted that the full knowledge of nature is only a limit "towards which man will strive forever, creating concepts, images and laws as he goes." But, against Deborin, he maintained that "for objective dialection, even in the relative there is an absolute."

Lenin has been harshly treated by the professional philosophers, but his theory of knowledge makes quite reasonable sense. He does acknowledge the difference between concept and sensation. What he does reject, and has to reject, is a purely intellectual theory of knowledge. Marx had already explained why, in his *Theses on Feuerbach*.

Knowledge is what happens when the mind comes to grips with objective reality, in order to transform it. Dialectical materialism refuses to think of separate inductive and deductive processes. The nexus that induction discovers among phenomena is not abstractly universal, there is no "uniformity of nature" to guarantee it; rather, there is a fluency in the interaction between nature and the mind, and an evolving "unity of opposites" which excludes any rigid classification inside reality. Marxists are not only transformists, they are universal transformists.

When the bimillennial of Epicurus was celebrated with great pomp in Moscow in 1937, many wondered why Democritus had not been chosen as the father of materialism. Yet the reason was not a secret. By introducing an arbitrary "swerve" in the fall of the atoms, Epicurus had created a philosophy that was not rigidly deterministic while being materialistic. He had qualified as the philosopher of freedom for the oppressed classes, in the very measure in which he was unscientific. His had been, in a way, the earliest *Anti-Dühring*.[5]

Soviet scientific philosophy has always resisted theories ultimately based on chance and discontinuity. It is easy to grow sarcastic about it, but there are reasons. "Chance" is a dangerous word, as we have seen in Plato's Laws and in Comte's program.

It is fairly well admitted in history that world views have gained acceptance in the measure in which they corresponded to the social philosophy of the times. The Aristotelian, the Newtonian, or the Darwinian theories, especially in their extrapolations, are clear cases in point. Behind Darwin there is Malthus, with his "law of nature" so convenient to the ethics of business. And so on. Therefore, it might not be senseless to suggest that the present statistical agnosticism and logical positivism of physical theory reflects something of a historical situation. Statistics is and remains something of a vicious circle philosophically. At least, this is what Einstein and others still suggest.

Lenin maintained this view with brutal vigor, but from the non-metaphysical end, in his polemic against Mach, the positivists and the "formalist-idealists." It has become a dogma. In physics, where requirements are strict and no alternatives are in sight, this philosophical directive has simply led in Russia to a provisional "double truth," as in the sixteenth century. In biology, however, there were openings. Also, the situation was more delicate.

Biology is far from being an exact science. It is still allowable to

---

[5] We don't mean that Dühring was a scientist, but that Engels in writing the book took an unscientific position.

feel unhappy about the picture of evolution presented by genetics. It is still, at best, a partial picture, and something is lacking. Whether it is more ideas along the same line, or an entirely different idea, no one knows.

The dialectician has decided that *he* knows. And he had to decide that way, because his metaphysics (like it or not, he has one) requires a real dialectical continuity between the lowest forms of life and the highest, based on interaction with the external situation. Otherwise the whole theory of the rise of the proletariat remains suspended in mid-air. Engels, no less than Spencer, did have a *Naturphilosophie*. It is we who have not, and that leaves us in the condition of "idealist-formalist bourgeois cosmopolitanism." Which is the impolite Soviet form of telling us that we do not know where we are going, nor, in fact, where we are.

Thus, the requirements were stated. Lysenko, a gentleman of copious illiteracy, satisfied them by going back (unbeknownst to himself) to the transformist ideas of Samuel Butler and G. B. Shaw. Then he began adding (again unsuspectingly) Semon's *mneme* theory of 1905 and Darwin's hypothesis of the pangenes dating back to 1860. Caught in his own dialectics, he retrogressed gradually from a firmly held Darwinism to Lamarck and beyond. His apologists in the West contend that this is a strategic retreat, as all war commentators have always done. We hold that it is a "bum steer." Meanwhile, however, many good scientists have been sentenced to death or to camp for raising objections to the new line, a thing which did not happen in the time of Galileo.

Clearly, our concern with these developments does not stem from a concern for Science as an entity. Science always takes care of itself. It is a concern for the status of the scientist. We keep saying, not without a shade of satisfaction, that Stalin has been killing the goose that laid the golden egg.

This is a point that I should like to see discussed. Nobody is really that foolish. Urban VIII did try to kill the goose, but then he considered the eggs simply bad. Stalin, like us, believed them to be gold; he only thought he could use new goose-conditioning techniques. So do we, in a way, although our techniques are milder.

This leads us back to Stalin as the ultimate maker of scientific policy as well as of all other policy. The liquidation of the Pokrowsky school in history, for instance, and the return to a more traditional and "voluntaristic" teaching, away from "abstract schematic" Marxism, was carried out after his pronouncement on the subject which came in 1939, and so was the liquidation of the Pashukanis school of legal theory in 1937. Let us not forget also his famous recent intervention in linguistics.

How this happens is also important. The limits and competence of the various bureaucratic instruments are not sharply defined. This corresponds to the nature of the administrative, non-juridical state, where decision from above must be able to override all separation of competences. The bureaucratic instruments now purposefully overlap within the framework of their ultimate unification in the dictator's hands (cf. W. W. Rostow, *The Dynamics of Soviet Society*). A large independent secretariat allows him to select the issues on which he chooses to intervene in detail. He can intervene intimately and directly at any level in the chain of command, and thus avoid a disproportionate accretion of power to any single subordinate group.

Let me try to reconstruct the policy behind such interventions, when it is a matter of scientific research.

Our free civilization wants results in general — one might say, in the abstract; "following the argument wherever it may lead us," as Plato would say.

The Soviet system has narrowed down this requirement to: (*a*) social-psychological results; (*b*) immediate concrete results. We might also say that it wants the results to be framed within a time program both for the attitude of the society and for the means at its disposal (the emergent "possibilities").

In science, this involves what we have already in this country, in James Bryant Conant's definition, as "programmatic research." Only, it is more decisively and brutally steered.

Steering seems to be done not by mere directive (this can be too easily eluded) but by setting in motion shock waves of new personnel embodying the new line. They roll and break with it, but meanwhile provide the dynamism required — a substitute for our "personal incentive" system.

This implies waste, no doubt. But that is nothing new. The purges of 1936–1938 implied a terrifying waste of able administrative and military personnel, even in the face of impending German aggression, yet Stalin seems to have thought that this was a fair price to pay for having a ship in good trim that responds to the rudder. He would have remarked, probably, that our cyclical depressions used to wipe out no less considerable amounts of working capital and of acquired positions, and yet were considered "good things."

The method of total purges seems to have been abandoned. The ship responds now to a flick of the rudder.

This seems to work in administration, in legal theory and so on. Can it be applied to science without destroying it utterly?

It is speculative to speak of a total demoralization of the scientific personnel, as H. J. Muller does, with his simile of the bear with the ring in its nose. There is some evidence that the suggestive force of triumphant orthodoxy and of the "forward-marching Soviet power" can keep young men in line. They simply have learned what to expect. An objective mistake is punished by death, as on the battlefield. But they also know, like the officer, that the ultimate criterion is not justice, it is delivering the goods. Lysenko is now riding high, and everyone talks Michurin language. But those who really believe in that language and make fools of themselves in practice are hauled up short, like the unfortunate Academician Greber who put pigs in booties to improve their foot heredity (it could not be a defective gene because Lysenko has decreed that genes are imaginary). But if Lysenko within a few years does not deliver the goods, he will follow the fate of Vavilov. Meanwhile the younger personnel, who were trying in various ways either to work with the new theories or to apply to them the concepts of regular genetics by means of a rapidly concocted doubletalk (interliner hybrids, etc.) will emerge with the new line, which might very well be a reversal to the old under the guise of a glorification of Timiriazev or what not. The idea (if we may assume that there is an idea) is that it will never really be the old, but a synthesis of the Lamarckian thesis with a Darwinian antithesis on a new and "progressive" level.

As for ourselves, we may follow a natural bent and predict that nothing will come of it. But we might also stop, look, and listen both ways. Since we enjoy the privileges of a free society, we can afford not to intone with the *Song of Roland*: "*païens ont tort et Chrestiens ont droit.*" This line has been intoned just a little too often, and as a result now genetics in America is stuck in the faintly embarrassing and unscientific role of Caesar's wife.

Yet it is fairly well known that our genetics, as it stands, is due for a serious reëxamination. I have no independent opinion on this, but I hope Dr. Bronowski will come out some day with a study that he has promised to undertake on the statistical foundation of genetics; for it is no mystery that there are serious difficulties, both as regards the time-scale available for evolution, and as regards the mechanism of adaptation. Mendel had phenomenal luck in choosing the sweet pea, but in the general theory of evolution often a series of characters mediated by separate genes have to be right before the animal has an advantage; and it takes more time than geology suggests. Lamarck had a point there, as some are beginning to suspect.

Moreover, there are some people who doubt whether mutation is a real process that creates new types, or whether it is not too uniformly detrimental; others wonder how it is that animals so different in nature and background as mammals and marsupials have such remarkable likenesses in their bodily apparatus; and there is still that curious question of continuous genetic variations (like height in a population) which can be explained, but not terribly well.

All these are merely points of doubt and discussion: but they suggest that a vigorous new approach *might* conceivably unearth some entirely new ideas. Whether the Russian scientists today are in a condition to do this is extremely doubtful. All we know is that new lines of research have to be started by men in desperation; they might hit upon something.

As for the scientific capital, personnel, and impetus which get lost in the process, it is safe to assume that they are considered expendable: (*a*) because the rate of renewal is considered more important than stable assets; (*b*) because those stable assets, under the form of continuous accretion, are provided freely by the scientific literature of Western countries. It does not take long for a specialist to get himself *au courant* of latest results abroad, if they are really "empirically sound." Thus, the shakeup in the system is made easier by a corresponding shakedown of the rival systems.

So much — briefly — for the general rationale. Does Michurinism become a normal *recursus* in this light, or is it one of those backfires like the Far East purge described by Beck and Godin, which started with the drunken self-accusations of a sergeant to spread through the whole Far Eastern Army, putting it out of commission and sweeping on towards its utter destruction, until there was no way to stop it except shooting the investigators? [6]

In the Soviet Union as everywhere else, initiative is rewarded, and Lysenko and his associate Present, the dialectician, seem to be the type of men that know how to catch Soviet fortune by the forelock. So was N. Ya. Marr, the linguist, however, and he even managed to die in power, which is the equivalent of immortality in the dialectical world. But the annihilating sentence of Stalin caught up with his work in 1950 and in terms which become a fierce irony on the present:

The slightest criticism of the situation in Soviet linguistics, even the most timid attempts at criticism of the so-called "new teaching" (that is, the doctrines of Marr) were persecuted and were suppressed on the part of the governing circles in the field of linguistics. For the critical attitude toward the heritage of N. Ya. Marr, valuable research workers in the field of linguistics were deprived of their jobs or demoted. Workers in the field of linguistics were promoted to responsible positions, not on the basis of merit but on unqualified acknowledgment of the teaching of N. Ya. Marr.

After giving an example of maladministration on the part of the bosses of Soviet linguistics, Stalin explained such practices by the fact that "an Arakcheev regime created in the field of linguistics cultivates irresponsibility and encourages such disorder."

Such words are surely being pondered over at present by many young geneticists and agrobiologists in Russia. The knife is being kept ready for Lysenko. What this does to a man's character can be described only in terms of Dante's Hell, but it does not mean that scientific research cannot go on under the mask of new behaviors.

When Lenin heard that the Bolshevik revolution had broken out in Hungary, he wired Béla Kun only four words: "Don't make my

[6] The role of sheer stupidity must never be underrated, and this might simply be a move dictated by the present atmosphere of brutal nationalism, as is said over here. After all, the Soviets did back Hitler's coming to power, and it was irretrievably stupid. But the positive and negative aspects of the prejudice and superstition inherent in great organisms can only be assessed in terms of what they *do* with them over a whole period, and this has caused me not to stress the "lazy hypothesis."

mistakes." This is how any serious Marxist is bound to think. Hence we may expect the colossal "bum steer" on genetics to feed back into the revision process sometime soon.

In conclusion, the analogy with the Galileo trial, which seemed so clear in the beginning, appears misleading. We are not facing a static idealist orthodoxy, but a moving operationalist one.

The scientific purges are an extreme application of operationalist views, in which whole ways of life are scrapped instead of abstractions, and what is considered expendable is not only theories, but the personnel that carries them.

14. Totalitarianism and History

BERTRAM D. WOLFE

I

For over two decades, Soviet historiography has been in steadily deepening crisis. Histories succeed each other as if they were being consumed by a giant chain smoker who lights the first volume of the new work with the last of the old. Historians appear, disappear, and reappear; others vanish without a trace.

Originally, only party history was subject to rigid prescription. Then Soviet history was added. Latterly, the area of command performance and commanded conclusions has spread outward to America and Asia and the wastes of Antarctica, backward to the Middle Ages, to Byzantium, to the shadowy origins of the Slavs and the pre-dawn of the Kievan state, to China's earliest culture. One day a given statement of events or interpretation is obligatory. The next it is condemned in words which seems to portend the doom of the historian who faithfully carried out his instructions. If it is a pronouncement of Stalin which he is following, all the more severely must he condemn himself — of course, without involving the Leader in his "self-criticism."

Often the central personages of an event become *unpersons*, as if they had never existed. The Civil War must now be rewritten as if there never had been a War Commissar named Leon Trotsky. The

Soviet theater, once the subject of so many histories, is historyless once more, until somebody contrives to write a new version without a trace of the great innovator-director, Vsevolod Meierhold. On February 15, 1951, *Pravda* accomplished the feat of "commemorating" the tenth anniversary of the Eighteenth Party Conference, in which Voznesensky delivered the main report, without so much as mentioning the name of the reporter!

Today the Balkarians are missing from Volume "B" of the new edition of the Great Soviet Encyclopedia; the Volga Germans have become an *unpeople*; and the Crimean Tartars, having been expelled from their centuries-old home to a region under the Arctic Circle, have had the place-names of their former habitations extirpated, and are now being subjected to the shrinking of their historical role in the Crimea to the point where they are gradually becoming an *unpeople*, too.

During the past spring even objects began to become *unobjects*, as *Pravda* and the regional press from February to May reported a grim and thoroughgoing purge of scores of local and national museums all the way from Lithuania to Kazaghstan. The Lithuanian museums were rebuked for failing to show the influence of Great Russian culture and the struggles and longings of their peoples for the extinction of their independence, while the Kazakh museums were condemned for the nostalgic splendor of their daggers, guns, harnesses, bridal costumes, and for failing to display any objects showing Great Russia's civilizing influence and the "progressive" character of her annexation of Kazakhstan.

If we seek to define the limits of this vast "Operation Palimpsest" we are struck by their continual enlargement: outward in space, backward in time, ever more profound in depth and ever more attentive even to minuscule detail. The operation tends to totality, as everything in the total state tends to become total.

II

History has become a "weapon," a "fighting science," an arm of propaganda, the first function of which is the justification of the shifting policies of the Soviet Government through reference to the "facts" and "documents" of the "past." The past has always been subject to the interpretive fashions of a changing present, but in the new history the past loses its pastness and firmness at a rate that is as dizzying as the changing policies of the Soviet Government.

Marxist historical scholarship, [says a keynote article in the professional journal, "Problems of History,"] must wage an incessant war against the falsification of history by the bourgeoisie. This war which places Soviet historians on the firing line, is being conducted, and must be conducted, in all fields of historical science . . . Soviet historical science develops under the constant and close leadership of the Soviet state, the Bolshevik Party, and Stalin personally . . .[1]

But to say that history has become a weapon and the historian a warrior is scarcely to touch upon what is essentially new in the new history. Historiography has been absorbed into ideology and must support and accord with and be pervaded by the ideology that justifies and takes its character from the regime. History is part of a myth or mystique, so that its actors, its forces and trends, its trajectory from past through present to the future, must be in keeping with the style that characterizes the whole system. Just as painting and poetry and music must conform to that "style," so history, which is once more a form of poetry in its primary sense of myth-making.

What the totalitarian is sure of is what the rest of us are most unsure of. Historians find it hard enough to determine what really happened in the past, more difficult to apprehend what is happening in the present, and impossible to foretell the future. It is the totalitarian's certainty about the future which makes him so ruthless in manipulating the present. To make the present conform to the inevitable future, he finds it justifiable to use force and fraud, persuasion and violence, to wage total and unending war on "all existing conditions," on all classes of society, on all realms of the spirit. Being thus ruthless with the present in the name of the future, shall he be more tender with the past?

Or, to put it purely in terms of "the record," shall a Vyshinsky who does not hesitate to rewrite the record of the North Korean invasion of South Korea even while it is occurring under our eyes,

[1] I. Kon, "K voprosu o spetsifike i zadachakh istoricheskoi nauki" (On the Problem of the Specificity and Tasks of Historical Science), *Voprosy istorii*, no. 6, 1951, p. 63.

be any more scrupulous with fact when the events of 1917 are concerned, events which are receding with explosive speed and suffering what the astronomer calls a "red shift" in the outer reaches of
the universe of history?

Shall the Dictator, who does not hesitate to sacrifice millions of
lives in the erection of a given state institution or the fulfillment of
a given state plan, be less harsh with facts and records than with
men? Should he be more tender with the traditions and men of
other lands and other times than he is with the men of his own land
and time? If he puts even the wayward artist into uniform, shall
he not do as much with the historian who has so often in the past
worn court livery or priestly vestments or other habiliments pressed
upon him by his patrons?

But this time the patronage, too, is total. It is not his to accept or
reject. There is no resignation from its service, no area that is remote
or neutral, no scope to educate or convince the patron who already
KNOWS, no chance to live in the interstices of society, to get away
with Aesopian language. Nor, if the total state has its way ("tomorrow the world"), will there be any ultimate possibility of remaining a historian-in-exile, or a historian-in-defeat, as were
Napoleon, Trotsky, and Machiavelli. The Inquisitor will thrust a
bayonet into the mattress, look for a false bottom in the trunk, rip
up the flooring in search of the hidden, unpublished, and unpublish-
able manuscript addressed to one's own conscience or a longed-for
and contingent "posterity." The Inquisitor knows that he represents
posterity. Therefore, he feels justified in searching the hidden recesses
of the soul for a lurking doubt, or he puts a bullet in the base of
the brain as a sure end to all refractory memory.

III

It is instructive to examine the first modest model of the new
totalitarian historiography, Lavrenti Beria's "On the History of the
Bolshevik Organizations in Transcaucasia," alternatively titled,
"Stalin's Early Writings and Activities." In it, all other parties and
factions save the Bolshevik faction disappear, or appear only as
deliberate but ineffectual opponents of the things they in many cases
actually sought or accomplished. Even other Bolsheviks are expropriated of their words and deeds — all, that is, except one. Just

as all the achievements of the Russian people, the canals, the bridges, the railways, the steel mills, the plans and the fulfillments, were the work of Joseph Stalin personally, just as he personally directed the war on all fronts and personally won the peace, personally cared for the scientists and directed the lines of their research, so "The History of the Bolshevik Organizations in Transcaucasia" is "Stalin's Early Writings and Activities." Title and subtitle are one. Actor and history are one. It is an early phase in the synthetic production of a charismatic leader that forms one of the central purposes of Soviet historiography.

Before Beria wrote, Yenukidze, one of Stalin's teachers, remembered one thing; Ordjonikidze, one of Stalin's cronies and comrades-in-arms, another; Makharadze, leading Georgian Bolshevik historian, yet another. There was confusion and uncertainty. But the Chief of the Georgian GPU gave a two day lecture in 1935 at a Party Conference. The lecture became a book and all confusion was dissipated along with the mists of conflicting evidence and uncertainty. The history of Transcaucasia was established, coördinated, streamlined. All important Transcaucasian organizations, it turned out, had been formed, all strikes led, all key thoughts thought and key articles written, by the youthful Joseph Stalin. Whoever remembered otherwise ended up with a bullet in the base of the brain and a footnote in later editions of Beria's book, reading: "So-and-so has since been exposed as an enemy of the people." Even the earlier editions of Beria's book were successively consigned to the great Orwellian memory hole, while all "prehistoric" documents were refurbished and reissued in new retroactive editions to accord with the new history. Need we wonder that so valuable a historian should in 1938 have been promoted from Transcaucasian to All-Russian historiography as the Chief of the NKVD, true guardian of Clio in her latest totalitarian incarnation?

IV

In the new historiography there is a startling reversal in the roles of history-maker and historian. In the pre-totalitarian epoch or in the free world, men make their history as best they can, and then the historians try to determine the relations between what they thought they were doing, what they said they were doing, and what they have really done. But the new rulers know what they are doing. They possess in their ideology and in their charismatic attributes a prophetic insight and an absolute key to the future. They are history-makers in a new sense, having banished all uncertainty and contingency from human affairs. They no longer need critical interpreters and assayers of their intentions, their words, their deeds, and the consequences of their deeds.

Furthermore, there is a reversal in the roles of history or experience and ideology or theory. The experimental thinker likes to believe that he derives his ideas concerning society and history from the facts of history as they have developed. But for the totalitarian his ideology is unquestionable and absolute, and history must conform with it, or rather, derive from it. "Who controls the future controls the present. Who controls the present, controls the past."

The totalitarian movement begins by being its own historian. It is a movement that, before it takes power, already aims at a total rupture with the past. It rejects the idea of organic growth, mocks at all traditional and inherited and evolving institutions and ideas and all their living representatives. Even the mighty dead must be made "usable," that is, made to conform, or they must be mocked, diminished, debunked, and retroactively purged.

The leaders of the totalitarian movements are essentially autodidacts who in their hearts have contempt for history. They are assured and certain men who have no place for uncertainty, contigency, tentativeness, no humility before the vastness of the unknown and the refractoriness and impermeability of the given, no sense of the precariousness and fragility of the accumulated heritage of culture and civilization. They are the "terrible simplifiers" whom Burckhardt foretold; monists who have no toleration for pluralism in theory or in life. Before they are in power they ignore, after they are in power they burn, the documents that might testify against their overriding ideology or call in question their version of any event, however remote. They are driven by a compulsion to ferret out and destroy or "edit" any documents that might sow the slightest seedcorn of doubt. Doubt — the tiniest shadow of doubt — is for the totalitarian intolerable. Nay more, it is menacing. Still more, it is treason. "So-and-so has since been revealed to be an enemy of the people."

The totalitarian leader, as Hannah Arendt has pointed out, finds his chief recruiting ground among untutored and inexperienced masses that have hitherto been inert and passive and have had no experience with programs or history. Life has recently roused them from their historyless limbo by inexplicably casting them out of a society that was at best inexplicable. There is real satisfaction in finding some one who can assure them that all the organic and traditional is as meaningless as it has seemed to them, that all the dignitaries are undignified and fraudulent deceivers carrying on a meaningless show which will stop the minute the sailor with a pistol dissolves the parliament, or the half-wit with the torch sets fire to the Reichstag building. Then "their" meaningless history will stop and "our" meaningful historyless history will begin.

v

Politicians have rarely been historians, and when they have, it has usually been in moments of exile or defeat or at least temporary dismissal. Their deeds no longer speaking for them, they have been moved to choose words. But in contradistinction to a Napoleon, a Thucydides, a Xenophon, a Josephus, or even a Churchill, who wait to turn their energies into the writing of history until defeat has deprived them of the opportunity of making it, Stalin engaged in the writing of history as one of the means by which he climbed to power. Then he used power itself as one of the means of writing, or rather "editing" and rewriting history. History having proved a useful weapon to assault the arsenals of power, his control of the arsenals showed him how the sword or pistol might guide the pen. This explains the ruthless political utilitarianism, the combative factionalism, the *partiinost* which he impressed upon history. That is why first "rotten liberalism" towards hitherto controversial matters, and then "objectivism" in dealing with historical fact became scholarly crimes.[2]

Having broken violently with the past and seized power by vio-

---

[2] *Partiinost*, literally, "partyness," may be partially rendered by the words "partisanship" and "party spirit." It is a demand made not only on history and the social sciences, but also on the natural sciences and art and letters. "Rotten liberalism" was first used by Stalin in a pronouncement on historiography. "Objectivism" is a reproach now in any of the sciences.

lence, the totalitarian regime has thereby broken the habits of obedience and service and the very fabric of legitimacy. It is therefore
perpetually driven to spin the web of its legitimacy out of its own
entrails and as constantly to break the web again, thereby giving to
historiography a vertiginous instability. It develops a mania for self-
justification and self-advertisement, which is as total as every other
aspect of its life.

In contradistinction to the limited and time-hallowed despotisms
of an earlier day, totalitarianism requires modern technology and
modern manipulative psychology as preconditions for its emergence.
It takes total organization and total power — not propaganda skill,
but the union of pen and sword or pen and pistol in a single hand —
to do so complete a job. Once the total state has concentrated in its
control not only all the mean of production of material goods but
no less of spiritual goods — all the modes of expression, communication, criticism, thought, feeling, all love and hate, all paper, ink,
type, loudspeakers, microphones, cameras, cinemas, montage and
cutting rooms, theaters, walls, churches, schools, lecterns, meeting
halls, all import and export of and traffic in ideas — it becomes possible to reshape the past, the ruler's, the party's, and the public past,
nearer to the heart's desire.

VI

Driven by the restlessness of its changing line, its unending penetration into all aspects of life and its tireless drive to revolutionize
everything from above, the totalitarian regime endlessly revises its
historiography to accord with its latest line and actions. Every such
revision has its resonance effects in a thousand unexpected places.
Because in totalitarianism's view, everything is relevant to its aims
and everything is connected with everything else, even each minor
revision is likely in the end to move outward in ever widening
ripples towards totality.

Totalitarianism is painfully, morbidly distrustful and susceptible
to suggestion from even the most remote analogy. Its cruelty and
resolute thoroughness are based on its own inner unsureness, whence
the astounding energy and hatred with which it may attack the
tiniest and most neutral seeming observation.

Thus, a morbid awareness of Russia's own backwardness in 1917

(making it Marxistically speaking inappropriate for a socialist revolution), and a morbid awareness of Russia's backwardness in many
spheres today, compels the totalitarian historian to revise the history
of the steppe tribes and their backwardness in relation to Byzantium,
to make Tadjikia more advanced than ancient Persia, and Kazakhstan more so than Arabia and Turkey. How Soviet historiography
is wrestling with the problem of rooting out the memory of the old
Slavic Chronicle which told how the Kievan Slavs asked Norsemen
to come and rule over them!

Because it is totalistic, totalitarianism assumes that every event,
every interpretation, every symbolical person or act, every thought
or institution, every element of the social system and our vision of it,
no matter how remote or insignificant, has implications for society
as a whole and for the ideology that rules it. This ideology saturates
life as water does a swamp. All politics, all institutions, all feelings,
are now "nationalized" and, what is more important, stylized, to
agree with the over-all style that characterizes the regime.

Hence the tribute which the official historian Pankratova paid to
the Supreme Architect of History and Lord of Life is literally true:
"Stalin has extended the limits of Soviet history by 1500 to 2000
years." The latest textbooks of "The History of the USSR" actually
extend Soviet history through the shadowy origins of the Slavs into
the Balkans; through the intercourse of the Slavs with Byzantium,
through the Transcaucasian kingdoms, and the fact that the Tigris
and Euphrates take their rise in the farther slopes of the Caucasus,
into Babylonia, Assyria, Greece, the Middle East, and even Egypt;
through the Mongols and the Central Asian peoples into the history
of Asia; through the Yakuts and their relations with Bronze Age
China into Chinese prehistory; through the Russian and Russian-
hired explorers of Alaska, California, and the Antarctic, into every
continent but Australia. (Can this explain the puzzling fact that the
Soviet bookstore in New York is named "Four Continents?")

Even nationalism is being curiously "nationalized" by the new
totalitarian historiography. The history of the Balkans and other
"People's Democracies" is being rewritten in the Slavic Studies Section of the Academy of Sciences of the Soviet Union. Bulgaria is
getting a new look. Rumania's animus toward old Russia is being
retroactively transformed and her language is being considered for

honorary Slavic citizenship. Non-Slavic Albania, it now turns out, has "longed for centuries for liberation from the Turkish yoke and has sought the friendship which now binds it to the Soviet peoples." Tito has become retroactively the eternal traitor, who in 1941 was simultaneously serving Hitler and Anglo-American imperialism. Two successive editings of Czechoslovak history have been scrapped, and the third, only a year old, is already under fire. The Polish historians are in continuous torment. Poland's culture must have been decisively influenced by the Great Russian, but not by Rome or the West, while all trace of Polish influence on Great Russian culture is being deleted or prefixed by a minus sign.

To the "memory hole" have been consigned all the works of Marx and Engels on the menace of Russian absolutism, on Russian imperial expansion in Europe and Asia, on Pan-Slavism, all their utterances in favor of the restoration of Poland "with the boundaries of 1772," in favor of Shamil and his struggle for Trancaucasian independence. After fifteen years of concealment, Stalin published a secret attack which he wrote in 1934 on Engels' last article "On Russian Foreign Policy." But Marxism is still needed as an ostensibly invariant philosophy to refer to in vindicating ever-shifting policies, so for the most part this censorship proceeds in silence.[3]

In 1934 Stalin could still rebuke a textbook for failing to brand "the annexationist-colonializing role of Tsarism . . . the Prison-House of Peoples"; its "counterrevolutionary role in foreign policy . . . as the international gendarme"; and for failing to show the influence of Western thought upon the democratic and Socialist revolutionary movements in Russia. To quote the 1934 Stalin in Russia in 1953 would be to take one's life into one's hands.

Now Great Russian nationalism is inextricably blended with "Soviet patriotism." Internationalism is for use abroad, and was defined by Stalin as "unconditional loyalty to the Soviet Union." At home it is "cosmopolitanism" and "servility to all things foreign." Nationalism of any other variety than Great Russian is "bourgeois nationalism" and is fatal. A Sosyura may not "love the Ukraine" unless he remember to love above all its yearning for annexation and

---

[3] For the writings of Marx and Engels that are now suppressed in the Soviet Union see *Karl Marx and Friedrich Engels, The Russian Menace to Europe*, edited by Blackstock and Hoselitz (Glencoe, Illinois: The Free Press, 1952).

the Great Russian imprint upon its culture. With each revision, the Balkan states move longingly another step toward incorporation.

Each of the "autonomous republics" is rewriting its history, revising its poetry, remaking its memories. Heroes become anti-heroes (Shamil, Kenessary); insurrections against tsarism until yesterday celebrated are today execrated; epics become anti-epics (*"Dede Korkut"*) or the versions that have lived so long in oral tradition and are the very national memory of illiterate peoples are purged and reissued in "new authentic texts."

The expurgation of the epic ["Manas"] should be strictly scientific and principled. It should take into account all the historical circumstances in the life of the people. This demands a suitable selection of variants, songs and episodes, a selection of which the fundamental principle must be the preservation in the epic of all the best elements inherent in the past of the Kirgiz people.[4]

Even so did Orwell picture a functionary in his Ministry of Truth whose task was to "produce garbled versions — definitive texts they were called — of poems which had become ideologically offensive but which, for one reason or another, were to be retained in the anthologies."

VII

Thus totalitarianism, which begins by being so sure of the future that in its name it declares war on all the existing conditions of the present, ends by making war on the entire past. Yet the past will not be mocked and takes its own peculiar revenge. It is wiser to approach the past with the "revolutionary" principle of the Apostle Paul: "Prove all things, and hold on to that which is good," than with all the slogans of Marx, Engels, Lenin, and Stalin. For the past shapes the present and nourishes it, and he who tries to throw it out indiscriminately will find the worst elements of his country's past reasserting themselves and enlarging their evil, while all that is best tends to be lost or destroyed. For what is the new order which tried to break once and for all with autocracy and bondage and the Tsarist Okhrana but a monstrous enlargement of police and autocracy and bondage into totality? And the great love of humanity in nineteenth-

[4] *Literaturnaya Gazeta,* May 27, 1952, p. 2.

century Russia that moved generous spirits everywhere has been lost or rather driven underground by this cruel indiscriminating war on the present and the past in the name of the future.

History may be but a feeble rushlight to illuminate the mists of the present and the obscurity of the future, but without a sense of history man cannot make a single step forward at all or even hold his precarious footing in the stream of time. That is why the hero of Orwell's *Nineteen Eighty-four* feared that he was going mad when all the objective landmarks by which he might get his bearings began to shift and crack and change into undependable and unrecognizable shapes.

DISCUSSION

Mr. Philipp Frank: One often wonders how the contemporary totalitarians can interfere with scientific research without losing at every point. We must, I think, differentiate the problem of politico-theological convenience from that of practical and technological importance. The former sort of consideration was relevant in the times of Copernicus and Galileo. Their theories were of very little immediate practical significance, but they did upset the theologians greatly. The issue was therefore one of ideological convenience.

The practical problem is quite different. The best twentieth-century illustration is probably relativistic physics. From the Nazi point of view, Einstein's theory was "Bolshevism in physics," but when they found it necessary for technological reasons to accep the formula $e = mc^2$, the Nazi ideologists decided to embrace the practical content while still rejecting the philosophical overtones. In Russia, much the same sort of thing happened. Relativity at first was flatly rejected, largely because of Einstein's sympathies with Mach and Machism, which Lenin abominated. Then, twenty-five years later, a paper in the most important Soviet scientific journal argued that relativity could be purged of the remnants of Machism and accepted as ideologically unobjectionable in its practical implications. In other words, to return to my opening remark, the totalitarians need not lose every time. They can prevent refutation of the ideology by the facts if they accept dissonant theories while ignoring their philosophical evaluations.

I have a question for Mr. Muller along these lines. Has Western genetics been "taken over" in the Soviet Union in its practical aspects, in divorcement from the completely unacceptable underlying theory?

Mr. Muller: Yes, it has, especially in the development of hybrid corn and in related fields. But, since they do not accept the general theory, they cannot extend the practical side on their own. They can only copy, and they therefore lag.

Mr. Carl Friedrich: I welcome Mr. Santillana's discussion of the Galileo case, for I submit that careful consideration of the facts will lead us to reject it as a parallel to totalitarian control of science. My reasons for saying this relate not only to our discussion of totalitarianism and science this evening, but also to the problems of totalitarianism and the personality which we were discussing this afternoon.

I think that we confuse totalitarianism with authoritarianism. I'm sorry to inject an apparently terminological issue, but this one is of fundamental importance. The use of the term "authoritarian" for the kind of personality inclined toward totalitarianism is rather unfortunate. (As in the use of such terms as "authoritarian family" and the implication involved that "authority" is bad.) Totalitarianism is precisely the opposite of authoritarianism, for it involves the elimination of all stable authority. Those psychologists, who have concentrated on the "authoritarian" personality and have linked "conformity" with "authority," must have missed this point. They have fallen into serious error if they tacitly assume that "authoritarian" is either synonymous with "totalitarian" or somehow closely related to it. I believe it is important to realize that every society must be "authoritarian" in some degree, every society must contain "authoritarian" personalities, every society must exact obedience to authority. But totalitarian societies attempt to shatter all traditional types of authority and to replace them with a new kind of social control. In a very real sense, in a totalitarian society true authority is altogether destroyed.

The case of seventeenth-century science in general and of Galileo in particular is an illustration of this distinction. We can distinguish two currents in seventeenth-century scientific research: the experimental, represented by Galileo and Harvey, and the mathematical and metaphysical, represented by Descartes and Newton. Kepler is perhaps unique, for he had a foot in both camps. To Descartes and Kepler, Galileo was a dangerous publicizer. In their view he brought difficult philosophical matters before people who could not understand them, always playing irresponsibly with "big questions" without the philosophical sophistication necessary to their consideration. This sort of behavior, they felt, disrupts society and strikes at the "authority" which helps to bind it together. Galileo ran into authoritarian opposition, if you like, but it was psychologically and institutionally nothing like the kind of totalitarian control over science which we have seen in our own century.

Miss Else Frenkel-Brunswik: May I reply to Mr. Friedrich on this matter of the term "authoritarian" in psychological research? We do not use the word, but I think we mean by it exactly what Mr. Friedrich means by "totalitarian." An authoritarian personality, in our usage, is one particularly susceptible to a totalitarian kind of ideology. Psychological studies have made it quite clear that such people are *both* excessively submissive to radically new assertions of authority *and* peculiarly destructive of established types of authority.

Mr. Karl Deutsch: If the so-called "authoritarian personality" is one susceptible to totalitarian appeals, we might all concur on the term "proto-totalitarian personality." This has one advantage which appeals particularly to those of us who have been trained as historians, for it focuses our attention on the formative stages of the totalitarian regimes.

With respect to the Galileo case, I would hesitate before implying that it is entirely removed from the problems of analyzing totalitarianism. It and the totalitarian phenomena have one thing in common, I think. In both situations we see a collision between two different rates of cultural change. I wonder if one could not say that both "proto-" and "fully" totalitarian societies are those in which the movement is attempting to impose on a society a faster learning process than that to which it is accustomed. The totalitarians try to hurry people along the road of history. The justification for this acceleration, and the indication of the route it is following, is the task of the totalitarian ideology.

Looking at totalitarianism this way may reveal to us some strains we would otherwise overlook. The differential rates of learning — that of the society before it goes totalitarian, and that of the totalitarian movement — create problems, for the gap must not be permitted to become too large and yet must be kept large enough to give the zealots of the movement a sense of historical mission. Furthermore, the very coming of the movement to power puts it into an international context and gives it governmental responsibilities, both of which may entail sudden "switches" in the official programs. These changes may leave the subordinate zealots on the ends of very shaky limbs: they vigorously pursue a line of historical acceleration which suddenly becomes obsolete if not heretical. Thus, within the totalitarian monolith there is a constant danger of fissures between the *Apparat* which executes plans and the leaders who must unexpectedly alter them.

Mr. Michael Karpovich: On the terminological issue which has been raised, I would suggest that we reserve "totalitarian" for situations where an all-embracing ideology is united with an all-powerful authority. This was certainly not the case in the time of Galileo, and we therefore merely delude ourselves if we call it totalitarian.

I cannot agree with Mr. Wolfe's implication that history was subjected to totalitarian controls from the outset of the Soviet regime. Intellectual activities were purified very gradually. Some disciplines — philosophy, then economics and sociology — were cleaned out very early, and history was being purged in the twenties. But not all history: literary history, for example, was out of step with the rest of the discipline until the attacks on "formalism" following World War II. And the natural sciences were not really rigorously controlled until the 1930's, and even there it is clear that biology was *gleichgeschaltet* before physics or chemistry.

That gradualism should appear is perfectly plausible. In the beginning, the "apparatus" is still rudimentary, and what there is of it is busy on more important problems than the control of the intellectuals. Only very slowly is learning attacked and in my own opinion this comes about not because of practical or operational considerations, but because of the inner dialectical workings of the regime.

I would also dissent from Mr. Wolfe's suggestion that history in the Soviet Union has been utterly perverted. Some good things still are being done. Even today, some Soviet historians are using the device of rendering homage to the regime in the first and last chapters of their books and publishing sound stuff in the middle. In party histories, the documents are dubious, but in other types of editing many important contributions are appearing which are untainted. Somehow, they get by the censors.

This leads me to remark that I doubt the possibility of completely effective, 100 per cent control of all scientific labor in totalitarian systems. Probably it can never be complete.

PART SIX

Totalitarian Social and Economic Organization

■

15. Totalitarian Appeal and Economic Reform

ALBERT LAUTERBACH

Both the Communist and the Fascist brands of totalitarianism contain certain principles of a program for economic reform. In fact, an economic program, in the alleged interest of labor or the "toilers," has officially been the principal rationale of Communism, and similar elements have been quite significant in the rise of Nazism. Measures against unemployment; programs of industrialization; expropriation of certain groups or types of property; redistribution of land; tax reforms; barriers to trade; all have been regular features of totalitarian programs, though none of these measures has been an invention or exclusive province of the totalitarians.

It would be quite misleading, however, to regard such initial ideas of economic reform as the real explanation either of the dynamics or of the wide appeal of totalitarian movements. Some people, it is true, are attracted to them mainly by those proposed remedies for economic evils, but this type of supporter is unlikely to stay with totalitarian movements very long. For the bulk of their followers, the economic reforms proposed represent a rationalization of deeper emotional needs, not the real basis for political support.

This fact emerges readily from a comparison between contemporary totalitarianism and older forms of autocracy. Through the ages, monopolies of power and of ideas, based on convictional certainty, have been very frequent. In many societies of the past, conformist exclusiveness was internalized to the point of making any deviant pattern of thought appear to the average person as sinful or insane. The medieval knight, serf, or priest could not even perceive any such thing as free thought — a freedom for "wrong" ideas to compete with the "right" ones.

In modern Western societies, however, the cultural and institutional setting of such attitudes is quite different. Individuals who have been brought up in the values of freedom and yet desire to escape from it, reflect extreme personal insecurity. The essence of totalitarian mentality in our period is emotional inability to bear criticism or even a real discussion, along with an uncontrollable urge for an unshakable frame of reference to which one can always hold on in the midst of an otherwise confusing world. In terms of the perception patterns concerned, such mentality reflects an excessive and rigid urge for definiteness and stability of the environment perceived, with intolerance of any perceptive ambiguity; and a constant if sometimes unconscious striving for absolute *certainty*, even at the risk of self-deception. Such urge for definiteness on the level of perception is often accompanied by impatience for action regardless of consequences: the title of a Nazi pamphlet was *Besser falsch handeln als gar nicht handeln*. At the same time, authoritarian-guided relief from responsibility, from necessity to make individual decisions, seems to promise a peace of mind which acutely insecure people often despair of finding in any other way.

Basically, persons with totalitarian propensity are characterized by deep unresolved frustrations, often rooted in family experiences during childhood. Such frustrations may lead to self-hating along with hidden needs for parental affection, which are then projected to the social scene; scape-goating and *Führer* veneration result. A political party, social movement, or economic panacea may offer an outlet for such needs, and may even put a premium on psychopathic traits. Blind authoritarian discipline and sacrifice come to be happily accepted by many in fulfillment of an unconscious craving for parental protection even if it includes punishment. (Hidden fear of children by parents, it is true, also appears to occur with some frequency in contemporary societies, thus adding a new source of personal insecurity in adults.)

Identification with the authoritarian leader or hero momentarily gives the insecure person some of the emotional hold he had been missing. At the same time, he tends to develop a perceptual block and strong resentment toward the mentality and aims of those who

resist a similar breakdown of their selves and a totalitarian resocial-
ization of their adult personalities. They are perceived as a danger to
society in refusing to join the ranks of the insecure with their collective fear of freedom, and in demonstrating implicitly that all human
beings need not be that way.

The excessively fear-ridden, as a group, are emotionally incapable
of bearing the presence of those who are not, or are so in a lesser
degree. At the same time, whenever totalitarians of any denomination succeed in spreading a mentality of fear and a receptiveness for
ideological panics, they have scored a victory for *all* such denominations no matter which one of the latter may win the next election or
immediate public support. Uncontrollable mass fears are the indispensable basis of any type of totalitarianism. Mussolini knew what
he meant when he said, paraphrasing what other authoritarians had
expressed before him: "I do not care about their love as long as they
fear me." [1]

Perhaps totalitarian propensity in a strict sense is not very frequent as yet in Western societies, but its nearest relative, the authoritarian mind, has been found to be fairly widespread. The features
of the latter have been described by Horkheimer as follows: "Mechanical surrender to conventional values; blind submission to authority together with blind hatred of all opponents and outsiders;
anti-introspectiveness; rigid stereotyped thinking; a penchant for
superstition; vilification, half-moralistic and half-cynical, of human
nature; projectivity." Similarly, Else Frenkel-Brunswik summarizes
as follows the traits of authoritarian personality, in the light of the
research carried out by the California group: "Self-alienation, mechanization, standardization and stereotypy, piecemeal functioning,
intolerance of ambiguity, lack of individuation and spontaneity, and
a combination of irrationality with manipulative opportunism"; "it
is this externally over-adjusted type of person who is internally much
less adjusted than the democratic-minded individual." [2]

[1] Carlo Levi, "For Freedom, We Must Conquer Fear," *New York Times Magazine*,
October 3, 1948. See also his book *Of Fear and Freedom* (New York, 1950).

[2] M. Horkheimer, "The Lessons of Fascism," in H. Cantril, ed., *Tensions that
Cause Wars* (Urbana, 1950), p. 230. See also T. W. Adorno and others, *The Authori-
tarian Personality* (New York, 1950). Erich Fromm, *Psychoanalysis and Religion*
(New York, 1950), pp. 31ff. José Ortega y Gasset, *The Revolt of the Masses* (New
York, 1950), esp. chap. x. H. D. Lasswell and associates, *The Comparative Study of*

In our period the totalitarian — an extreme version of the authoritarian — is quite likely to use economic programs more frequently than did his forerunners in earlier periods of society. Essentially, however, economic arguments or institutional programs of any kind provide in this case mere rationalizations; for totalitarianism is essentially a primitive religion with some totemistic traits, a perverted messianic element, and a relapse into barbaric mob behavior. This substitute-religion shares with some older creeds an anti-scientific, anti-intellectual attitude which is basically at odds with the requirements of genuine economic reform. This particular creed, however, has not learned as yet any tolerance — or at least, understanding of other people's mentality — as many others have in varying degrees.

It is true that initial economic improvements under a new totalitarian regime do sometimes occur where it takes over a society ridden by economic backwardness or disruption. It remains to be seen, however, whether any totalitarian regime can survive in the long run unless it keeps the bulk of its people in poverty, in humiliation, and in the ignorance that so often goes with them. Thus far, recent history shows conspicuous instances of totalitarian regimes which started out with the promise of economic progress in the sense of increasing equality but wound up with extreme inequality to the point of establishing a class of slave laborers.

In modern Western societies a high incidence of strong personal insecurities, often expressed in totalitarian propensities, has accompanied processes of social disorganization and, especially, of economic instability. Contemporary society, however, with its background of pronounced encouragement of intellectual individuality, cannot take totalitarian attitudes for granted as some earlier societies did, nor can it afford to accept the rise of such attitudes as unavoidable in any socio-psychological situation. For any sweeping disintegration, in the wake of totalitarianism, of the social norm that are usually asso-

---

Symbols (Stanford, 1952). Else Frenkel-Brunswik, "Interaction of Psychological and Sociological Factors in Political Behavior," *American Political Science Review*, March 1952. On the perception processes concerned, Robert R. Blake and Glenn V. Ramsey, eds., *Perception: An Approach to Personality* (New York, 1951), chap. iv (E. R. Hilgard), chap. iv (W. Dennis), chap. ix (J. G. Miller), and chap. xiii (E. Frenkel-Brunswik). B. Bettelheim, "Remarks on the Psychological Appeal of Totalitarianism," *American Journal of Economics and Sociology*, October 1952.

ciated with civilization; any revolution of nihilism; any wide appeal
of psychopathic heroes who take care of people's personal fears by
making them the prevailing and, indeed, the only recognized pattern — any such trend can be fatal in a period of mechanized large-
scale production with its striking instruments of mass communication.

Once a totalitarian atmosphere has developed, any discussion of
economic reform is immediately displaced from the level of intellectual evaluation to that of a primitive version of theology; the suspicion of unorthodox economic ideas or reform preferences becomes a
favorite starting point for heresy hunts. Not that such hunts depend
on the actual occurrence of unorthodox thought or behavior. Their
essential element is the uncontrollable emotional *need* for witches
that characterizes the totalitarian mind. If it cannot find anything
resembling real sinners it will create them in its own imagination.
Witches and confessions are indispensable as an outlet for the fears
and security needs of the totalitarian; whoever declines to confess
refuses the accusers relief from their insecurities. Lack of "coopera-
tion" on the part of whoever happens to be accused thus comes to
mean sabotage and betrayal — of the security needs of the totalitarians. The "sense" of forcible confessions, regardless of whether the
coercion is physical or mental, is to enhance the beliefs and security
feelings of the accusers. Sometimes this comes to apply to insecure
or totalitarian-minded defendants, too, regardless of possible innocence — simply by relieving them of any hidden guilt feelings, especially those stemming from lack of successful resistance toward the
inquisitors.

Essentially the purpose of obtaining such confessions is to "explain" the root of evils and to make sure, by the confession as such,
that these evils are now removed. Confession thus serves as a kind
of incantation; to plead innocent means to invite the wrath of the
demons. The factual guilt question involved — in our period quite
often economic beliefs and their meanings — is irrelevant and serves
as a mere irritant if brought up by old-fashioned defendants who
have not caught on to the game. That is why any denial of charges,
or any criticism of totalitarian investigators, is automatically considered a proof of subversions: it means refusal of personal security
to them.

The witches are most effective in their security-promoting function if they were originally of the accusers' own breed, if they were
considered "loyal" in the past; Satan was originally an angel.[3] The
mutual tension-relief operates best if an underlying community of
emotional starting-points underlies it. In addition, this type of collective tension-relief also serves the purpose of creating a particular
kind of "mass" — the one that only a community of fear can cement.
Refusal to confess, that is, to share these mass fears, is thus interpreted by the totalitarian as an anti-social act.

Basically, we repeat, totalitarian mentality reflects the emotional
inability of excessively insecure persons to bear criticism. Here discussion of controversial ideas or institutions in the economic field,
in particular, is perceived as a tool of propaganda if not subversion.
Totalitarianism itself "solves" economic and other problems by removing any possibility of a legitimate alternative to its own pre-
conceptions, not only legally but psychologically — by denying the
very existence of such problems under its own rule outside the perverted imagination of deviants who supposedly are always few but
never are allowed to die out.[4] It is a part of the tragedy of our time
that such mentality has spread in the name of Communism and
anti-Communism alike; and that it has often met only weak or brief
resistance among the rank and file toward the compliance requirements concerned. Such requirements were at the same time rationalized, with the help of restructured perception, into individual beliefs
or assumed objective needs of society. It is the ultimate aim of totalitarianism to make an accomplice out of every individual, at least
in the psychological sense of coming to share all the guilt with the
totalitarian movement and, especially, with an established regime of
this type.

In practice, the psychological difference among the various denominations of totalitarianism has been slight even when their eco-

[3] See Alexander Weissberg, *The Accused* (New York, 1951). Marion L. Starkey,
The Devil in Massachusetts (New York, 1949). Carey McWilliams, *Witchhunt* (Boston, 1950).
[4] Karl Mannheim, *Freedom, Power, and Democratic Planning* (New York, 1950)
pp. 231ff. I. Berlin, "Political Ideas in the Twentieth Century," *Foreign Affairs*, April
1, 1950. For a historical comparison, J. L. Talmon, *The Rise of Totalitarian Democracy* (Boston, 1952), esp. pp. 249ff.

nomic programs or political semantics seemed to be irreconcilable. In Western countries, at least, the choice of denomination appears to be a secondary matter (or to show oscillations) in persons who have a strong totalitarian propensity. The most elaborate brand of totalitarianism in our period, however, is undoubtedly Communism. The key to the understanding of its role in the present-day world is not in the intellectual, political, or economic origins of that movement but in its psychodynamics, including attitudes and beliefs. Undoubtedly there are strong, if mostly hidden, elements of an attitudinal and belief system in the original structure of Marxism itself, despite its claim to purely scientific analysis. It would be quite hopeless, however, to look in the writings of Marx and Engels for an explanation of the twists of Soviet ideology and policy in our period. Only censored editions of Marx are available in the Soviet Union today; and there is much reason to believe that Stalin or Malenkov would have liquidated Marx, had the latter lived long enough to see what uses had been made of his doctrine.

Moreover, the socio-economic starting-point of Communist movements should not be confounded with their subsequent features. Justified grievances of the working class in industrialized areas (especially in newly developed ones) and, above all, the exploitative legacy of feudal and absolutist regimes in backward countries, are frequently at the root of an initial mass appeal of Communism in the parts of the world affected. Nevertheless, its institutional origins in actual needs and goals of economic reform should not blind anyone to the subsequent shift of Communism into an international tool of Russian power policy and, at the same time, into an all-embracing substitute-religion in its psychological meaning to the individuals afflicted.

Actually the common cover of Marxian or pseudo-Marxian semantics conceals the existence within the world of Communism of three phenomena of quite different orders. First, there is a genuine movement for economic reform with radical methods, mainly in countries with a feudal-aristocratic legacy, landless rural masses, and a need for sweeping redistribution of land and for protection of workers from ruthless exploitation. Such reform goals are not essentially Communist in character, but the Communists easily manage to appropriate them, largely by defaults of other political and ideological groups. In recent years, the combination of such economic ideas with nationalist slogans has been especially effective.

Second, there is the Communism in the Soviet Union of the fifties, after three or four decades of unchallenged power position and ideological monopoly. In the Soviet Union today — and, in a lesser degree, in some of its satellite countries to the West — the Communists represent largely the conformist or indifferent types, not the revolutionaries or malcontents. In a monolithic structure like the Soviet regime, with a large majority of people who have never known any other order of things, it must take quite an unusual amount of independence, non-conformity, or rebellious personality to oppose Communism. Essentially it is the individual with a conformist or, at least, a conservative personality, who supports Communism in the Soviet Union in our period, although the continuance of new industrialization must leave some outlets for imaginative initiative for the time being.

Third, there is the person with totalitarian propensity in Western countries which have long known freedom of thought and democratic discussion. To go totalitarian in a free country takes an extreme amount of personal insecurity resulting in a pressing need to hold on to someone who supposedly will always have all the answers. Frequent occurrence of such needs in a country with traditions of intellectual freedom indicates strong disruptive influences in social life such as a high degree of recurrent economic instability. Any wide appeal of either Communism or other shades of totalitarian mentality under conditions such as these is a symptom of a sick society.

The three kinds of Communism overlap in some places and are subject to shifts in their relative importance within the various countries affected. The Kremlin, of course, holds them together and utilizes them for its own power purposes as thoroughly as it can. But this political fact should not be allowed to obscure the different roots, characteristics and, therefore, future prospects of the various attitudes that go under the name of Communism.

On the individual level, it is true, totalitarian identification, no matter in which of the ways mentioned it was originally acquired, often continues long after a person has been purged: he is afraid of

losing his frame of reference without being able to replace it by a
new one. The following description of the rise and fall of a Russian
Communist, by a fellow-prisoner, is illustrative: "The Party gave
him a psychological backbone which he did not otherwise possess.
He was a man without initiative and he felt safe in the Party; it
offered him a certain position he could never have won on his
own. . . During the revolution and the years of civil war they had
been attracted by its revolutionary ideas and, once inside, a cleverly
devised system saw to it that they never drifted away again. Their
choice was between membership of the dominant group, which included a comfortable and secure position, and the terrible threat of
complete moral and physical destruction if they ventured to depart
by as much as a hair's breadth from the Party Line." [5]

The material aspects of defection are, of course, different in countries where Communism is not in a dominant and perhaps not even
in a legal position. But the psychodynamics of its current or past
supporters do not necessarily differ in the same way. On the individual level totalitarian identification, no matter in which of the various
ways mentioned it was originally acquired, often tends to be quite
persistent in a hidden way, at least. This fact explains the paralyzing
impact of totalitarian purges upon many supporters who are objectively innocent of the charges raised against them. They can fight
against perceived enemies but not against perceived brethren even
if the latter made a "mistake." Conversely, the accusers perceive suspected heretics as "suffering from a psychological dichotomy which
will split and destroy them 'spiritually' . . . The internal strains to
which they are subject will be too much for them both as individuals
and as a party." [6]

Among the various types of totalitarian propensity in Western
countries, the people most likely to be attracted to Communism

[5] Weissberg, pp. 123ff. Compare H. D. Lasswell, N. Leites, and associates, *Language of Politics* (New York, 1949), esp. chap. x. S. K. Weinberg, "Personality and
the Soviet Society," *American Journal of Economics and Sociology*, October 1952.

[6] Hamilton Fish Armstrong, *Tito and Goliath* (New York, 1951), p. 157. Com-
pare Jan Stransky, *East Wind over Prague* (New York, 1951), esp. part III. For other
interesting aspects of the Soviet mentality, see Barrington Moore, Jr., *Soviet Politics —
The Dilemma of Power* (Cambridge, Massachusetts, 1950), esp. pp. 390ff; Margaret
Mead, *Soviet Attitudes toward Authority* (New York, 1951); Sidney Lens, *Counterfeit
Revolutions* (Boston, 1952); Ypsilon, *Patterns of World Revolution* (Chicago, 1947).

(rather than to other shades of totalitarianism) are strongly guilt-ridden persons. Communism, as distinguished from fascism, has its institutional starting point in lower-class aspirations, and it keeps rationalizing the emotional needs of its followers in this old way — a practice which tends to attract certain individuals from upper and middle groups of society who unconsciously wish to repent for individual or group sins felt. Driving the Communists underground probably increases this masochistic attraction and strengthens the allegiance of the initiated, the "knowledge," to each other and to the cause. At the same time, Communists appear to have a basic contempt for fellow-travelers who do not commit themselves to the movement formally and, above all, psychologically; and who may even be really interested in economic reform chiefly, rather than in an all-embracing substitute-religion.

The fascination that Communism holds for its active members, we repeat, often continues after they have been expelled or have left the Party on their own. Ideologically, the positive charge in their minds shifts into a negative one, but psychologically little changes in such cases: the black-and-white mentality continues, and in their perception of the world there still is nothing more important than Communism. The explanation, of course, is in the fact that the same personality traits that led them into Communism in the first place are still there even though their good standing with the ruling party clique of the moment has been impaired.

The social and historical starting-point of Communism, we pointed out earlier, is in lower-class aspirations. Fascism, on the other hand, originates typically in aspirations of upper and middle classes, especially where the middle classes are of pre-capitalist origin. It then comes to attract a number of persons from various strata who identify themselves with a social elite, but who are frustrated in their conscious or unconscious desire for high social status. Here again a program for economic reform serves to rationalize basic totalitarian propensities, even though society may objectively *be* in need of actual reform. While the socio-economic roots of fascism are different from those of Communism, however, the psychological disposition of the individuals afflicted is (or comes to be) very similar. Actually, interchange of ideas, methods, and allegiances between these twin movements is by no means infrequent despite the blood-thirsty language they like to use against each other.

The socio-economic conditions which typically enhance a mass appeal of fascism include national inferiority feelings based on perceived humiliation (in the wake of military defeat or foreign exploitation, for instance); uprooted pre-capitalist survivals in an industrialized society, such as aristocratic landowners or small handicraft; disgruntled intellectuals who form a frustrated would-be elite; an aimless or cynical youth in search of leaders and goals; strong concentration of economic power along with failure of the economic system to function properly, especially a sequence of depressions and inflations; actual or imagined threat to the economic order from radical currents or an extensive labor movement, along with collective guilt feelings of the upper classes; cultural and national characteristics that favor conformity, especially in the absence of deeply rooted experiences in democratic give-and-take; and, last but not least, any factors that generally foster a high incidence and intensity of personal insecurities.

Economic reforms, we repeat, often rank high in the official programs of fascist movements and in the initial policies of fascist regimes (employment policy, community improvements, housing, drainage and irrigation, land reforms, and monetary changes, for instance). Basically, however, such reform programs are entirely subservient to the emotional urge to find outlets for the mass fears found or aroused. Reform goals are cynically sacrificed to this urge whenever they are no longer required for purposes of plausible rationalization. Persons who are attracted to a fascist movement mainly by its economic program, and not by its images of hatred and power, will soon run afoul of its demands and mentality.

Fascism cannot be genuinely interested in economic reforms because of its consciously anti-intellectual character, its endeavor to arouse strong and blind emotions in its followers, its "know-nothing" attitude toward any scientific approach to human problems. The persecutory mob, not the revolutionary, is characteristic of fascism at an even earlier stage of development than in Communism. Economic factors — not excluding real goals of status defense of individuals or groups — are only of indirect importance in the rise and policy of fascism, to the extent that economic frustrations contribute greatly to the state of fear that underlies Fascism.

These considerations also apply to the related area of attitudes usually summarized under the heading of group prejudice. Attributed traits, and various stereotypes concerning certain groups (especially minorities) may be offered as "explanation" of high prices, bankruptcy, exploitation, or inequality. However, the underlying state of mind is not really rooted in any specific shortcomings of the economy (or in lack of economic information), although tensions resulting from socio-economic instability influence it greatly in a longer run. Ackerman and Jahoda describe the emotional predispositions to group prejudice as anxiety; confusion of the concept of self; conformity and fear of the different. The corresponding defense mechanisms transform the underlying anxiety into aggression against a collective scapegoat.[7] Fascism attempts to drive such displacement processes to the extreme, on a mass scale: it sets out to change and broaden the scale of social distances in its followers in such a way that actual economic relations and needs are distorted sadistically in their minds. This or that minority group permanently or periodically becomes the great villain, replacing the concept of objective economic conditions to be studied and changed.

Some experiences are now available concerning the legacy of a defeated fascist regime, and they are not very encouraging. Despite disappearance of the institutional structure of fascism in Germany, Austria, and Italy, the same insecurities that brought it about in the first place tend to continue or to reappear. Shortly after the war, an American psychiatrist found the following situation in Germany: The psychological effects of the twelve-year Hitler regime are seen most commonly in a variety of anxiety states, cautious manner, ap-

---

[7] N. W. Ackerman and M. Jahoda, *Anti-Semitism and Emotional Disorder* (New York, 1950), pp. 25ff, 88ff. B. Bettelheim and M. Janowitz, *Dynamics of Prejudice* (New York, 1950), chaps. iv and ix. UNESCO, *The Race Question in Modern Science*, pamphlet series (Paris, 1951). Hannah Arendt, *The Origins of Totalitarianism* (New York, 1951). T. W. Adorno, "Freudian Theory and the Pattern of Fascist Propaganda," in G. Roheim, ed., *Psychoanalysis and the Social Sciences*, vol. III (New York, 1951). Gordon W. Allport, *ABC's of Scapegoating* (New York, 1948). A. Forster and B. R. Epstein, *The Troublemakers* (New York, 1952). Muzater Sherif, *Outline of Social Psychology* (New York, 1948), esp. chap. xiv. Hadley Cantril, *Psychology of Social Movements* (New York, 1941), chap. iv.

prehension, diminished energy, reduction of social contacts, a host of psychoasthenic symptoms, and exaggerated submissive attitudes." [8]

My own observations in Germany and Austria in 1947, 1948, and 1950 indicated at first the impact of the negative selection which fascism (plus war destruction and hunger) had brought about. The courageous, independent, responsible types had become rare; most people seemed tired and interested only in the most immediate needs. Fear of some kind of new totalitarianism persisted and often resulted in shunning any active politics. The generation between twenty and forty seemed more anxious to play safe than older people — those who had retained a pre-fascist frame of reference. The conception of social activity of the people themselves as the root of progress was rare; they had been liberated by others and expected protection and initiative from others.

The former Nazis often presented themselves in a charming, cooperative, "non-political" vein; perhaps they had made some mistakes, but were the Americans (or any other people) really any better? This attitude did not prevent many of them from wishing to emigrate to the United States; they took it for granted that they would be welcome. Avowed Nazis were almost impossible to locate for a while. Demoralization, cynicism, and fatalism prevailed and usually resulted in readiness to conform with anybody — with a new fascism, with Communism, even with democracy. The only real novelty was a widespread disinclination to undergo any new rearmament and militarization.

After the currency reforms in these countries, a marked shift from demoralized submissiveness to nationalistic aggressiveness occurred, not only in terms of regained self-confidence but in terms of renewed receptiveness of many toward Fascistic slogans. Needless to say, unwarranted generalizations should be avoided, and currency reform was not the basic reason for such attitudinal changes; but this reform symbolized the beginning of speedy economic recovery and, with it, of important steps toward national self-assertion.

These observations do not, of course, claim universal validity, but they appear to be confirmed by many objective data. Neither the

[8] David M. Levy, *New Fields of Psychiatry* (New York, 1947), p. 108. Compare David Riesman, "Some Observations on the Limits of Totalitarian Power," *Antioch Review*, Summer 1952.

collapse of the fascist state nor the beginnings of economic recovery had automatically removed the roots of totalitarian mentality, although both measures were indispensable steps in that direction from a long-run point of view. By May 1951 fascist forces in eight countries of Europe, including Germany and Italy, had sufficiently recovered to hold an international meeting in Sweden, at which a world alliance of fascist groups was founded — an international league of nationalists.

In summary, any serious spread of totalitarian mentality — either of the Communist or of any other type — in contemporary Western societies indicates a wide incidence of strong personal insecurities. Such insecurities, in turn, reflect in large part a recurrent socio-economic instability. Yet totalitarian attitudes are not genuinely directed at economic reforms which might in due course remedy such instability. Essentially totalitarianism mirrors a psychic state of fear on a mass scale. Its Communist variety has its historical starting point and frame of reference in the lower classes; in the fascist variety, upper-class values are used in a comparable way. However, in the essential traits of the mentality and psychic needs concerned there is relatively little difference between the various brands of totalitarianism. In each case economic reform is used as an initial or periodic device to gain attention and support among masses who actually *are* in need of institutional improvements. Sooner or later, however, economic reform becomes a mere object of rationalizations — if not conscious deception — on the part of totalitarian movements.

The question that emerges from these experiences of our generation is how to replace totalitarian mentality, especially when it occurs on a large scale, by genuine striving for needed reforms. Reduction of socio-economic instability is likely to help diminish eventually the incidence of personal insecurities that foster totalitarian propensity; but this might take a generation or longer, and in the meantime the vicious circle of instability and totalitarianism might continue. Attempts to "disprove" the delusions of real totalitarian addicts, to show that their fears are objectively unjustified, would be psychologically hopeless. Such a procedure, however, may influence some persons who have no real totalitarian propensity and who got into the orbit of totalitarian movements by accident or by genuine mistake.

Well-meaning liberals, who have been trained in logical argumentation and who strongly believe in its power, are quite likely to be ineffective in counteracting real totalitarian mentality. Likewise, turning the fears and hatreds of those afflicted against each other, thus leading their mentality *ad absurdum*, is an uncertain and hazardous procedure, although it has sometimes been effective in history when a mass hysteria had nearly run its course and merely awaited a final blow.

The real task is to eliminate fear as a mental condition — not fear of anything in particular — as a snow-balling occurrence among the masses. By far the most promising method is action through key persons, reference groups, and legal devices, which demonstrate to those afflicted that prejudice, hatred, and violence are at odds with basic values of society; and that the totalitarian, far from being embraced by a new fraternity, is likely to find less acceptance and assurance than the democratic person. In this process, an attempt could also be made to imbue the unhappy totalitarian souls, as a group, with a greater degree of personal security than they have had. Institutional reforms — prominently including economic ones — can eventually contribute much to changing the attitudinal framework of many persons with totalitarian propensity and, still better, to preventing the rise of such propensities on any mass scale in the future. This, however, is likely to be a lengthy, continued process, rather than a quick cure once for all.

At any rate, the real decision about the course of society lies today between the totalitarians of all brands on the one hand, and people with productive orientation of any kind on the other. The task is to channel the prevailing frustrations of a period into genuine reform attitudes instead of unrealistic images or destructive hatreds disguised as programs for economic reform. The nineteenth century erred in assuming that economic reform was a purely intellectual showdown, to the neglect of emotional problems involved; the twentieth century is up against pseudo-reform attitudes which are mainly guided by hidden emotional needs, to the neglect of intellectual processes.

Regardless of the economic semantics of totalitarianism, its suc-

cessful spread spells sooner or later the death of any genuine movement for needed economic reforms. On the other hand, economists
today can learn something from this tragic predicament of our generation. Expert advice for economic improvement was often disregarded in history because it did not take the attitudinal and emotional dynamics of economic reform into sufficient account — thus
leaving a vacuum into which totalitarians moved only too easily.
In order to be realistic, genuine economic reform in a free society
must involve productive changes in human attitudes and emotions
no less than in the intellectual and institutional equipment required.

16. The Economy of the Soviet Zone of Germany

J. P. NETTL

The importance of the Soviet Zone in a study of totalitarianism lies in the fact that it has provided a trial ground for the
two most extreme forms of totalitarian organization in the political
and economical field which we know today. This has the definite
advantage that we can watch, as it were, the golfers go over the
same terrain one after the other, dealing with the same obstacles and
bothered by the same circumstances. Moreover, we are dealing with
an advanced society, industrially organized and efficient with a long
tradition of development along the lines which a Marxist dreams
about when considering prospective objects for the exercise of his
particular wizardry. It is an important country in the sense that
what happens has significance in the economic and political development of Europe, and therefore, is a more meaningful line of study
than the backwaters of the Balkans. Finally, there is the important,
although perhaps ephemeral, fact that we know quite a lot about
Eastern Germany, which is a not altogether unhelpful point in any
academic discussion.

We can, therefore, take Eastern Germany as an instance (*a*) of
Nazi economic organization, (*b*) of Communist economic organization, (*c*) of totalitarian economy in general (if there is such a thing,
to decide which is one of the objectives of this paper).

It will be unnecessary to discuss Germany's Nazi economic organization in any detail since the material is all familiar. Its salient features for the purpose of this discussion were the absence of any basic economic program, and its corollary, the availability of economic policy and action as political ground bait to catch votes. Thus, the Nazi party could promise at one and the same time destruction of chain stores and other monopolies to one group and vitiation of the trade-union movement to another. Going on from there, the system believed implicitly in improvization, as is evidenced by the sudden price stop of 1936; the purely *ad hoc* government investment, as a last resort when private investment failed; the varying and haphazard policy of government borrowing, and so forth. The reason for all this is to be found in the opportunist purposes of Nazi economics, which were to get the German economy in shape for the war which was the main object, to alleviate en route the results of the depression, and to pay off supporters in the form of profits.

The Nazi system made use above all of private organizations as much as possible (Chambers of Commerce, and so forth) and enforced its will by an artificial hardening of the arteries of economic responsibility, making purely private and personal organizations, originally responsible only to their members, a definite tool in the enforcement of government policy. At the same time centers of resistance to this process were destroyed by political means, thus insuring, to use the term of a recent author, the destruction of the organs of countervailing power. One of the most vivid features of this policy was the importance of the *Betriebsgemeinschaften* (works or factory units), which circumvented the normal economic process of employer-labor relationship. (The idea was that by forming one single unit of economic production in opposition to the existing dichotomy between labor and management, a common goal to both, that is, maximum production and minimum friction, could be achieved. It was hoped that to play on a loyalty to the firm would result in competition and struggle between one firm and another in the same production process rather than between capital and labor.) I would like to point out at this stage one interesting feature of this. Incentives, which became important once a full-employment position had been reached and passed, took almost entirely the good old-fashioned form of pay envelopes. An attempt was made to work by patriotic slogan, but emphasis was always on the principle that the more you worked, the more you earned. Employers were asked to stimulate production on a works or unit basis, which seems to show that the Nazi government and the Nazi theoreticians were only too glad to avail themselves of the good old-fashioned type of loyalty which workers had for their firm. Naturally, no such refinements were necessary, once an increasing proportion of the labor force came to be recruited after 1942 from the occupied countries in the form of slave labor.

As regards the organization of labor, we find that in this field, and in this field alone, both the underlying spirit as well as the form of Communist and Nazi action are very similar. In both cases the unions created from the voluntary association of trade groups for collective-bargaining purposes were taken over into a state-controlled labor organization. At a very superficial glance the form of association and the object of the unions remained the same as in capitalist society, but the independent power of labor was destroyed, so that the organization of the unions could be used for the full mobilization of labor and for the political pressure required to align labor fully behind the objectives of the government. Moreover, the very chain of command of unions served a useful purpose in destroying the means by which labor imposed its collective will on its bargaining partners and on the community generally. Instead of pressure from below for the purpose of ameliorating wages or conditions, the government imposed its will downward and made protests impossible. The larger the union, the more effective government control could become, and consequently there was a tendency in Nazi Germany and in Soviet Russia for the actual units to be larger and larger. All the time, however, the illusion of continued labor confederation and representation was kept alive in both systems. It is therefore true to say that the treatment of the labor question is fundamentally similar in all types of totalitarian economy and provides to some extent the exception to the various fundamental differences which have been mentioned elsewhere in this paper; so much so that it is possible to argue that on this vital question the two systems show an over-all similarity which must apply to all totalitarian systems. On the other hand, it may be due to the more limited though nonetheless important fact that in modern industrial states labor unions do represent perhaps the most powerfully organized popular force, and that therefore on a purely political basis alone control and reorganization of the labor unions is an immediate imperative for all totalitarian systems.

Apart from these considerations, in turning to Communist economic organization, we are immediately up against some vital differences. The Communists have a very definite economic theory which is part and parcel of their rigid all-embracing faith. They had, therefore, little use in the long run for convenient or inconvenient forms of economic organizations which they found on taking over. (Not only did they realize that their purpose could not easily be carried out with a system of economic organization based on free-market mechanism, but they went much further than this. The whole essence of Communist theory is based on the fact that the political dictatorship of the proletariat, which is the touchstone of the entire technique, cannot function unless there is a radical change in the economic organization. Consequently, in order to make real totalitarianism possible, any economic system other than that envisaged by Marxism must be first destroyed and then completely remodeled.)

Moreover, the Communist purpose was very different from that of the Nazis. As a matter of fact, they had two purposes in Germany, and their inability to decide on a permanent priority for one or the other, and their inability to combine the two satisfactorily, always dogged their economic effort in Eastern Germany and still dogs it today. The first purpose is the one that they have shown in the satellite countries, which is briefly to build a Communist society as quickly as possible along the lines pioneered in Russia. The other purpose is unique to Eastern Germany and consists of an attempt to enter into a competitive economic race with Western Germany on capitalist terms and according to capitalist rules. The reason for this was the declared policy of inducing the weight of German public opinion to choose the better system, and this, therefore, resulted in the need for the Communists in Eastern Germany to prove themselves the better system in terms of bourgeois economic and nationalist preferences. The measurement of success in this daring and unusual effort were efficiency, gross product in comparison with prewar real wages and the other paraphernalia of measuring economic achievements. (In

this connection it can be noted how all production figures in both
East and West Germany are always calculated in terms of per-
centages of the equivalent 1936 figure. The convenience of this arose
from the fact that in that year the German Central Statistical Agency
conducted a thorough and complete statistical survey of the German
economy. The yardstick which 1936 provided was also useful because it is also generally reckoned as the last year in which the
German economy achieved a maximum peace-time production before it turned over more and more to a war economy. Thus the full
employment position of 1936 was something to be emulated after
the war by both sides of the inter-German frontier, and provided a
sort of goal to both. In the last resort, of course, this Communist
purpose was purely political and purely temporary until success had
been gained, and might be described as the serjeanty to politics
which economics was called upon to perform. Theoretically, there
seemed no reason why this effort should not succeed, and the most
authoritative German Communist politician, Walter Ulbricht, expected it to succeed.[1] However, the very nature of Communist economic development made success impossible. The concentration on
developing capital-intensive industries at tremendous real cost, even
in favor of neglecting existing and viable industries which were considered less vital — to take only one example — and the insistence
on a small holder's land reform made the highly competitive race
in efficiency with a booming Western Germany hopeless. (By the
same token however, the full-scale mobilization which is fundamental to Communist economics gave at the outset a flying start to
the East. Where West Germany was wallowing in ineffective controls, and was being held back by reluctant producers and distribu-
tors, the effort of and political pressure on the East German economy,
inspired moreover by a real enthusiasm for reconstruction, resulted
in considerable economic activity and far greater approximation to
the 1936 figures of production and distribution than in the West.
Nonetheless, the East German economy was bound to lose the race
as soon as the necessary incentives to go ahead were available in the
West.) So East German policy has since 1945 been teetering between
one object and the other and has fallen heavily in between two

[1] See Walter Ulbricht, *Lehren des Demokratischen Staats und Wirtschafts Aufbaus*
(Berlin, 1949).

stools; for which someone — never the person really responsible — is shortly to pay the price. (It will be noticed that the purges which have been announced for East Germany, one of whose prominent victims appears to be the late Minister for Trade, are motivated by economic failures primarily.) Most recently, the hopeless bankruptcy of trying to impress Western Germany with economic development in the East has resulted in a more rapid straight-forward development along orthodox Communist lines, since it is clear that West Germany will not vote itself Communist in a daze of political and economic admiration. There is now no reason to keep back the remains of the old economic order which were intended to show that East Germany was not a doctrinaire Communist state, and the representatives of this old economic order are being mercilessly chased into West Berlin.

I want now to discuss differences and similarities between Nazi and Communist economy as evidenced in East Germany and to draw some tentative conclusions possibly applicable to all forms of totalitarianism as covered by the brief of this conference.

Such purpose as there is in Nazi and Fascist economies is *ad hoc* designed to achieve limited given objectives in short periods. From recent historical experience, it seems clear that the object of most existing and recent fascist-type economies has been the preservation of the economic *status quo*; indeed, a case can be made for both German National Socialism and Italian Fascism as partly designed to provide a political shield to preserve an existing economic organization against economic revolution. Such changes as were made in economic structure could perhaps more accurately be described as a sacrifice of small items in return for leaving undisturbed the main trends, rather than as an attempt to impose some sort of a totalitarian economic system on the countries concerned. The nature of totalitarianism, which so often seems to lead to wars, does necessarily mean that the shape of totalitarian economy must be designed to make war possible, but this again is a symptom of totalitarianism, limited in scope, rather than a *conditia sine qua non*. (It is necessary to make a distinction between the form of control which we have come to associate with a war economy and that which might be described totalitarianism *per se*. To fight a modern war successfully it is essential that an economy be not only mobilized more completely than mere investment policies make possible, but also planning on a vast scale is essential. But, in all war economies which consist of a superimposition of planning and control on an economy designed to function on the whole according to the market mechanism, it is necessary to assume a voluntary compliance of the people who have economic responsibilities with the political powers that be, bearing in mind that a full-scale coercion would probably not be possible. With the Soviet economy, on the other hand, things are exactly the other way around. The economic structure, aided by the political control organization, attempts to shut out the voluntary element as much as possible, but makes for the tightest possible centralized control in the hands of the really reliable elements. This does not mean that the voluntary element is or can be entirely shut out, but it is reduced to a minimum and is assumed by the very nature of the organization to act necessarily against rather than for the political objectives of the regime. Thus where a Communist government will base its policy on the assumption that factory management, presidents of trusts, and so on, cannot be allowed more than the minimum essential discretion as they may be guided by diversionary motives, the Nazi economy inevitably assumes that the upper levels of management are politically behind the regime. It is here that the view which holds that differences between the Nazi and Soviet economies are only a matter of degree or of time allowed for full development seems to ignore an important difference between the two systems.)

Communism, on the other hand, implies a fundamental economic theory and has a specific, if broad, economic purpose. It aims at establishing a particular type of economy and visualizes economics as one of the most important features of the political development desired. It will not be necessary to discuss what this purpose is, but no one will disagree about its existence. One of the particular features which Communist economics entails is a tremendous emphasis on production and a compensatory lack of emphasis on distribution. This is the main reason why Communist economies are "inefficient" in terms of capitalist judgment and why the Communist effort to enter the lists, which have been described above, failed so signally. One of the important questions a study of East Germany has raised is the eventual shape of such an economy. As things are at present, the satellites are really appendices of the Soviet economy and likely to remain so, but what is to happen if the ambitious plans for East Germany are fulfilled and yet no satisfactory solution of the present hand-to-mouth attitude toward trade in practice and in theory is reached? There is at present no room behind the iron curtain for organized trade as we know it, based on a tendency toward maximum efficiency and maximum mutual rather than one-sided benefit.

We have noted that Nazism used existing economic developments to further its purposes and tried to avoid the creation of special agencies or bodies. Communism starts the other way round, with definite forms of economic organization, the adoption of which are imperative and to which economic development has to be fitted. It is almost the first task of any Communist regime to take into its hands by far the greatest sector of production, followed by the imposition of a collective system of farming in several stages. One of the results of this difference between National Socialism and Communism is in the relationship between politics and economics. In fascist and Nazi countries, the economy works quasi-independently under a political shield, and economic responsibility is, as in liberal capitalist economies, limited to those who are active in production or distribution, always providing that the over-all result is not against government policy. In Communist economies, however, one of the objects of economic organization is to achieve a pure political responsibility for economic activity. (This is really the corollary of what was stated above with regard to the attempt of the Communist system to reduce the discretion of executives to the minimum. Political pressure will then take care of the unavoidable but reduced discretion which remains.) That is the reason for the otherwise inexplicable tendency in Communist countries to deal with the fulfillment of plans in terms of political sabotage. The distinction is a vital one and provides one of the really serious and fundamental differences between the one type of totalitarianism and the other. It is this which is radically new in the present regime in East Germany, and it is this which provides the main reason for resistance to Communism in East and West Germany. Thus, whereas political orthodoxy, control of thought and action, rigid and universal obedience to a political party line for all proved fairly acceptable to large numbers of people in East Germany, and might so prove in West Ger-

many, the same masses of people refuse to swallow the translation
of their purely economic activities into political terms. East Germany
has shown most clearly that not only Communist economic practice but also Communist economic theory break down when trying
to deal with capitalist economies in a capitalist way. The attempt
to run the East German economy on a basis of competition between
the nationalized sector and the private sector proved impossible
since it was more than any Communist could do to treat economic
results in economic terms. Thus when a privately owned factory
failed to fulfill its production plan, the manager was automatically
hauled before a court, attacked on political grounds by party news-
papers and punished by the law. The result was that no one except
on the highest level would make important decisions. When the
rules of a game are not observed, the game cannot be played.[2]

The Communists have provided a very interesting and important
answer to the question of competition without economic reward
among the lowest paid groups by their development of a really
unique and interesting contribution to the existing forms of incentives. Whereas the Nazi economy worked basically in the way that
we know in Britain and the United States — leaving aside the last
resort threat of personal punishment in case of failure — the Communists have experimented with non-monetary incentive. The be-
fuddling meetings, councils, statistics, and other magic with which
the Communist worker seems to be burdened have actually provided one of the most powerful weapons of enforcing the "Law of
Socialist Development," which insists that the worker will produce
substantially more than is returned to him in the form of remuneration.[3] In East Germany, where the game of competing along
capitalist lines with West Germany has only recently been abandoned, the introduction of the Soviet type of incentives is fairly new

[2] It is, of course, ridiculous to suppose that every important economic decision in
Russia is taken by the Politburo. But as long as former capitalist managers are still
in charge before being replaced by the new type of "bureaucrat," the inevitable
political suspicion which their very presence arouses must gradually stifle their remaining economic initiative.

[3] This "law" is a model perfected by Koslov and other Soviet economists, and is
supposed to embody scientifically those very principles which Marx considered to be
the central injustice of capitalism. Soviet economists claim, however, to use their
law as an eventual means of equating the value of work and the value of wages,
through a cumulative decrease of real costs.

and for that reason especially interesting to watch in its undiluted and urgent form. Even immediately after the war, it was impossible for Communists to bring themselves to introduce a straight-forward wage system in relation to the nature and the amount of work performed; instead they fiddled the issue by letting the private sector of the economy work on money wages, the value of which was infinitesimal in real terms, but insured a considerable advantage for their public sector by coupling money wages with a scale of availabilities of consumer goods at controlled prices which greatly enhanced the real wages of the workers concerned. Now the latter system is still in force, but the vital factor in the great strides of output which have to be made if existing ambitious plans are to be fulfilled, without any likelihood of return in terms of personal gain, must be the incentive offered by purely social advantages. I have seen in Poland and in Germany the tremendous effects produced by the four-story-high placards advertising the weeks' winning factory, shift in the factory, and worker in the shift. Given concentrated application and absence of outside influence, this system can have tremendous effects and can fill, in non-monetary terms, the gap between work done and remuneration for it. In passing, it is interesting to note that this gap originally gave rise to Marx's indignant flourish of the labor theory of value, and it is doubtful whether he would have approved of the present Communist method of filling it.

Another important difference between the two types of totalitarianism arises from the question of transition. Politically the Communists in East Germany were greatly helped by the spade work of their Nazi predecessors. The organization of the Socialist Unit Party, the transformation of trade unions into a form of state supertrade union, the effect of plugged political slogans were all easy meat for a people accustomed to this kind of thing. The political transition from National Socialism to Communism was fairly easy, just as the transition from Nazism to liberal democracy in the West is frightfully difficult. Not so the economic transition. What resistance there has been in East Germany to Communism was on economic and hardly at all on political grounds. The majority of refugees from the East until recently were not political but economic cases. The chief resistance in West Germany to Communism in the East is not so much political in the sense that they resent the destruction of liberty, but is based on solidarity and sympathy with the class which many Germans consider the backbone of the nation and which the Communists are destroying: the economic middle class. It is also significant that centralized planning in West Germany from 1945 to 1948 was a hair-raising disaster, while the almost excessively free economy since that time operated smoothly beyond the expectations of all the occupation officials and of the great majority of economists. Fundamentally the difference between the controls with which the economy was burdened before and after 1945 is small. In both cases the over-all objective of economic policy was clearly laid down and within its framework planning reached down into even the lowest levels of the economy. Not only production was prescribed, but the disposal of this production was allocated rather than left to the free initiative of the individual producer or merchant. It is, therefore, difficult to draw any other conclusion from the relative effectiveness of even the last stages of Nazi planning and the ineffectiveness of the economic planning of the Western military occupation than to point to the discretion which both systems left to the individual entrepreneur. This discretion was thrown into the scale on the side of government and its policy during the Nazi period — though to a decreasing extent as can be seen from the rapidly expanding black market during the last years of the war — while during the allied military occupation this same discretion operated in the direction of almost deliberate sabotage. It was clearly recognized by the allied military authorities that even greatly enhanced political pressure would probably have been ineffective in altering this lack of co-operation.

This might be taken, therefore, as tentative evidence for the view that even the whole political apparatus of totalitarianism is not necessarily effective in achieving economic results unless a fundamental change from a liberal type of economy is undertaken.

Furthermore, we have the ease with which that same German economy after years of so-called total war and rigorous allied economic planning adopted without difficulty an unusually free market system. Thus the changeover after the currency reform, in terms of economic organization, was very small. The same firms and the same people easily fell back into the operation of a system which came naturally to them, once the superstructure of controls had been re-

moved. The reason can only be that there was no great and fundamental chasm to be bridged between the Nazi economy and the
Ehrhard economy. But in the East Zone the Communists moved
very carefully and as late as 1950 were talking of limited socialism
in Germany, of the irrevocability of the land reform which created
many small holdings out of large ones, and they were promising
the continued existence of private economic enterprise. For a moment
they even teetered on the edge of one of the greatest Communist
heresies: that of producing a special native brand of Communism
peculiar to their own environment and different from the example
of the Soviet Union. Therefore, it is reasonable to suggest that the
Communists found it unexpectedly difficult to combine their relatively easy political task with an equally easy economic effort in
picking up the threads from the defunct hands of the National
Socialist state. It proved simply not true that fascism or imperialism
as existing in Germany is the highest form of capitalism as described
by Lenin, and therefore the one most suitable for easy transition to
socialism.

CONCLUSION

From a very sketchy outline of some of the salient features of the
economy of the East Zone, it is suggested that whereas on political
grounds the difference between Communism and other types of full-
scale totalitarianism is limited to degree and method, the difference
between Communism and other types of totalitarianism is fundamental as far as economics are concerned. The whole idea of communist economics is so interwoven with political ideology that the
result must, it is felt, be fundamentally different from any other
form of political and economic organization. Indeed, it might even
be suggested that the very similarity in politics between all forms
of totalitarianism, which have been discussed in other papers, will
to some extent break down once the economic objects of Communism
begin to be realized. Such is Communist theory, embodying the
proposition that the state and its organs will wither away. Whatever
one may think of this theory, it does imply a dynamic development
as economic conditions change — and they are intended to change —
a development which might lead and is intended to lead to a change
in the political structure as we know it today. This is not true of

any other known form of totalitarianism. It is here that we reach
the most important difference of all between economic Communism
and other totalitarianisms. Communism is changing and was always
intended to change, whereas it is very clear that any major changes
in other forms of totalitarianism have been synonymous with its destruction. And now perhaps the death of Stalin will prove me wrong.

17. Cracks in the Monolith: Possibilities and Patterns of Disintegration in Totalitarian Systems

KARL W. DEUTSCH

Is there a pathology peculiar to totalitarian systems? Are
there, that is to say, specific ways in which established totalitarian
governments or cultures tend to be destroyed, divided, or otherwise
basically changed by their own inner development?

Are there, in particular, any recurrent tendencies to stagnation or
division, to schisms, heresies, or secessions — social, regional, or ideological — *which can be traced to the fundamental structure of totalitarian government*, and which could be tested, at least in principle,
against available data from concrete cases? If so, what inferences for
policy expectations and research programs in the free countries could
be derived from them?

All that will be offered in this paper in answer to these questions
will be a scheme of analysis drawn from the theory of communication and control, and to some extent from the theory of organization,
and brought to bear on a problem in political thought, so that it may
be confronted with data from history and from comparative political
research. To gather these data in detail, to use them to test the specific theory, and to modify the theory in their light will of necessity
have to be the task of later work.

SOME CHARACTERISTICS OF TOTALITARIANISM

Before we even approach the questions we just asked, we must
first pause briefly to deal with a preliminary one. Is there a "totalitarianism" in the abstract, or as an ideal type, somewhat in Max
Weber's sense, or are there only particular totalitarian systems? [1] In

[1] Terms such as "total state" were used by some spokesmen of the Fascist regime

this paper it will be answered tentatively that there are particular totalitarian systems which are comparable among each other to the extent to which they have certain limited performance characteristics in common.[2]

The three most important of these characteristics are perhaps extreme *mobilization of effort, unity of command*, and effective *power of enforcement*. These three characteristics, perhaps more than any others, make totalitarian systems perform differently from other systems of social and political decision-making. Their loss is conspicuous whenever totalitarian governments succumb to stagnation or disintegration.

Totalitarianism characteristically involves the extreme mobilization of the efforts and resources of population under its government. "In a democracy," runs a well-known joke, "everything that is not forbidden is permitted; under an authoritarian regime, everything that is not permitted is forbidden; under totalitarianism, everything that is not forbidden is compulsory." The citizen of a totalitarian state or culture has no time and no possessions that he could truly call his own. His free time after working hours should be spent digging victory gardens, or volunteering for a work brigade, or attending party meetings, or in some other activity or campaign prescribed by the regime. His home and goods, if any, must likewise be devoted to the cause. Ideally, he is expected to be unceasingly active, with all his time and all his resources.

As with the individual, so with the country. Nothing must be held back, and none may withhold themselves. Whatever the avowed purpose of the cause or the regime, it must now be served and pushed forward "with all thy heart and all thy strength," "unstintingly and

in Italy and the Nazi government in Germany in referring to some of their own political institutions since the late 1930's. Since then, opponents of Communism and Fascism have gradually popularized the term "totalitarian" as a means to emphasize certain similarities between fascist and Communist one-party governments.

[2] For some discussions of totlitarianism, see Sigmund Neumann, *Permanent Revolution: The Total State in a World at War* (New York: Harper, 1942; Hans Kohn, "Fascism and Communism — A Comparative Study," in *Revolution and Dictatorships* (Cambridge: Harvard University Press, 1939), pp. 179–199; Hannah Arendt, *The Origins of Totalitarianism* (New York: Harcourt Brace, 1951); and the excellent account of the use of the concept of the "total state" in the rivalry between state and party bureaucracies in Germany and Italy, in Franz Neumann, *Behemoth: The Structure and Practice of National Socialism* (New York: Oxford University Press, 1942), pp. 47–82.

unflinchingly," "not sparing our own blood or treasure," "without
mental reservation or evasion," "rejoicing to be damned for the glory
of God." As the old inscription of the Hanseatic sailors had it,
navigare necesse est, vivere non.

This is the language of enthusiasm. Every phrase just cited can
occur, and indeed has occurred, in a non-totalitarian context. In a
non-totalitarian setting, however, such total commitment, even if it
should be demanded, remains transitory, or it remains limited to
some particular sphere of activity, or to some particular group of
people. The more totalitarian a culture or regime becomes, the more
permanent and all embracing become its demands for mobilization
and commitment,[3] and the more thoroughly are they reinforced by
the two other characteristics of totalitarianism: singleness of command and a significant probability of enforcement.

The term "singleness of command" is used in two different meanings. It may mean that all commands in the system originate from a
single source, or are at least controlled by a single source, whether
or not these commands are consistent among themselves. Or the
term may mean that all commands in a system are consistent among
themselves, whether they originate from a single source or from
several sources. It is singleness in this latter sense of mutual consistency of commands which is essential for the operation of a totalitarian system.

The third characteristic, the probability of enforcement, requires
the existence of sufficient power to enforce all decisions within the
totalitarian system, and to prevent all effective interference from outside; although it does not necessarily require sufficient power to
achieve some avowed external goal of the regime.

Each of the three characteristics or functions which we have listed
— mobilization of resources, singleness of command, and power of
enforcement — is dependent on some underlying conditions without which it cannot be maintained.

THE EMBARASSMENT OF PREVIOUS COMMITMENTS

Thus the mobilization of resources required by totalitarianism
presupposes that these resources have already been freed from pre-

[3] For some suggestive observations on the growing psychological readiness for
totalitarian mobilization, see Ernst Jünger, *Die totale Mobilmachung* (2nd ed.;

vious commitments, both from commitments of custom and from commitments imposed by previous political systems or even by earlier stages or policies of the totalitarian regime itself. Totalitarianism thus must destroy previous custom, even where its spokesmen may profess to defend it. Its leaders must divert resources, manpower, and attention from past institutions, even where these institutions are supposed to be preserved. Finally, totalitarianism must take away resources and attention from its own past policies and past demands of consistency wherever these past policies or past commitments threaten to cut down the range of resources available to it presently for recommitment.

Changes in the previous political line, or in the old guard of decision-making personnel, are therefore not peripheral or accidental in totalitarian regimes, but seem likely to recur. As soon as the new commitments of resources mobilized by totalitarianism tend to become permanent, these resources are no longer completely available to the totalitarian regime. The more permanent and irrevocable the commitment of its resources, the less totalitarian in the long run must a regime become. Either, that is to say, its resources become frozen in commitments to an unusual strategy for an improbable goal — in which case the regime loses much of its capacity to maneuver and to learn, and thus to preserve itself, and risks stagnation or destruction — or else its resources become ever more firmly committed to patterns of activity which are quite capable of being carried on repetitively and within the limits of a self-preserving and self-maintaining society. In this event, the totalitarian regime begins to erode into an increasingly traditional society. In either case a totalitarian regime is to some extent threatened by the permanence of its own memories and of its own traditions. Either these traditions force it to persist in some ever more unrewarding strategy or pattern of behavior, or else they turn into a new network of customs and established expectations which increasingly limit the range of decisions still open to the totalitarian command.

In order to maintain the mobilization of its resources, a totalitarian regime needs therefore some machinery, formal or informal, to

---

Berlin: Junker, 1934), esp. pp. 10–18, 29–31. See also Hans Kohn, *Force or Reason*: *Issues of the Twentieth Century* (Cambridge: Harvard University Press, 1937), pp. 35–38, 132–133.

counteract the hardening of its own abstract traditions or professed ideologies, such as creeds, dogmas, philosophies, political doctrines, and the like, and it needs similar machinery to counteract the hardening of its own past preferences for particular geographical centers or particular groups of personnel. Traditions of doctrine, as well as preferences for geographical centers or for sociological groups of personnel, can easily become matters of heresy in totalitarian systems; but it is one of the paradoxes of totalitarianism that excessive orthodoxy in one of these three matters may have anti-totalitarian consequences and expose the die-hard orthodox partisan of the regime to some of the same penalties which threaten the heretic.

THE PROBLEM OF CONSISTENCY OF COMMANDS

The second function, unity of command and of intelligence, requires some machinery either to insure a single source of decision, or a set of arrangements or devices to insure consistency of decisions among several sources. A single source of decisions is in effect an arrangement by which all important incoming information available to the system is channeled to a point where it can be confronted with data recalled from a single integrated memory pool. The outcome of the interaction of these collected data from the outside world and the data recalled from an integrated set of memory facilities are then the current decisions of the system.[4]

In its extreme or "ideal type" form, a totalitarian decision system would need to have five properties: (1) *transitivity*,[5] that is, the property that each decision was either clearly superior or clearly subordinate to some other decision, and that no sequence of such hierarchically ordered decisions could be circular; (2) *rigor*, that is, uniqueness of outcome of each step at all the relevant stages of decision-making below the top; (3) *awareness of intake* and facilities for its simultaneous inspection, that is, arrangements to make

---

[4] For a further discussion of the theory of communication and decision-making used in this section, see Norbert Wiener, *The Human Use of Human Beings: Cybernetics and Society* (Boston: Houghton Mifflin, 1950); and Karl W. Deutsch, "Communication Models in Social Science," *Public Opinion Quarterly*, XVI, No. 3, Fall 1952, pp. 356–380; and "Communication Theory and Social Science," *American Journal of Orthopsychiatry*, XXII, No. 3, pp. 469–483.

[5] Cf. John von Neumann and Oskar Morgenstern, *Theory of Games and Economic Behavior* (2nd ed.; Princeton: Princeton University Press, 1947), pp. 38–39.

sure that all important items of incoming information are confronted with each other and with data recalled from the memory facilities of the system; this involves the labeling of important items of incoming information by means of secondary symbols attached to them, and it involves the bringing together of these items for simultaneous inspection; (4) *self-awareness*, or the internal intelligence function, that is, arrangements to make sure that information about internal changes within the system itself are brought to bear on the system's current decisions; there must be symbols for the constituent sub-assemblies, organizations, resources, or personnel of the system itself, which are processed and brought to the memory facilities of the system in such a manner that the system "knows" what is going on within its own organization, and is capable of acting on this information; (5) *learning capacity*, that is, the ability to recombine items of incoming information with items recalled from memory in new patterns, so as to produce new combinations of symbols sufficient to survey, test, or devise new strategies of behavior, as well as the ability to produce new combinations of actual physical resources and manpower in such a way that the new strategies can actually be put into action; systems with this capacity will have the power to initiate new courses of behavior.

Actually existing totalitarian systems of government may well be deficient in any or all of these respects. Yet to the extent that they are so deficient, they will be less effective as totalitarian systems, and their chances for survival or expansion may be correspondingly lessened.

THE DEPENDENCE ON COMPLIANCE

The third characteristic of totalitarian government, the enforcement of decisions, depends to a large extent on the compliance habits of the population. Compliance and enforcement are interdependent; they reinforce each other, and the varying proportions in which they do so, form as it were a continuous spectrum. At one end of this spectrum, we could imagine a situation where everybody obeys habitually all commands or decisions of the totalitarian regime, and no enforcement is necessary; at the other end of this spectrum, we could imagine a situation where nobody obeys voluntarily any decision of the totalitarian system, and everybody has to be compelled to obey at pistol point, or under conditions of literally ever-present threat and ever-present supervision.

In the first of these cases, enforcement would be extremely cheap and, in fact, unnecessary; in the second, it would be prohibitively expensive, and in fact no government could be carried on on such a basis. Even the behavior of an occupying army in wartime in enemy territory falls far short of this standard; even there, many of its orders are obeyed more or less habitually by an unwilling population in situations where immediate supervision is not practicable. If the occupying army had to put a soldier behind every man, woman, and child of the local population, it would be extremely difficult for the army to keep sufficient numbers of its men detached from such occupation duties to continue with further military operations. Somewhere in the middle between these extremes of universal compliance and ubiquitous enforcement is the range of effective government. There a majority of individuals in a majority of situations obeys the decisions of the government more or less from habit without any need for immediate supervision. Yet the probability of supervision and detection, though possibly small, is still large enough to strengthen and reinforce the habits of obedience; and the habits of obedience, in most individuals and in most situations, are widespread and strong enough to make enforcement in the exceptional situations both practical and probable in its success. The higher the probability of voluntary compliance among the population, the greater therefore is the probability of enforcement in the exceptional cases. This will be so particularly if the enforcement facilities of the government are supported by voluntary efforts of the population in giving information, and in rendering voluntary assistance to the police and the troops of the government, and in their voluntary armed support of the government in case of necessity, as in the mobilization of a militia, the activities of guerillas, or the case of a posse of deputy sheriffs.

These considerations apply to totalitarianism as they apply to all types of government, but in their application to totalitarianism they again suggest a paradox. Totalitarian power is strong only if it does not have to be used too often. If totalitarian power must be used at all times against the entire population, it is unlikely to remain powerful for long. Since totalitarian regimes require more power for dealing with their subjects than do other types of government, such regimes stand in greater need of widespread and dependable compliance habits among their people; more than that, they need to be able to count on the active support of at least significant parts of the population in case of need.[6]

What are the sources of such compliance and support? As under all systems of government, they cover a whole range of social and psychological motives. At one extreme, we find mere passive acquiescence to the acts or commands of a government for which its subjects have no shred of sympathy but which they are too apathetic, too exhausted, or too disillusioned to resist. Further up the scale, we may find individuals supporting the government, still without any liking for its institutions or policies, but for what its current supporter may consider reasons of their own cold self-interest. Such men may support a government in the belief of using it for their own ends, as an instrument to procure some advantage to themselves or to inflict some damage on their enemies.

Still further up the scale of political support, we may find persons looking upon the government as in some manner an extension of themselves, or upon themselves as an extension of the government. Here we find self-identification and ego-involvement: the triumphs and successes of the government — or the state, the flag, the nation — are felt as personal triumphs by its subjects; its defeats are experienced as personal dishonor or misfortune; the prestige of the regime, the ideology, the state, the nation have become criteria for the self-respect of the individual subjects or citizens who have made this identification. Such ego-involvement need not necessarily involve considerations of general morality or religion, and thus in one sense what Freudians call the "superego." The ardent patriot may be well aware that his government's action is immoral: "Our country!" ran Stephen Decatur's toast: "In her intercourse with foreign nations may she be always in the right; but our country, right or wrong."

[6] A comparison of the relation of compliance habits and enforcement probabilities in different countries was included in the checklist for comparative political studies, suggested by the Research Seminar on Comparative Politics of the Social Science Research Council. On the work of this seminar, and its implicit suggestions for the study of totalitarianism, see Roy C. Macridis, "Comparative Politics: Method and Research," *Social Science Research Council Items*, VI, No. 4, December 1952, pp. 45–49.

Men with such views prefer, sometimes quite wittingly, their symbol or group identification to their conscience. They find it easier to transgress against their general morals than against their collective self-esteem. Or else they may accept the theory of Machiavelli and his successors: the doctrine of the double morality, one applying to relations among individuals, based on honesty and peaceable dealings, the other applying to relations among states, governments, or peoples, and based on force, deceit, and fear.[7]

Finally, at the extreme top of the scale of political support, we find those persons who have identified obedience and support to their government not merely with their self-esteem but also with their general beliefs and convictions of morality and even of religion. Here we find the men — so often satirized by George Bernard Shaw — who always succeed in believing sincerely that the commands of Providence coincide exactly with the currently proclaimed "interests" of their state and the current policies of its rulers. Here we find, too, the men who sense that there is a tension between blind and complete support for all policies of a government and the highest commands of morality and religion, but who have decided to resolve this tension in favor of the deification of the political institution and its symbols.

Totalitarianism clearly endeavors to elicit wherever possible this most complete type of political support in which each individual unites a state-made self-respect with a state-made morality and a state-made religion for the support of the regime.

This state of affairs, however, is not easily achieved. As most students of the learning process know, loyalty taught through indoctrination, through what men are told by their rulers, does not go very deep. It is by their own experiences and actions that men learn most thoroughly. It is by what they themselves can tell their government, and do within its framework, and elicit a response to their own questions or appeals, that they learn to feel at home in it and to identify themselves with it. To elicit full identification and loyalty, therefore, a government must be to a considerable extent accessible

---

[7] For the general problem of such a split between personal and political morality, see Gerhart Ritter, *Die Dämonie der Macht* (6th ed.; Munich: Leibniz Verlag, 1948). On the extreme reliance of National Socialism on this split and the resulting use of *arcana dominationis*, see Franz Neumann, pp. 464–467.

and predictable.[8] It must be accessible to the questions, problems, needs, desires, and communications of its subjects; its office must be accessible to personnel recruited from their ranks; the minds of its decision-makers must remain open to the hopes, fears and wishes of the population; and their commands and actions must be predictable in their impact on the lives and fortunes of its citizens. Any government under which life becomes unpredictable in some really important matters — even a democracy in an extreme economic depression becomes suspect as arbitrary and may become feared and resented as alien or tyrannical. The well-known substitution of "they" for "we" in people's conversational references to their government may well occur in such situations.[9]

Totalitarian governments need at least the appearance of accessibility and predictability if they are to hold the active support of a large portion of their subjects. But the accessibility of a government interferes with its need to hold down the burden on the time and attention of its decision-making personnel, and we have seen that totalitarian regimes may be already prone to overload their central decision-making institutions. Predictability, in turn implies the commitment of manpower and resources to the repetition of previous patterns of behavior which now have become expected, or to the carrying out of policies which have been previously promised. Totalitarian regimes thus need to elicit identification from their subjects while tending to produce feelings of alienation among them. The more predictable and expectable a government becomes, the less totalitarian is it likely to remain; and the more totalitarian a government remains, the less likely it is in the long run to retain the active support of its population. Obviously, these inherent conflicts in the basis of the political support of totalitarian regimes can be sustained for considerable periods of time; but as these periods lengthen into generations the fate of most totalitarian regimes should become increasingly dubious. In order to function, the power machinery of totalitarianism requires the voluntary support and active help of a

[8] On the relationship between unpredictability and alienation, see Karl Mannheim, *Man and Society in the Age of Reconstruction* (New York: Harcourt Brace, 1948); and Karl W. Deutsch, *Nationalism and Social Communication* (New York: John Wiley and Massachusetts Institute of Technology Press, in press).

[9] E. H. Carr, *Conditions of Peace* (New York: Macmillan, 1943, pp. 36–37.

significant part of the population; but this very dependence upon the habitual and voluntary support of a relatively large part of the people makes it more difficult for any totalitarian regime to preserve for two other conditions for its own functioning: its unity of command and its freedom from previous commitments.

Each of the three major characteristics of totalitarianism thus gives rise to a peculiar set of difficulties. The totalitarian mobilization of resources, human and material, depends on a freedom from previous commitments which is constantly threatened, not only by the possibility of a relapse of the population into apathy or resentment, but also by the previous political, organizational, or ideological commitments of the totalitarian regime itself. The totalitarian unity of command and the consistency of decision-making depends on a unity of memories and a coördination of information channels and communication processes, which is constantly threatened by the tendency toward a diversification of memories, on the one hand, and the danger of overloading the undiversified centralized decision-making facilities on the other. The enforcement function, finally, of totalitarianism is threatened by its dependence on at least limited popular support, and by the tendency toward a downward migration of power which is inherent in most hierarchial systems of command.

Some of the weaknesses peculiar to centralized decision-making and to hierarchies of power may now be discussed somewhat further.

THE LIMITED CAPACITY OF CENTRALIZED DECISION-MAKING

The conflict between centralization and delegation of decisions is fundamental in many systems of government, but it is perhaps most critical in totalitarianism. Centralization of decisions means, essentially, that responses to incoming items of information are made in terms of data recalled from a single pool of memories, such as the memories carried in the head of a single man, the decision-maker; such a single decision-maker may of course consult other individuals and their memories, but these memories are then data which are to be used or rejected in terms of the data which his own memory is supplying to himself. Where the range of memories carried by a single individual is no longer large enough for the type of decision-making needed, the single decision-maker or theater commander may be replaced by a central committee of some sort. In this case incoming messages of major importance are brought to the attention of all committee members who all recall from their individual memories pertinent data for suggesting a response. These suggestions are then discussed and in effect simultaneously inspected in the course of the discussion of the committee, and the "sense of the meeting," or the collective decision, may emerge. It is possible, of course, that a particular committee member carries most influence in the committee, and the borderline is fluid between decisions made essentially in terms of the memories carried in the head of a single individual, and decisions made in terms of the memories and agreements of a whole committee.

All centralized facilities for decision-making, however, committees as well as individuals, can only give attention to a very limited number of items for decisions at the same time, and can therefore be very easily overloaded. The distributive attention of individuals is notoriously limited, and so is the amount of business any committee can transact within a given time. Julius Caesar has been renowned for his legendary exploit of dictating seven letters at one and the same time; and chess masters who can play forty games simultaneously are objects of admiration. Major military decision systems or political decision systems, on the contrary, may easily require decisions of many hundreds of problems in substantially the same interval of time.

A simple example of the difficulties involved can be found in the problem of the plotting room of an anti-aircraft defense center in a city under air attack; by means of a number of ingenious arrangements, it may be possible there to represent at one and the same time the attack of several hundred enemy aircraft and to make decisions about how to oppose most effectively every one of them. Nevertheless, the decision-making capacity of even a very good anti-aircraft plotting center is quantitatively limited. These quantitative limitations become particularly sharp and painful when the question arises of how to defend a warship against aerial attack. Here the attacking enemy aircraft can be represented on radar screens but the number of tracks symbolizing attacking aircraft may very soon become too large for the decision-making capacity of any single individual; it is possible from this point of view to saturate not merely the physical, but rather the intellectual or cognitive defenses of the ship. Just as a massed attack of aircraft coming simultaneously from many different directions may overload the capacities of a directing center for anti-aircraft defense, so the amount of problems requiring urgent decision may overload the decision-making capacities of a government.[10]

Moreover, the more absolute, dictatorial, or totalitarian such a government is, the more likely it is to politicize, that is, to make subject to decisions, an ever larger sphere of life, and therefore the more likely it is to be thus overloaded with decisions with which it can no longer cope, except at the price of either intolerable delays or an increasing probability of potentially critical mistakes.

The answer to this problem of the overloading of centralized decision-making facilities has been, of course, decentralization. Classes of decisions have been delegated to sub-assemblies of the system, where they are made in terms of separate pools of memories. These subordinate decision centers with their subordinate facilities for the storing of data may in turn be controlled more or less closely from some common decision-making center. Such control, however, is apt to be incomplete. Once the subordinate centers have been delegated some authority, and once they have been given their own facilities for storing memories, these subordinate centers and memory pools will in the future receive only part of their imput from the supreme government. A significant part of their future experience will be local, in terms of their own peculiar local, regional, or functional situations, or in terms of their own probabilities of internal recombinations, their own ideas, preferences, customs, or habits of behavior, as they may evolve from the internal workings of their own smaller system. The more imperfect the facilities for the pooling of experience among all the subordinate centers — and all pooling of such experience is necessarily imperfect to some extent — the faster will be this increase of the share of diversified memories and diversified experiences in each subordinate organization.

The result will be a steady drift to a peripheralization and pluralization of the centers of decision. In the long run there is thus perhaps inherent in every totalitarian system of government a tendency

[10] On possible strategic uses of this overload problem, see K. W. Deutsch, "Game Theory in Politics: Some Applications of Games Theory to International Relations."

either toward overloading of its central facilities for the making of decisions, or toward an automatic corrosion of its original centralized structure and its disintegration into increasingly separate parts.

THE INSTABILITY OF HIERARCHICAL POWER

The difficulties that militate against the viability of any permanent system of totalitarian centralization are paralleled, in a sense, by the difficulties in the way of any permanent hierarchical distribution of power. A hierarchy of power requires that all power should be located at the apex of a pyramid, and that all power should lead downward in terms of a transitive chain of command, transmitting orders from the single power holder or the few power holders at the top to the many soldiers or policemen at the bottom. However, every such pyramid of power is inherently unstable. To maintain transitivity it must be steered by orders coming from the apex. Yet the shortest communication routes to all relevant sub-centers and sub-assemblies of power is not from the apex, but from some location farther down, let us say one, two, or three tiers farther down in the chain of command, according to the size of the pyramid and the speed with which the number of power holders increases from each layer of authority to the next lower one.[11] In all such pyramids, the Prime Minister, Shogun, Grand Viziers, Major Domus, or Police Chief, is closer to the real deposits of power than the king or prince whom such an official is supposed to serve. Power may very well then migrate from the king or dictator to some of his subordinates; it may migrate from the marshals and generals in the army of some small dictatorship to the brigadier-generals or colonels, or in a small country even to the captains or sergeants. The lower an officer or official is in such a pyramid of power, the closer he is to the ultimate facilities of power, the common soldiers or policemen, provided only that he succeeds in organizing for himself the support of a sufficient number of his peers on his own level.

If several strata of power holders in a hierarchy of command, such as, say, generals, colonels, and captains, may be thought of as po-

[11] Suggestive small group experiments on the relation between the location of power and the shortness of communication lines have been carried out by Alexander Bavelas and associates at Massachusetts Institute of Technology.

tential competitors for power, then the stratum most likely to emerge victorious may well be that which best fulfills the interplay of two conditions: (1) Among its rivals, it is sufficiently low in the hierarchy to be "close to the people," or at least to the soldiery; (2) it is still high enough in the hierarchy to have sufficiently small numbers so as to facilitate the effective organization of a proportion of its members sufficient to isolate all higher levels in the chain of command. Power may thus migrate from the apex a small way down the pyramid; if so, the old apex may shrink to a ceremonial shadow of its past, or may disappear altogether. In effect, a new, somewhat lower apex then has come into being; and the pyramid of power has been made somewhat less steep. But the new apex is again located above the point of shortest communications with the entire pyramid. Again it is liable to be challenged and superseded by a shift of power to the incumbents of the central strategic positions on some lower level; and the pyramid of power may remain unstable through several repetitions of this process. Theoretically, this process might stop when power has shifted so far down the hierarchy and the pyramid of command has become so broad and blunt that the remaining distance between the last apex of the pyramid and the point of shortest communication is no longer significant.

At this stage, however, the center of command may find itself again overloaded with the flood of current decisions to be made. After all, the reducing of this burdensome volume of decisions — through suitable screening, delegation, and selection of matters to be decided at different levels of command — had been one of the primary advantages of the original pyramid of power. Some of the conditions for reducing the burden of communication and decision-making are thus the opposite of the conditions for preserving the stability of power. The steeper the pyramid, and the more numerous the intermediate layers between the bottom and the top, the less is the danger of overloading the information-processing and decision-making capacities of the men or groups at the apex. The blunter the pyramid and the fewer screens or layers of delegated authority between bottom and top, on the other hand, the greater is the danger of such overloading. Since it takes less communicative and decision-making capacity to seize power at a favorable opportunity than it takes to exercise such totalitarian power for longer periods, it may well follow that the problem of the pure power pyramid — the pursuit and location of power per se in a transitive chain of command — has none but unstable solutions.

TOTALITARIANISM AND SOME LIMITATIONS OF TECHNOLOGY

Thus far we have listed a number of weaknesses and conflicts inherent in the working of totalitarian systems and making for their eventual stagnation, disintegration, or corrosion. But have all these tendencies not been overbalanced by the impact of new technological developments which might increase the power of dictatorial governments far beyond all precedent and all previous political and social limits?

Will not the future development of microphones and television cameras supply every totalitarian regime with cheap and ever-present spies, just as the development of tanks and airplanes has supplied them with weapons which can be concentrated in the hands of a few, and as barbed wire has supplied them with facilities for inexpensive concentration camps?

Several reasons seem to suggest that no presently indicated development of technology is likely to increase significantly the stability or cohesion of totalitarian regimes. In a world of rival powers, the concentration of effective weapons in the hands of a trusted few men is a luxury no great power can afford. Throughout all advances in military technology, governments have become more dependent, not less, on the support of millions of their citizens. Armies, navies, air forces, tank corps, civil defense and production organizations all require hundreds of thousands or millions of persons in their ranks, and the day of the quasi-aristocratic war, carried on by small groups of highly skilled professionals, seems even farther away than at the time of its early prophets in the 1920's.

To the extent, on the other hand, that decisive instruments of military power should become concentrated in the hands of a few specialists, some additional positions would be created for the power struggle within the totalitarian regime. None of the potential rivalries between the political leadership, the propagandists, the administrators, the army, the police, and any other major power group — rivalries of the kind instanced by the executions of Soviet Marshal Tukhachevsky and Soviet Police Chief Yagoda in the 1930's at the behest of the Politburo — could be wholly abolished by any techno-logical development. The problems of mobilizing mass support for national military strength, and of insuring unity of command and cohesion among the different parts of the regime, are all essentially political in nature. They are fraught with the hopes and fears, the expectations and motives of individuals. They involve, therefore, all the difficulties of totalitarian regimes which were discussed earlier; and no increase in the gadgetry of violence will solve them.

If totalitarianism can expect no decisive aid from the technology of violence, neither can it expect such aid from any improvements in the gadgetry of supervision or persuasion. Electronic devices can be used to improve the reception and transmission of information in these processes, but they can do little or nothing to facilitate its use and thus its ultimate effectiveness. Even if supervisory television de-vices and microphones were to be installed in the home of every citi-zen, the totalitarian state would still have to find the huge numbers of officials necessary to look at and listen to the vast amounts of in-formation thus obtained — a difficulty from which the dictatorial government in George Orwell's nightmare world of 1984 seems to have been conveniently free.[12] Anyone who has tried to wade through several hundred pages of the transcript of a tape recording of a con-ference will have at least an inkling of the quantitative problem involved. Human greed cannot be listened to with understanding at very much higher speed than it can be spoken, and the talk and gossip of even one person's lifetime may well require something resembling half a lifetime's listening on the part of some luckless policeman.

The introduction of universal electronic supervision, even were it technologically feasible, would drown the totalitarian regime in an ocean of trivialities, and the addition of automatic transcription de-vices would merely convert their output of trivial noise into a flood of paper. Political supervision is a feedback process in which incom-ing information must be responded to in terms of behavior that reaches back to the citizen or subject. It thus consists in its essence in the paying of attention and the exercise of judgment and neither of these functions can be mechanized with any equipment likely to exist for the rest of this century or longer.

[12] George Orwell, *Nineteen Eighty-four* (New York: Harcourt Brace, 1949).

Similar considerations apply to the problem of persuasion. As noted earlier, persuasion is not a one-way process, except on the simplest levels of advertising designed to change none but very minor habits of its addressees. More deep-reaching persuasion requires again listening, responsiveness, and the creation of learning situations. None of these functions can be readily mechanized by presently indicated technological developments.

Finally, electronic devices may speed the transmission of orders and reports, and exchange of information among top-ranking personnel of the regime, and facilitate to some extent the pooling of information essential to maintain unity of command. However, while radio during World War II could transmit reports from the German armies in Russia to Adolf Hitler's headquarters, no electronic device could force the Führer or his staff to make intelligent use of them. Television conferences may leave men as self-centered, quarrelsome, or antagonistic to each other as did simpler methods of communication. Some of the most bitter conflicts in both Germany and Russia occurred among groups or leaders living and working relatively near to each other.

The heart of the matter is perhaps in the tendency of economic and technological progress thus far to increase the decision load of governments as fast or at a faster rate than the means of governments to cope with them. By "decision load" is meant the total volume of social and political decisions to be made, and the extent and number of their probable consequences to be taken into account, by a given organization within a given time. Because of this growth in the decision load of governments, the business of governing has become harder instead of easier during the last fifty years, just as driving an automobile through rush-hour traffic has become harder, and this growth in the decision burden has been greatest in the case of totalitarian regimes. Confronted with such pressures and demands, their crucial difficulty is still in the limited capacity of the individual human mind to pay sufficient attention to a large number of other individuals and to learn significantly from the whole range of their memories and preferences. All these are matters of the give and take of human learning and human communication, and in all these matters so crucial in resisting disintegration, totalitarianism as such is not stronger, and may well be weaker, than democracy.

TOTALITARIAN POLICIES TO RESIST DISINTEGRATION

If the trends and conflicts making for the loosening or dissolution of totalitarian regimes are not counteracted effectively by technological developments, we may well ask how any totalitarian governments have managed to maintain themselves for longer periods of time. Perhaps the persistence of totalitarian governments or movements, and of social institutions having at least some totalitarian features, over several decades or even several generations, may be due in part to their development of a whole series of resources for the maintenance of the unity of command. Such unity of command, or consistency of decisions, depends to a large extent upon the unity of consistency of the memories, both of factual data and of operating preferences, in terms of which all such decisions must be made. The problem of maintaining unity of command is thus essentially that of maintaining a sufficient unity of memories, and it is by providing for a larger share of relatively uniform memories, and of relatively uniform processes for adding new but uniform, or at least compatible experiences, that totalitarian governments or movements have attempted to persist over larger expanses of space and over longer periods of time.

The first and most obvious method of totalitarian regimes to maintain unity among their subjects and subordinate organizations consist, of course, in setting them a common goal. It is such a goal in terms of which totalitarianism carries out its attempts to bring about the mobilization of all material and human resources which is so characteristic for its workings. Since the totalitarian goal is by definition overriding, its imposition resolves many, though not all, possible conflicts with established habits of procedure, or even with lesser policies of the regime.

Such unification through an overriding goal which is then to be sought spontaneously by all loyal subjects of the government is based on the hidden assumption that the government knows, and that its subjects can know easily, just which actions will in fact bring the country nearer to the goal, or will in fact promote the best interests of the regime, nation, or ideology. This totalitarian assumption often proves unwarranted. As the inhabitants of the ruined cities of Germany have had occasion to find out, the usefulness of Nazi policies to the German people had been greatly overrated. Yet without certain and easily available knowledge of how to promote in fact the proclaimed goal, the united striving for a common purpose is likely to degenerate into endless wrangling over means and methods, made only more bitter by the total devotion and intolerant zeal which totalitarianism enjoins upon all its followers.

Another method of promoting unity might consist in standardizing common rules of procedure for the finding of facts and the making of decisions, either in addition to the stating of goals, or even in place of them. The Koran of Mohammed, the Corpus Juris of Justinian, the Corpus of Canon Law and the Code Napoleon are all examples of pre-totalitarian or in some cases perhaps proto-totalitarian, attempts to insure the unity of far-flung or long-lasting organizations or regimes. All of the codes listed have been successful in some measure, although their success has at times been greater, and their life span longer, than that of the regimes which gave them birth. No such codes were lastingly established by the totalitarian regimes of Italy and Germany. Whether the growing body of Soviet law shows any signs of playing a similar unifying role in the eventual development of Russian society might well be an interesting question for research.

A more far-reaching attempt to insure effective unity of memories consists in the imposition of a common ideology. Such an ideology may be couched in secular or in religious terms. In either case it includes not only common statements of value, common assertions of supposed fact and some common rules of procedure in decision-making, but it also contains often a common epistomology, at least by implication. Its inherents are told which kinds of knowledge, which sources, and which methods of gaining it, are to be trusted and which ones are to be shunned. With common goals, common procedural values, common memories, and common methods for screening and acquiring new information, the probability of maintaining consistency among future decisions and commands is greatly enhanced, even if these decisions have to be made by individuals cut off from communication with each other.

Despite the potential effectiveness of ideologies, most people are more likely to respond to personal experiences and personal contacts than to abstract thoughts or even to colorful symbols. Totalitarian regimes, like other governments, may attempt to maintain their unity by creating a common pool of leading or decision-making personnel — perhaps in the form of a common political party — or of particular institutions, formal or informal, for the training and rotation of leaders. They may make a point of drawing to the capital leading personnel from potentially doubtful outlying districts, somewhat as the Nazis brought wittingly or unwittingly an unusual number of Catholics and Bavarians to Berlin, or as the Soviets put some Georgians, Armenians, and Jews on their central decision-making bodies. They may send their officials from one district to another, so as to maintain the unity of a service corps among them even at the expense of making more casual and distant their relations to the population among whom these officials reside during any particular tour of duty; or they may even command their officials to do two potentially contradictory things at one and the same time: to retain absolute loyalty to the common center and yet to develop numerous deep and intimate contacts with the people among whom they work as in the case of model Communist Party workers extolled in Soviet literature.

Perhaps the most effective way of insuring a community of memories is one over which totalitarian regimes have only very limited control. It is the community of memories that derives from the possession of a common universe of experiences as they are produced by a new way of life, a new fundamental pattern of culture, a new economic system, or a new religion. To the extent that a totalitarian regime becomes established in the course of such a fundamental rearrangement of society, and to the extent that it draws its personnel from those who share in the common ensemble of continuing new experiences resulting from that fundamental change, it can count on at least some significant degree of similarity or uniformity in the outlook both of its decision-making personnel and of its underlying populations, not only in the central regions of its territory but throughout the areas over which the full effects of the fundamental social changes have become extended.

What is perhaps even more important, a totalitarian regime that has arisen in the course of such a fundamental change can count on the unifying effect of the antagonism of the populations and groups of personnel among whom these changes have become accepted against the outside world which has remained skeptical or hostile to the new dispensation. Foreign threats to the totalitarian regime appeal then readily as threats to the new way of life, the new gospel of salvation, or the new institutions of society, and even the remaining domestic opponents of the regime appear in the eyes of the converted population as aliens or infidels.

The contrast between the two types of totalitarianism becomes reinforced by the differences between the psychological and educational techniques employed by each regime. The main emphasis of Nazism was on hardness, will and action; on obedience and command; and on the subordination or annihilation of inferior races. Nazi theories of learning were rudimentary; inventiveness and creativity were considered biological rather than psychological categories. Little if anything in the Nazi education encouraged listening to other people. The circular flow of information from the led to the leaders and from the leaders to the led was to be replaced by a one-way arrangement of commands coming from the top down. In the Nazi world the loudspeaker thus outgrew the microphone and the mouth the ear; and the result seems to have been a gradually increasing bias throughout the system against discovery and against learning.

The Soviet rulers, too, like all dictators, have been eyeing rather warily the human capacity for new discoveries and new social learning, but instead of ignoring it, or trying to stifle most of it outright as the Nazis did, the Soviets have tried to control this capacity and use it for their purposes. Soviet literature in education, psychology, science, and the arts constantly urges individuals to display resourcefulness, initiative, and creativity, while at the same time insisting that they should keep closer to permitted patterns. This double insistence cannot but burden the individuals concerned with a good deal of constant strain and tension; and, to the extent that genuine learning capacity and initiative can survive and grow under such strained circumstances, they may well in the long run contribute their share toward the undermining of the conformity that is essential for the continuation of the totalitarian regime. The strains and stresses inherent in these aspects of Soviet life, terrible as they are for many of the individuals concerned, are occurring on a higher level of complexity and are leaving a wider range of resources available to the regime than did the comparable educational and psychological practices in fascist countries. These differences do not make the Soviet dictatorship less of an opponent of democracy and of the Western world; rather they make it a more formidable one.

SOME TENTATIVE PROSPECTS

Considerations of this kind bring us back to the problem of assessing the capabilities and performance characteristics of different governments and types of government. In many cases, the communicating of information and the reaching of decisions may be as vital to the survival of governments as the functioning of the nervous system would be to the survival of some complex organism. Governments, of course, are not organisms, and the metaphor should not be pushed too far. Even so, different political systems may be profitably compared in terms of the performance of their "nerves of government," and particularly in terms of their ability to maintain political cohesion and unity of decision-making under conditions of social, political or economic strain. Applied to existing governments, an analysis of this kind reveals major differences between totalitarian and democratic governments in general, as well as between different types of totalitarian regimes, and perhaps between different kinds of democratic policies and institutions.[13]

At this stage, any inference from our survey of the patterns of disintegration of totalitarian systems must be tentative and provisional. Thus qualified, they will be indicated here, at the risk that readers will call obvious those findings which fit in with their views, while calling unsound those which do not. Both strictures may turn out to be correct; yet perhaps it may be hoped that they will be imposed only after some careful testing. If treated thus as inferences to be tested, rather than as conclusions to be believed, the following suggestions may yet fulfill some useful function.

[13] A brief survey of some of the unifying or unity-maintaining techniques and policies of the totalitarian regimes of Soviet Russia and Nazi Germany was presented to the Conference on Totalitarianism of the American Academy of Arts and Sciences as part of the present paper. The length of this survey precluded its inclusion here without disturbing the balance of this book; and it may be published in due time elsewhere. Some of its findings, however, have been used in the section which follows here; and the indulgence of the reader is asked for omitting references to specific policies and cases, which were presented to the Conference.

1. Totalitarianism is by no means immune from processes of disintegration; on the contrary, many of the dictatorial techniques which are intended to combat schism or disintegration may in fact tend to accelerate and intensify these very processes.

2. The basic processes of political integration and disintegration occur on a more fundamental level than that of mere political, military, or police techniques, or of government-run propaganda. This is even more true in the occurrence of schisms and secessions of supra-national philosophies or ideologies. Research on the probability of a future split — for instance, between the Communist regimes of Russia and China — might most profitably be aimed at these more fundamental levels.

3. Although there are significant analogies in the behavior of different totalitarian systems, the aims of particular totalitarian regimes may make a considerable difference to their ability to maintain cohesion for a longer period of time. The same seems true of the nature of the underlying social changes in the course of which a totalitarian regime may become established; and further considerable differences may be due to the specific practices and institutions by which particular totalitarian regimes may attempt to combat their own automatic drift toward pluralization and disintegration.

4. For all these reasons, no schematic predictions can be made concerning a general probability of all totalitarian regimes to split up or disintegrate within a short period of time. In particular, a number of important performance characteristics of Russian Soviet totalitarianism, on the one hand, and of German Nazi totalitarianism on the other, differ radically from each other. What imperfect data we have surveyed seem to suggest that the Soviet dictatorship in Russia still disposes of substantial resources to stave off its own disintegration or pluralization for a considerable time.

5. These considerations apply, however, only to time scales of about twenty to fifty years. Most of the major economic and social changes in history which were violent enough to give rise to regimes with some totalitarian features were substantially completed within a period of the order of fifty years, and with the slowing down of the rate of major changes there has usually followed a period of pluralization and a dwindling of totalitarian expansiveness. If similar considerations should apply to the totalitarian regimes of Russia

and China, which established themselves in consequence of revolutions which disrupted the *status quo* in these countries as early as 1911 and 1917, respectively, then we might well expect the 1970's or 1980's to bring a slowing of the expansive pressure from these two regimes, or a growing divergence of policies between them, or among some of their constituent regions, or some combination of all these changes, leading in either case to a diminution in "classic" patterns of totalitarian behavior.

6. In the meantime, the free countries of the world cannot rely on the disintegration of Soviet-type regimes to rid them of their present opponents; nor does there seem to be much evidence that any propaganda or underground activities short of all-out war could influence the course of events behind the Iron Curtain decisively in favor of freedom. Even the political results of an all-out war against totalitarianism might be hazardous to predict, quite apart from its probable atomic devastation, so long as even the final results of our "reëducation" of the German and Japanese peoples are by no means clear. The prospects seem to indicate, therefore, a period of prolonged tension until at least the 1980's, followed perhaps then, with luck, by a slackening of pressure.

7. Throughout this period it will be essential to maintain the political, economic and moral strength of the free world. This involves the maintenance of adequate military strength for defense, and the protection of the territories of the democratic countries. In the long run, such Western power will be not very much aided by centering our whole attention on the task of confining the Communist regimes to a particular line or perimeter drawn somewhere on the map of Asia, nor by borrowing doubtful strength for the cause of the democracies from a motley crew of minor totalitarian regimes who detest our ideals but offer us support for pay. Rather the essential strength of the free world in all likelihood will have to come from the genuinely free countries within it, and our best defense during the next thirty years may well consist in the strengthening of the free world from the ground up and from the inside out, through the growth and strengthening of centers and core areas of genuine freedom.

In geographic terms, this might mean particularly the strengthening of the English-speaking countries, the democracies of Western

Europe, and on the Asiatic continent perhaps India and Pakistan. Within these areas, and in terms of politics and economics, as well as of our whole cultural, moral and spiritual climate, it might mean the insistence on the continuing growth of freedom and democracy in all their dimensions.

DISCUSSION

Mr. Ivo Duchacek: The major element in commanding mass conformity in a totalitarian society is the power of the political authority to assign or withdraw employment, that is, the means to live. The modern welfare-garrison state makes an individual absolutely dependent on absolute political power. In these circumstances, one need no longer speak of a desire to conform: it becomes instead a *necessity* of conforming. Simply by living in a totalitarian society, one commits oneself to it. One can escape only by dying or emigrating. Simply trying to live is already a first step in active collaboration with the regime. There may be a quantitative difference, but hardly a qualitative one, between the man who accepts a factory job in a totalitarian society and one who becomes an official in the party.

Thus, anyone who survives in a totalitarian regime also conforms. As a result he may suffer psychologically, and in particular may feel a rather complex sort of guilt. Interviews with refugees who in 1953 succeeded in escaping the totalitarian society of Czechoslovakia after living in it for five years seem to confirm the existence of such a complex of guilt.

Mr. N. S. Timasheff: One of the great difficulties of conceptualizing totalitarianism arises from the great differences between the economic aspects of the Soviet system and those of the Nazi state. Both, nevertheless, have one thing in common. Both assert that the state has the right to direct all economic life, and in this they differ radically from laissez-faire liberalism. In the details of their activity, the two totalitarian regimes display striking economic differences; for example, the Soviet technique was expropriation, whereas the Nazis relied on extremely detailed regulation. In consequence, the political institution is the only employer in the Soviet Union, something which was not true in Germany.

A comparison of the traits listed by Mr. Deutsch with those earlier advanced by Mr. Friedrich leads me once again to point out the difficulties of definition by means of juxtaposing selected characteristics. On Mr. Deutsch's grounds, one would be forced to classify the government of Peter the Great as a totalitarian one, while Mr. Friedrich's criteria would exclude it.

Mr. George Denicke: I think one can overemphasize the technological element as against the human one. It is perfectly true that the totalitarian movement must have machine guns, but let us not forget that it must also be able to control the machine gunners.

The human aspects of totalitarian movements are well worth more careful study. In the early phases one needs zealots, but zealots become a source of danger once the movement is in power. They are usually friends with their fellow zealots, and they are reluctant to assist in their purging. In Russia, many of the Bolsheviks disliked and resisted the attempts to dispose of their old Menshevik comrades-in-arms. Once the regime is established it requires, as Dzerzhinsky once put it, "dirty hands to do dirty jobs." This raises a serious problem: where is it to recruit them?

Mr. Paul Kecskemeti: I have two remarks to Mr. Deutsch's paper.

He emphasizes, quite rightly I think, the absolute necessity for the totalitarian leadership to remain autonomous with respect to its own past commitments. There must be flexibility for sudden changes in totalitarian policy. And he furthermore stresses the importance of the learning process in the totalitarian setting. I merely wish to point out that there is a latent contradiction here. A stable learning situation, totalitarian or otherwise, requires a stable frame of reference, and if the leaders are to be free to abandon their past commitments, the conceptual framework must be subject to sudden change. The learning process, in other words, is not merely accelerated, as Mr. Deutsch has pointed out, but it is also segmented. Those who learned too well in an earlier segment of the learning situation *must* be purged if a new sequence is to be initiated. This raises a very interesting problem: who is able to survive such sudden shifts, and what are the conditions of their survival?

In speaking of unity of command, Mr. Deutsch has pointed to the need for a transitive relationship. But surely it must be more than that. It must be nonsymmetrical as well, that is, it must be ordered. But there is a danger of analytical oversimplification here. Quite probably, the hierarchy of decision-dominance is not unilinear or unidirectional. We should probably be mistaken to hypostasize the dictator as pure will; instead he is most surely an arbiter who decides between undeterminate orders of decision-making. This, one should insist, does not weaken the importance of the dictator, for under such conditions the arbiter is essential if any "unity of command" is to be maintained.

Mr. Waldemar Gurian: On Mr. Nettl's grounds, we should be forced to drop "totalitarianism" as a generic term and confine our attention solely to the Soviet system. This seems to me to go too far; there is perhaps a case for excluding Fascist Italy from the totalitarian category, but surely Nazi Germany must be granted membership.

I grant that there are evident differences between the Nazi economy and the Soviet one, but I should believe these not to be differences in formal structure but rather of historical context and of developmental phase. For example, the Bolsheviks wanted to transform the economy at once to an ultra-radical degree, and the Nazis did not. In Russia, the pre-revolutionary elites were eliminated at once with the sole exception of the "old specialists"; in Germany, the totalitarian movement was often masked as conservatism and it promised to bring the old elites back to their prior positions of power. The distinction, I suggest, is not one of kind, but simply a matter of the divergent historical conditions under which the two totalitarianisms arose.

Mr. Deutsch has raised some highly significant problems in the techniques of totalitarian administration. I should concede that the decentralization he mentions is inevitable in any complex society, but certainly unity of command is equally necessary in any totalitarian society. The key to the paradox is terror, which holds the regime together even though "pools of power" may compete and conflict within it.

Mr. Bertram Wolfe: This matter of historical phasing seems to me to be something which we cannot afford to overlook. The Soviet system is now thirty-five years of age, but the Nazi regime had been in power only six years at the start of World War II and hardly had an opportunity to "develop" during the course of it. And the Soviet government had been established for more than a decade before Stalin, late in the twenties and into the early thirties, began to impose totalitarian controls upon it. In Germany the totalitarian features were perfectly clear within four years.

I would fully agree with Mr. Nettl's suggestion that we view the totalitarian economy as a war economy, provided that we view the war in turn as one on two fronts. It is directed against the subjects of the regime first and against foreign enemies second.

Mr. W. W. Leontief: I have the impression that the Conference is perhaps too optimistic.[1] The tone seems to be that we have only to wait and the internal stresses will tear the totalitarian system apart. I am most skeptical of this approach. Perhaps we are paying too much attention to theoretical disintegrating forces, and not enough to the practicalities of the time-scale involved. It's a little like the stable owner who tells his jockey not to worry about the horse in the next race with the favorable time-trials, for, after all, all horses die sometime.

We must remember that the Soviets are doing very well indeed in their economic expansion. In fact, they are doing better than we or anyone else. In only a very few decades, if the present rates of growth continue, they will overtake and surpass us. I am not at all sure that the disintegrative tendencies — and surely they are present — will prevent this, and perhaps they will not even delay it. The Soviet rate of expansion of economic output cannot be dismissed and probably will not be halted.

Miss Hannah Arendt: I too think that Mr. Deutsch is overoptimistic, though the economic reasons Mr. Leontief pointed out do not entirely convince me. Politically, one may say that under normal circumstances the chain of command may indeed be "overloaded"; the specific question regarding totalitarian circumstances, however, is whether or not the *Führerprinzip*, which is expressly designed to take care of this situation, works. As far as I can see, it works rather well; we should remember that Hitler, up to the very last days of the war and deprived of nearly all means of communication as well as of real power, remained completely in charge, while the Kaiser, for instance, whose chain of command certainly was not overloaded, did not fare half as well the moment it was clear that he had lost the war.

I very much agree with the remarks of Mr. Duchacek. Universal

[1] Mr. Leontief was present only at this meeting of the conference.

complicity, that is, organized guilt, helps to hold the system together even if the individuals concerned still feel pangs of conscience. Conscience under these circumstances unfortunately cuts both ways: people who joined the party for essentially economic reasons and without any convictions whatsoever, then began to feel guilty of their "opportunism"; the result was that they became *gleichgeschaltet* in true earnest. There are very few people who have the strength of character to remain "cynical" enough to keep their personalities intact. And even people who did not comply at all but only lived in the country that happened to be totalitarian are trapped in universal complicity. As Karl Jaspers said in 1945: "Our guilt is that we are still alive." This is not a sentimental exaggeration, but a precise description of the situation as it really is.

Mr. Duchacek's emphasis upon the sheer force of necessity leading to total compliance is very important. One must eat, and in modern societies one must work to eat, and in totalitarian societies working is a political act. In other words, we live in a society of job holders, not of property holders. This is true regardless of the social system operating in a given country. No matter what our political convictions with regard to property are, it is a fact of the first importance that only property can materially guarantee individual freedom. With the withering away of this material guarantee, which seems inevitable and can be watched in all countries, the need for legal protection of individual liberties and constitutional guarantee for civil rights is greater than ever before.

On one of our general problems I should like to add a word. We have looked for similarities and differences between Nazism and Soviet Communism. One of the differences is so obvious that it seems we overlooked it, and this is the Bolshevik institution of the purge. The purges were originally a revolutionary device for preventing corruption and bureaucratization of the Party; they were even intended to give the people an opportunity to fire incompetent or corrupt officials. Very early, they were used as political weapons, first only within the party itself, then on a gigantic scale throughout all services and offices. Since 1936, the purges have become part and parcel of this system and occur by now in regular intervals. Nothing of this sort existed under the Nazis. The closest the Nazis ever came to a "purge" was the liquidation of the Roehm clique, but it remained without consequence and was not repeated. The extermination of ethnic groups can of course not be considered a purge. In view of the great importance of the purges for the functioning of the Soviet system, this difference seems to be more significant than many others which are frequently stressed, such as differences in ideologies, historical traditions or economic systems.

Mr. Sigmund Neumann: I wonder if we aren't concentrating too much on techniques and institutionalized devices. Totalitarianism, among other things, is an institutional form, but it is also a force in itself. Once the institutional manifold is in operation it develops a momentum all its own. But this does not mean that it is simply a homogeneous force, working on everyone in the same way. Some groups and classes are more ready to comply than others; some groups are involved in different ways from the involvement of others. We need a kind of diagnostic approach, a catalogue of warning signs which we can apply to our own society. And, beyond that, we need a basis for social integration which will not destroy essential human traits. So long as we can neither diagnose nor prescribe we are in danger.

Mr. Carl J. Friedrich: I have two factual footnotes, so to speak. Mr. Lauterbach has contrasted the "lower-class" support of the Marxists with the "middle-class" basis of the Nazis. I think this is mistaken. In Germany, as in Italy and in Spain, what mass support there was came from the peasantry, a stratum which stands outside the usual three-fold classification. Peasants are neither upper- nor middle- nor lower-class folk as those groups are customarily defined.

I would also warn the Conference against the dangers of concentrating too much on Germany under the Nazis and Russia under the Soviets. The Russian satellites today are definitely totalitarian.[2] China seems to be heading in that direction if she is not already fully there, and Japan from the mid-thirties to the end of the war was a totalitarian society under the domination of the militarists and a mass party subject to their control.

Mr. Lauterbach: Let me answer the comments on my paper in the order in which I have jotted them down.

First of all, in response to Mr. Duchacek and Mr. Timasheff: in-

[2] See in this respect the "additional comment" of Andrew Gyorgy below on page 381.

troducing the scope of "state" activity, whether it be the welfare state or the classically defined state, as the yardstick of totalitarianism simply begs the question. The totalitarian economy *is* a power economy, but power under totalitarianism is *not* merely state power. Moreover, if one is to talk of the state, one must make up his mind *who* "the state" in question is and what social forces it actually mirrors. At any rate, certain power concentrations develop in totalitarian systems entirely apart from anything that can be called a "state" according to any customary definition of that term.

I fully agree with Mr. Leontief's misgivings concerning assumptions of early economic disintegration of the Soviet regime. I don't anticipate its purely economic collapse. But I do think that the essence of the Soviet type of totalitarian economy is an attempt at rapid industrialization at a pace far surpassing any the world has ever seen; and that this kind of economic policy may in turn lead sooner or later to political and psychological consequences of a disruptive nature. The real problem here will be that of how fast they are going to industrialize, how they will go about it, and what the impact will be on different groups within Soviet society.

Miss Arendt's remarks on job-holding as against property-holding seem to me to be sound. But I would add that the real difference is one of function, not of ownership title as such. The contrast of the Soviet as against the Nazi system makes this quite clear. The Russians expropriated, whereas the Nazis left legal ownership rights virtually untouched but took actual control of economic decision-making. The techniques were quite different in their intensity, but the upshot was about the same: the owners no longer controlled.

As for Mr. Friedrich's comments on the role of the peasantry in the rise of certain totalitarian regimes in Europe, I agree that this role has been important. I would add, however, that on the basis of its land-holdings the peasantry may be considered part of the middle class, at least in the European meaning of this term, which includes an important element of pre-capitalist structure and mentality.

Mr. Nettl: Let me reply seriatim too.

I also find Miss Arendt's remarks about job-holding and property-holding most acute. Might I add a historical footnote? Medieval society was also one of "job" holders, not of property owners, though medieval men wouldn't have used the term "job." The point I want to make is that property-holding as a strategically important social function is of limited historical duration, and our society is not the only one that diverges from the property-holding patterns.

To say, as Mr. Timasheff does, that a totalitarian economy is one where "the state entirely controls the economy," is in effect to include the Soviet Union, to exclude Nazi Germany, and then to sweep in some clearly non-totalitarian economic systems. During World War II, for example, state control of the economy was far more tight and more detailed in the United Kingdom (and, I gather, though I cannot speak from my own knowledge, in the United States), than it ever was in Nazi Germany. But surely neither the American nor the British economic mobilization was "totalitarian."

Mr. Leontief, it seems to me, is entirely correct in laying heavy emphasis on the success of the Soviet economy. But the success itself creates all sorts of political strains. This factor tends to differentiate the Soviet from the Nazi and Fascist situations, where economic dynamism of this kind was wholly lacking. Neither the German nor the Italian leaders ever set out to transform the basic structure of the economy; indeed, they used much of their political power to preserve it. The transformation in the Soviet Union, I believe, might be fully successful from the economist's standpoint and yet highly dangerous from the political point of view, because it will bring as yet unpredictable social changes in its train.

Mr. Karl Deutsch: I am not attempting anything so ambitious as a "definition" of totalitarianism. I am merely trying, like Mr. Friedrich, to select a coherent set of traits which will serve certain specific purposes. In the case of my own selection of three traits, these purposes are to concentrate on the development of the totalitarian regime and to highlight certain problems in its functioning. For Mr. Friedrich's purposes, I am perfectly willing to accept his set of traits instead of my own.

I welcome Mr. Kecskemeti's contribution. The contradiction he sees appears to be entirely probable, and to call for further empirical research. I also believe that the arbitral function he assigns to the totalitarian leader is probably the correct one; in assigning to the dictator absolutely consistent willful control we are perhaps being deluded by the totalitarians' own claims to infallibility.

With Miss Arendt's reliance upon the leader-principle as an assurance of unity of command I cannot agree. The record of Hitler's decisions — especially his strategic ones — makes it fully evident to me that the principle did not work at all well. Decentralization as a technique also has it dangers, for it may all too easily lead to power rivalries whose elimination is most expensive to the regime.

PART SEVEN

TOTALITARIANISM
AND THE FUTURE

■

18. Totalitarianism and the Future

PAUL KECSKEMETI

I

There was a time when many people, both admirers and opponents of the totalitarian form of government, were inclined to see in it the "wave of the future." Let us recall the two decades preceding the Second World War. During that period Soviet totalitarianism was perfected and consolidated; and outside Russia, fascist totalitarianism and more or less similar anti-democratic, authoritarian regimes engulfed one European country after another. Democracy seemed to be doomed, destined for extinction. Then war came, and the early triumphs of Nazi Germany seemed to confirm this forecast. But since the early forties the picture has changed. Nazism, Fascism and the Japanese military autocracy have been eliminated by armed force; their place has been taken, in part, by new democracies. On the other hand, the totalitarian Soviet system emerged as a world power. The Communist type of totalitarianism holds sway from Central Europe to the Pacific; since the war it has extended its dominance over China. The world is split among the Soviet bloc and the group of free nations, facing each other across the Iron Curtain in mounting tension. There is real strength on both sides: no irresistible "wave," carrying one side from triumph to triumph, is in evidence. Whatever the future may bring, it will not, so far as we can see, repeat the one-sided pattern of the twenties and thirties. The main question we face is, rather, whether the two "worlds," the free and the totalitarian, will coexist in tense equilibrium, or whether they are headed for a fearful clash that may well spell the doom of civilization.

I shall not try to answer this question: I think both coexistence and conflict are possible, and do not see any rational argument excluding either possibility. When we try to think about our political future rationally, we have to take our departure from some trend we have observed in the past; when such a trend suggests itself, we must ask whether it can be extrapolated to the future with any degree of confidence. Now the present bipolar tension is too novel a situation to permit such thought experiments. Hence I shall not speculate about its probable future course, but take up, instead, some other problems connected with "totalitarianism and the future" — problems that do lend themselves to the kind of thought experiment I have described.

II

Two such questions come to mind, both of a hypothetical nature. The first is: what can we expect, in the light of past experience, in case there is conflict? The second is: what can we expect if there is coexistence?

As regards the first questions, it seems clear that past experience does not enable us to say much about the course or the outcome of a possible future conflict, unless we specify some of the exact initial conditions prevailing at the time when conflict breaks out. I shall not speculate about these conditions; they are outside my competence, since I know little about either strategy or military technology. But I think I can say something about the political consequences of a possible conflict. To begin with, it seems practically certain that if a total conflict breaks out, the political regime of the losing side will be eliminated. This, indeed, has been the dominant "trend" of the last two wars, and there is no reason why this trend could not be extrapolated to the future. If, as is often said, there will be no "victors" in a future war, the regimes of *both* sides may collapse or undergo drastic changes. At any rate, we cannot expect the trend toward correlation between "defeat" and "collapse of the political regime of the defeated country" to be reversed.

III

This in itself is almost a truism; nobody would expect anything else. But there is a more interesting political question we can raise in this connection. A regime can "collapse" or be "eliminated" in various ways. It can be removed by direct intervention of its victorious enemy, or it can fall as a result of internal upheaval — either "revolution" or "*coup d'état*." Now in this respect the unfolding pattern of twentieth-century total wars shows an extremely interesting trend. The role of "internal upheaval," and particularly revolution, grows less and less; that of "forcible removal by the victor" grows greater and greater.

For one of the regimes defeated in the First World War, that of Russia, the change, indeed, assumed the form of a "revolution" of elementary, explosive dynamism. Direct intervention by the victorious power, Germany, played a small role in the shaping of Russia's new regime; at any rate, Russia was not transformed in the winner's image — the revolution followed its own internal dynamism. In all of the other defeated countries, too, revolution broke out; but these revolutions were far more subdued than the Russian. They started only after the regimes in question had officially acknowledged defeat; and they showed a considerable tendency to imitate the fundamental institutional pattern of the victorious democracies. In the Kaiser's removal, moreover, the Allies' refusal to treat with Germany as long as he was in power played a more decisive role than purely German opposition to him. In this sense, though the German monarchy, in appearance, was abolished by "revolution," in fact it was removed by "intervention."

In the Second World War one phenomenon, which does not seem to have attracted enough attention, stands out: the complete absence of revolution in the belligerent countries. It is customary to speak of the twentieth century as an age of revolution, and this way of speaking is correct, insofar as the depth and the extent of social and political change is concerned. But it is significant that in mid-century even the most radical changes were no longer brought about by what is meant by the classic term "revolution." The ferment of the masses, the dissolution of ties of discipline in the military and administrative machinery, the dramatic transfer of allegiance from old to new centers of power surging from below — all these classic concomitants of "revolution" were absent at the end of the Second World War (in contrast to the First). The changes were imposed, dictated from above; nothing was left to spontaneous revolutionary dynamism. The countries of Central Europe, overrun by the Soviets, traversed an astronomical distance within a few short years, moving from a semi-feudal traditional order to a surrealist, lunar landscape of bureaucratic super-discipline, austerity, and double-talk. Every step in this transformation process was meticulously planned and imposed by the Moscow authorities; and the transformation was effected without any interruption in the continuity of economic life (which had been an outstanding characteristic of the Bolshevik revolution in Russia). The representatives of the "new order" could make no move without asking permission of a central authority already entrenched — a thing violently at variance with the classic image of revolution. Can we imagine Danton, Robespierre, or Lenin waiting for "authorization" before storming ahead? In the middle of the twentieth century, however, this is how "revolutionary" changes were effected — they had to be rubber-stamped in advance.

Essentially, the downfall of losing regimes in the Second World War came about through "intervention" of the winner rather than through internal "upheaval"; and insofar as the pressure of the military winner induced "upheaval," that upheaval invariably took the form of *coup d'état* rather than revolution. (The two most conspicuous examples of such *coups d'état* were those of France in 1940, and Italy in 1943.) All this suggests that the twentieth century — the most "revolutionary," perhaps, of all history, insofar as the rapidity and intensity of social and political change is concerned — has discarded "revolution" as a form of political change. Insofar as the outward *form* of change is concerned, the century since the close of the acute stage of the Russian Revolution has become the most *unrevolutionary* of all epochs.

One might suggest that all this holds true of Europe only; did the Second World War not "revolutionize" a large part of Asia? The Asian pattern certainly differed in some respects from the European one — but not in the sense that "revolutions" of the classic type occurred in Asia. There, too, the political process was dominated by centers of military and political power already in existence. Chiang's regime, for instance, was "removed" by war — the Communists took over through military conquest of the territory of China.

Some further observations we shall have occasion to make about political change in the twentieth century will provide additional evidence in support of our thesis about the waning of "revolution" as a characteristic feature of the twentieth century. Before we turn to this subject, however, we have to take up briefly the question of whether one can *extrapolate* to a possible future war the trend just discussed — the trend toward "removal" rather than "upheaval," and particularly "revolutionary" upheaval, as the dominant type of the elimination of losing regimes in the twentieth century.

IV

It is not entirely certain that this trend would still assert itself in a possible future war. It is true that even the most massive and destructive attacks directed against civilian centers in the Second World War failed to provoke "revolutions." Both in Germany and Japan the masses remained docile to the end; if anything, air attacks increased their dependence on the authorities which alone were in a position to organize emergency relief. Now we do not know whether the social and psychological effects of the far more destructive weapons provided by nuclear technology would not be more disruptive. Nuclear attacks might paralyze political and police controls; they might frustrate all efforts at providing emergency relief and thus create really anarchic conditions. This may be the case; we do not know — and we can only hope that we shall never have occasion to know. But at any rate, we should guard ourselves against facile assumptions concerning the "revolutionary" potential of nuclear attack. There may be such a potential — and nuclear attacks might also precipitate "*coups d'état*" in the countries affected. All these effects, however, depend on extremely complex psychological and political factors; and it would be particularly dangerous to assume that *totalitarian* regimes would necessarily be *more* vulnerable to nuclear attack than democratic ones. Unfortunately, the reverse might be the case. It is by no means impossible that in a "symmetrical" air war, a "peace offensive" launched by the *totalitarian* enemy would have a more disruptive effect upon a *democratic* opponent than "liberation" propaganda launched by a democratic belligerent would have upon the totalitarian enemy. It is an extremely dangerous illusion to believe that a totalitarian war regime could be removed, so to speak, by "remote control," that is, by air attacks precipitating upheaval. In spite of the unknown psychological and political potentialities of nuclear weapons, I would tend to assume that no totalitarian regime would succumb to war without being completely defeated. Essentially — as the losing totalitarian regimes of the Second World War — it would have to be "removed" by a victorious opponent. The spontaneous self-liberation of peoples under totalitarian rule, either through "revolution" or through "*coup d'état*," is unlikely to occur under war conditions. This is what the past record suggests; and nuclear weapons are not certain to reverse the trend.

v

Let us now turn to our second question: what have we to expect, in the light of past experience, if there is coexistence instead of conflict? Which form of government is likely to show greater stability and vulnerability respectively in the face of internal forces of disruption *in peacetime*, that is, in the absence of violent attack from without?

The trend of the past hundred years also seems to confirm our finding about the "waning of revolution" as a form of internal change. If we disregard the Iberian peninsula, we have to say that the last *peacetime* revolutions occurred in Europe in 1848–49. Since that time there were revolutions touched off by defeat in war; the biggest wave of such revolutions was, of course, that of 1918–19. Since then, a large number of political regimes collapsed "in peacetime," that is, some time after the end of the First World War. In these cases, however, we have to do, not with revolutions but with *coups d'état*. The parliamentary and democratic form of government was suppressed and replaced by totalitarian or authoritarian government — and this new form of rule was either directly exercised or at least fully sanctioned and supported by those groups which had already possessed full legal authority and controlled the decisive power positions in the society before the *coups d'état* took place. The transition in most cases was smooth; no violent upheavals, no drastic interruption of economic activities and administrative routines took place.

What is particularly impressive is that events conforming to this type occurred in the vast majority of the countries that had emerged from war in Central Europe, from the Balkans to the North Sea and from the Mediterranean to the Baltic. Another feature of the period was the contrast between the brittleness of democracies and the stability of the totalitarian and authoritarian *coup d'état* regimes that succeeded them. This suggests that during the period in question parliamentary democracy suffered from a specific and fatal vulnerability, to which the authoritarian regimes were immune.

Is it possible to account for this vulnerability in terms general enough to fit all the cases? Of course, the factors underlying the wave of counterrevolution that swept over Central Europe in the twenties and thirties were exceedingly complex. They had to do, in part, with the radiation effect of the Russian Revolution, which called forth counterrevoluntionary reactions; in addition to this, specific social, economic, ethnic, political, and psychological tensions arose in every single one of the countries involved, and these were of different nature from one country to another. A full analysis of the counterrevolutionary process would take us too far afield; but it is possible to single out one factor which seems to have been of major importance at least in the most highly developed countries affected by the trend.

The critical problems left behind by the war led to the emergence of a vast potential of mass violence. Large numbers of people were unwilling to let the problems facing them be solved by compromise and majority decision. They were ready to become "mobilized," to mass for direct, violent action; they gave their allegiance to leaders and symbols of all-out struggle. At the same time — and this point is generally overlooked — there was also, throughout the societies thus divided, and even within the ranks of the "mobilized" masses themselves, an intense and extraordinary *fear* of wholesale, acute violence and disorder. This was particularly true of the *urban* masses which were instinctively aware of the extent to which their very existence depended on the continuous functioning of the vastly complicated and interlocked machinery of industrial production and public administration. In cities, also, there was little chance for rebellious masses either to overpower or to escape from troops wielding modern weapons. For all these reasons, Western cities in the twentieth century ceased to represent a revolutionary potential.

On the level of symbols and gestures, however, there was a cultural lag. The urban masses and their leaders tended to revert at times to thinking in the nineteenth-century terms of barricades, street battles, general strikes, and victorious revolutions. This symbolism was hollow: nobody really expected to engage in fatal and destructive struggles. In the "revolutionary" camp, the symbols and gestures of revolution were expected to achieve success by "magic," as it were: the walls would crumble before the embattled emblems of revolution. It was on this basis that masses became "mobilized" for revolution: they marched, but only on condition that the transition would be smooth and easy, and victory instantaneous and without cost. When "magic" did not work, they were all too ready to go home.

This gave counterrevolution an extraordinary opportunity. The "revolutionary" masses were unable to achieve their aim by "magic," at one stroke — this was obvious, since they did not control any of the centers of real power and influence. Victory was possible, if at all, only through fearful struggle in which the masses did not want to engage. On the other hand, counterrevolutionary leaders were also able to "mobilize" masses which felt threatened by revolution (and shared the illusions of the "revolutionary" leaders and masses concerning the efficacy of revolutionary gestures). But the counterrevolutionary leaders were able to offer their followers prospects which were free from the "inner contradiction" besetting revolutionary strategy. The counterrevolutionary masses were not expected to challenge *real* power centers for all-out combat. They could restrict their violence to weak, marginal, and unprotected opponents. Final victory, the conquest of supreme political power, could be achieved at one stroke, without critical battles — simply by *arrangement* with those who already controlled the armed forces and the decisive economic and administrative positions.

I do not assert that counterrevolution everywhere followed this pattern; the actual course of events was, as I said, extremely varied. Besides the type of counterrevolution described — which is predicated upon the existence of mass parties both of "revolutionary" and of "counterrevolutionary" character — there were also direct *coups d'état* in which political power was not *handed over* to a counterrevolutionary mass leader and demagogue but taken away from parliament and concentrated, say, in the hands of a monarch and his henchmen. But these variations are of secondary importance. In every case, the critical factor was the masses' unwillingness to disrupt order, and their willingness to go along with any existing authority that could guarantee continuity and tranquility. This also explains the stability of counterrevolutionary regimes. Obviously, the exponents of constitutional democracy could not challenge these regimes; it was not possible to remove them, except by revolution. But revolution had become discarded as a form of political change — for the masses were more interested in order than in violent change.

Since revolution was already an extinct political form in the early twenties, none of the European counterrevolutions was "needed" to forestall a threatening revolution — nor would it have succeeded, if revolution had been a *real* threat, i.e., if the masses had been in a mood to fight. When Hitler came to power in Germany, there was not a shadow of a chance for a successful Communist revolution, or even for a serious attempt at revolution. Twelve or eleven years earlier, when Mussolini was climbing to power in Italy, revolutionary effervescence was undoubtedly greater — Marxism challenged the political order in Italy quite effectively in some of the provinces. But we must note that the *élan* of the revolution had fizzed out when the march on Rome took place: the occupations of factories had been lifted; the workers had "gone home."

VI

We must now ask whether in our own period, the aftermath of the Second World War, the rules of the game are still the same. Are the dice still loaded in favor of counterrevolutionary *coup d'état* and against parliamentary democracy? Or are the chances, either of revolution or of the maintenance of democracy, now better? And finally: is the stability of authoritarian and totalitarian regimes still guaranteed by the "rules of the game," or has totalitarianism become more vulnerable?

Unfortunately, in our own time, the field of experimentation is greatly restricted: parliamentary democracy exists only this side of the Iron Curtain in Europe, in the new Asian republics, in Japan, and in parts of Latin America — and in some of these areas it exists under the highly artificial conditions of military occupation. Further, we cannot say whether, say, in Europe the existing parliamentary regimes *could* weather a really severe economic crisis. Since the war ended, full employment has been fairly steadily maintained in the democracies, and there was no runaway inflation. This *may* mean that in one respect, the democracies have gained in vitality: they now know how to ward off dangerous economic crises. Whether this gain is permanent or not, we do not know; only the future will tell. But regardless of this, it is unmistakable, I think, that the whole psychological and political atmosphere of the forties and fifties is very different from that of the twenties and thirties. There are still tendencies toward political polarization and radicalization; and as I said, these *might* again assume critical proportions if there should be an economic crisis. But so far at any rate, the established democratic order, where it exists, seems to be *less* acutely threatened than it was between the two wars. The dice are still loaded against revolution: it still is an "extinct" form, and even more so than before the last war. On the other hand, *coups d'état* on the fascist and authoritarian pattern also seem to be on the wane. At any rate, none has occurred in the eight years since the war ended, unless we count the Czech *coup d'état* of 1948 as an example.

First, let us consider the problem of revolution. The assertion that the likelihood of democratic regimes being overthrown by revolution is *smaller* now may appear surprising, in the light of the extraordinary growth of the French and Italian Communist parties. Surely, this indicates an *increase* of the revolutionary potential in those countries, does it not?

The answer is that it does not, and the very strength of the French and Italian Communist parties is a proof of this. Revolution is so "extinct" that even its nominal upholders either cannot or do not care to launch it. The Communist parties — whether large or small, whether powerful or outlawed — have become parties of *coup d'état*, of subversion from above and from within, rather than parties of *revolution*.

The behavior of the French and Italian Communists after the war provides a convincing illustration of this. Revolution in France and Italy was feasible; the Communists had broad support among the masses, far beyond the ranks of urban labor, as well as well-disciplined organized cadres; they had all but monopolized the patriotic glory of the Resistance. The probability of direct Anglo-American armed intervention — as in Greece in 1944 — was remote. This is not to say that the revolution would have succeeded; perhaps, in spite of all these favorable circumstances, it would have failed in the end. But there can be hardly any doubt that if before the Second World War any Communist Party had found itself placed in circumstances as favorable to revolution as those prevailing in France and Italy at the end of the war, they would not have hesitated for a moment.

Yet, in actual fact, the French and Italian Communists, in sharp contrast to Lenin's revolution strategy of 1917, entered coalition governments alongside Marxist and non-Marxist parties; and while they remained in the government, they did their best to suppress industrial unrest and to avoid organic social reform. The reason for this was not that the Communists had abandoned their ultimate objective, the introduction of totalitarianism on the Moscow model, and sincerely embraced democratic compromise and coöperation. Rather, they intended first to occupy key positions in the government, place their agents in all strategic spots, and then to turn upon their partners and annihilate them. This appeared more promising and safer than the technique of "revolution." Moscow apparently discarded this technique, both because it shrank from its risks and uncertainties, and because it did not relish the prospect of a revolutionary process creating independent leader figures with a *charisma* of their own. Moscow had no use for such leaders — it preferred *controlled* transformation, guided by strategic advice and kept under firm bureaucratic control at every stage.

According to the present "rules of the game," which have been laid down, in part, by the Communists themselves, a democratic regime could be "taken over" by the Communists only by *coup d'état*, that is, only *after* the Communists had secured control of *all* decisive power positions in the state. These rules are extremely stringent, and they may be expected to work — barring unforeseen developments, such as a sweeping electoral victory of the Communists and their friends — in favor of the established democatic regimes. We would do well in America to pay more attention to *these* implications of the correctly diagnosed "conspiratorial" character of the present-day Communist movement. It is quite true that the Communist strategy aims essentially at infiltrating governments and subverting them from within. But it is not true that isolated individuals who can worm their way into the government could actually pull this off.

The strategy can succeed only where the means of power are already securely in the hands of Communists. Or, to put it in different words: it is said that the aim of the Communists is to overthrow democratic governments "by force and violence," and nothing could be truer. But nothing could be more erroneous than to translate this formula into the mental image of bomb-throwing Bolsheviks surging from nowhere and "overthrowing" the government. The "force and violence" which the Communists would have to apply and want to apply consists in the use of the *armed potential of the community* which they must control openly before they can exercise the kind of "force and violence" they are hankering after; it is also quite possible that they consider direct intervention by Soviet forces as necessary to insure success. This is not to say, of course, that Communists who succeed in infiltrating the government are harmless — spies are not harmless, and Americans who give their allegiance to an unfriendly foreign government can do plenty of damage, particularly in wartime. We must be vigilant to ward off such damage, but we must not lose our sense of proportion: we must not indulge in the fantasy that in flushing out Communists we are saving our democratic system from being bodily overthrown by them. By the Communists' own decision, the only way to power open to them is the way of the *coup d'état*, and this can be undertaken only by people who already control the army, the police, and the key civilian authorities, besides having the loyalty of "mobilized" mass elements. No *coup d'état* has ever succeeded where these conditions were not fulfilled. And in the democratic countries, it would seem difficult indeed for the Communists to create conditions under which they would be able to manage a successful *coup d'état*. They were able to effect the necessary preliminary concentration of power positions only in the countries under direct Soviet control or within range of Soviet guns, as in Czechoslovakia. In Western Europe, the democratic groups were able to shake off their Communist coalition partners before the critical stage had been reached.

What about the possibility of counterrevolutionary *coups d'état*? A fateful series like the one we witnessed between the two world wars also seems to be extremely unlikely. The waning of "revolution" as a form of political change is being slowly recognized by the masses as well as by the decision-makers. The Communists have repudiated revolution as a political strategy, and nobody seems anxious to pick up the flag of mass rebellion they have thrown away. Hence, there is no mass mobilization on the counterrevolutionary side either, and the opportunity for an "arrangement" among the power holders and vested interests on the one hand, and counterrevolutionary demagogues on the other, does not arise. Things might change if, for instance, a severe economic crisis were to arise; but this merely points up the importance of the recently developed techniques of governmental intervention — on the national and international scale — which serve to maintain economic stability.

Where the military represents an independent power center, capable of transferring its allegiance from one supreme authority to another without encountering serious resistance, the possibility of military *coups d'état* exists; we have seen examples in certain countries of the Middle East. But in Europe, the position of the military is neither independent enough nor strong enough to permit such a course.

We have to conclude, then, that in our present postwar era, constitutional democracy is relatively less threatened than it was before the Second World War. Not that it is completely secure: the existence of Communist cadres and masses, driving — or being manipulated — toward the strategic goal of *coup d'état*, does represent a challenge, and there is, of course, the supreme menace of war. But the rules of the game have changed, and the cards are no longer stacked one-sidedly against democracy.

VII

The next question is whether the "conditions of the game," while now more favorable to the preservation of democracy, are not, on the other hand, also still such as to secure the stability of totalitarian regimes already established. Or are totalitarian regimes becoming somewhat *less* secure than they have been up to now?

To begin with: we have no reason to suppose that upheaval "from below," revolution, is a more serious possibility in totalitarian countries now than in the past. We see, as the counterpart of the unduly pessimistic fantasy that clandestine Communists could overthrow *our* government, the unduly optimistic fantasy — often entertained by the same people — that a revolution might break out spontaneously behind the Iron Curtain, or be touched off by vigorous propaganda campaigns launched from this side. The totalitarian police system is effective enough to suppress even the smallest beginnings of such self-liberation; but police terror is not even needed to prevent large-scale revolution. Even if opposition were less savagely repressed, the people of the totalitarian countries, no matter how bad off and dissatisfied they are, would not want to engage in any large-scale struggle — they seem to feel that disorder, chaos, and destruction would make them even worse off. People may dislike being regimented and exploited, and still be afraid of disorder and uncertainty more than of anything else — and if they live near the subsistence level, this fear can only be greater. Facile assumptions about the engineering of mass uprisings behind the Iron Curtain are, then, out of order. We can only harm ourselves by banking on them.

But then, what about the possibility of *coup d'état* as a form of subversion within Communist regimes? Is there no possibility of an internal rift, setting one part of the Soviet power apparatus against the other, and bringing the edifice down? We know that intra-party conflicts and purges have occurred in the past, and something ominously similar seems to be brewing now. Could such disturbances within the "monolithic" structure of totalitarianism not lead to a fatal explosion?

We must be extremely cautious in assessing the likelihood of such developments. A Soviet "purge" is, indeed, a kind of *coup d'état*; its mechanism is in many respects the same as that of the counter-revolutionary coups which we have analyzed. But this means that, in this purge, too, all means of power are safely concentrated on one side before the blow is struck at *nominal* power holders. No *real* power is being challenged; the intended victims are being isolated before they are struck down. The technique involves no real risk: it can set off no chain-reaction.

After Lenin's death, both power (control over the means of coercion and pressure) and the policy-making process (control over the content of governmental decisions) were divided in Soviet Russia. This might have led to fatal internal conflicts; Stalin forestalled this, first by concentrating all real power in his own hands, and then eliminating plural authority over policy-making. This is the pattern of the *coup d'état*; by putting the government on this *coup d'état* basis, Stalin assured its stability. But the question is whether the system can survive him. If a system is stable because all power is concentrated in the hands of one individual, can its stability not be fatally impaired when that individual dies?

The problem is one of "rivalry." Neither Lenin nor Stalin had any "rivals" in the Soviet system: nobody in authority thought of challenging either the one's or the other's leadership. (In a consolidated democratic regime, too, power is "undivided": the legal government has no "rival" in positions of authority willing and able to challenge and subvert it. Power is "plural" only in the sense that it can pass from one group to another, depending on the way the popular or parliamentary vote goes; but once vested in a government, it is undivided.) In a totalitarian system, however, the possibility of the splitting of power into independent rival centers does arise when a successor has to be found for the central figure. A successor may be designated by common accord among all those having formal authority; but in spite of this, real "rivalry" may develop, as it did after Lenin's death. The dictator's power cannot be inherited: it must be founded anew by each incumbent. In this respect, constitutional power is superior to dictatorial power: it can be passed on from one generation or group of power holders to another, without running a serious risk of becoming split each time. Power *may* become divided in a democratic regime, as we have seen; it is unlikely to become divided in a dictatorship as long as the dictator is alive. But dictatorship has a transition problem which democracy does not face.

A dictator who is newly elevated is always faced with the necessity of eliminating rivals: if he can achieve this by the *coup d'état* technique, as Stalin did, his tenure will be secure. But this depends on the new dictator's ability to make an arrangement with all those who formally control the means of power. If he does not succeed in making such an arrangement, he will have to challenge *real* power, and be challenged by it. Whether Stalin's successor will succeed or not, we do not know, but we believe the transition of power does represent a source of instability for dictatorial regimes. The period ahead of us may disclose a pattern radically different from that of the twenties and thirties.

It is possible that — as long as coexistence lasts — the "wave" of totalitarianism has reached its high-water mark. And it may well be that in the not too distant future it will start rolling back.

19. The World Revolutionary Situation

HAROLD D. LASSWELL

The purpose of this paper is to consider the relevance of the conception of the world revolution of our time that was originally formulated in the middle thirties. It is appropriate to the theme of the present conference since the hypothesis was put forward of the probable emergence of a world of one or more garrison states.

A "developmental construct" is a speculative model in which the present is characterized as a transition between a selected pattern of events located in the past and a pattern imputed to the future. No claim of scientific validity is made for the model, although the present state of knowledge is taken into account in setting up the hypothesis. The developmental construct is not a simple extrapolation of recent trends, but a critical weighing of future outcomes considered as an interacting whole. By highlighting some major possibilities we may be led to revise our previous estimates of the situation, and to guide research and policy activities with a view to taking advantage of emerging opportunities for analysis, insight, and perhaps control.

Imagine that the Marxist conception of our epoch as one moving from capitalism to socialism were free from dogmatic claims to embody scientific truth. We would then have a "developmental construct." Some terms refer to a hypothetical profile of future relationships (in the example, socialism). Other terms refer to events at some cross-section of the past (capitalism). By characterizing the past-future as a manifold of events passing from one pattern to the next, it becomes possible to classify all intervening events as approximations toward the new, or as repetitions of the old.

In considering the context of events including the future as well as the past, we are especially concerned with the fate of human dignity. Until recently, it was not fantastic to imagine that the next few decades would witness the triumph of free societies everywhere throughout the globe. Today there is no mistaking the possibility, or even the probability, that anti-progressive tendencies will win. We may confront the two developmental constructs with one another:

Alternative One: The historic trend away from caste societies will continue until the free man's commonwealth is achieved on a global scale. A commonwealth is free, of course, in the degree that values are maximized for the many rather than the few.

Alternative Two: The direction of history is reversing itself, in the sense that it appears to be moving toward the restoration of caste, though in new forms. More specifically: assuming that the world crisis of insecurity continues, power and other values will be further concentrated in a few hands in the name of providing for the common defense. As the world is bipolarized between the United States and the Soviet Union, perpetual crisis favors the loss of freedom, and the eventual consolidation of garrison and of garrison-police states. As power and other values are taken into the hands of the soldier and political policemen, other groups decline in weight, perhaps disappearing entirely (notably the businessman and the free professional man). In the end, if the process is carried to the logical (thinkable) conclusion, the leaders of the garrison-police state constitute the active elite of a new caste system.

The first alternative generalizes the course of history since, let us say, the eighteenth century; the second alternative — concerning the return to caste — may be roughly dated from the 1930's to the decades immediately ahead. The former construct is substantially the forecast of both liberals and socialists after the "bourgeois revolution" ran its course.

THE MEANING OF WORLD REVOLUTION

Our conception of the nature of a world revolution turns upon symbolic and elite criteria. A "revolution" is a relatively rapid change in the characteristics of the wielders of power, and of the symbols ("myth") in the name of which they wield it. A "world revolution" marks the appearance in the world arena of an elite that possesses a novel composition, a novel outlook, and a novel vocabulary. There is, however, a further distinction to be made between the "world revolution of the center" and the "world revolution of the epoch." The former is exemplified by the Revolution in France of 1789 or the Revolution in Russia of 1917. The second is suggested by the words "bourgeois revolution" and "proletarian revolution." The latter terms characterize widespread transformation in social structure and perspective that occurred during a given historical period, of which the "world revolutions of the center" were phases.

The following pages characterize the world revolution of our time according to the sharing of social values in a few or in many hands, and according to the institutions that are likely to prevail. Since the least welcome outcome is regarded as more probable than the desired alternative, it is characterized at more length. (The unwelcome outcome from my point of view, perhaps needless to say, is the world of garrison prison states.)

THE PRIORITY OF POWER AND THE EXPECTATION OF VIOLENCE

The hypothesis is that continuing crisis brings profound transformations in the structure of societies that have emphasized the peaceable pursuit of prosperity. The conditions once stated by de Tocqueville are becoming actual. He wrote, "If a military government were to be established among any of the nations of our times . . . the result would be a regular, clear, exact and absolute system of government; the people would become the reflection of the army, and the community regimented like a garrison."

DEMANDS AND EXPECTATIONS OF WORLD DOMINION

Our epoch is characterized by at least one major ideology that predicts the inevitability of collective violence as an incident to the rise to world dominion of one system of social organization. Why do we not take such ideologies literally and say that World War III is inevitable?

In part our caution comes from skepticism about any claim to infallibility in predicting the future. But in this case the grounds are more specific. We know that confidence in a mission of world conquest is nothing new in history. And it is instructive to recall that ideologies of world imperialism have by no means met with uniform success. . . .

Soviet doctrines are sufficiently ambiguous and contradictory to provide ample justification for the decisions which are regarded as expedient by the active elite of a given moment. Granting that total war is not "inevitable" even in Soviet ideology, the issue is whether the decision-makers of the Soviet world will eventually come to regard World War III as expedient. Several considerations touching the Soviet elite must be borne in mind in evaluating the use of war as a means of internal control. Will the Soviet leaders take big chances in the foreign field, and allow themselves to be goaded into "adventurism"? For the most part available evidence points in a contrary direction.

In estimating the prospect of total war we must not neglect the effect of the Soviet threat upon the leading circles of non-Soviet states. Since 1945 Soviet intransigence has transformed the outlook of many influential elements in the non-Soviet world. Exasperated by the Soviet, they have accepted the thesis of "inevitable" war (providing, incidentally, another example of a fundamental mechanism in human relations; namely, the "partial incorporation" of an opponent's pattern of life). Will the impression gain ground that vigorous action is necessary in order to put an end to the "unbearable tension" of a world divided against itself in a perpetual preparation for fratricide?

Even "moderates" may decide that a "policy of ultimatum" is indispensable if progress is to be restored and mankind liberated from the garrisoning process. They may see in this policy the best prospect of peace on the theory that the Soviet leaders will be sufficiently alert to the facts of relative strength to discount these developments in advance of their completion, and join in acts of peaceful coöperation before the moment of ultimatum actually arrives, thus rendering it superfluous.

The interpretation just referred to places an extraordinary amount of reliance upon the assumption that the Soviet leaders will continue to apply their alleged calculating proclivities to the world scene, and that they will arrive at the particular inference that they should prevent the ultimatum by concession rather than "preventive" war.

The assertion that World War III is highly probable, though not inevitable, gains credibility when we ask the following question: During these dangerous years can relations between the two worlds be conducted without "mistakes"? The weapons of modern warfare

are quick-acting and devastating when compared with the weapons of even the recent past. Local "incidents" can precipitate a chain of countermoves that bring total war, although *not* "according to plan."

MILITARIZATION AND THE REDUCTION OF POLITICAL UNITS

The foregoing discussion has taken high levels of militarization for granted. Our forecast of militarization carries with it the implication that the trend toward reducing the number of effective political units in the world arena will continue. More specifically, the prediction is that the globe will be rigidly split into two garrisoned camps, until a body politic is eventually evolved which includes them both. As indicated before, this may come about by conquest; but we hold open the possibility that it may occur gradually through a resumption of coöperation within the framework of a progressively more effective United Nations.

Until recently it was customary to speak of the Western state system as comprising several powers of about equal strength, the "Great Powers," and lesser states. By the end of the Second World War the pattern of world politics had undergone a substantial transformation, so that the leading characteristic appeared to be the bipolarization of the globe around the Soviet Union or the United States. Hence "polypolarity" in the world political arena has been followed by "bipolarity"; and this in turn, it is suggested, will give way to "unipolarity."

THE UNIVERSALIZATION OF SCIENCE AND TECHNOLOGY

A key factor in calculating the future of bipolarity and unipolarity is interpreting the impact of science and technology. The arts of production are interchangeably the arts of destruction, and we project into the future a rising curve of science and technology, seeking to estimate the effect in a context in which social change is discounted according to actual or potential fighting effectiveness. Today it appears that only two centers of power command the resources to compete with another in applying nuclear energy on a scale sufficient to deal a devastating series of blows anywhere on the globe. Nuclear technology calls for vast investment; and it is only by the discovery of a technology requiring small outlays that we can cut down the present and prospective supremacy of the Soviet Union and the United States. Such developments are not in sight.

Despite the "universalizing" implications of modern science and technology, they have been held in check by "parochializing" factors which restricted the new industrialism to the locality, the province, the nation, or the region. Thus, the strength of the "self-reference effect" militated against universal identifications with "class" or "humanity." By the "self-reference effect" is meant the tendency to pay more attention to the "nuclear" than to the "peripheral" features of the self whenever one is confronted by something new.

GOVERNMENTALIZATION

Inside each political unit we expect to find parallel processes, notably in the trend toward governmentalizing all organized activities of the community. Militarization carries with it the focusing of the points of decision in the hands of government even in the societies which have been most resistant to "encroachment" by the state.

We forecast that the following closely related developments continue: *centralization, concentration* (focusing of power at a given level in a few hands), *bureaucratization, regimentation* (of individual choice).[1]

THE EXPECTATION OF HIDDEN MALEVOLENCE

One consequence of the overriding expectation of violence is suspiciousness. The expectation of hidden malevolence is by no means an unrealistic attitude during periods when ideological differences exist. The news of enemy intentions and capabilities provides a sufficient provocation for counter-hostility. But these hostile impulses cannot be directly discharged. In many societies guilt feelings are automatically aroused by the adaptations which individuals feel impelled to make as the situation deteriorates. If they have ideals of outspokenness on controversial matters, they feel guilt and self-contempt when they restrain themselves. If they have ideals of personal courage, they hate themselves for feeling reluctant to visit

[1] The following points, discussed in the original version of this paper, are omitted here: The stabilization of employment, the reduction of living standards, the gradation and stabilization of income, the compulsion to work, the requisitioning of talent and skill.

friends who may be under suspicion. To the degree that anti-self attitudes become unbearable, the choosing of an external scapegoat becomes a more frequent occurrence. The individual may eventually give up the struggle to conform to his former ego-ideal and resign with more or less bitterness to the practice of deceit and denunciation, all in the name of "you've got to live somehow," and "I have my family to think of."

The government, of course, contributes to the atmosphere of suspicion by broadening the role of the political police.[2]

THE ADMINISTRATION OF HATE

In crisis societies the psychological problem is comparatively simple: hostility must be diverted from the top and directed outward against external targets, and downward against pariah castes.

People can defend themselves to some extent from regimentation by withdrawing affection from remote objects, and choosing targets which are much nearer home. But this cannot be relied upon to block the garrison process. Withdrawal may be accompanied by generalized hostility against all persons who fall outside the small circle with which the individual permits himself to stay identified. A posture of indifference or hatred leads to cruelty and inhumanity in the carrying out of "superior orders."

The process of withdrawal can go to the extreme of cutting off significant ties with any human being. Resentment against "excessive interference" on the part of others can elicit many indirect forms of revenge; and the individual may inflict some damage upon himself at the same time. I refer to the many forms of internalized destructiveness, such as incapacitating illness or accident, unconscious sabotage of machinery and materials, and unconscious withholding of the energy needed to perform a task with full efficiency.

THE DOMINANT-SUBMISSIVE CHARACTER

The character structures favored by garrison-police conditions contribute to the consolidation of the regime. It is not only a matter of recruiting the leaders from egocentric and ruthless personalities, but

---

[2] Omitted: Discussion of the requisitioning of loyalty: (a) The direct demand for loyalty; (b) Undermining the family; (c) "Teams" versus "comrades."

of fostering acquiescence among the mass. The characteristic personality emphasizes the "either-or" of dominance or submissiveness.

THE POLITICIZATION OF RECTITUDE

The stress on power carries with it a considerable shift in the specific standards of rectitude that prevail in a society whose traditions emphasize human dignity. In a free society individuals are expected to assume responsibility for the self-policing of their conduct in accord with the requirements of human dignity. Driven by the sense of imminent threat, the active elite of a garrisoned society may be expected to emphasize negative rather than positive sanctions of public order. Hence the punishment of "ordinary" crimes will become more coercive, which reverses an outstanding trend of modern industrial society.

THE POLITICIZATION OF ENLIGHTENMENT

One consequence of crisis is the cutting down of the stream of information which in a free society is made accessible during less critical times. Civilians, legislators, and private-opinion leaders are blinded as the curtain of secrecy descends. Sensing the evaporation of the sources of trustworthy information it is probable that men of independent judgment will retire from the field of active opinion-making, and leave the forum to agitators who have little of a constructive character to offer.

Where the instruments of public enlightenment are wholly under the domination of the active elite of power, the controllers of the media develop a fantasy world in which the images communicated to the people have little relationship to reality. The stream of public communication becomes dogmatic and ceremonial to such a degree that it is inappropriate to think of communication management as a propaganda problem. It is more accurate to think of ritualization than propaganda, if we use "propaganda" to designate a situation in which contradictions are permitted.

THE REQUISITIONING OF TASTE

As the scope of dogma is expanded, all details of taste submit to authoritative criticism. Alert to the slightest sign of opposition, the eyes of the top elite and its advisors are quickened for minor innovations. The standardization of taste is a means of forestalling the emergence of a secret language of criticism which can be read by those who learn to decipher it.

THE POLITICIZATION OF RESPECT

The garrisoning process carries with it the subordination of respect to power, a process which is most clearly exhibited at the top and bottom of the social structure. At the top we find a towering pinnacle of respect for the head of the state, who does not necessarily hold much effective power. However, such symbolic elevation is required as psychic tension mounts in the social system. By one of the reversals which we often see in human behavior, the humiliation of the primary ego of the members of a community results in the prodigious magnification of a central object of respect. As the subordinated ego descends it obtains indirect compensation by exalting the image to which it kneels in self-abasement. The sources of this response are varied. To some extent an ego appears to be gratifying the desire to believe that, after all, goodness and wisdom and irresistible power do exist somewhere.

At the lower stratum of society are the targets of negative sentiment against whom the contempt and indignation of loyal elements are directed. The need for a soaring pinnacle is matched in reverse.

THE STRATIFICATION OF POWER AND SOCIETY

Summing up the significance of the shifting equilibrium for the sharing of power, there is a tendency to stratify power within a given body politic in reference to military ends, and eventually to focus effective power in the hands of a small elite, which tends to become a self-perpetuating class (caste).

THE GARRISON STATE VERSUS THE POLICE STATE

Our forecast includes the probability that an intense struggle for power will be carried on between the military and the political police. Several advantages are initially on the side of the military. The war crisis calls for continuous calculation and preparation for partial and total conflict. Hence it is reasonable to turn to the professional soldier for advice in planning and operating defense programs, which greatly enlarges the scope of this particular group of "specialists on violence" in the making of decisions. However, the continuation of the crisis tilts the balance toward the political police. This is likely to occur first in the elites possessing a revolutionary tradition. In a bipolar system, ideological differences are magnified by each elite in order to seal off its domain from penetration by the other, and to drive a wedge between the opposing elite and its supporting rank and file. When the accent is put on ideological differences, the problem of loyalty is greatly magnified in importance. The atmosphere of suspicion and the comprehensive scope of military preparations call for the surveillance of the entire community. Whoever prepares the intelligence reports upon the basis of which loyalty determinations are made comes to speak a deciding word in decision-making, which brings the political police to the fore.

THE NEW INSTRUMENTS OF SURVEILLANCE

A factor in forecasting the ascendancy of the political-police group is the emergence of new technological devices of surveillance. In modern times many inventions have enlarged the scope of detection. The microphone, the infrared camera, and the one-way glass are new instruments; but they pale into insignificance beside narco-synthesis (the use of drugs) and hypnosis in order to ascertain the past history and present outlook of a subject.

Dictators are anti-psychological in the sense that they continually seek to reduce the hazards of persuasion. Words are used to indoctrinate, rather than to inform or discuss. The ideal of indoctrination is to train the population to respond to a limited supply of "cue" words, when these cues are invoked by the proper authorities. The freezing of doctrine into dogma, and of dogma into ritualized reiteration, is a step congenial to dictators. If cheap physiological means can be found for reducing the uncertainties of response, it is likely that the holders of concentrated power will use them.

IDEOLOGICAL ADAPTATIONS

Every society that possesses a tradition of freedom at the beginning of our epoch must undergo profound transformations if it is to become a stabilized garrison or garrison-police state. We are especially conscious of the cost of these transformations in the United States, and in all countries possessing the inheritance of Western

Europe. But the global distribution of the culture patterns of freedom must not be overestimated. Where they exist (beyond Western
Europe and Great Britain, North America, Australia, and New
Zealand) the practice of democratic participation in power, in the
making of important decisions, is often restricted to the local affairs
of the peasant community or the family. The "overhead" structure
is traditionally autocratic; and the carriers of the Western democratic inheritance did not usually appear as apostles of freedom during the nineteenth century as they extended their empires through
the globe. Among most of the folk cultures of Africa, for example,
the dominant patterns of power were anything but democratic.

There is no space to do more than characterize some of the ideological emphases that we expect to find on the part of the major
elites. "Freedom" and "democracy" are terms likely to be invoked
during the transition to totalitarian forms. "National" symbols of
identification will also be treated with great deference while the
structure of world power is in fact consolidating larger units. "Economic" limits such as "socialism" and high "levels of productive
employment" or "industrial democracy" will outcompete themes
that are couched in the "formalistic" symbols like "monarchism" or
"republicanism." Because of the role of religion in intermediate
zones in the bipolar conflict, "religious" symbolism will play an important part during the transition. They will diminish to the extent
that the Soviet-centered world gains the upper hand. Symbols of
"race" will have only a local future unless the garrison prison-state
is ultimately realized in a form that gives overwhelming importance
to one ethnic element (if "colored" rulers are ever dominant over
"whites"). And during the period of transition some of the conceptions that have often been stigmatized by the Communists as "sentimental" will be used by all elites in order to soften the harsh facts
of life. ("Peace" and "justice" are examples.) "Revolution" is a limit
that will be invoked so long as it is believed that discontented elements can be appealed to in the enemy fortress.

THE POSSIBLE RESUMPTION OF THE PEACEFUL MARCH TOWARD
WORLD FREEDOM

Turning now to the other major construct for the epoch, the peaceful resumption of the trend toward freedom, what are the circum-

stances in which the elites of the key states and state combinations will expect to be better off by peaceful coöperation than by continuous military crisis? If we assume that the top leadership of the Soviet world is highly disciplined in the calculation of political possibilities, it is reasonable to forecast that should the Soviet leaders come to believe that they are being out-produced, out-armed, and out-persuaded by the opposing coalition, they will call off the armament race, agreeing if necessary to arms reduction and inspection by United Nations agencies.

The consolidation of the non-Soviet bloc calls for political creation at every level, whether military, economic, diplomatic, or ideological. The building of strength calls for simultaneous action in managing each major instrument of policy. Since the persuasiveness of words in foreign propaganda depends to some extent upon how they harmonize with deeds, the industrial democracies of the Free World will need to make convincing demonstrations that they know what they mean and propose to give active support to their ideals. It will become increasingly apparent that the "ex-colonial" peoples must have confidence that the way to better their lot is by working with the industrial democracies. The United States and Western Europe must be willing to use their influence to bring about the "delayed social revolution." No other policy will carry conviction. Otherwise the elites of the Near and Far East, for example, will try to support themselves against the growing disaffection of their own people with the help of United States soldiers and equipment, thus giving ocular proof of the Communist thesis that the capitalistic powers will prop up every reactionary element throughout the globe as part of the "encircling" and "war mongering" assault upon Communism.

It should be made explicit that the present construct is intended to apply to world developments, whether World War III occurs or not. If the war occurs, and if organized Soviet resistance is broken without great human sacrifice on both sides, the ruling elites then in control of the world will not necessarily adopt enlightened measures to restore and consolidate a free world commonwealth on a global scale.

We conclude by recalling once more that it is a question of the possible, even of the probable, and not of the inevitable. Under present circumstances the garrison-police alternative is more probable than the resumption of progress toward the full realization of human dignity. The act of recognizing this sinister potentiality, and of evaluating the factors contributing to it, may influence the historical process, since an act of insight may evoke sufficiently powerful initiatives to affect the course of policy. In our epoch, at least, the task of mankind is to combine industrialization with freedom and safety on a global scale.

DISCUSSION

Mr. Geroid Robinson: The paper by Mr. Lasswell has launched our discussion of totalitarianism and the future on a very high plane indeed. I want merely to try to restate some of his conclusions in a different way, while attempting to maintain the level of the discussion where Lasswell has placed it.

Our fundamental problem, it seems to me, is the question posed early in a certain Christian catechism, well known to me: "What is the chief end of man?" Departing from the catechetical answer, I would suggest (I have just formulated this definition, by the way) that man's chief end is to mature and develop himself and others as morally responsible decision-making individuals. This phraseology is, I think, merely a more precise refinement of Mr. Lasswell's "full realization of human dignity."

But, though I can agree with Mr. Lasswell's definition of the chief end of man, I cannot agree that there has been a clear trend toward its fuller realization since 1789. From my standpoint, historical "trends" since that date are very unclear. The Industrial Revolution — the critical phases of which postdate 1789 — has given birth to production by machines which cannot be operated by individuals in isolation; these machines can be operated only by crews of workers. This development entails group economic activity under discipline, and in this there is bound to be some obliteration of the individual, whether the boss of the group productive operation is a capitalist boss or a Communist boss.

Jefferson, I think, would have been most unhappy to have witnessed these economic changes, but Marx and Lenin welcomed this packing of individuals into working crews. Factory discipline, in their view, was a most promising preparation for socialist discipline. It strikes me that they were right. When the individual is no longer in a position to make numerous responsible decisions every day in the course of his work, this loss cannot be compensated for by giving him the right to make a responsible decision once a year when voting in a democratic election.

Can anything be done about this? I wonder. There are many suggestions, such as rural coöperatives, a greater share in management for the laborer, and the like, but these attempts clearly reflect, in their pattern of decision-making, the *group* nature of productive activity. They do not in themselves restore fully a sense of *individual* dignity and responsibility in the making of important decisions.

Mr. Edwin Land: I have not previously intervened in the discussions, but here I think I may have a thought to contribute. May I assure you, Mr. Robinson, that the machines are designed by human beings in the first place, and that it is entirely possible to design machines which will provide a means of fulfilling the purposes you have mentioned?

Mr. Paul Lehman: Professor Robinson has raised the question: "How can we in a democratic society at the present stage of mechanized industrial development achieve the maturity required for responsible decisions?"

This question is a very central and far-reaching one. It brings the many-sided discussions of this conference to a rather sharp, functional focus. And it bears very directly upon the future before us, the future not only of totalitarianism but the future of alternatives to totalitarianism. I should like to comment upon only one implication of the question which Professor Robinson has raised, and that is the possible contribution of religion to the future before us.

Let me submit that religious and theological analysis of the present situation in the light of the future may provide a fruitful "developmental construct," in Mr. Lasswell's sense of the phrase. What considerations would be relevant to such a "construct"? Obviously, this is not the occasion to do more than to make certain hints in the direction of an answer.

The first point I would make is that religious and theological analysis leads to a cultural and social matrix which can provide a genuine alternative to totalitarianism. There has been a certain tendency in our discussion to "give hostages to fortune." Absorbed as we have been with the complex phenomenon of totalitarianism, with its nature, its operation, its dynamism, we have, so to say, allowed the "enemy" to choose the ground of debate. Under the terms of the problem and of the conference this procedure has, of course, its propriety. I do not question this at all. My thought is that the analysis and discussion up to this point requires a sufficiently long and comprehensive view in order both to understand the present situation and the future. It is important, I think, that the present predicament of democratic society, to which Dr. Robinson referred, is related to a basic shift in the cultural matrix of that society. Broadly stated, the shift could be described as a shift away from a theocentric to an anthropocentric orientation of culture. More specifically, this shift could be described as the displacement of the Biblical strain by the humanistic and rationalistic strain in the Western democratic tradition.

My second point is that the weakening or loss of Biblical and theological insights and images involves a loss of important memories which imperil the "developmental construct" of the future by isolating it from an important segment of the past. This does not mean that since totalitarianism has exposed the anthropological predicament to which Professor Robinson referred, we are to be advised to "go back to God." On the contrary, the Biblical understanding of the relations between God and man and the world rejects the notion that God can ever be significantly related to human affairs "from behind." This was the fatal mistake of Lot's wife, who has been in a dehumanized state of immobility ever since. A study of the perspective and the thrust of the Biblical images would show, I think, that the meaningful understanding of what in the Bible is called "the promises of God," and in theology, "the purposes of God," requires exactly that openness toward the future which enables one to explore the present without illusions, without anxieties, but with a responsible confidence in the day and the outline of deliverance. We are, so to say, not to "go back to God" but "ahead toward God," toward what He may be up to next.

A third remark that suggests itself to me is a pragmatic one. The rediscovery of Biblical memories is the special province of theological reflection. But as this conference has already clearly shown, scientific specialization, important as it is, is not adequate to the future of totalitarianism. What is required is a common universe of discourse and of action. The particular memories and insights with which theology is concerned are laden with common elements of meaning and action which can be creatively related to the insights and images with which other sciences work. The symbolic interrelation of theological and non-theological images in a "developmental construct" of totalitarianism, especially in relation to democracy, would seem to be a fruitful and immediate task. The problem is partly a semantic one. But it is also a matter of a fresh exploration of the creative content of Biblical and theological images. Perhaps such a conference as this could further conversations between theologians and specialists in the several sciences who are participating in these discussions. Understanding would not come easily or quickly. It would, therefore, be desirable for the theologians and the sociologists, the economists, the psychologists, the historians, to see how far they could understand each other first. If the theologians and psychologists talked together, for instance, or the theologians and the sociologists, and then, in turn, the rest, what creative clarity might emerge on precisely such matters as have engaged us here. I am thinking, for example, of the problem of the "time-scale" mentioned by Professor Deutsch; of the problem of basic trust and mistrust mentioned by Dr. Erikson; of the relation between authority and autonomy; of the relation of responsibility to complexity and change.

It could be that the phenomenon of totalitarianism is pressing upon us the task of an adequate cultural matrix in order to find the answer to exactly the question which Professor Robinson has raised. Suppose that one gave to Professor Robinson's catechetical question, not his answer, but the one which occurs in the catechism from which his question was drawn. Suppose one said that the chief end of man is to "glorify God and enjoy Him forever." What difference would such an answer make in a "developmental construct" for a future which so far as we can now see, lies under the prolonged shadow of totalitarianism?

Mr. Carl Friedrich: Mr. Lasswell describes totalitarianism as "the garrison state." You have read and heard how I feel about using the word "state" in connection with totalitarianism, and I am forced to add that the totalitarian system is not a "garrison" either. Hence I must differ with Mr. Lasswell on terminology: "Garrison state" won't do, since neither "garrison" nor "state" is applicable.

Mr. Lasswell makes two projections into the future. He argues that the world of the future, two or three decades hence, will be either a group of competing garrison states, that is, totalitarian systems, or an amiable world commonwealth under law (he doesn't mention law, but I think we can assume he means us to take it for granted) in the best tradition of classical liberalism. Of these two possibilities he considers the first the more likely.

I don't agree at all. Neither, it seems to me, is probable, though either is certainly possible. I think it is a better bet to predict a world of 1980 more like that of 1950 than like either of Mr. Lasswell's constructs. But that is far from certain, too. In any event, neither Mr. Lasswell nor I have any data to support his hunches, and both of us know full well that one of the key characteristics of Western society during the past three generations has been its extraordinary unpredictability. Who, in 1902, or even 1922, could have foreseen the world of 1952?

It is, of course, entirely possible that the world may come to an end altogether. But the fundamental lesson, I think, is the complexity of the problem. There is such a great multiplicity of factors, related one to another in such a variety of ways, that rational analytical constructions are extremely difficult, and dependable prediction thereby rendered almost impossible. Our world is one of several different types of cultures impinging upon one another in new and unknown ways, with unforeseeable results. In particular, I would point to the severe difficulties involved in predictions of an economic nature. The economic factors of 1902 or 1922, extrapolated fifty or thirty years, would certainly not have yielded an accurate prediction of the economic situation of 1952.

Mr. J. P. Nettl: I think that we face three alternatives in the struggle against totalitarianism on the international level. (This, today, means in effect the struggle against the Soviet.) We can do any one of these three things: (1) Quit the struggle, because the other side won't follow our rules for playing the game; (2) stay in the game, by adopting their rules, which means going totalitarian ourselves in international policy, perhaps at the cost of going totalitarian at home; (3) stick to our own conception of the rules, even though it may cost us some temporary tactical advantages.

My own choice, of course, is the third, but I think there are more than a few signs that we are going in for the second. One striking indication is the degree to which we have adopted the vocabulary of our opponents: we have accepted the term "bourgeois" as mildly perjorative, and "capitalist" even with us is a defamatory word. Or, to cite another example, take the groundnuts scheme of the Labour Government in my own country. When the idea was first broached, the leaders of the Labour Party carefully sought out the best advice available. It was almost unanimous, to the effect that the government should proceed slowly, adapting the technological changes in Africa to the social situation of the native population there. Instead, the government approached the problem as one of will alone — provided that the intent was firm enough, the difficulties could be surmounted. The result was an abysmal failure. My point in citing this illustration is the adoption, in a democratic setting, of the totalitarian emphasis on will in economic problems. Once we do that, we have embraced our enemies' rules of the game.

One of the phenomena which worries me is the number of people who are engaged full time, in their professional capacities, in fighting totalitarianism by propagandist means. This, to my mind, is a totalitarian sort of activity, and it worries me.

Mr. David Riesman: I want to follow up Mr. Nettl's remarks, but I ought to explain first that I am speaking in a context of my own recollections. Six years ago, in 1947, I participated in a conference of this sort addressed to the problem of relations between the Western powers and the Soviet bloc. I am most encouraged to witness the progress we have made in the subtlety of our thought, if the proceedings of this conference as compared to those of the earlier one are any test. Six years back, there were two schools of thought. On the one hand we had the geopolitical strategists, who thought that the problem was one of naked power on the model of the power situation as it was, say, in 1914. On the other hand there was what I would call the Ruth Benedict school of thought: "After all, the Russians have a culture too." The first group misinterpreted what "power" means in the contemporary international situation, and the second group failed

completely to comprehend the significance of power structures however one defines them.

Our insight, as the conference this week-end reflects it, has become
much more serious and supple. But I wonder whether our imagination, so far as alternatives are concerned, has broadened very much.
We still think — as Mr. Nettl seems to believe — that it is either a
matter of embracing the other team's rules, or clinging tenaciously
to our own traditional rules, or resigning the game. I don't think we
need confine ourselves so much. Some time ago, I proposed what I
called the "nylon war," or "Keynesianism in reverse." Why don't we
perform where we pretend to be really good? Why don't we produce
consumer goods to the utmost of our capacity, and then flood the
Russian population, by aerial bombardment, with all kinds of stuff:
jeeps on Odessa, nylons on Moscow, and so forth, instead of spend-
ing all this effort trying to convince the world that we have sym-
phony orchestras too? The whole point of our system is its produc-
tivity; let's show the world that it really can produce. These really
are "our rules."

Mr. Michael Karpovich: I'm not sure I agree with Mr. Nettl's
mutually exclusive alternatives. We are, after all, engaged in a worldwide political and military power struggle, and I don't see how we
can avoid using military force and political propaganda in such a
conflict. But this does not necessarily imply that we fail to remain
ourselves, that is, that we must adopt totally the techniques of our
opponents. We are fighting a political machine rather than an idea
or a new sort of man. Since this is the real struggle, we can conduct
it on a military and political plane without becoming tainted with
totalitarianism. The need is for a negative opposition to the Soviet
abroad while continuing a positive program of building a new and
better society at home. I don't understand why these two objectives
must be viewed as antithetical and therefore impossible of simultaneous support.

Mr. Kecskemeti: Mr. Lasswell, I think, underestimates the complexities of social change and the resilience of social systems. It is
not a simple matter of "either we go their way, or they go ours."
Instead, it is a matter of reciprocal interpenetration. In some respects,
to a partial degree, we will manifest totalitarian symptoms (they
are present in all modern industrial societies in any case), and in

other ways the Soviet system will perhaps begin to show liberal or constitutionalist features. If we assume that the rules of the game assumed on either side will change completely, we radically over-simplify and hence distort the problem, just as William Graham Sumner did when he argued that Spain had really won the Spanish-American war for the reason that the United States had purchased victory at the price of going militaristic and thereby adopting Spanish patterns.

There is a related danger which I wish to mention. Mr. Lasswell appears implicitly to accept a pair of monolithic conceptions of totalitarian and liberal society. I have argued that this assumption over-simplifies the issues. A similar assumption is the uni-causal one: that our difficulties with the Soviet totalitarianism are all reducible to a single factor with respect to which we must fight totally. This approach, I submit, is a true case of adopting the rules of the other side, and hence of fighting the opposition on its own ground. Such overconcentration on an aspect of a highly complex situation weakens our capacity for defense against a wide variety of possible attacks. The most striking contemporary illustrations are, of course, the present ridiculous emphasis on loyalty to the exclusion of everything else and the spectacle of senators who want to go all-out on the verbal level while cutting appropriations for the armed forces.

Mr. Lasswell: I should like to respond to the several criticisms of my "developmental constructs." The critics all agree on the point that they oversimplify the problem, and it is to this charge that I wish to reply. I shall therefore not single out any particular participants in the discussion this afternoon.

Of course the constructs oversimplify the problem. All constructs do. My intent in my paper was to provide an illustration of a methodological device, which is that of building intellectual models in terms of which we can approach the task of prediction. I am very sorry that there is always a flavor of intellectual arrogance inherent in such attempts; I can only plead that it is unintended, and that such constructs are worth the price of possible offensiveness only if they stimulate further inquiry and in that way lead to the working-out of better constructs. Several speakers this afternoon have pointed out some short-comings of my own first approximations, a fact which leads me, at any rate, to believe that the constructs have served their purpose.

The fabrication of such constructs requires in particular one type of sophistication which has not, I think, been mentioned today, although Mr. Wolfe spoke of it at an earlier session. We must be very careful to distinguish the differences in historical phasing between the Nazi and the Soviet cases of totalitarianism. This requirement makes a construct-construction very difficult indeed, but it also makes specifically developmental constructs absolutely essential if we are to attain a real understanding of totalitarianism.

Our immediate practical policy problem is that of deciding what our objectives are (that is, of defining our goal-values), and then of devising the most practicable means of reaching these goals. Here again, I submit, we must tackle the problem by means of analytical constructions which make the complexities manageable.

Our conference as a whole has shown our awareness of the differences between the totalitarian way of life and that manner of social living which we sum up as "freedom." I submit that the Academy of Arts and Sciences might well proceed to schedule a Conference on the latter topic; for it, like totalitarianism, is much more complicated than we sometimes believe.

Mr. Erwin Canham: In response to Mr. Robinson's remarks at the opening of this session, I should like to add some comments to those of President Land and Mr. Lehman. We not only have both our ability to design machines for human needs and the resource of our Christian heritage, but we have as well one institutional recourse which totalitarianism cannot provide. I am thinking of the voluntary organization, through which we widen the creativity of ourselves and our society. These spontaneous, unplanned groups of human beings are a kind of *"free* collectivism" which counterbalance that deadening of the human spirit otherwise inherent in an industrial society. Mr. Robinson overlooks, I think, the desire of human beings not to live as isolated individualistic atoms, but rather to be members of meaningful groups. Our society is one which can be permeated by such voluntary groupings which preserve the values of individuality and yet transcend them by coöperation. This potentiality cannot be present in any totalitarian system, and is our greatest source of strength in the contest with totalitarianism.

Comments

ANDREW GYORGY

I would like to make a few informal comments concerning three of the principal papers delivered at the American Academy of Arts and Sciences Conference on Totalitarianism. My remarks are addressed primarily to Professor Carl J. Friedrich and Dr. Bertram D. Wolfe. They also involve comments on the stimulating paper presented by Professor Waldemar Gurian.

In general terms I would like to express my appreciation of the high level of doctrinal significance and intellectual interest of these papers which have made this conference an unusually stimulating event. I was somewhat surprised, however, that in three days of intensive deliberation so few references were made to emerging totalitarianism in the satellite societies of the contemporary Eastern European political scene. Although there were a few scattered remarks on Tito and some of the structural features of Yugoslavia, I imagine that the doctrinal, and distinctly non-geographical, orientation of the papers excluded further reference to individual political areas, even if they were of a high degree of relevancy and immediate interest to the political scientist.

My first point is to emphasize strongly both the obvious and the more latent possibilities inherent in a detailed study of the *partialitarian* (semi-totalitarian) features of the typical Eastern European society. The contemporary satellite state reflects totalitarianism in its formative stages, and presents a unique spectacle of Stalinism in transition, full-blown in some areas, badly lagging in others. A study of the course of its general evolution offers challenging possibilities for clinical laboratory observations which may give us further insight into the nature and characteristics of modern totalitarianism in action.

Professor Friedrich outlined the five "closely linked clusters of characteristic features" which are basically shared by all totalitarian societies of our time. While the partialitarian societies of Eastern European satellites seem to possess fully the second, third, and fourth features stressed in Dr. Friedrich's paper — the single mass party, the technologically conditioned, near-complete monopoly of control of means of armed combat and of the means of effective mass communication — they are endowed with distinctly limited equipment on Points One and Five. The first factor refers to an official ideology, consisting of a body of doctrine covering all vital aspects of man's existence, and the fifth feature stresses a system of terroristic police control, systematically exploiting scientific psychology. In terms of an official ideology, the armature of satellite doctrine is far from complete; features absolutely essential to the dogma of Marxism-Leninism are missing, while on other points there is considerable hesitancy, uncertainty in method and ambivalence in objectives. Official self-criticism, this Eastern European variant of a more exotic oriental "brain-washing," is practiced with alarming frequency and by the highest echelons of a rigidly stratified Stalinist hierarchy which is anxious to point up doctrinal deficiencies and accelerate the painful transition period from "people's democracy" to a full-fledged "Soviet democracy." [1]

The incompleteness of satellite theory is most clearly reflected in the vacillation and inconsistency concerning the attitude of the vari-

---

[1] Each of the top-level Communist leaders of the Eastern European satellite states has enthusiastically participated in this process of competitive excoriation. Among the more notable efforts were those of the late Klement Gottwald criticizing himself and his government with respect to their lenient and mistaken attitude toward Rudolf Slansky (December 6, 1951), and the important policy-making speech of Mátyás Rákosi, delivered on February 10, 1950, to the Central Committee of the Hungarian Workers' Party. Steeped in the critical approach reminiscent of the *samokritika* pattern of the USSR, Rákosi's speech lashed out against the party members' indifference toward doctrine. He bitterly denounced lax or negligent party members and high government officials who were too easy-going to understand the theoretical postulates of Marxism-Leninism or to put up with strict party discipline. Cf. Mátyás Rákosi, "Erősítsük Pártunk kapcsolatait a tömegekkel, fejlesszük a pártonbelüli demokráciát, a kritikát és önkritikát" (Let us strengthen the relations of our Party with the masses, let us develop intra-party democracy, criticism, and self-criticism), *Társadalmi Szemle* (*Social Review*), Budapest, February 1950, vol. V, no. 2, pp. 89–109.

ous Workers' Party leaderships with respect to the "perfect" social structure of the *ideal* Eastern European state. Social lines are drawn and redrawn, classes included in and excluded from the makeup of a utopian one-class society which as yet is barely in its formative stages and still unable to distinguish between the flexible categories of class friends and class enemies. There is a purely arbitrary, and theoretically unjustifiable, random selection between *Klassenfreunde* and *Klassenfeinde*. In spite of the leaders' frantic efforts to set up an ideologically purified social cadre for the entire population, the Leninist-Stalinist framework for a contemporary Socialist Society, where *Society = Workers + Peasants + Progressive Intelligentsia*, has not crystallized as yet in the countries of Eastern Europe.[2] This doctrinal uncertainty has, in turn, been responsible for the significant fact that the satellites have never really progressed beyond the political phase of inexorable implication in one domestic conspiracy after another, in the staging of one purge after another, while moving from crisis to crisis and from tension to tension. Their postwar Communist movements emerged into full legality through the systematic exploitation of an alleged need for "combatting reactionary conspiracies." Somehow, the craving for conspiracies has never abated, and satellite politicians seem to have adopted the *leitmotiv* of institutionalizing *counterconspiracies* carefully pre-arranged by the regime on a fairly permanent basis. To use Hannah Arendt's felicitous phrase, Stalinist society lives in an aura of "successfully subduing conspiracies plotted in broad daylight."

On the fifth aspect described by Professor Friedrich as basically shared by the totalitarian societies of our time, we again intend to stress the Eastern European variation of the general theme outlined

[2] There are numerous relevant illustrations of the *Stalinism in suspended animation* aspects of Eastern European Communism. It is probably in order to paraphrase here briefly Professor Gurian's excellent remark on "absolute total domination" which he fully interpreted in his paper delivered at this conference. In the politics, government, and social structure of the contemporary Soviet satellite we seem to witness a case of *relative total domination*, with the interesting possibility of proving that totalitarian domination can be a limited one. In our opinion it does not have to embrace the whole of life and society. It does not necessarily have to determine all the realms of individual and social existence. There can be private life outside, and finally, in many cases, passive acceptance is sufficient, while active and enthusiastic support seems unnecessary. The *partialitarian* makeup of the six Soviet satellites in Eastern Europe forcefully points up the manifold limitations inherent in the theory and practice of Stalinism as one of the contemporary variants of totalitarianism.

here. The system of terroristic police control is not fully established in the satellite state where *partial subversion* appears as a necessary preliminary to *total subversion*, and where the police have not succeeded as yet in displacing the armed forces or in relegating them into the background. The methods of police control are only partially worked out and frequently prove ineffective, particularly when compared with the formidable superstructure of the secret-police system in the USSR. Since the identity of the class- and state-enemy remains confused, police terror is occasionally inverted and explodes in large-scale *intramural purges* within the domestic security forces themselves. Witness the recent shakeups in Hungary, where the Minister of Justice, the Chief of the Political Police and at least seven or eight department heads of the dreaded ÁVH were swiftly and silently purged in February and March 1953. The relatively partial, incomplete, and frequently self-devouring characteristics of the police control system are some of the several significant variations, both in time and place, so concisely stressed in Professor Friedrich's paper.

In connection with Dr. Bertram Wolfe's paper, I would chiefly like to emphasize that the intellectual agony of Soviet historians is interestingly matched by the agony of some of the more respectable Eastern European historians. The professional pride of the latter is currently lacerated by two "Operations Rewrite," conducted in different areas of satellite culture and historiography, and yet permeated by the same spirit of indiscriminate crusading for the ultimate triumph and full recognition of Stalinism. One of these "Operations Rewrite" is harnessed into the production of new textbooks in history, language, and literature, while the other concentrates on the retroactive idealization of the national Communist parties of Eastern Europe.

In "Operation Textbook Rewrite" we witness frantic efforts to appropriate for Communist purposes literary heroes and prominent public figures of the past. This mass appropriation of nationalist symbols seems an essential prerequisite for legitimizing the dubious origins of post-World War II totalitarianism. While the theory of cultural sovietization is fairly clear-cut, in practice it creates total chaos in the teaching of national language and literary surveys. According to recent information from Hungary, a textbook in literature adopted in September 1951, at the beginning of the academic year, had to be discarded twice and a third book substituted by the end of December 1951. The reason for this triple change in the "pedagogical line" was that the authors of the first and second books committed errors in their political discussions, and these deviations apparently went unnoticed by the board of educational censors. Thus "reactionary" phrases were used in the biographies of several prominent Hungarian literary figures. The second textbook was discarded for "misrepresenting" the political views of two popular Hungarian heroes, Sándor Petöfi and Lajos Kossuth, and for not living up to the educational requirements of a people's democracy. There are numerous incidents illustrating the arbitrary superimposition of a new culture of total aspirations over individualized civilizations with a body of national traditions.

For want of space we have to summarize briefly the principal objectives of the historians' campaign to offer an embellished *ex post facto* version of the past activities and ideological makeup of their own brand of a Communist Party. In their dialectically inspired professional agony satellite historians stress the following features:

1. In the pre-World War II period their Communist Party was the only anti-fascist, anti-German, anti-ruling class and anti-Social Democratic force active on the domestic political scene.

2. Neither the party hierarchy nor the rank and file of its membership had ever been involved in the Spanish Civil War, which, in more recent Soviet and satellite historiography, has become synonymous with an illicit anti-Stalinist excursion unsuccessfully staged by the Titoist clique and such "pocket-revolutionaries" as the late Béla Kun.

3. During World War II the Communist Party was the only group actively interested in waging effective guerrilla warfare against the "fascist invader" or the "reactionary occupying power." Party members not only performed brilliantly in such partisan guerrilla operations (considerably out-Titoing Tito), but they also succeeded in linking their forces engaged in *active, armed* resistance with the rapidly advancing Red Army.

4. Throughout these climactic months, claim present-day satellite historians, the Communists were alone, unaided, and *almost unwillingly* cast in the role of founding fathers responsible for a better future. In Hungary, Czechoslovakia, and Rumania local nuclei of

Stalinist leadership strongly emphasize the regretful "we were alone" *leitmotiv*, proudly pointing to themselves as the only patriotic, democratic, and enthusiastic citizens of their much-tortured countries.[3]

5. Although individual Communist parties were nationalistically minded at first, in the anxious perspective of their historians, the national-patriotic veneer disappeared in June 1948, when Tito's defection cast the aspersion of dissidence or deviation on all national Communists everywhere. The memorable date of June 28, 1948, was thus directly responsible for a frantic antedating of all nationalist inclinations in the satellite Workers' Parties of Eastern Europe. As an interesting incidental feature of totalitarianism in action, we should note that it succeeded in creating the concepts of *terminal patriotism* and *terminal nationalism*, with the obvious sanction of total excommunication from the family fold.

The satellite historian faces a seemingly endless series of crises. Will he succeed in depicting his country's Communist movement as ardently chauvinistic and fanatically nationalistic up to a given date of contemporary history? Will he then be capable of appraising the most recent five-year span as uninterrupted progress in the direction of total loyalty and absolute subservience to Cominformist ideals and expectations?

[3] In his colorful pamphlet on *Harcunk Budapestért* (Our Fight for Budapest; 1946), the Hungarian writer Lajos Fehér bitterly complains that the Communists have to do everything themselves and that they are receiving little support from the working classes of Hungary. The author here expresses a characteristic disappointment mingled with surprise at the fact that literally nobody was willing to help the Communists.

CARL J. FRIEDRICH is currently Eaton Professor of the Science of Government at Harvard University. Born in Germany in 1901 and educated at the Universities of Marburg, Frankfurt, Vienna, and Heidelberg, he came to the United States in 1922. Among Professor Friedrich's numerous works are: *The New Image of the Common Man, The Philosophy of Law in Historical Perspective, Constitutional Reason of State,* and (with Z. K. Brzezinski) *Totalitarian Dictatorship and Autocracy.*

A SELECTED LIST OF TITLES IN THE
Universal Library

HISTORY AND POLITICAL SCIENCE

LITERATURE, CRITICISM, DRAMA, AND POETRY

PSYCHOLOGY

TITLES OF GENERAL INTEREST